In Him Was Life

In Him Was Life

THE PERSON AND WORK OF CHRIST

Trevor Hart

BAYLOR UNIVERSITY PRESS

Cover Design by Savanah N. Landerholm
Cover image: Monographia of the cathedral of Chartres, Chrome
lithography of the stained glass window: The life of Jesus, Paris,
Imprimerie impériale, 1867 - Complete window, Original size 12605
x 30236 px. Retouched and combined from 5 single sheets (1:6), this
window has a height of more than 10 meters. Wikimedia Commons.
Book Design by Savanah N. Landerholm

The Library of Congress has cataloged this book under ISBN
978-1-4813-1015-4.

Printed in the United States of America on acid-free paper with a
minimum of thirty percent recycled content.

Ἐν αὐτῷ ζωὴ ἦν

For Geoffrey Edward Hart (1939–2016)
in grateful memory

Contents

Preface   ix

Introduction   1

I
Revisiting the East

1   Hellenization   19

2   Recapitulation   35

3   Divinization   55

4   Deification   79

II
Reconsidering the West

5   Satisfaction   115

6   Substitution   151

7   Mediation   167

8   Sanctification   189

9   Revelation   205

10 Filiation   227

III
Christology in Contemporary Context

11	Impeccability	243
12	Universality	257
13	Particularity	277
14	Availability	291
15	Imagination	309
Notes		337
Works Cited		393
Credits		407
Index		409

Preface

Over the years I have written and published numerous pieces on Christology and soteriology. The focus of many of these essays has been historical, while others have addressed questions of particular concern to our own contemporary context. Most have been published in academic journals or as single chapters in edited collections, where, by definition, they have tended to reach a focused rather than a wide readership. Repeatedly, I have been asked where particular essays are to be found and why they are not more readily available. So, somewhat grudgingly at first and feeling like the hapless dog of Proverbs 26:11, I have gone back to them to see whether, combined into a collection, they might have more integrity and overall force than the fact of their common appearance alongside my name in library catalogues otherwise affords them. Not all of the essays available for consideration made the cut, but I am content that those represented here do all belong in a single volume possessed of its own proper shape and with a singular contribution to make. Many of the pieces are concerned with the fructifying interplay and cross-fertilization between Christology and soteriology that has preoccupied me over the decades. Others also explore the significances of the doctrine of the incarnation for constructive Christian theology more widely.

Several of the pieces included in this volume have undergone significant reworking in the interests of stylistic conformity and to accommodate what the book seemed to me to require in order to secure balance of coverage and some semblance of completeness. Others, although based on scholarship conducted several decades ago, appear here in print for the first time. With very few exceptions, little attempt has been made to bring individual chapters up to date in terms of the continuing industry of scholarly publication in their respective fields, each being permitted simply to reflect the state of things at the point of its original composition. Readers are asked kindly to make allowances for this, for such brief repetition of ideas and material as may occur here and there due to the scholarly convention of occasional "self-sampling," and for the fact that the overarching scheme indicated by chapter titles is to some extent a conceit born of convenience—intended to draw attention to larger continuities and existing connections but certainly not to suggest any attempt at exhaustive or even thorough treatment of some of the themes as such. I hope that, such potential irritants notwithstanding, both individual chapters and the collection as a whole may be of interest and value to a new generation of theological readers, as well as to those who may have stumbled across some of them previously in earlier incarnations.

Much of the material in this book originated in invitations to deliver papers at academic conferences or events, or to research seminars. For most busy academics (certainly in the UK) it is mostly in such self-imposed interruptions to the daily grind of teaching, examining, filling out grant applications, or submitting to the demands of yet another institutional audit process that opportunities and the justification for time invested in fresh scholarship arise. The lists of publications accompanying many academic CVs or adorning personal websites are thus typically the fruit of the accidents of history rather than any carefully imagined scheme of research intended to shape a career. When, therefore, looking back over several decades of such happy opportunism, some of those products seem to cluster naturally and helpfully together, and even to gesture toward a greater whole of which they might form a valuable part, the result is both a sense of pleasurable surprise and a deepened conviction in the reality of divine providence. Nonetheless, I should express my gratitude here to those who have, over more than thirty years, issued those invitations humanly and then, humanely, engaged with the eventual products of their acceptance. Thanks are also due to the several colleagues and the many PhD supervisees with whom engagement over the years has provided opportunity or occasion to discuss and further develop my own thinking about these things. I am grateful, as always, to Carey Newman and the staff at Baylor University Press for publishing my work, and for doing so with such obvious commitment to high production values, a personal and supportive relationship with authors, and a vision for the future of serious scholarship and academic writing in the field of Christian theology.

Trevor Hart
St. Andrews
Feast of the Holy Innocents, 2018

Introduction

The notion of redemption or salvation is a basic constituent in the plot of the story that Christian faith tells about human existence in God's world. The characteristic designation of this story as "gospel," good news, already bears within it the assumption of a human race in some serious need or lack or crisis, whether it is aware of it or not. To unpick this central thread and seek to remove it in order to accommodate the more optimistic and comfortable stories furnished by the cultures of premodernity, modernity, and postmodernity alike would be to run the risk of unraveling the tapestry of Christian belief and self-understanding, so vital is it to the design and structure of the whole. Humans, Christians contend, need to be rescued from a plight that currently distorts and ultimately threatens to destroy their creaturely well-being under God, but which lies utterly beyond their control or influence. But just what sort of threat is this? And by what means are we to think of it as having been met?

§1. Salvation, Language, and Reality

The history of Christian doctrine reveals a remarkable variety and diversity of answers to these questions, and this for two chief reasons. First, the biblical text itself (which furnishes the raw materials for the theological craft) offers a striking kaleidoscope of metaphors in its attempts to make sense of and develop this central theme of the gospel. Second, these

1

images have in turn been taken up, interpreted, and developed within a vast range of different social and historical contexts, each bringing its distinctive questions and concerns and expectations to bear on the text. Not surprisingly, as each age, each socially located group, has interrogated the apostolic tradition afresh, it has found that some parts speak more naturally and immediately to its particular world of meaning and, understandably, has sought to develop these aspects rather than others in fleshing out an account of salvation relevant to its context.

Particular ways of construing salvation, then, are closely linked to particular social contexts and human situations, both in terms of their origins and the ways in which they are later taken up and developed. What this amounts to in practice is that some human communities find it easier to identify with a particular element of the human plight as described by Scripture—guilt, alienation, impurity, mortality, ignorance, oppression, or whatever—than others, and therefore find it easier to own the correlative metaphor of salvation—acquittal, forgiveness, sanctification, bestowal of new life, illumination, liberation, and so on. In a sense this is relatively unproblematic, and the cornucopia of biblical imagery provides something for everyone, a gospel to fit all cultural shapes and sizes. If this provides a convenient way for the theologian to lead his contemporaries into the riches of the biblical tradition, then, we might suppose, so much the better. But things are a little more complicated than this, and there are some problems lurking not far beneath the surface.

The plurality of biblical imagery does not seem to be intended purely or even primarily as a selection box from which we may draw what we will according to our needs and the pre-understanding of our community. To be sure, there is some evidence within Scripture itself of such pragmatic eclecticism; thus the writer to the Hebrews develops at length the imagery of priesthood and sacrifice, and of the Servant of the Lord, while Paul, writing for a predominantly gentile community, unfolds the gospel chiefly in terms of more accessible cross-cultural concepts. But in general terms what we find is that particular writers addressing particular groups may nonetheless draw within the space of a few sentences on a wide variety of images, suggesting that the plurality is no mere indication of the cultural diversity of biblical texts, writers, and readers but points to the multifaceted nature of the redemptive activity of God itself, which no single metaphor can adequately express. In this case the metaphors are not to be understood as exchangeable, as if one might simply be substituted for another without net gain or loss, but complementary, directing us to distinct elements in and consequences of the fullness of God's saving action in Christ and the Spirit. To select a particular metaphor from among those available, therefore, and to develop it in isolation from or at the expense of others, is to risk a partial and inadequate grasp on the reality of redemption.

This danger is exacerbated further by the fact that the scriptural metaphors do not seem to be intended by the writers as all possessed of equal weight and significance. Some appear to be much nearer to the heart of the matter than others. Thus, for example, to select the theme of redemption as illumination, the bestowal of truth and understanding to remedy ignorance, at the expense of an adequate handling of more personally and morally focused metaphors such as reconciliation and forgiveness, would seem to be to risk a truncated and inadequate account of things. Picking redemptive metaphors to match the felt needs of our culture, therefore, while it may provide a starting point, is unlikely to be sufficient to bear the weight of responsibility attaching to the call to transmit the full gospel of Jesus Christ from one context to the next. There is good reason to suppose that those felt needs themselves may need challenging and broadening in the light of the biblical text.

This leads to a further point, namely the danger that, rather than drawing on the rich diversity of biblical thinking about salvation in order to speak to our context, we may fall instead into the trap of tearing biblical images and symbols away from their proper location and the network of cultural and theological associations in the midst of which their primary meaning is to be discerned, and employ them as empty labels that we subsequently attach to perceptions of the human situation and of the meaning of "redemption" obtained in advance and quite independently of Scripture itself. In other words, we allow our own self-diagnostic skills (or those of our culture) to tell us the best and the worst about ourselves, decide what measures must be prescribed to deal with the situation, and then seek suitable biblical terms in which to dress this up as a version of the Christian gospel. This is prone to happen especially when the scandal of the cross and what it signifies meets with a pre-understanding more than usually resistant to the news that God's response to humankind and its achievements involves radical judgment and re-creation rather than basic affirmation and some suggestions for improvement here and there; that redemption is, as the Scots theologian P. T. Forsyth observed, more than a mere matter of "grouting the gaps in nature," and that the spirit of the age should not be confused with the Holy Spirit. Whenever the story that the church tells appears to dovetail neatly with the stories that human beings like to tell about themselves and their destiny, it is likely that the church is cutting the cloth of its gospel to fit the pattern laid down by the *Zeitgeist* rather than the *heilige Geist*. However much we rightly wish to be open to discern the activity of God outside the church and in the intellectual and cultural currents of the day, historical observation and theological judgment suggest that the gospel faithfully transmitted will always arouse some level of opposition and discomfort. It was not meant to do otherwise. If "Jesus is the answer," nonetheless, in exploring the themes of fall and redemption, of human need and God's action to meet it, we need to be constantly reminded precisely what the question is. If we assume that we already know, and approach the Christian tradition looking only for answers that fit with our prior questions, then again we shall be in danger of transmuting the gospel message into something else.

No one metaphor, image, or model of God's saving activity has ever been exalted to the status of a formal credal orthodoxy within the church. But this should not be mistaken for a sign that the church has a divided mind where the matter of salvation and its concomitant doctrines are concerned. To be sure, some of the descriptions, when set directly alongside one another, do seem to take us in quite different directions, and even to conflict with one another. Yet, as various studies have reminded us, we shall misunderstand the relationship between them if we do not distinguish carefully between the reality of salvation itself and these various symbolic and linguistic representations in which its mystery is approached. If we insist on thinking of the relationship between reality and representation as a precise 1:1 correspondence, a mapping of coordinates that in some sense captures and "speaks" reality as it actually is, then we shall quickly run into insuperable difficulties here. For in this case two divergent accounts can only amount to rival claims to truth. But once we recognize the inherently metaphorical nature of our language in its relation to reality, then, while the questions of truth and falsity certainly still arise, we can see things in a different light.[1] The metaphors which are to be found in Scripture, and those which are derived from biblical ways of thinking and speaking, may be construed as complementary rather than alternative or conflicting accounts. None grasps and renders forth the reality of salvation in its essence. How could it? Language is language. But each points us beyond itself to some aspect of this saving economy, something that, *mutatis mutandis*, it has in common with a victory, a sacrifice, a bearing of judgment, a purification, a redemptive payment, and so on. It is, of course, vital that we seek to discern where the discontinuities between the reality and these various ways of thinking of it lie. Failure to do so has frequently been the cause of unhelpful developments in theologies of atonement.

§2. Salvation and the Person of the Savior

What the metaphors and models all have in common, if they are faithful developments or translations of the apostolic tradition, is a specific focus in history, namely the life, death, and resurrection of Jesus of Nazareth. They do not drift freely across the plains of history as universal truths of reason, or recurrent religious myths in which the global hopes and aspirations of humankind are expressed. They are rooted here, in the awkward particularities of God's dealings with actual men and women, inseparable from the specificities of time and place to which the Christian Scriptures bear witness, although transcendent of these in their significance. There, indeed, is the rub for many whose sensitivities are finely tuned to the wavelengths of modernity with its historical consciousness and relativistic outlook. God, the Christian gospel insists, has acted decisively for our salvation *here* rather than elsewhere. It is in the personal particularities of the story of Jesus, a historically and culturally remote figure for most of the human race, that our own personal stories collide with God's story, that they are somehow taken up into his story and transformed. Here particularity and universality refuse to be prized apart. Scandalous as it may be to contemporary pluralism, this claim is intrinsic to the identity of the Christian gospel. In the fortunes and fate of this historical figure we have to do neither with a convenient visual aid for universal ideas of truth, beauty, and goodness, nor a local and culturally contained expression of "religion," but, the church has always insisted, the fulcrum of God's redemptive activity with respect to his entire creation.

The subject of Christology, or consideration of the "person" of Christ, is often disentangled from his "work" to be tackled under a heading of its own. But unless handled with care this bit of doctrinal tidying can be misleading and, in theological terms, potentially dangerous. As we shall see throughout this volume, there is a proper sense in which questions about the identity of Jesus and those concerning his work refuse to be separated. The designation "Christ," we need constantly to remind ourselves, is itself first and foremost a title, a job description that locates this man's life and death within the particular framework of God's dealings with the nation of Israel at a specific stage in her history, and within the broader context of his God's redemptive purposes for his creation. And so it is with many other christological titles. For, the key question in soteriology, as my doctoral supervisor and mentor James Torrance constantly reminded his students, is not so much "how?" but "who?": "Who is this one who acts in this way, who says these things, to whom this happens?" This, though, is a question the answer to which probes much deeper than the multiple images, titles, and institutions of Israel's social and religious culture alone can take us, driving us relentlessly toward a stammering identification of the Savior that will finally blow them wide open and demand their reinterpretation. The answer that we give to this question, in fact, will shape our entire understanding of the content of biblical soteriology, and determine the shape of the gospel that we bear into our own context.

The hallmark of Christian understandings of salvation, then, may be said to be that they have at their center not a metaphor but a personal history: the life, death, and resurrection of the one whom the apostles referred to as, among other things, the Christ, the Son of God, the Lord. And within this history it is to the compound event of the death and resurrection of Jesus that particular attention is directed. Here is the heart of the mystery, expressed in the ancient catholic confession that humankind is redeemed "by the blood of Christ." It is in the church's attempts to unpack the meaning of this event, and to relate it to the wider texture and structure of human history and existence under God, that Christian soteriology has its distinctive origin.

§3. Salvation in Biblical Perspective

The New Testament is concerned with redemption from the first page to the last. Attempts to sum up briefly the gist of its message are, however, notoriously difficult because of the bewildering array of metaphors pressed into service by its writers in their efforts to unfold the meaning of God's action in Christ. In general, these are drawn from the religious, political, and social institutions and understanding of the Jewish nation—not simply because these lay conveniently to hand as illustrative material, but in the conviction that the fact and form of Israel's existence was itself a God-given matrix within human history for the eventual irruption and interpretation of God's redemptive act. But the fulfillment that Jesus' ministry brings is located within a story of divine promise and preparation stretching beyond the boundaries of the covenant people to embrace the whole human race and the wider creation. Thus the secret kept hidden for long ages is at last revealed (Rom 16:25, 1 Cor 2:6, Col 1:26, NRSV), the mystery of God's will not simply to redeem Israel, but—in, with, and under the fulfillment of the covenant and the establishment of God's kingdom—to gather up all things in heaven and earth in Christ (Eph 1:10), and to reconcile them to himself (Col 1:20), the creator, in whom we live and move and have our being, thereby fashioning in his own humanity a new covenant, a new humanity, a new creation. These are the ultimate parameters of the New Testament vision of redemption, the broader horizons within which other metaphors find their place.

First, there are metaphors of release. Thus Christ has come "to destroy the works of the devil" (1 John 3:8), to break the hold of him who holds the power of death (Heb 2:14), a theme reflected in the synoptic tradition and its vivid portrayals of Jesus' struggle with dark and demonic forces from his baptism to the cross where the "prince of this world" is finally disarmed and driven out (Col 2:15, John 12:31). The metaphor of "redemption" (*apolutrosis*) draws on a similar pool of ideas. Just as a person sold into slavery might be redeemed or ransomed by a blood relative able to pay the price specified by law (see Lev 25:47–55), so now Jesus' life, death, and resurrection bring release to captives (Luke 4:18–19), constituting a ransom (*lutron*) for many (Mark 10:45, cf. 1 Tim 2:6), which sets them free from slavery to sin (Rom 6:6, John 8:34) and sin's use of the law as a device of restraint rather than blessing (Titus 2:14, Gal 4:4, Eph 2:15, Col 2:14, Heb 9:15, etc.).

Second, there are metaphors of transformation, of change in the human condition. So, for example, Christ brings healing and immortality through resurrection to transform our sickness and death (1 Cor 15:20–21, 2 Tim 1:10, John 5:24). Salvation does not only release us from that which binds and inhibits us, it bestows on us new and unimaginable blessings: eternal life in union with the Son of God (1 John 5:11), the personal indwelling of God's Spirit within us (1 Cor 3:16), the moral fruit of the Spirit in changed and Christlike lives (Gal 5:22–23), the eventual glorification of our humanity (1 Cor 15:43, Eph 2:6, Phil 3:21), and (perhaps the most enigmatic verse in the New Testament) participation in the divine nature (2 Pet 1:4).

A third group of metaphors have to do with the facilitation of a new, confident, and joyful access to God for those estranged and separated from him by sin and its consequences (Matt 27:51; Eph 2:18, 3:12; Heb 10:19–20), and the provision by Jesus of an atonement (*hilasterion*) that facilitates and secures this. Here the language of both cult and legal code are appealed to. Thus Jesus' life and death are construed in terms of the sacrificial cultus of Israel, likened variously to the covenant sacrifice

(Matt 26:28, 1 Cor 11:25), the Passover (1 Cor 5:7), and the sin-offering
(1 John 2:2). Christ purifies us from the ritual defilement of sin and mediates between the most Holy God and sinful humans (Heb 9:15). The theology of sacrifice is notoriously difficult to determine, but it seems clear
from prophetic denunciations of *ex opere operato* ritualism that what is
manifest in its symbolism above all is the complete self-offering of the participant, and not the death or immolation in and of itself. Thus the atoning thing here has an irreducibly moral dimension: it is the offering of a
perfect reciprocal holiness from the human side of the covenant relation,
a fulfillment of the demand to "be holy, for I am holy." Jesus' suffering and
death are also construed as a bearing of divine judgment on human sin (a
theme the precise relation of which to that of sacrifice is disputed). Thus
the crucifixion is a bearing of the curse of the law (Gal 3:13) in which Jesus
was "made sin for us" (2 Cor 5:21), God's nailing the claim of the law over
us to the cross of his Son (Col 2:14); his death crucifies or circumcises and
thereby does away with the sinful nature (Col 2:11, Rom 6:6), the wages of
sin finally being paid, and the wrath or judgment of God being dealt with
(Col 3:6, 1 Thess 1:10). Somehow, in and through his obedient life and
his death, Jesus justifies us (i.e., establishes us in a right relation to God
within the new covenant) and sanctifies us (i.e., makes us ritually acceptable as an offering to God). And all this is complemented and qualified
by the most intimate and personal metaphors. What God desires above
all is that we should be reconciled to him, receiving the forgiveness that
he longs to lavish on us, and, through union with his only begotten Son,
embracing the status of sons and daughters, loved with an eternal love in
his Fatherly heart. This draws our attention to something vital in the apostolic message, namely the realization that *God is not the problem from which
we have to be rescued*; he is the one who graciously gives his all to rescue us.
Redemption is his idea and his greatest gift to us.

The terse statement that "Christ Jesus came into the world to save
sinners" is developed in all these and many other ways in the apostolic
writings. The brightly colored threads of metaphor are woven into an
eschatological fabric in which God's saving activity unites past, present,
and future: redemption is a historical achievement in Christ's life, death,
and resurrection for us; it is an ongoing activity of the Holy Spirit in us
who unites our present with that redemptive past; and it is a future hope
yet to be realized and in the expectation of which Christian lives are lived.
The New Testament, we should observe, knows nothing of the later careful distinction between objective and subjective aspects of this complex

package, perhaps because such terms presume hard and fast individual boundaries where it takes for granted a relatedness and solidarity among human beings. The apostolic mind seems to assume what Colin Gunton has referred to as a perichoresis of time and space in which we, as the particular persons that we are, and without ceasing to be particular, are nonetheless constituted as such by our relatedness to all that has been and all that will be, as well as all that is.[2] Thus, for example, for Paul salvation is fundamentally a matter of being "in Christ." We *were* in Christ in his historical redemptive acts; we *are* in Christ through faith and the indwelling of his Spirit; and we *shall be* in Christ when the final consummation of all things comes to pass. Salvation, then, is not a commodity that we can obtain at will on the free market, or an insurance policy which we can cash in on the last day, but a matter of our personal relatedness, past, present, and future, to the Savior in whose very person and being it has been fashioned, and thereby to God.

§4. In Him Was Life

Rethinking Person and Work

In this book I consider some different attempts to make sense of the apostolic claim that God, in Jesus, has redeemed us. Each of these attempts is from a quite distinct historical and cultural circumstance, and each reflects in its own way the struggle to translate the heart of the gospel for a world whose outlook and experience is constantly changing. Each, therefore, bears the inevitable imprint of its cultural location as well as that of its Christian identity, and offers the fruits of a transaction between the two. The volume's underlying concern is the ways in which accounts of Christ's person and of his so-called work are related to one another, with the implications of faith's ultimate confession of the one who undertakes that work as Lord. How should we imagine and speak of what "salvation" (itself an intrinsically *negative* image) finally means in positive terms if, indeed, in Jesus we have to do with a God who, as various theologians over the centuries have dared to suggest, has not simply effected a cosmic salvage exercise through some cleverly devised moral or legal transaction but effected a "marvelous exchange" in which he has become what we are so that we might share in what he is, taking our flesh and making it his own so that, together with it, we might be "promoted into" God's own being and life?[3] What does all this mean for our understanding of who God is, of our own creaturely nature and capacities, and of God's ways of relating to us and realizing God's own creative purposes? And, significantly, what might Christology itself have to say about the nature, possibilities, and constraints of "theology" (our thinking and speaking about God) itself?

The book falls into three parts, the first of which invites Western readers in particular to revisit and explore some of the characteristic themes of the soteriologies of the Christian East, especially in their connection with the development of incarnational theology and the establishing of christological orthodoxy in the first five centuries of the church's history.

The soteriology of the early Christian East has often been supposed (by Western scholars) to be in large measure the fruit of some unhappy liaisons between biblical themes and the religious and intellectual milieus of Hellenism. In the apologetic task, it has been held, the church granted too much sway to the contemporary cultural mores, resulting in a distorted account of the nature of salvation. More precisely, the results of metaphysical speculation about the person of Christ were allowed to shape soteriology in a problematic manner. Chapter 1 traces this influential line of interpretation, reckoning in particular with its application to the second-century writings of Irenaeus of Lyons (typically identified as an early culprit), and argues for the need for a more nuanced approach.

Continuing from the argument of the previous chapter, chapter 2 offers an alternative exposition of Irenaeus' work, presenting it as a largely faithful development of the apostolic gospel, albeit now translated into and enriched by the categories of a new cultural context. We see how, in his hands, Christology and soteriology do indeed begin to be woven together, but not, as suggested by advocates of the Hellenization thesis, in a manner that departs significantly from apostolic images and emphases. Rather, in his development of the image of the "recapitulation" of humanity in Christ, key strands in biblical theology are held together in a manner that earths an account of the person of Christ (as God incarnate) in an understanding of his saving accomplishment.

Like many flawed and misleading scholarly paradigms, the interpretation of the Greek fathers as incautious Hellenizers of the gospel gains its plausibility and influence from the fact that it is not wholly false. There were indeed some who sought apologetic traction and intellectual respectability not just by borrowing terms, images, and ideas from Hellenic culture but by endorsing the frameworks of meaning within which these were habitually made sense of. Chapter 3 attends in particular to the theology of Clement, near contemporary of Irenaeus and one of the so-called Christian Platonists of Alexandria. It argues (against the Liberal

Protestant suggestion that orthodox incarnational Christology has its roots sunk ultimately in Greek soil) that his account of the person and work of Christ respectively is actually *incapable* of sustaining a truly incarnational perspective precisely *because* of its entanglements with Middle Platonism and Neoplatonism.

Chapter 4 brings the argument of part 1 to a close with a reading of the fourth-century Christology and soteriology of Athanasius of Alexandria. Concentrating in particular on his insistence that in Christ "God became human so that we might become divine," I argue for an interpretation of Athanasius' key christological terms and phrases that forbids any interpretation of this statement that permits or encourages a soteriological blurring of the boundaries between God and the creature, either in Christ or in redeemed humanity. Instead, "deification" (*theopoiesis*) is, I maintain, to be understood for Athanasius as our redemptive sharing in the incarnate Son's filial relation to the Father (*huiopoiesis*) in the power of the Spirit. This vision is maintained in direct opposition to the reductionist and dualist impulses that duly led to Christologies such as those of Arius, Apollinaris, and Nestorius—the true christological heirs, I suggest, of Platonizing tendencies in Christian theology.

Part 2 of the book attends to some of the familiar images and categories that have been prominent in Western treatments of the person and work of Christ, but it concentrates in particular on ways of appropriating and reading these that resist or complicate more mainstream and familiar presentations, not least by their holding of person and work closely together. So, for example, chapter 5 argues that, despite ways in which it has been used in the mainstream, the original heart of the soteriological image of "satisfaction" is not essentially penal but has closer resonance with the biblical image of sacrifice. Christ offers to the Father what we cannot offer, rather than bearing a punishment that we cannot bear. Tertullian, Anselm, and John McLeod Campbell are all considered in this connection, and a closing section offers a theological reflection linking this strand of atonement theology with creation, worship, and Trinity.

The first of two chapters to address issues of abiding contention in the post-Reformation West, chapter 6 begins by considering the difference between Protestant and Roman Catholic accounts of "grace" in the context of a doctrine of redemption as, in broad terms, concentrating on "extrinsic" and "intrinsic" categories, respectively. A close reading of French Reformer John Calvin (in both the 1553 edition of the *Institutio* and his commentaries on Scripture), and of his dispute with the Lutheran theologian Osiander in particular, suggests a different paradigm in which Christ substitutes his own humanity for ours at every point (both in justification and sanctification), but in doing so unites us to himself so that "participation" is the natural obverse of this vicarious self-giving. Grace, therefore, is never merely external to us, nor yet the infusion of something into us, but a transforming function of the humanity of Jesus who binds us to himself by taking our flesh and becoming a man who has God in common with us.

Chapter 7 focuses on the image of Christ as mediator, an image central to Reformed theology and to the Westminster documents and the writings of theologians in the Westminster "federal," or covenant, tradition. The chapter interrogates Westminster's use of the image, setting it in the context of biblical considerations and probing the role it plays in casting the mold for the Confession's understanding of divine-human relationships. It also considers the influence of English and Scottish political life in the sixteenth and seventeenth centuries in informing Westminster's biblical hermeneutic. I argue that the image is insufficiently modified here by the reality of the incarnation, a reality that for Christian theologians both fulfills and should transform our thinking about how God and humanity are related, and thereby points to a quite distinct way of modeling what mediation in Christ means.

Chapter 8 is a study of the doctrine of atonement developed by the Scots theologian P. T. Forsyth, considering the way in which his distinctive approach holds together the doctrine of God ("Holy Love"), the doctrine of creation (as a moral as well as a physical order into and through which God's character is directly woven), and the doctrine of the cross as the point in history that is the self-realization of holiness in the sphere of the human. While holding to an account of the cross articulated in penal terms, Forsyth nonetheless ruptures traditional categories and refers us to it as the point where our humanity is sanctified, made holy, and thus established in its authentic creatureliness precisely in its submission to judgment. Against the background of his original devotion to Ritschl, and with more than a dash of Hegel thrown in for good measure, the result, I argue, is a profoundly Christian account of the matter.

Chapter 9 begins by posing a question about the relationship between the man Jesus, known by the application of historical methods to the Gospels, and the divine Word about whom faith claims finally to speak. The question was first posed by D. M. Baillie in 1948, accusing theologians of the day of a practical Nestorianism in which a separation had been allowed to open up between history and faith. In exploring this further, I consider charges laid at the door of Barth's Christology along similar lines and respond to them by offering a reading of his account of the place of the "flesh" of the incarnation in revelation. Following on appropriately from a reckoning with Barth, chapter 10 is, straightforwardly, a study of the relationship between person and work of Christ in the theology of T. F. Torrance. Torrance provides a perspective from within Reformed theology, which, due to his extensive study of patristic theology, draws too on the tradition of Irenaeus and Athanasius discussed in earlier chapters. Thus, consistently with emphases treated in chapters 5, 6, and 7, he offers an account in which in an important sense the person of Christ *is* his work, since it is the atoning reality in which others are given to participate.

In part 3 I explore some issues that bear the intellectual stamp of the twentieth and twenty-first centuries in particular. Thus chapter 11 grapples with an ancient christological question but brings to bear on it some very contemporary categories. Could Jesus have sinned? That he did not do so is a conviction of faith. But was he capable of doing so? And if not, as the theological mainstream has generally supposed, in what sense can we hold him (as faith also insists) to have been genuinely obedient? This question (should we confess either *non posse peccare* or *posse non peccare*, in the terms of older Western theologies?) is explored in relation to wider christological and soteriological issues, drawing in the process on some recent philosophical and theological discussions of human freedom.

One "scandalous" element in the Christian gospel, according to both modern and postmodern intellectual milieus, is its particularity, linking that knowledge of God which is redemptive to particular events in history and to the times and places in which a faithful response to those events can meaningfully be supposed to have been possible. Against the enormous scope of the history of humankind such particularism seems, it has been held, inefficient and (granted what is at stake) unjust. Various attempts have been made to respond to this problem theologically, some abandoning the particular claims of Christianity in preference for a religiously plural version of things, and others remaining steadfastly within the Christian paradigm, and seeking a response rooted in its distinctive aspects. Among the latter, one of the most careful is that offered by John A. T. Robinson. Chapter 12 revisits the case Robinson makes in his book *In the End, God . . .* , and considers in detail the robust criticism of it by T. F. Torrance. Robinson's argument, I hold, whether it finally persuades or not, is better than Torrance's account of it suggests and is certainly deserving of the epithet "Christian."

Another facet of the so-called scandal of particularity is highlighted prominently in the writing of feminist theologians of one stripe or another. Here, it is not Jesus' historical and epistemic remoteness from the bulk of humankind that is the sore point but his maleness, which, it is held, renders him salvifically irrelevant to those who do not have masculinity in common with him—that is, women. Other versions of the same claim (focusing on other particulars, such as Jesus' ethnicity) are found here and there. Some theologians respond to this by emphasizing the shared genus "humanity" as that which bridges the relevant distances. Jesus, they say, has redeemed our "human nature." There are two problems with this response: (1) "human nature" itself is a suspect category in our postmodern times, and (2) such Christologies tend necessarily to draw attention away from the very particulars of Jesus' life, teaching, ministry, suffering, death, and resurrection, which the four Gospels seem determined to share with us, and so distance Christology from its biblical base. In chapter 13 I offer a critical reading of an essay by Richard Bauckham in which he attempts to answer the question "How can a particular Jesus be of universal saving significance?" and insists that it is precisely *in* his particularity (the things he did, said, and suffered as related in Scripture) rather than despite it that his universal significance is to be found.

A further feature of the modern/postmodern response to the world and to its own Christian intellectual heritage is "a vivid sense of the absence of God." What is intended by this inevitably varies, though it is usually distinct from the simple atheist claim that God does not exist other than as a figment of humanity's religious imagining. In this sense, at least, absence is both apprehended and measured by a lingering sense of presence. Chapter 14 traces some of the trajectories of talk about divine presence and absence and does so in relation to traditional Christian claims about God's presence to and distinction from the world, in creation, in the incarnation, and elsewhere. It offers a critical rejoinder to attempts by some Christian theologians to identify significant traces (universally available apprehensions) of God's presence outwith the gracious condescension of God's own self-giving and the forms that takes. Again, universality is held to be contingent on rather than despite the particular forms of God's revealing, understood biblically under the rubric of the doctrine of divine "election."

The final chapter in this volume tackles the question of the conditions of our human knowing and speaking about God. It offers a programmatic case for the inevitability and vital importance of acts of imagination in the theological task and in liturgical/devotional practice. And it does so precisely on christological grounds. Aquinas, Austin Farrer, and Janet Soskice are set in counterpoint with T. F. Torrance's plea for an "imageless relation" between human words and their divine referents. I argue instead that this is neither possible nor doctrinally warranted as an ideal in a properly Christian theology. Using christological paradigms, I maintain that the status of the verbal image, albeit necessarily broken and always made new by its application to the reality of God's being and life, is nonetheless such that the "flesh" of the relevant image (in a manner analogous to the flesh of Christ) remains securely in place, and plays a vital part in the revelatory economy within which our knowing of God is held to occur.

I

Revisiting the East

1

Hellenization

§1 Gospel, Apologia, and Context

The relationship between the Christian gospel and the intellectual, religious, and cultural milieu of any given community or society has posed a challenge for the church in every time and place in relation to missionary practice as well as theological enterprise. How, in attempts to hand on the message received from Scripture and tradition, ought Christians to deploy the language and appeal to the thought forms current in their day? How ought they to interact with what sociologist Peter Berger refers to as the "plausibility structure" of particular cultures (namely that combination of beliefs and assumptions that determines what a society can accept as plausible)?[1] How far should they permit the mores of such worldviews to affect the message or, conversely, to be affected by it? Answers given to these evangelical and methodological questions cannot but determine the shape and substance of theology itself, for they are not simply questions about communication, but ones that force us back to consider the very nature of the theological task and, ultimately, the nature of the gospel.

It is easy to forget, in reading the early fathers, that their writings were motivated and shaped by precisely these existential concerns and by the ways in which they responded to them. They too belonged to cultural contexts into which the gospel entered as something essentially alien (as it always is) rather than familiar, a hard saying both to hear and to utter.

19

They too desired to present this "strange word" about Christ to their contemporaries in ways that were clear, compelling, and persuasive. They too faced the difficult question as to how this was best to be achieved. In what follows I am concerned with the nature of the responses made to this challenge by some representatives of the eastern patristic traditions, and with the ways in which these responses shaped their respective presentations of what lies at the heart of any account of the gospel, namely, what the neat categories of Christian doctrine identify as the "person" and the "work" of Christ, respectively. As we shall see, it is precisely in testing the putative boundaries of such categories that the early theologians of the Christian East are at their most interesting, suggestive, and challenging.

It is not uncommon for modern studies of the doctrine of redemption in the patristic East to conclude that in its broad outlines, it represents a decisive shift away from the language and thought-world of the Old and New Testaments. The eastern fathers, we are told, began their dialogue with the plausibility structure of what was chiefly a Hellenic culture by ceding too much too quickly to its basic presuppositions, baptizing core elements of its cosmology, its metaphysics, and its religious imagery, with the result that it is hardly recognizable any longer as continuous with the apostolic concern with our human entanglement in sin and death, and the overcoming of these through an act of atonement divinely purposed and provided. The plausibility of this analysis rests, as is so often the case, in the fact that it embraces grains of truth as well as falsity. The Greek fathers do employ the language of the philosophers and of contemporary religious understanding in expressing their understanding of the Christian gospel. We ought not to expect it to be otherwise. The question is, however, not whether they used the language of their day but how they used it and what they meant by it when they did.

In these opening chapters I am concerned with answering this question as it applies to three bishop-theologians, Irenaeus of Lyons (c. 120–140–c. 200 CE), Clement of Alexandria (c. 150–c. 211–215 CE), and Athanasius (c. 297–373 CE), the fourth-century Bishop of Alexandria best known for his disputations with the Christology of the Arians and for championing the Nicene *homoousion*.[2] All of these theologians deploy Greek language, images, and ideas in their apologetic and polemic. In considering them carefully, though, the ostensive similarities prove to conceal at least two very different styles of theology, and two quite different accounts of salvation and how it is related to the person of the Savior. This chapter embarks on an account of Irenaeus' theology, treating it as a convenient case in terms of which to introduce and respond to the wider suggestion that the Christology and soteriology of the early Greek fathers involved a "Hellenizing" of the apostolic gospel.

Irenaeus was born in Asia Minor sometime between 120 and 140 CE. He left there for Gaul, becoming a presbyter in Lugdunum and ultimately succeeding the martyred bishop of Lyons, Pothinus, in about 180 CE. Tradition suggests that Irenaeus himself was eventually martyred, but the precise date and circumstance of his death are not known. According to Eusebius of Caesarea, Irenaeus had, as a youth, heard Polycarp (Bishop of Smyrna until his martyrdom in 155 CE), who had in turn been personally acquainted with the apostle John and others "that had seen the Lord."[3] Irenaeus is known to us primarily for his major treatise the "Refutation and Overthrow of *Gnosis* Falsely So-Called,"[4] on which we still rely for much of our information concerning the various "gnostic" systems of religious thought. In this polemical and apologetic work Irenaeus seeks to defend the integrity of the Christian gospel in relation to a view of the cosmos and of the relationship between God and humankind in Christ that he holds to be alien to it.

This avowed concern for the authentic gospel notwithstanding, there has been no shortage of scholars willing to understand Irenaeus himself as departing significantly from the forms and substance of apostolic faith in the person and work of Christ. Indeed, he has been held by many to evince an early tendency among the theologians of the Christian East to do so, a tendency which arises in various forms common to which is an undue reliance on contemporary cultural and religious mores, resulting in a notion of redemption as the "divinization" or "deification" of our humanity, a type of soteriology which, such interpretations contend, is essentially Hellenic rather than biblical in its substance as well as its expression, and which duly has an impact on the estimation of the nature and status of the person of the Savior.

So, for example, in the late nineteenth century the historian of doctrine Adolf von Harnack begins his exposition of Irenaean theology with precisely this assumption. The theology of Irenaeus, he claims, will inevitably remain a riddle to us if we do not discern those elements that it borowed directly from the thought of Gnosticism. Granted that Irenaeus' purpose was the utter refutation of the gnostic systems, we should be aware that, like all apologists and polemicists, in order to achieve this end he was himself compelled to adopt some of their most characteristic themes and presuppositions, clothing the claims of faith in terms of a conceptuality more Hellenic than biblical in its resonances.[5] Harnack is not dissuaded from this reading of Irenaeus despite the fact that, unlike his North African near contemporary Clement, for instance—whose apologetics is unashamedly syncretistic, and whose "Christian Platonism"[6] depicts a world cast identifiably in Hellenic terms (despite his clear determination to populate its landscape with distinctly Christian and biblical ideas)—Irenaeus makes no deliberate attempt to baptize any Hellenic or gnostic conceptions. Indeed, he has nothing positive to say about Gnosticism at all, insisting repeatedly that his own intention is to be utterly faithful to the Scriptures interpreted in accordance with the Rule of Faith, and mocking those who seek to build their theology on any other foundation as striving "to weave ropes of sand."[7] Such insistence, though, Harnack contends, is simply the well-intentioned consequence of "a happy blindness to the gulf which lay between the Christian tradition and the world of ideas prevailing at that time."[8] Irenaeus may not have intended any syncretistic dalliance with Hellenic conceptions and doubtless believed himself to have remained pure from taint in this regard. But in reality his version of the gospel was just as surely dependent for its articulation and argument on the cultural forms furnished by the dominant Zeitgeist as were those of the gnostics that he sought to demolish. His Hellenism may have been more moderate than that of his opponents, but in the final analysis it was Hellenism nevertheless and "promoted the gradual Hellenizing of Christianity."[9]

Driving Harnack's reading of Irenaeus is a methodological assumption of his own, namely that the theological task can never finally escape syncretistic entanglements with the dominant culture within which that task is undertaken. After all, he reminds his readers at the outset of his massive historical survey, "it lies in the nature of theology that it desires to make its object intelligible," and it can do this only by being willing to reconfigure that object in terms that the wider world will find acceptable, that is, the terms proper to the plausibility structure or intellectual spirit of the time.[10] Syncretism at some fairly basic level, in other words, is a necessary condition of the successful rendering, appropriation, and spread of the gospel, and the purist idea that "theology is interpreted faith,"[11] nothing more and nothing less, is hermeneutically naive. As such, the theologies of Irenaeus and the Eastern fathers in general, while they may differ from one another in detail, are all bound to reflect "the work of the Greek spirit upon the soil of the Gospel,"[12] for even in the age of Roman empire and in Gaul, it was Greek culture that continued to dominate the life of the intellect, and much else besides.

Where Irenaeus is concerned, I suggest duly that Harnack's reading (which enjoyed some influence in patristic scholarship throughout the last century) is considerably wide of the mark. There is a quite different way of interpreting Irenaeus' Christology and soteriology than the sort Harnack's approach champions, one that both makes better overall sense of what Irenaeus says and manages to avoid characterizing him either as methodologically inconsistent or else blithely unaware of what he is actually doing (charges which ought to be laid at the door of authors only after every effort has been made first to read them on their own stated terms). On the whole, I argue, Irenaeus' handling of texts and different ways of reading them (his own or those of his opponents) suggests anything but "happy blindness" to the complexities of the task of interpreting and contextualizing meaning.

§2. Falsifying the Oracles of God

Of course, Harnack's interpretation of Irenaeus as a closet Hellenizer would have found little purchase even in the Liberal Protestant imaginations of his readers had there been nothing in Irenaeus' own writing capable of bearing an essentially Greek or gnostic interpretation. In fact, there is an abundance of language that may be so interpreted, should we choose to do so. So, for instance, while Irenaeus does not yet use the technical vocabulary of "deification" (*theopoiesis* or *theosis*) to describe the redemptive impact of God's joining of himself to humankind in the incarnation, he does speak of man "passing into God" and being "promoted into God,"[13] language that at first sight seems to bear a similar range of possible interpretations and thus to merit careful interrogation. When, therefore, he goes on to refer to salvation as the bestowal of immortality (*aphtharsia*) and incorruptibility (*athanasia*) on humankind by Jesus Christ through the divine act of incarnation,[14] and as the realization of the image of God in humanity such that we have genuine knowledge (*gnosis*) of God and are united with God,[15] Harnack has little hesitation in referring us immediately to the problematic influence of gnostic and Hellenic schemata, bound gradually to obscure rather than illuminate the *fides credenda* of the apostolic and subapostolic church.

This, though, will not do. To begin with, we should certainly acknowledge that, despite his polemical intent and the invective he reserves for his gnostic antagonists, Irenaeus is content to engage nonbiblical forms in the task of doing constructive theology. So we ought not to take his binary rhetoric at face value. But nor need we impute to him any blindness to the considerable differences between the thought world of Scripture and Christian tradition on one hand and the world of ideas prevailing in Greco-Roman culture on the other in order to account for this. Like most of the catholic fathers he is perfectly capable of differentiating between various levels and modes of engagement between cultures and between linguistic forms and the range of meanings that, used variously, these may bear. So, while he is certainly content, when it suits his purposes to do so, to appropriate words, images, and ideas from the reservoir of Greek language, life, and thought, Irenaeus is careful both in his selection and ways of using these. In broad terms, he remains averse to the introduction of Greek notions[16] where they bear no legitimate biblical or Christian analogy and thus cannot serve, *mutatis mutandis*, helpfully to render or faithfully to interpret basic Christian convictions and realizations, and he understands perfectly well that at certain key points the intellectual spirit of Hellenism may prove toxic rather than fertile for any attempt to tell the story about God and the world that the church has been mandated to tell. Sweeping gestures with regard to "Hellenism" will not suffice, therefore; the devil, as always, is in the details of particular instances of use and the possible meanings arising from these.

Thus, in his handling of texts, Irenaeus demonstrates ample awareness that meaning is not a static quantity bound up with particular terms and combinations of terms independently of their context and manner of use, and that theology is therefore always a responsible exercise in which terms are deployed in ever new contexts and endlessly creative ways that either illuminate or obscure their proper object. It is no good simply reiterating biblical statements, as if truth resided in them as statements. Like many groups judged by history to be heterodox,[17] the gnostics familiar to Irenaeus were perfectly capable of appropriating biblical language and themes, and citing them at length. In doing so, though, he complains, "They disregard the order and the connection of the Scriptures, and so far as in them lies, dismember and destroy the truth. By transferring passages, and dressing them up anew, and making one thing out of another, they succeed in deluding many through their wicked art in adapting the oracles of the Lord."[18] Whether intentionally or erroneously, "these men falsify the oracles of God and prove themselves evil interpreters of the good word of revelation," a hermeneutical failing all the more subtle and dangerous than any outright departure from Scripture, since "their language (*lalountas*) resembles ours, while their sentiments (*phronountas*) are very different,"[19] a difference easily lost on the neophyte.

This, then, is the supposition or principle on the basis of which Irenaeus proceeds both in his criticism of gnostic schemes of thought and in his own attempt to articulate a theology faithful to Scripture and to a hermeneutic informed by the Rule of Faith. Language and meaning, letter and spirit may and must not be conflated, a fact that in the same moment both liberates and binds, enabling words to be ever fresh and new in their impact rather than bound to the corpses of prior semantic transactions, and at the same time forcing on us the question of their accountability to something beyond themselves—some objective state of affairs or "truth" to which they refer us, faithfully or otherwise. Hence, for Irenaeus, there are no absolutely "true" biblical statements or "false" unbiblical ones. There are right ways of interpreting Scripture and wrong ways; right ways of translating it and wrong ways; right ways of contextualizing it and wrong ways. The criteria lie not in the words, images, and categories themselves (and Christian theology itself may and must use all sorts of terms, images, and categories if it is to remain alive and dynamic), but in the ways in which these are used and adapted to (and, in their turn, adapt us to) the shape and substance of reality,[20] either referring us to it in illuminating and fruitful ways or not. Theology done well—whatever language it may appropriate in the task—provides a prism through which the message of Scripture may better be grasped, a matrix on the basis of which that message may be further unpacked, extrapolated, and applied, and a symbolic *habitus* via the active indwelling of which our relation to God is sustained, nourished, and constantly adjusted.

§3. Incarnation and "Physical Redemption"

Let us return, though, to the way in which Irenaeus was widely interpreted in the wake of Harnack's influential representation, namely in terms of what came to be referred to as the physical theory of redemption. The essential idea is summed up conveniently by another interpreter from the Liberal Protestant stable, Friedrich Loofs (his theological formation having been influenced both by Harnack and by the great Albrecht Ritschl). The physical theory, Loofs tells us, is at its core "the understanding of redemption as the removal of *phthora* (mortality) from human nature, completed through the union of humanity and Godhead in Christ."[21] The suggestion here is that Irenaeus substitutes the categories of metaphysics for moral ones in his presentation of the gospel, reflecting a typically Greek interest

in ontology (the status of our human "being" as regards the complex schemata of material and spiritual essences) rather than a more biblical concern with our standing in relation to categories such as sin, judgment, and
guilt. Accordingly, the human plight is understood primarily in terms of
the consequences of sin for our creaturely "nature" (*physis*)—mortality
and physical death—rather than the moral condition and consequences of
sinfulness and the commission of sin itself.[22] Salvation is thus construed
as the administration of an antidote to mortality—the attributes of *aphtharsia* or *athanasia*—rather than the relational and personal realities
of forgiveness, atonement, and reconciliation of which the Bible speaks.
Already here the telltale influence of Ritschl's explicit distaste for metaphysics and his attempted amputation of it from theological constructs in
favor of moral categories[23] can be identified at work—a disjunction which,
as posited, seems quite alien to the world of the biblical writers and which,
I argue duly, indeed finds little traction in Irenaeus' way of thinking. But,
for now, let's allow the exposition to continue.

The way in which the transfusion of humanity with immortality was
conceived as having been accomplished is vaguely described by such
scholars as "realistic" or "physical." Immortality and incorruptibility are,
according to the Greek outlook on which Irenaeus is supposed to have
drawn, conditions proper to God himself alone, that is, to "divine" nature,
or *physis*.[24] Nevertheless, through the joining or union of divine and
human substances in the person of the "God-man," these same qualities
are duly communicated to humankind, infused first into the humanity
of Jesus himself and passing thereafter in a "naturalistic" or "mechanical"
manner to the whole race by virtue of a mystical union with the Redeemer.
So, following in the influential Harnack-Loofs vein of interpretation, Robert S. Franks insists that "absolutely fundamental to Irenaeus is the notion
of humanity as an organism into which Christ enters, and in which all that
he is and all that he does are as a leaven permeating the mass."[25] The incarnate Word of God is thus in effect the metaphysical bridgehead through
which a divine inoculation enters the race, a point of contact via which
humanity is given to share in the attributes of divine *physis* in a "deifying"
act. This, argues Wilhelm Bousset (another early disciple of Harnack, and
a prominent figure in the so-called history of religions school), is the idea
that dominates the "Hellenistic mystery piety" of Irenaeus' day, and so
determines the shape of his articulation of the Gospel. "The characteristic
thing," Bousset maintains, "is that here all boundaries between divine and
human fade away in an utterly astonishing fashion.... Christian piety was

more and more filled with this striving for deification, with the longing for the higher, heavenly manner of being.... Irenaeus is the first one decisively to put these ideas into the centre of his interpretation of Christianity."[26]

The redemption is accordingly seen as all but complete in the very act of joining Godhead and humanity in the virginal conception, the acts of Christ being obscured here by a concentration instead on the peculiar ontology of his personal existence, incarnation successfully displacing atonement and the cross as the focal point of Christian soteriology. As Hastings Rashdall (another English follower of the German Liberal Protestant lead) asserts in his 1915 Bampton Lectures, redemption, for Irenaeus, was "effected primarily by the incarnation, and the theory is not brought into any very close connexion with the death of Christ, except in so far as the death was necessary to the resurrection."[27] The impetus of such interpretations of patristic soteriology and its christological concomitants continues to find adherents across the decades of the twentieth century, arising in some form or other even in much more moderate and sympathetic accounts. Eastern soteriology from the early centuries onward, it is widely supposed, tended toward a view of salvation variously expressed and articulated as essentially a sharing in the divine nature,[28] communicated by a Savior who was himself necessarily both divine and human, his "person" and his "work" being, if not identified with one another, at least intertwined in a manner that tended to relativize the significance of his acts, suffering, and death on the cross within the scheme of salvation. If, though, these soteriological variations on a theme can all be classified as unhelpful intrusions of Hellenic ideas as Harnack suggests, what implications might follow from their close entanglements with Christology?

§4. Soteriological Axioms and Christological Conclusions

It is Harnack himself who takes the next step. "So far as we know," he writes, "Irenaeus is the first ecclesiastical theologian after the time of the Apologists . . . who assigned a quite specific significance to the person of Christ and in fact regarded it as the vital factor. That was possible because of his realistic view of redemption.... This conception suggested to him the question as to the cause of the incarnation as well as the answer to the same."[29] In other words, it was a particular way of understanding what salvation consists in (a "realistic" one drawn largely from Hellenic rather than biblical images and categories) that drove Irenaeus to posit a full-blooded incarnational Christology. Human beings can be infused with the qualities and condition of immortality and incorruption only if at some point their mortal nature is conjoined with God's own, to which alone such qualities properly (*kata physin*; "by nature," or, we might say, "naturally") belong. Ergo, God becomes human, uniting us to himself in Christ so that we in our turn may share a "divine" or immortal existence. A particular metaphysic leads first to a notion of redemption that in its turn becomes both the premise and the driver for a Christology; in this the Hellenization of the Gospel is more or less complete, and the way opened to a version of Christianity far removed from the theological heart of the New Testament, even though it continued to draw on its vocabulary and to claim its authority.[30]

A more recent argument in the same mold is to be found in the writings of Maurice Wiles, applied now to the more developed and precisely nuanced formularies of what emerged from various doctrinal convulsions in the fourth and fifth centuries as christological orthodoxy. Anyone reading the history of the relevant debates, Wiles notes rightly, might well suppose that Christians of the day were "excessively preoccupied with the detailed niceties of a correct intellectual formulation of their understanding of Christ's person," and become impatient with or indifferent to the endless quibbling over Greek propositions, dipthongs, iotas, and conceptual hairs capable of being split by those minded to do so. What should transform our interest, though, Wiles argues, is the realization that, despite appearances, the primary concern in all this was *soteriological*, as the fathers sought "to understand as fully as possible the nature of their Saviour and thereby of the salvation that he had brought"—something we might suppose all Christians to be properly concerned with. Thus, he concludes, "the most fundamental reasons for the rejection of Arianism and Apollinarianism were soteriological reasons."[31]

For the theologians of the ecumenical councils that pronounced on matters of Christology and so defined the substance of orthodoxy,[32] Wiles suggests, two "fundamental axioms" were at stake, each having to be held together with the other in some sort of equilibrium: first, only one who is himself God can save us, and second, whatever is not assumed by (and thereby joined to) God remains unredeemed. The first axiom drove the church's rejection of Arius (for whom the human Son of God was the incarnation not of the most high God himself but of a lower, creaturely species or stratum of "divine" or angelic being) and the second its insistence, against Apollinaris, that in Christ God became fully human rather than uniting himself to a suitably modified edition of human nature lacking in some of its less-than-godly features. The importance of positing a genuine, simultaneous union between "full Godhead" and "full humanity" duly led to the rejection of Nestorianism and to the eventual formulation of the Chalcedonian Confession, according to whose seeming theological algebra the one "person" (*hypostasis*) of the Savior subsists in two distinct "natures" (*ousiai*): "without confusion, without change, without division, without separation (ἀσυγχύτως, ἀτρέπτως, ἀδιαιρέτως, ἀχωρίστως); the distinction of natures being in no way abolished because of the union, but rather the characteristic property of each nature being preserved, and concurring into one Person and one subsistence, not as if Christ were parted or divided into two persons, but one and the same Son and only-begotten God, Word, Lord, Jesus Christ."[33] All this, to repeat, is to secure the underlying soteriological conviction that only a Savior who is himself fully God and at the same time fully human, who unites in himself genuine deity and true humanity, is able to deliver redemption as Christians in the patristic East had come to understand and think of it.

But what is this notion of salvation, and where does it come from? Like Harnack before him, Wiles is quite clear. Both axioms arise out of a particular (essentially Greek rather than essentially biblical) notion of salvation as "the impartation of the divine nature." Thus "it is within the context of an understanding of salvation as θεοποίησις," he writes, that the first axiom finds "its first clear and rigorous expression in Christian thought in the arguments of Athanasius against Arius."[34] If redemption consists in the deifying conjunction of our humanity with the nature of God himself in the person of Christ, then it follows that the one in whom that union occurs must possess or embody that nature, that is, must himself be God and not some lower species of "divine" or angelic being, let alone a mere man. Likewise, "if this is the real nature of man's salvation, it certainly seems natural to say that for man to be healed (= divinized), man" (i.e., the whole man and not something less than fully human) "must first have been 'assumed' into special hypostatic relation with the Word and thereby divinized."[35] What we have here, then, according to Wiles, are soteriological axioms derived from categories drawn primarily from the fathers' cultural, religious, and intellectual context, on the basis of which strong inferences are drawn or deductions made about the person of the Savior. Soteriology drives Christology, and the Chalcedonian doctrine of "hypostatic union" between "two natures" in the incarnation is the eventual result.[36] But with the question of the *origin* of this soteriology, Wiles observes, must go the question of the truth or falsity of the two fundamental axioms themselves, and thereby of the theological necessity of the particular christological formulations reached.[37] "Saving faith in Christ," he concludes, "is not so closely tied to an accurate understanding of the nature of his person as orthodoxy has normally assumed,"[38] and judgments about that person cannot be made on soteriological grounds, but on other, "essentially intellectual" grounds instead.[39] Having shown that classical christological orthodoxy is derived from a contextually specific notion of salvation that can or need no longer be entertained, Wiles frees himself from the constraints of supposing it to be "a criterion of genuine Christian faith" and, on the grounds of "intellectual propriety," to embrace "a very wide variety of conclusion" where the doctrines of incarnation and Trinity are concerned.[40]

§5. "Deification"

Discriminating Difference

Before coming to grips with some actual patristic texts, it may be helpful if I sketch the outlines of a broad response to the claims of the Liberal Protestant schema unfolded above, indicating precisely where I judge its interpretative insights and missteps to lie. By way of substantiation of the sketch, of course, I can only offer here the several close readings of Irenaeus, Clement, and Athanasius that I attempt in chapters 2 through 4, commending them for consideration as ones that make better sense of what each actually has to say. That, when all is said and done, is the best substantiation any interpretative hypothesis can hope for.

First, there can be no doubt that from very early on the theology of the Christian East typically discerns a very close relationship between the person of the Savior and the nature of the salvation that he brings, and that this relationship might fittingly be described as one of virtual identification: in some sense, in other words, for this theology the person of Christ *is* his work, the incarnation *is* the atonement or redemption, and so on. The question is, In what sense is this the case, and how are we to unpack and evaluate the claim? We should not rush to misunderstand it or presume its falsehood simply because it threatens to overturn the neat categories in terms of which much Western theology has typically proceeded.

Second, it is true enough that the heart of this theology finds expression in terms, categories, and images that sound foreign to the Western ear. Talk about "divinization," "deification," or "union with" or "sharing in" or "partaking of" the "divine nature" is not wholly without biblical root and warrant, and not without instance among the theologians of the West, either in the patristic era or subsequently.[41] It is, though, remote enough from the center of Western soteriology to provoke questions among those more used to the relational, ethical, pecuniary, sacral, and forensic imagery that has tended to coalesce there (albeit all, at their best, to be duly qualified by a christological and Trinitarian hermeneutic). The bold formula of Athanasius according to which "the Son of God became human so that we might become divine"[42] will possibly occasion surprise and even resistance from those more used to picturing salvation as at root a relational matter to do with sin, forgiveness, reconciliation, faith, justification, holiness, and the like, and having its center of gravity decisively in the event of Christ's death and resurrection. Such talk, we may be tempted to suppose, does seem at least to have shifted the soteriological focus, and to be unduly concerned now with the "metaphysics" of divine flesh-taking rather than the moral heart of the gospel (the "work" for the sake of which, we might be inclined to insist, the "becoming" or "assuming" or "tabernacling" of the Word among us occurred at all), not to mention its apparent willingness to soften the boundary between God and the world, the Creator and the creaturely. Might it not be *correct*, therefore, to ascribe this shift of emphasis to the contexts within which the gospel was here being proclaimed and explored—an essentially apologetic gesture designed to persuade a world to which such things mattered religiously and philosophically that the Christian message was designed to scratch their particular itch, or answer the sorts of questions they were prone or willing to put to it?

This seems to me to be a natural enough train of thought, and a reasonable question to ask. I want to suggest, though, that a straightforward answer to it is impossible and misleading to attempt to give in general terms, and that sweeping allusions to the soteriology of the east as "Hellenizing" (as though there were anything approaching even a broad theological consensus lying behind the many and varied uses of this litany of non-Western terms and images) is therefore as unhelpful as a sweeping denial of the same. The reality, I suggest, is that the language of deification, divinization, participation in God, and the rest is not simply "patent of many different nuances," as Turner puts it,[43] but situated by different authors within quite different theological economies or frames of reference that grant it its peculiar meaning, and that will bear very different soteriologies and Christologies as a consequence. In brief, my claim is that there is quite literally a world of difference between the way such terms arise and the force they bear within the writings of different theologians.

The catechetical tradition of the aforementioned Christian Platonists of Alexandria, Clement and Origen, are, I will argue, aptly so named, their apologetic zeal having certainly permitted the current "rationalities" of the academy (Middle Platonism and Neoplatonism) a determining voice in their construction of an intellectually compelling Christian theology. Clement's Logos is thus one who enters the world in order to enable the participation of human beings in the realm of divine Forms—their "deification" though the elevation and fulfillment of their rational souls by withdrawal from the world of particular material and historical realities. Correspondingly (and contra Wiles' model), Clement's Christology is driven by the conviction of God's radical transcendence, and the natural progenitor not of a properly incarnational orthodoxy but of tendencies which, in their more developed form, would duly be proscribed as heterodox.[44]

We have already seen how sensitive Irenaeus is to such hermeneutical concerns. His theology, I argue next, is of an altogether different stamp, one that I take to be determined by a Hebraic and biblical rather than an essentially Hellenic backdrop, and in broad continuity with the later thought of Athanasius and Cyril in the Alexandrian episcopal tradition, and Basil and the Cappadocians (among others) in the wider Christian East. Failure to discriminate between these quite distinct treatments of the vocabulary of *theopoiesis* has led and can only lead to an indolent failure to appreciate the force and depth of what this particular theological tradition grasped and expressed about the relationship between the person and the "work" of the incarnate Son (a grasp that, precisely in its "alien" presentation to Western readers, affords a vital corrective or counterbalance to the familiar schemas of Western theology). To trade on such indolence in order to justify the easy abandonment of such intellectually and existentially challenging ideas as the apostolic claim that God has entered the world which he created as one of his own creatures is, to my mind, altogether too convenient, and at best (to appropriate Harnack's own phrase), the result of "a happy blindness to the gulf which lay between the Christian tradition and the world of ideas prevailing at that time."[45]

The tradition embodied in the second-century writings of Irenaeus of Lyons (and furthered by Athanasius and others in the theological mainstream in subsequent centuries) was, I believe, not one in which a contextually derived model of salvation was permitted to drive christological considerations—incarnational Christology being, in effect, the child of peculiar Hellenic interest in the "divine" provenance and destiny of the

human soul. On the contrary, theological judgments about the person of
Christ were made on other grounds altogether. Christology and soteriology were, to be sure, understood by such theologians to be organically
linked, but the grounds for christological beliefs were not, for them, to be
sought ultimately in a vision of salvation (be that pagan, biblical, or otherwise). Nor, though, were they the "essentially intellectual" grounds craved
by Wiles,[46] if by that is meant the judgments of some independent rational scheme. They were (or at least they were believed to be) the grounds
of God's own self-revealing in the person of Christ as borne witness to
in the apostolic testimony in Scripture and its authoritative transmission
through the Spirit-led tradition of the church. Biblical and cultural notions
of salvation alike, in other words, were all to be *radically reinterpreted* in
the light of the climactic claim of the apostolic and subapostolic witness,
namely, that in the man Jesus of Nazareth (his life, ministry, death, and
resurrection), God himself had entered the flow of human history with
redemptive intent. The burden of such reinterpretation was such that, for
the Christian East, only the language of "union with" God, "participation
in" the life of God, or "deification" would suffice to express the enormity of
the soteriological circumstance apprehended. Some strove and managed
to encompass and make sense of such radical language within the framework of a biblically derived cosmology (thereby heightening rather than
lessening its theologically explosive connotations). Others, as we shall see,
transferred it more conservatively into a culturally acceptable account of
the world's situation vis-à-vis God, and in the process diluted it.

2

Recapitulation

§1. Redeemed Relationality

If, now, we turn to a closer engagement with Irenaeus' theology itself, perhaps the first thing to establish is that, despite the generalizations and caricatures, his account is by no means one in which Hellenic interest in the "physical" consequences of human mortality and sin are permitted to displace a *theologia crucis* or any notion of redemption as involving an atonement between God and humankind. On the contrary, he has plenty to say about our standing before God as moral agents, and of the consequences of sin for our relationship with God. "According to nature," he writes, "we are all sons of God because we have all been created by God. But with respect to obedience and doctrine we are not all the sons of God: those only are so who believe in him and do his will."[1] In other words the question of our obedience or sinfulness is bound up with the question of our personal relationship to God as Father. Sin and disobedience do not result merely in "physical" consequences but serve to separate us from that fellowship with God for which we were created. As humans we are creatures placed under the obligations of life in the presence of our Creator, and our failure to fulfill these same obligations has led to our condemnation and guilt, and our slavery to sin and the Devil, from which we now require to be set free. Irenaeus' account, in other words, gives plentiful recognition to "relational" categories as well as those which have been termed "physical."

Nor, secondly, does Irenaeus allow organic and impersonal imagery to supplant the biblical demand for faith and repentance, driving him inevitably in the direction of a mechanistic or "mystical" redemption automatic in its mode of efficacy and universal in its scope. The name of Christ, he maintains, confers benefits on and cures thoroughly and effectively "all who anywhere believe on him."[2] Likewise it is those who believe in the name of Jesus Christ our Lord who are made children (huioi) of God by him[3] and who, uniting themselves to God,[4] are made perfect by him because they acknowledge his advent. Those who, on the other hand, choose disbelief in the face of Christ's self-revelation will suffer the consequences of God's righteous judgment, being shut out into the darkness which they have chosen for themselves in preference to the light.[5] Thus "the righteous judgment of God [shall fall] on all who, like others, have seen, but have not, like others, believed."[6] God has indeed acted for the salvation of humankind, "thus making peace and friendship with those who *repent* and turn to him . . . but preparing for the *impenitent*, those who shun the light, eternal fire and outer darkness, which are evils indeed to those persons who fall into them."[7] Far from suggesting the endowing of the race with the physical quality of immortality via some mechanism or automated process, such language gives the fullest place to human response in the appropriation of and participation in the salvation which has been worked out by Christ for us.

Accordingly, Irenaeus also has much to say about our restoration to a relationship of *koinonia* with the Father through the mediation of the incarnate Son. It is in such contexts that we find a wealth of reference not just to the incarnation but also to the suffering and death of Christ as God's way of dealing with the existential breach opened up by human sin. "The Lord," Irenaeus writes, "has reconciled man to God the Father, in reconciling us to himself by the body of his own flesh, and redeeming us by his own blood."[8] It was, in fact, for this very reason that the Son of God "became a man, subject to stripes, and knowing what it is to bear infirmity."[9] How, he asks, if Christ had not undergone that birth which is proper to human beings "could he forgive us those sins for which we are answerable to our Maker and God? And how, again, supposing he was not flesh, but was a man merely in appearance, could he have been crucified, and could blood and water have issued from his pierced side?"[10] Here, then, we certainly find Christology in the foreground of his soteriological reflection and driving his rejection of gnostic docetism. Christ was, is, and must be fully human if salvation is to have been accomplished.

Whatever else may yet have to be said, though, this soteriological concern with the full humanity of the Savior is intended precisely to secure proper recognition of the importance of Christ's passion and death, and not to sideline them.

Correspondingly, Irenaeus insists too that the one who suffers and dies is to be identified with the very one who is himself offended and wounded by human sinfulness. "He was himself the Word of God made the Son of man, receiving from the Father the power of remission of sins, since he was a man, and since he was God, in order that since as man he suffered for us, so as God he might have compassion on us and forgive us our debts, in which we were made debtors to God our Creator."[11] "Therefore," Irenaeus writes, "in the last times the Lord has restored us into friendship through his incarnation, having become 'the Mediator between God and men'; propitiating, indeed, for us, the Father against whom we had sinned, and cancelling our disobedience by his own obedience."[12] In this way God himself puts his own words into deeds and loves his enemies, praying even for those who crucify him.[13] Such statements (and they are plentiful) resist any suggestion that Irenaeus sees the bare fact of incarnation itself as the sum or even the greater part of Christian soteriology; saving us "through his incarnation" is unpacked in relational categories, as something entailing an atonement or reconciliation between God and humankind wrought through the entire course of Christ's life, ministry, suffering, death, and resurrection.

It would be possible, à la Harnack, to dismiss the presence of such themes in Irenaeus' writing as little more than occasional lapses, habitual adherences to bits and pieces of a received biblical and theological heritage situated awkwardly within a wider depiction of the world to which they neither properly belong nor make any substantial difference. My purpose is to insist, to the contrary, that these familiar motifs, rooted as they are in Johannine, Pauline, and other strands of apostolic imagery and modes of expression, lie at the heart of Irenaeus' theology and are both wholly compatible with and serve to qualify his use of more Hellenic-sounding language, once the latter is properly interpreted.

§2. Irenaeus and the "Classic" Idea of Atonement

Despite the continuing influence of Liberal Protestant readings, the middle decades of the twentieth century produced a number of interpreters of Irenaeus who sought deliberately to move beyond that heritage and, in doing so, achieved more balanced and helpful accounts of his thought,

albeit ones needful in their own right of some adjustment and recalibra-
tion. One such was Gustaf Aulén, whose provocative essay *Christus Victor*
traced an overlooked or neglected emphasis in the history of treatments
of the person and work of Christ, an emphasis that he identified as present and active in the thought of various church fathers including Irenaeus.
Rather than identifying the dogmatic center of Irenaeus' theology in the
bare fact of the incarnation, Aulén argues, due recognition must be given
to the vital soteriological significance he ascribes to the whole life and
ministry of Jesus, the "acts" of Christ being far more important than any
mere "joining" of divine and human natures. Nor, therefore, for Irenaeus,
can we simply shift our attention from the virgin's womb to the cross of
Golgotha, from an essentially "physical" to an essentially ethical and
forensic understanding. There are, Aulén correctly discerns, elements of
his theology which resist the reduction of his thought to either of these
putative alternatives. He notes in particular the emphasis that Irenaeus
places on the active obedience of Jesus throughout his life, as well as on
the events surrounding his passion and death. "The earthly life of Christ
as a whole," he argues, "is . . . regarded as a continuous process of victorious conflict" over the powers of evil and death which hold humanity in
their grip, his death being understood as "the final and decisive battle."[14]

While Aulén's account (geared as it is toward his personal concern to
discredit the "Latin" model of atonement in favor of what he calls the "classic" idea)[15] might be judged to overstate its case, it succeeds at least in demonstrating the presence of the "victor" motif in Irenaeus' theology. Thus
Irenaeus writes: "Our Lord . . . fought and conquered; for he was man con-
tending for the fathers, and through obedience doing away with disobedience completely: for he bound the strong man, and set free the weak and
endowed his own handiwork with salvation, by destroying sin."[16] Again,
this is a redemption which Irenaeus understands as requiring the incarnation: "For it behooved him who was to destroy sin, and redeem man under
the power of death, that he should himself be made that very same thing
which he was, that is, man; who had been drawn by sin into bondage, but
was held by death, so that sin should be destroyed by man, and man should
go forth from death."[17]

What Aulén's analysis conveniently draws to our attention, then, is
the fact that in the theology of *Adversus Haereses* it is not merely the consequences of human sin that are dealt with in the saving economy (whether
these be understood in physical, ethical, or forensic terms) but rather
the condition of sinfulness itself as it is undone in the recapitulatory[18]

ministry of Jesus: obedience replacing disobedience, victory over evil replacing defeat by evil, freedom replacing bondage. A new humanity emerges in Christ, characterized by its freedom from the determinacy of evil. In short, the human nature which Christ shares with us is transformed through his obedient and victorious indwelling of it, so that we too might share in a life liberated from the powers and principalities that currently hold us in their thrall.

There are two points in Aulén's exposition, though, which are problematic. The first is the answer he gives to the obvious question as to how Christ's victory actually accomplishes or generates ours. Granted that Jesus lives a victorious life in the face of temptation and thereby establishes a new sort of human existence in the world, in what sense can this be understood to be "for us"? By what mechanism or process of redemptive influence is his victory communicated so that we, too, share in it, rather than its disappearing again from the face of the earth with his eventual return to the Father's right hand? Aulén's answer resorts to the language of pneumatology and eschatology, respectively. For Irenaeus, he maintains, "the Recapitulation does not end with the triumph of Christ over the enemies which had held man in bondage; it continues in the work of the Spirit in the Church." Furthermore, "the completeness of the Recapitulation is not realized in this life: Irenaeus' outlook is strongly eschatological. . . . It remains true, however, that in the process of the restoring and perfecting of creation . . . the central and crucial point is the victory of Christ over the hostile powers."[19] In other words, the ministry of Christ sees the beginning of a process in which the Spirit empowers individual men and women, enabling piecemeal victories over the powers of evil which, for now, are limited in scope, the full reality and presence of "new humanity" being hidden with Christ in God's future, the subject of divine promise and human hope. While all this may be true enough for Irenaeus, it does not quite capture the distinctiveness of his vision, something I seek to redress below.

The second problematic element in Aulén's account is his understanding of the christological frame within which Irenaeus perceives redemption as occurring. He rightly notes what we have already seen, namely that in *Adversus Haereses* "incarnation and atoning work are . . . set in the closest possible relation to one another." Yet in the instant that he affirms the importance of the victorious obedience of Christ as a transforming of our nature from within, Aulén calls this into question again by an undue emphasis on the God-humanward dynamic of the incarnation—namely its function as a coming of God "from above," as distinct from its aspect as encompassing a corresponding movement "from below" toward God by the now enfleshed Son. Thus, he insists, Irenaeus "does not think of the Atonement as an offering made to God by Christ from man's side, or as it were 'from below'; for God remains throughout the effective agent in the work of redemption."[20] When, therefore, "Irenaeus speaks in this connection of the 'obedience' of Christ he has no thought of a human offering made to God from man's side, but rather that the Divine will wholly dominated the human life of the Word of God, and found perfect expression in his work."[21]

Aulén's concern here is to avoid what he realizes to be the danger of any suggestion that Christ acts as Savior in a purely human capacity over against a God who is understood to be the object rather than the subject of the atoning event, a danger which Aulén sees realized in the Latin model. Irenaeus would certainly concur with the concern, but his way of averting the danger, I suggest, is a rather different and more nuanced one. He is clear throughout that the active subject in the incarnation is God himself in the person of the Son, but he is equally clear that in the economy of incarnation God enters into our creaturely nature in such a manner as to be susceptible to genuinely creaturely experience and capable of genuinely human acts. So, for instance, he condemns various gnostic texts in which a Hellenic divorce between divine and human, spirit and matter renders such claims nonsensical, resulting in one or another form of docetism or proto-Nestorian dualism, with a human "son of Joseph" on whom the divine Christ descends and enacts works of divine power but from whom he departs again, being incapable of such merely human experiences as suffering and death.[22] By refusing to predicate creaturely experiences and actions of the one who is himself the Word of God, invisible, incomprehensible, and impassible,[23] Irenaeus insists, such theology loses its grip on the most radical and remarkable thing, the thing that is indeed a scandal to Jews and foolishness to Greeks because it refuses to be dictated to by prior religious sensibilities or philosophical schemes, but the thing that alone finally makes the story of Jesus *good* news as well as shocking news. That is, of course, the claim that here, uniquely, God himself becomes his own creature ("He is man, the formation of God"[24]) precisely so that, indwelling humanity as its proper subject, he may be capable of human actions and passions because "in *every respect* . . . He is man, . . . the invisible becoming visible, the incomprehensible being made comprehensible, the impassible becoming capable of suffering,"[25] and thereby "He took up man into Himself."[26] We might express the matter, therefore, by saying that, for Irenaeus, it is certainly God who is the agent of salvation from first to last, but in Christ it is precisely *humanly* that God acts, and the fully human integrity of his agency is essential to what occurs redemptively. What this entails for Irenaeus we shall see duly.

§3. Divine Victory Humanly Wrought

Another scholar who emphasizes the soteriological import for Irenaeus of the whole scope of the incarnation, culminating in the cross and the empty tomb, is Aulén's fellow Swede, Gustaf Wingren. Drawing on the same key themes of conflict and victory in *Adversus Haereses*, Wingren, however, stresses precisely the fact that it is *as a human being* that Christ is presented throughout the struggle, and that his obedience and ultimate victory are therefore essentially human ones. Thus, he writes, for Irenaeus "Jesus Christ is a man. He belongs to our race. As a man he must confront both sin and death. In his temptation he takes sin upon him, and on the Cross death itself finally enfolds him. But neither of the two enemies of humanity can get this man into its power. Christ resists temptation and he rises from the dead. And when a man forces both evil and corruption to turn away from him, as Jesus does, the purpose for man is realized, for man was ordained to live and to live in righteousness."[27] No matter what we may have to say about the nature of God's involvement *as God* in the particular struggles and triumphs of this human life, therefore, it cannot entail the elision or displacement of a fully human experience of and mode of engagement in them by the incarnate Son. It is precisely Christ's genuine identity with us in the weakness and bondage of our nature that gives his ultimate victory its integrity and thus its redemptive significance for others, for, Wingren suggests, it is in this very conflict with the forces of evil (both those within and those without) that human nature is actually recreated and redeemed.[28]

The issue at stake here is the same one that would arise in later patristic debates over whether or not Christ could be said to have had a human soul/mind or possessed a human will.[29] Irenaeus' supposition anticipates the soteriological concern lying behind the eventual orthodox insistence that he must indeed have had such, since it is precisely through the conforming from within of a human will, mind, soul, and body to God's own holy character that "at-one-ment" is effected, and humankind reconciled and restored to wholeness and life. The "victory" is salvific precisely and only because it is won humanly, and not simply by divine power wielded by fiat through the instrument of an essentially passive human form. Yet, in affirming the full integrity of Jesus' humanity in Irenaean theology, Wingren sees no need to question his conviction that it is God himself who acts humanly here, or that God is indeed fully involved also a second time *as God* in the complex dynamics of the incarnation, creating, sustaining, and bringing to fullness the obedient response of a humanity being "made anew." Unlike Aulén, he is sensitive to the fact that, as we have just seen, Irenaeus perceives no yawning ontological gulf between Creator and creature of the sort which Platonism typically posited between the divine and the human. On the contrary, if the proper distinction between Creator and creature is maintained, the fact of the incarnation excludes the possibility of any such radical divorce, pointing instead to the openness of the created order to the working of God, and to God's continual presence to and involvement in, with, and through its processes.[30] The God who has taken flesh is precisely the God who formed our humanity in his own hand, and in his own image and likeness, and while we cannot measure or comprehend his greatness, he is nonetheless close to us rather than far flung from us on some putative spectrum according to which Creator and human creature cannot coinhere or cohabit.[31] Thus it is not the case that we must affirm the absence of divine action in order to preserve the presence of a fully human action. Were it so, Christology would indeed be bound to collapse variously into some version or precursor of docetism, Ebionitism, Arianism, Monophysitism, or Nestorianism, all of which are born ultimately of the ill-advised attempt to ground Christianity's incarnational claim on a dualistic metaphysic in whose grammar the adverb "humanly" (ὡς ἄνθροπος) does not meaningfully qualify any verb having God as its subject.

For Irenaeus, though, Jesus is both the God who redeems and the man who is redeemed; both the God who pours out his Spirit and the man who receives and is transformed by it; both the God who judges and the man who bears the judgment for others.[32] The relationship between Creator and creature is understood in dynamic terms as a bilateral exchange which begins in God and elicits response from his creatures; for Irenaeus, in the enfleshing of the Son this dynamic as a whole is drawn across the threshold into the life of God ("He took up man into himself"),[33] becoming now a function or quality of the eternal relationship between Father and Son. Thus, Irenaeus writes, "The Word of the Father . . . having become united with the ancient substance of Adam's formation, rendered man living and perfect, receptive of the perfect Father, in order that as in the natural [Adam] we all were dead, so in the spiritual we may all be made alive."[34] While, therefore, we must be clear that Christ's response to the Father is precisely one we could not make (hence its redemptive quality), we must be equally clear that it is nothing less than a fully human response (in an important sense, the first and *only* fully human response), and that in Christ's making it—throughout his life and in the moment of his death—the human circumstance as a whole is altered decisively.

So, the union of God and humanity in Christ is no "bare fact" but rather the dynamic interweaving of divine and human existences in a particular life lived humanly and offered from moment to moment and at its end to the Father by the Son. In this self-offering, Irenaeus avers, the Son's purpose was to "accustom man to receive God and God to dwell in man,"[35] a reception and indwelling to be configured not in static, substantialist terms but as "attaching man to God by his own incarnation, and bestowing upon us at his coming immortality durably, and truly, by means of communion with God."[36] Such communion with God is itself the communication of "immortality,"[37] and death or nonexistence is precisely its absence.

§4. Improvising on an Apostolic Image

We have, I hope, reached the point where we can discern the inadequacy of any interpretation of Irenaeus in which all that matters for the salvation of humankind is some static linking or fusion of two inert "natures," divine and human, such that the proper qualities of the one might invade or infect the other redemptively. For Irenaeus, the "joining" of our humanity to God is effected in no such abstract and timeless manner but rather by the assumption and transfiguration of the dynamics of divine-human relationship within the life of God himself, conforming the pattern of our humanity to the contours of God's own character in the life of Jesus and thereby "recapitulating in himself his own handiwork."[38] Yet we have also seen that Irenaeus can and does speak of salvation as accomplished objectively in the dynamics of this particular man's "union" with God for our sakes. How, then, are we to think of this particular transforming and conforming of our humanity as being genuinely redemptive for others? The answer lies precisely in Irenaeus' distinctive appropriation of the metaphor of a "recapitulation" (ἀνακεφαλαίωσις) of the universal history of humankind in its relation to God in the particular history of the man Jesus, the metaphor to which we now turn.

Irenaeus speaks repeatedly of Christ's having recapitulated or "summed up" the human race in himself and thus, in his particular actions, endowed the whole with salvation.[39] We today are familiar with the image from its deployment, for instance, in the vocabulary of musicology where it denotes the return, within classical sonata form, to the exposition of a main musical theme after its varied melodic and harmonic development, often entailing the resumption of the tonic or "home" key after the creative tension generated by modulations of one sort or another. Such usage suggests the reiteration or revisiting of the basic pattern, the head (κεφαλή), original fount, or sum total (κεφάλαιον) of something with a resolution of some sort involved. While Loofs in particular wanted to find in Irenaeus' use of the image dependence on an earlier theological tradition already well established in Asia Minor,[40] most scholars have been content to see Irenaeus as borrowing consciously from the usage of the apostle Paul in Romans 13:9 concerning the "summing up" of the entire law in the "second greatest commandment," and in Ephesians 1:10 concerning the Father's intention in the fullness of time to "sum up" or "gather up" (NRSV) or concentrate all things (in heaven and earth) in Christ, this being "the mystery of [God's] will" in creation and redemption.[41] Irenaeus' frequent juxtaposition of such language with other Pauline imagery (such as the parallelism between Christ and Adam in Rom 5) no doubt reflects his close familiarity with the apostle's thought. Yet, even were commentators to be in broad agreement about Paul's use of the verb ἀνακεφαλαιόομαι and its cognates,[42] this would hardly suffice to determine our interpretation of Irenaeus. Continuity of meaning between the apostolic writings and the second-century bishop (let alone between Irenaeus and modern compositional techniques) cannot simply be presumed, and we should permit Irenaeus' own use of the word in context to guide our attempts to fathom his distinctive understanding of it.

§5. Recapitulation as Reiteration and Reversal

When we turn to the text of *Adversus Haereses* there seem, in fact, to be two main emphases in Irenaeus' use of the vocabulary of *recapitulatio*.

First, the recapitulation effected in Christ involves a reiteration of the history of humankind's relationship with God. Christ is the new human, the *eschatos Adam* who fulfills the creaturely destiny of the first. Yet in view of the oft-expressed view that Irenaeus holds only to a token "Fall,"[43] it must be emphasized that this reiteration is no mere perfecting of something essentially good in itself, no realization of a potential toward which humankind has aspired and strived but of which it has fallen short. On the contrary, for Irenaeus the recapitulation calls humankind into account, functioning as judgment as well as grace, because it takes the form of a radical reversal of the dynamics of human life before God, from disobedience to obedience, from sin to faith, from apostasy to fellowship, and hence from death to life; it is in this very reversal that salvation is achieved. In the history of the new human the sinfulness of Adam is undone and its horrific consequences eradicated.

In the man Jesus, therefore, God effectively creates a new point of contact between himself and his fallen creation. This theme of a new beginning, a fresh start between God and humankind, and Irenaeus' own polemical concern to hold together the themes of creation and redemption in opposition to the gnostics (who typically polarized them and ascribed creation the status of a botched job by a "demiurge" rather than the handiwork of the God revealed in Christ) lead him to make substantial use of Paul's Christ-Adam parallel in Romans 5. Thus he presents Christ's life of obedience as restoring what had been damaged or destroyed through the sin of Adam. "When he became incarnate, and was made man, he commenced afresh the long line of human beings, and furnished us . . . with salvation; so that what we had lost in Adam—namely, to be according to the image and likeness of God—that we might recover in Christ Jesus."[44] Unlike the first Adam, who was defeated by the devil, Christ, entering the same situation, emerges victorious from it, "waging war against our enemy, and crushing him who had at the beginning led us away captives in Adam."[45] In so doing he offers and commends our humanity to the Father,[46] and renders it receptive of the Father,[47] thereby restoring it to that communion with the Father in which life and immortality properly consists.

The parallelism is developed, occasionally at length and in what may sometimes seem a fanciful manner,[48] in order to drive home the point that Christ was "himself made the beginning of those who live, as Adam became the beginning of those who die."[49] Thus, for example, "as by the disobedience of the one man who was originally moulded from virgin soil, the many were made sinners, and forfeited life; so was it necessary that, by the obedience of one man, who was originally born from a virgin, many should be justified and receive salvation."[50]

A further motive for Irenaeus' extensive appropriation of Pauline Christ-Adam typology was perhaps his determined embrace of Christ's full humanity, attacking the docetic tendencies of the followers of

Valentinus, for example, who, he insists, by denying the integrity of the "flesh" which the Son of God assumed effectively "exclude[s] the flesh from salvation."[51] It is Adamic nature in its entirety that is the object of divine salvation, Irenaeus maintains, and Christ "would not have been one truly possessing flesh and blood, by which he bought us back, unless he had summed up in himself the ancient formation of Adam."[52] In laying hold of our humanity and making it his own, Christ's purpose is to restore immortality to it, endowing it once again with that image and likeness to God which had been twisted beyond recognition as a result of Adam's fall into sin. And his obedience unto death, therefore, is no mere Anselmian *satisfactio* rendered to salve the offended divine honor, nor the payment of a redemption price, but rather itself a positive gift bestowed on our nature as human creatures, a sanctifying of humanity which lifts it up from its fallen and alienated condition and establishes it so that it may participate freely and fully in the divine life and will. Furthermore, the bestowal of this gift comes not by external donation but through a particular human struggle with sin and evil, and a victorious wrestling of the "flesh" into its proper condition. This clearly could not occur unless the humanity of Christ was indeed the same humanity that had perished in Adam, and not some other, discreetly modified or truncated humanity. "He had himself, therefore, flesh and blood, recapitulating in himself not a certain other, but that original handiwork of the Father, seeking out the thing which had perished," and making it his own and the object of his redemptive indwelling.[53] And again: "It behoved Him who was to destroy sin, and redeem man under the power of death, that He should Himself be made that very same thing which he was, that is, man; who had been drawn by sin into bondage, but was held by death, so that sin should be destroyed by man, and man should go forth from death."[54] For Irenaeus, just as surely as for the Cappadocian fathers in a later century, the soterio-logic here was the same: that which has not been laid hold of and "recapitulated" in Christ's victorious struggle must remain estranged and fallen. The unassumed is the unredeemed. Hence, Irenaeus concludes, "*Flesh* is that which was of old formed for Adam by God out of the dust, and it is this that John has declared the Word of God became."[55]

At this point it is natural to inquire whether, given Irenaeus' clear emphasis on Christ's sharing fully in our human condition and redeeming it from within, he understands the Adamic "flesh" of the incarnation as one participant in our fallenness, or the prelapsarian humanity with which Adam was created. In response, we might note first that these are not terms in which Irenaeus himself frames things, and any answer we give must therefore be based on inference from other things that he does say. Studies of this question vary in their willingness to ascribe the idea of fallen humanity to Irenaean Christology,[56] and again this reflects the ambiguity inherent in the question itself as well as the sorts of things he has to say which might be deemed relevant to an answer. At least one study insists that, together with several other patristic theologians, Irenaeus' soteriology asserts "a principle that forcefully advances" the conclusion that Christ's flesh must have been fallen rather than free from the taint and consequences of sin:[57] the principle, namely, that what is not assumed in the incarnation is not healed and drawn into the life of God.

Of Irenaeus' thought we should remind ourselves of several things. First, as we have seen, he takes the idea of a fall and its terrible impact on our humanity fully seriously, rather than softening or mitigating its force as has sometimes been suggested. Second, as we have just seen, the sort of humanity that had been drawn by sin into bondage and made subject to the power of death is precisely the sort of humanity that, in the incarnation, the divine Word or Son assumed, so that he might recapitulate it in himself. Third, it was by struggle and victorious obedience, and by offering himself up to God's holy judgment on the cross that Christ's victory over sin and death was won and the refashioning of our humanity accomplished. There is no suggestion anywhere in Irenaeus' writings of a fresh start for humankind accomplished by the generation *de novo* in Jesus of a new humanity untainted by sin and its effects. Instead it is by the regeneration from within of our own "old" humanity, entangled as it is in bondage and death, that this is understood as having been accomplished. And yet, of course, fourth, Irenaeus insists equally on Christ's redemptive difference from us at every point, and his Christology needs (as all Christology does) to be able to account for this too. Jesus does what we do not and could not do, and does it in our stead. On the whole, though, Irenaeus is far more concerned to emphasize Christ's solidarity with us in all things, eschewing gnostic docetism, than he is with the danger of a Christology that makes him *too* human or "*only* human." In this he seems content to live with the tension already implicit in the statement of the Epistle to the Hebrews that Christ was "in every respect tested . . . as we are, yet without sin" (Heb 4:15, NRSV).[58] To admit the latter would be to explode Irenaeus' soteriology just as surely as to deny the former.

So much depends on the particular parsing of technical theological categories (What does "fallenness" amount to? What is its precise impact on our human capacity and incapacity? To what extent is it an individual and to what extent a corporate or social phenomenon? Is it inevitable that a "fallen" creature, bound up in "original sin," will in fact *commit* sin?) that it is perhaps more illuminating to rest content instead with the terms in which Irenaeus does express himself rather than speculate about how he might have used those which, for whatever reason, he chooses not to.

So eager is Irenaeus to insist that our shared creaturely nature in its entirety was laid hold of redemptively in the dynamic of the incarnation that he tends occasionally to forms of fancy which depart identifiably from the particulars of what the Gospel accounts tell us of Jesus' life, ministry, and death and, in doing so, run the risk of turning his humanity into something of an abstraction. So, for instance, he refers to Christ's

> not despising or evading any condition of humanity, nor setting aside in himself that law which he had appointed for the human race, but sanctifying every age by that period corresponding to it which belonged to himself. For he came to save all through means of himself—all, I say, who through him are born again to God—infants, and children, and boys, and youths, and old men. He therefore passed through every age, becoming an infant for infants, thus sanctifying infants; a child for children, thus sanctifying those who are of this age. . . . So likewise, he was an old man for old men . . . sanctifying at the same time the aged also.[59]

Quite apart from stretching historical credulity in counting Christ among the aged ("over 50 years old") at the point of his death, the logic here will appear problematic to modern readers on other grounds too, seeming as it does to suggest that Christ must share certain levels of human particularity (in this case, age) in order to redeem those characterized by them. The same logic in our own day has been used variously by feminists, advocates of black theology, and others to pose questions about their own potential exclusion from a salvation wrought by a Savior whose humanity is admitted to be irreducibly particular (and in its particularity different from theirs). This is an issue we revisit later in this volume.[60] For now, though, we can be content simply to note again the antidocetic impulse that drives Irenaeus to venture on this affirmation that Christ shared in the fullest sense in the humanity of his creatures, leaving, as it were, no corner of human existence and experience unexplored and thus unredeemed.

Before moving on we should note that for Irenaeus the reiteration of our humanity in Christ includes a retrospective, negative aspect too. Christ assumed flesh and blood not just to wrestle it into conformity with his own divine character but in order to suffer and die too, because this same flesh and blood stood properly under the divine judgment. Thus it is in his death as well as in his life that Christ sums up ours.[61] The complete refashioning of our fallen and broken nature is accomplished in this willing submission to divine judgment, which comes as the summation of a life lived at one with the Father's judgment and will: "The Lord has restored us into friendship through his incarnation, having become 'the Mediator between God and men'; propitiating indeed for us the Father against whom we had sinned, and cancelling our disobedience by his own obedience; conferring also upon us the gift of communion with, and subjection to, our Maker."[62] The incarnation of the Logos, therefore, sees the old humanity assumed, wrestled into submission, and put to death, and the new humanity raised up in its place. All this takes place in the particular humanity Christ assumed and made his own. But that, of course, raises the question, In what sense is this redemptively effective "for us"? How is it that Irenaeus can refer to Christ's "saving in his own person" what had originally perished in Adam, as if in this same event others too have been saved?

§6. Recapitulation as Solidarity and Substitution

This question leads us naturally to consider the second identifiable strand in the metaphor of recapitulation as Irenaeus uses it, namely the sense in which Christ "sums up" or includes within himself and his actions the larger whole of the human race. The new humanity is forged in a manner which not only reiterates and reverses the gestalt of humankind's fallen existence, but is inclusive of others, what he is and does being for their sake, and they being implicated in it. His particular humanity is the part which represents the whole, and the whole is included within what he is and does so that it is theirs too. Thus he came "and gathered together all things in himself . . . summing up all things in himself,"[63] the Creator summing up his own handiwork in himself by becoming part of it,[64] that in his reiteration and reversal of the pattern of its history before him, "all flesh" may be raised up and renewed.[65] There is, then, an ontological bond or solidarity between this one man and all other members of the race (perhaps even with all creation) by virtue of which what is his may properly be predicated of them too. This is how Irenaeus understands the repeated biblical insistence that Christ is "for us."

Such language and imagery do not resonate naturally with the more individualistic sensibilities of our own intellectual *milieu*, and it is tempting to seek to account for it in terms of some primitive or now outmoded

philosophical outlook. Before doing so, though, we need to reckon fully
with the fact that similar assumptions are to be found woven through the
canon of Scripture, and not least in texts closely associated with Israel's
emergent messianic hope and the church's eventual reception and interpretation of the same. Time and again we find expressions and trains of
thought that indicate that wholes are taken to be included in a very concrete sense within representative parts, and groups concentrated within
particular individual members of them;[66] this comes to a particularly
striking and seemingly extraordinary head in the New Testament's witness to what one helpful treatment of the subject calls "an understanding
and experience of Christ as corporate."[67] Central to this witness, of course,
is the first chapter of Ephesians and the use of this same image of recapitulation, this being set, though, against the backdrop of a far wider Pauline
theology of "incorporation" (such as his ways of using the images of the
body and the temple, and his idiosyncratic use of the phrase "in Christ,"
the force of which has certainly perplexed some biblical scholars)[68] and
alongside the development of discrete but similar themes and images
in the Johannine writings and the presence in the synoptic traditions
of motifs concerning the Son of Man, the suffering Servant, and others.
Despite its extraordinariness, therefore, there is a good case to be made
that Paul is nonetheless being faithful in his development of such ideas to
a significant mode of thought in the heritage of the Hebrew Scriptures and
their testimony to the shape and substance of God's promise. And it seems
to me, too, therefore, that a similar case can be made that Irenaeus, rather
than drawing on the categories of esoteric mystery religions or particular philosophical suppositions about "concrete universals," is at this point
doing little more than be faithful to something lying at the heart of Christian Scripture and foregrounded in particular in the writings of Paul, and
that the second-century bishop gives us the clue to this presumed heritage precisely in his extensive use of the Pauline term ἀνακεφαλαίωσις.
We may continue to find such notions perplexing, but as C. F. D. Moule
notes, "What causes the puzzlement is a phenomenon that undoubtedly
does present itself in the New Testament, explain it how one may,"[69] and
we cannot therefore resolve our sense of perplexity at its appearance in
Irenaeus' theology by presuming it to be incidental, or part of a cultural
husk from which his gospel can be liberated. It is not that. It is essential to
the apostolic gospel as he understands and presents it.

　　Since we cannot here explore further the biblical background to this
aspect of Irenaeus' thought, we concentrate next precisely on clarifying the

way Irenaeus himself presents and seems to understand it. First, it does not seem to involve any compromising of Christ's individuality. Indeed, as we have already seen, in an important sense it is precisely his individuality, his particularity, his difference from all others that is redemptive. The technical distinctions drawn in later soteriological discussions may help to sharpen the point: for Irenaeus Christ is not merely our representative before God; indeed, in a vital sense he is not *representative* of us at all, being radically different in his human response to God, and saves us by *substituting* his difference to us at every point in our relationship with God—doing what we do not and cannot do, both in his life and his death. All this is done, as we typically say, *instead of* us, because we were incapable of doing it ourselves. So, there can be no confusion of his humanity and ours. He is not to be thought of as one in whom humanity's best and highest aspirations to godliness are at last fulfilled and ably "represented" in a champion. On the contrary, he comes to judge our aspirations and our accomplishments, to put them to death, and to replace them with his own. In this much, he stands not with us but over against us.

Despite this careful and consistent disentangling of the Savior from the saved, though, Irenaeus clearly does perceive a real and unbreakable bond between them, a solidarity that goes far beyond the ordinary ties of nature and kinship, and which enables him to be and to act in their place in such a manner that they themselves are implicated or included in his being and actions. If substitution is indeed a relevant category, therefore, it is nonetheless a substitution that includes rather than excludes those in whose part it is undertaken. Only thus can we make sense, for example, of the claim that Christ "sanctifies his nature for us."[70] Such a statement makes no sense if we seek to force it into the mold of an external transactional relation between Christ and others. Yet once we recognize that for Irenaeus the relationship is instead one of inclusive solidarity and participation, we can begin to grasp how Christ's obedience, righteousness, and holiness can genuinely be said to *belong to* others, as he gives his soul for their soul, his flesh for their flesh, attaching them to God, as Irenaeus says, by his incarnation.[71] In him, all the divine promises to humankind find their concrete fulfillment,[72] and so it is only insofar as we are united to him and have a share in him that we are given to share in those promises. In this sense Christ may indeed be said to represent the whole race as the new human, the one in whom for the first time the covenant between Israel and God is fulfilled, and fulfilled from both sides;[73] but this representative status rests wholly on his own decision to redeem his own handiwork by taking flesh and making it his own, and so summing up the totality of all flesh in himself—the one who, as its Creator, is of course "always present with the human race" sustaining and holding us in being, now present with and to us humanly too, "united to and mingled with His own creation."[74]

§7. Recapitulation, Regeneration, and Response

A final point to clarify is that this emphasis on the objective accomplishment of salvation in the dynamics of the incarnation, where a new humanity is wrought for all and all are drawn into the Son's human relationship with the Father, does not lead Irenaeus to any easy universalism or an antinomian lessening of insistence on the imperatives of the gospel (faith, repentance, and baptism). On the contrary, such things become more rather than less urgent, as what we are now in Christ renders our continuing unbelief and sinfulness all the more problematic, and Irenaeus is damning, for instance, in his criticism of gnostic ideas according to which the truly "spiritual" nature need not fear pollution by the indulgence of our bodies in the "lusts of the flesh." Such things, he insists, can have no place in the kingdom of God, nor those who practice them.[75] But for Irenaeus our sanctification straddles the boundaries between what modern analysis might identify as the "objective" and the "subjective" dimensions of redemption.[76] It is an established fact in the humanity of Christ which he laid hold of and transfigured through his life, death, and resurrection, and whose humanity was and is "for us"; on what must be admitted to be a second-order level for Irenaeus, it gradually works itself out in our lives as the Spirit unites us ever more fully to Christ and enables our participation in the image and likeness of God.[77] Thus, in the wisdom of God, God's ancient handiwork, "incorporated with [corporatum] and conformed to [conformatum] his Son, is brought at last to perfection."[78]

It is the theme of the solidarity of humankind with Christ in his regeneration of our nature that, when coupled with the acknowledgment of who Christ himself is, provides the key to Irenaeus' talk of salvation as a matter of being united with, or joined to, or even "promoted into" God,[79] talk in which, we have seen, some scholars have sought and found justification for classifying his soteriology as more Greek than biblical. It is instructive, though, to read further in the passage just alluded to, where it becomes clear that "promotion into God" is no matter of blending or bolting together abstract "natures," or the elevation of the human creature to some "semi-divine" status. Instead it is all about our union with the Word who has taken flesh, making our humanity his own, restoring in it the divine image and likeness, and so lifting it (and us together with it) into his own filial relationship with the Father within the life of God.[80] By virtue of that radical divine "becoming" which Irenaeus is at pains to insist on, but which genuinely Hellenic thought could neither stomach nor make intelligent sense of, the humanity of Jesus (with which we are all united and of which we each partake) is precisely the humanity of God, yet there is never any suggestion that it becomes "divine" or even "semi-divine" as a result. It is taken up into the life of God, because the eternal Son becomes a human Son as well, living out his relationship to his Father from within our broken humanity, empowered by the gift of the Holy Spirit, and so making it anew through his history of victorious obedience and holiness. It is in this sense that Christ unites us to God by his incarnation,[81] uniting us with himself (the human Son), drawing us into a relationship that falls properly within the very being of God, pouring out that "paternal grace" which belongs by nature to him alone in his knowing of the Father,[82] and which is itself the substance of immortality and life in all its fullness.

The lack of appetite for such fundamental Christian claims amid a predominantly Greek intellectual culture was not one that was easy to remedy or overcome. In chapter 3 we shall see how attempts nonetheless to cater for Hellenic tastes could all too easily go wrong, modifying theological recipes in ways that would surrender the piquancy and distinctive flavors of apostolic Christianity, and serving up instead something altogether more predictable and bland.

3

Divinization

Where philosophical and religious ideas were concerned, Alexandria in the late second to early third centuries CE was a melting pot.[1] The ascendancy of Platonism was very apparent, though, whether that be in the academic guise of Middle Platonism or explicitly religious as in the Hellenistic Judaism of Philo.[2] The peculiar fusion of philosophy and religion in which a broadly Platonist description of how it is that we come to know the truth coincided with an account of what it means to be redeemed had begun already with Philo, but it came to fruition in the philosophical theology of the Neoplatonists, not least in the writings of their chief exponent, Plotinus.[3] In Plotinus in particular, therefore, we are dealing with a prominent pagan peer of the early Alexandrian fathers, and with a system of redemption that may be held conveniently to embody the influences of the contemporary intellectual milieu, thus affording a useful control for our reading of his Christian contemporaries.

§1. Keeping Body and Soul Apart

The hallmark of all types of Platonism is the division of reality into two self-contained and to some extent mutually antagonistic categories. First, there is the realm of reality proper (κόσμος νοητός), the world of perfect, eternal, and universal Forms or ideas where true being, and hence truth, is to be found. Second, there is the imperfect realm of phenomena (κόσμος ἀισθητός), the particular objects of sense experience, ever in a state of flux and "becoming" (rather than "being"), and so never the locus of truth in the proper sense. Offering his own take on this ontology,[4] Plotinus posits a complex hierarchy of realities with "the One" (or the Good, or the First) at its apex and sensible matter at its base. All is conceived as having emanated from the One, and each stratum of being is simultaneously generated and generating with respect to what is situated above and below it in the pyramid of existence. The "Intellectual Principle" (or "Divine Mind") is the first emanation and the image of the One. With it begins the existence of multiplicity and complexity, or "being." It is the highest knowable reality and contains within itself the divine "ideas." Immediately below it is the "World Soul" (or simply "Soul"), which includes within itself all souls. It emanates from the Divine Mind, and is directly responsible for generating all "lower" existence in accordance with the ideas.

Plato's positing of the existence of an objective order of universals or "forms" had been a response to a problem epistemological and linguistic in origin. How, if the realities of which we speak and claim to know are forever changing, can we ever claim to know or speak of them *truly*? For in this case the words we use to refer to them will never apply to them in the same sense on two or more separate occasions but must themselves constantly be changing in their meaning. For there to be stability in our knowing and speaking, therefore, there must be some third thing, some reality distinct both from the material particulars of experience and from the words we apply to them, something to which our minds attend and our words apply appropriately if not exhaustively on each occasion of their proper use. In the writings of his middle period[5] in particular, Plato moved away from the suggestion that the "form" (to which the mind attends and our common names apply) was an element to be identified *within* material particulars, and instead came increasingly to insist that the form or idea of something had an existence wholly transcendent of the material realm and held in an awkward tension with it.

Thus, for example, in the *Phaedo*[6] Socrates does more than *distinguish* between particulars and universals; he goes much further, arguing that the former are but *imperfect copies* of the latter and fail to embody them properly or precisely. Thus, he argues, while sticks or stones of equal length or size may suggest to us the abstract, universal form of equality, they do so not because they are true embodiments of it but rather because the mind is already familiar with this form and is reminded of it by the sight of its imperfect correlate in sensible objects. Plato's argument concerning the epistemic process of *anamnesis*[7] is based squarely on the same contention that it is impossible to come to know the form of a thing through abstraction and induction based on empirical experience, insisting instead that the mind's a priori familiarity with the forms or ideas is the basis for our capacity to recognize ("remember") and classify things appropriately at all. The parable of the cave in the *Republic*[8] presses the point further. Here, immersion within and attention to the world of material particulars is likened to a state of illusion, and exposure to the truth is held to require not the bringing of the "shadows" of empirical experience into sharper focus, but a form of epistemic μετάνοια which literally turns its back on them and seeks reality in a different direction altogether. Here, particulars are related to their respective forms by a relation of "participation" or "imitation" that is characterized by shortfall and distortion, and if the human soul is ever to attain truth in this life it must therefore be by a painful and disciplined process which consciously withdraws from the empirical and transient in order to attend instead to the perfect ideas, truth being available, in fact, only in inverse proportion to the extent of our entanglement with the empirical and historical.

Like all transcendentalist philosophies, Plato's persistent dualism between material and intelligible reality poses all manner of problems, especially in its more robust statements. That Plato himself began to reconsider the starkness of his account of the "mimetic" relation between particulars and their forms is apparent from the *Parmenides*, though the matter is left unresolved there, and remains unresolved in his later and last works. The basic framework of Plato's thought, meanwhile, and the problematic status ascribed to the material world within it, was handed on as a point of departure to those who, like Plotinus, would identify themselves as his intellectual heirs.

§2. Radicalizing Transcendence

Echoing Plato's ontology, therefore, Plotinus posits a hierarchy of entities stretching from that which is "beyond being" to that which is "below being." All reality (spiritual and material) is perceived in terms of emanation from God and as in a state of gradual return to its source, yet God remains for Plotinus absolutely transcendent.[9] Indeed, the radical transcendence of the First or the One in God is perhaps the most distinctive aspect of Neoplatonism, opening up a gap just as profound in its theological consequences as the one Plato had posited between matter and form. Strictly speaking, Plotinus envisages God as a triad of divine hypostases:

the First, the Intellectual Principle, and the Soul. Hierarchy is already present even in this triunity, though, with the First being posited as the source of the godhead of the other two hypostases (and thereby of all reality). Thus, for instance, the Intellectual Principle (which is the expression of Godhead's thought) "is that which sees the One on which alone it leans while the First has no need whatever of it."[10] The World Soul, down one rung farther on the ladder of existence, duly emanates from the Intellectual Principle and is Godhead's point of contact with creation.[11] The gap between all three divine hypostases and creation is, of course, considerable, but for Plotinus the gap between the One and all else (including the Divine Mind and Soul) is greater still, and of more far-reaching significance. Insisting on Plato's maxim that the One is "beyond being" (ἐπεκέινα τῆς ὀυσίας), Plotinus presses the notion much further, opening up a gap between finite and infinite that falls not between God and the world but *within the very "being" of God* himself, with Intellectual Principle and World Soul both falling on the same side of it as that finite sort of existence which creatures enjoy.[12] These subordinate hypostases belong precisely to the realm of "Being" or authentic existence, compared favorably with that which is "less-than-being" or "Becoming," but nonetheless distinct from the One who is alone "beyond Being." Whereas Plato seems to hold that the One or Good is in principle *knowable* by the mind, being the Absolute and the summit of the epistemological pyramid to which the mind or soul of the disciplined aspires to ascend, Plotinus, therefore, insists instead that the One is so far removed from finite existence, so far beyond being that we cannot truthfully say that it or he "is" anything, not even that it is "One" or "Good" in fact! All positive attribution is strictly inappropriate, not because the One lacks anything but precisely because it is beyond all circumscription. Thus, even to say that the One "transcends Being" "assigns no character, makes no assertion, allots no name, carries only the denial of particular being" since "to seek to throw a line about that illimitable Nature would be folly, and anyone thinking to do so cuts himself off from any slightest and most momentary approach to its least vestige."[13]

The epistemic consequences of this stringent dualism are every bit as far-reaching for Plotinian thought as those that follow from Plato's separation of Form and particular. Because the One is beyond being it must also be beyond the reach not just of sensory engagement but of rational thought and speech too. Thus, "As one wishing to contemplate the Intellectual Nature will lay aside all the representations of sense and so may see what transcends the sense-realm, in the same way one wishing to contemplate

what transcends the Intellectual attains by putting away all that is of the
intellect, taught by the intellect, no doubt, that the Transcendent exists,
but never seeking to define it. Its definition, in fact, could be only 'the
indefinable': what is not a thing is not some definite thing."[14] The One is
precisely that, one, an undifferentiated unity transcending all antinomies
in itself, and thus beyond the reach of positive affirmations that, according to Proclus, "cut off reality in slices."[15] No name can properly be given
to the One, and no thought or activity can be ascribed to it, since activity
(and intellection is an activity) presupposes a distinction between subject
(agent) and object.[16]

Despite such radical statements of transcendence, Plotinus does not
understand this as *remoteness* from the world; on the contrary, the One
is "present" to the created order, and there is a "trace" of the One in all
things, such that they may have some intuitive awareness or apprehension
of the One.[17] Furthermore, the ineffability of the One should not be taken
as a reason for silence. Plotinus himself has plenty to say of the One, and
urges that we must continue to try to speak the unspeakable, not because
he believes that some appropriate description or definition will ever be
found but because the concepts, categories, or images we reach for and
deploy analogically in expressing our intuitive glimpses may act fruitfully
as signposts diverting us from error as we first cast them up for consideration and then negate them again, confessing their final inadequacy and
inappropriateness to the circumstance. Our knowing and speaking of the
One are therefore always of a quite different sort than the cognitive and
descriptive modes of engagement proper to intellection (which takes a
long way but reaches its legitimate terminus with the Intellectual Principle or Mind). Of the One, therefore, there is more truth to be had in silence
than any amount of cautious predication or logical deduction. Even the
name "the One" must not be misunderstood or misused in this regard,
for, strictly speaking, the One is equally "not One."[18] This, of course, is the
heart of the approach which has come to be known as negative theology
or apophaticism. But we shall not have grasped its most important and
most radical point if we understand by this a theology which defines God
in terms of what God is not (gradually articulating a space within which,
sooner or later, a more cataphatic approach may legitimately pick up the
baton and proceed). For Plotinus, at any rate, the point is more profound:
he insists that we must go beyond simply saying "God is not x" to acknowledging that "God is not *not* x" either![19] For the point is that the One is
altogether beyond predication, whether positive or negative, and that all

language concerning the One must therefore be understood in a wholly different manner. It has, we might properly say, a certain sort of poetic quality which eschews positive and negative predication altogether and equally. Its analogies are not ones laying claim to definition or even the tabulating of proportionate likenesses between God and the creaturely world, for their proper object is not the One as such but the shape and substance of our noncognitive intuitions and experience, of which they are in effect poetic expressions.[20] In the moment that we seek to objectify and to express it in conceptual terms, such apprehension slips from our grasp.[21] As Armstrong notes, what we find in Plotinus is a dialectic between intellectualism and mysticism, a philosophy or theology which, remarkably, "could profoundly influence both Augustine and William Blake"[22] and which is, we might add, the precursor to much in the theology of the nineteenth and twentieth centuries as it grappled with Kant's radical distinction between *phenomena* and *noumena*.

§3. The Soul's Flight

Losing the Body and Becoming Divine

The closest Plotinus comes to anything resembling a soteriology is his teaching concerning the human soul's transport within the divine realm of Forms and its natural striving for union with God. His anthropology follows the typical Greek pattern, dividing humanity cleanly into its binary constituents of material and spiritual aspects—body and soul, the latter of which he further divides into three "phases," the "Intellective soul," the "Reasoning soul" and the "Unreasoning soul."[23] These map neatly onto his larger metaphysic, the Intellective soul being that element of humanity which alone contemplates "authentic existence" ("being"), untouched (and unpolluted) by direct contact with sense experience, while the Unreasoning soul is lowest, compromised by its necessary "Couplement" with the materiality of bodily existence.[24] The soul (Intellective and Reasoning) belongs naturally to the divine realm, such that Plotinus can even refer to the Intellectual Principle or Divine Mind as "the summit of our being."[25] His dying words, recorded by Porphyry,[26] are in effect a personal application of his own appeal to the counsel of the *Iliad* to "flee then to the beloved Fatherland,"[27] the Fatherland for Plotinus being precisely the realm of being, Intellect, or Mind, and beyond that the One to whom the soul belongs, from whom it originates, and to whom it must ultimately return.[28] This return is accomplished through knowledge and contemplation, but, for reasons already indicated above, while acts of intellection may be vital, they cannot suffice. The One in particular lies beyond the reach of any and all such acts of cognitive "knowing" yet may perhaps be "known" in a different manner, by means of a "participation" (μέθεχις) in which the soul escapes its confinement in the body and seeks to become godlike (θεῷ φησιν, ὁμοιωθῆναι).[29] It does so through sharing in virtues that have their origin in the Divine Mind, but such divine qualities have a deeper, more ultimate source in God even than this, and Plotinus can suggest that in its purified state the human soul is "simply God [θεὸς μόνον], and one of those gods who follow the First. For he himself is the god who came Thence, and his own real nature . . . is There."[30] There is, he indicates later, the existence in us of a likeness (ὁμοίωσις) of "that which transcends the nature of the intellect" in ourselves, such that we may have intuitive knowledge of it, "for there is something of it in us too; or rather there is nowhere where it is not, in the things which can participate [μετέχειν] in it."[31]

Such purification of the soul from its contamination by the world is effectively its divinization or, we might better say, its return to that state of "likeness to God" which is its proper nature and its promised destiny. Furthermore, it consists in a likeness not just to the Divine Mind (through acts of pure cognition) but, Plotinus indicates, to the One or First who is present in it from the outset. Here, then, the robust and radical notion of transcendence that so marks his account of the One elsewhere is tempered by the suggestion that the One, too, is susceptible to some form of approximation via noncognitive, intuitive, and participatory modes of apprehension. The strict distinction between Divine original and divine copy may remain in theory, but it can be and is compromised in Plotinus' more "mystical" moments. In fact we might go further. The human soul, it might be claimed, is capable of participating in the One in a manner which even the Divine Mind itself cannot, the former being capable of an intuitive mode of participation that the latter (by definition, being precisely "mind") is incapable of.

The soul's pilgrimage back to the One from its state of immersion in the realm of the sensory is variously described by Plotinus as an ascension,[32] a withdrawal into the inner life[33] and a return to the soul's origins.[34] It takes the soul beyond intellection into a state of contemplation or "vision,"[35] a metaphor apparently intended to suggest both the continuing separateness of human subject and divine object and a state of union in which that separation is nonetheless transcended, "for to be god is to be integral with the Supreme."[36] This trajectory, resulting in a form of "beatific vision" which is the soul's divinization, is one which, like its Platonic forebear, involves the effort of disciplined stripping away of the world's distractions (good though these may be in and of themselves for Plotinus). Yet in an important sense it is a natural occurrence and not, like the Christian notion of rescue from a state of fallenness and sin and death, a peculiar accomplishment either on the part of God or the creature. Thus, as Armstrong argues, while we ought not to exclude altogether something equivalent to the notion of "grace" from Plotinus' scheme, such divine assistance is not salvage but something built into the "original creative impulse," albeit an impulse that continues active in the present moment.[37] Thus "the soul loves the Supreme Good," Plotinus writes, "from its very beginnings stirred by it to love."[38] While there may well be a "conversion" of sorts for the soul to undergo, therefore, it is of a less radical sort than that U-turn of mind and soul envisaged by the Plato of the *Phaedo* and the *Republic,* and quite different again in its nature and implications from the μετάνοια of the Gospels and Pauline epistles.

§4. Christian Platonism

We embarked on the above, all too cursory sketch of Plotinian Neoplatonism as a way of illuminating at least some of what we find in the philosophical theologies of figures such as Clement and Origen. Both in its broad outlines and in some of its detail something very like this was what confronted these Christian apologists as they considered how best to present the gospel in ways that might commend it to and persuade their readers. As we shall see, some of their characteristic modes of expression and emphases are ones that will now have a familiar ring to them. As Salvatore Lilla notes, rather than disregarding the cultural and religious milieu of their Alexandrian context, these were theologians who sought deliberately to incorporate elements of it into their own theologies, thereby the better to win acceptance for it.[39] It is this boldness which has earned them the label Christian Platonists. The manner in which they did this was, though, I shall maintain, unduly incautious, embracing not only discrete elements, ideas, images, and terms in the service of constructing an apologetic but permitting the larger plausibility structures of Hellenism a degree of influence which both left these themselves unchallenged at key points and also, therefore, made it difficult to accomplish the task of genuine evangelism or even pre-evangelism. Intellectual persuasion is a fine thing in the service of the gospel, but if what one ends up commending is a system that cannot bear the distinctive claims of the biblical gospel itself concerning God and God's ways with the world, then one's theological method must be revisited and reconsidered.

Clement (Titus Flavius Clemens, c.150–c. 211–215 CE) was a "Greek" both by birth and by education. Converted through the persuasive force of the teaching of Pantaenus in Alexandria, he eventually succeeded him as master of the Apologetic School there. Known to us chiefly as the author of three significant works, the *Protreptikos*, the *Paidogogos*, and the *Stromateis*, Clement clearly saw a clear enough distinction between his own ideas and those of the various Greek systems, suggesting that he was anything but uncritical of them and their potential. "The Hellenic truth," he writes rather sweepingly, "is distinct from that held by us . . . both in respect of extent of knowledge, certainty of demonstration, divine power and the like." For, he adds with a flourish, "we are taught of God."[40] Divine provenance, though, is something Clement is willing to ascribe to the views of the Greeks too, despite what he sees as the partial, provisional, and relatively unconvincing quality of their overall outputs. Indeed, this very incompleteness is proper to their nature as he understands it, being directly analogous in this respect to the writings of the Jewish Scriptures, and given by the same God to the Greeks as "a covenant peculiar to them," paving the way and preparing them for the coming of Christ, and furnishing them with their own culturally congenial set of categories in terms of which to receive and make sense of this.[41] Given this assumption, and given Clement's own heritage, his enthusiastic endorsement of much in Hellenic intellectual culture is hardly surprising. Far from requiring a paradigm shift, embrace of the message about salvation in Christ was, he believed, precisely what Greek philosophy had been grooming this gentile culture for all along, being in God's hands "a preparation, paving the way for him who is perfected in Christ."[42] Thus, as Charles Bigg notes, "The Gospel in [Clement's] view is not a fresh departure, but the meeting-point of two converging lines of progress, of Hellenism and Judaism."[43] The result is, in Hastings Rashdall's words, that "here for the first time we can feel in reading the pages of a Christian writer that we are conversing with the intellectual fellow countryman of Plato and Aristotle"[44] and, we might venture to suggest, in many respects their soulmate.

Clement's primary concern in his writings is thus with demonstrating how the Christian message is not only compatible with but the natural and proper heir to and fulfillment of principles of truth unfolded in the Greek intellectual tradition. The principles themselves, he insists, are incapable of demonstration, being instead the object of intellectual assent (συγκατάθεσις) due to their self-evident character, and this assent, which provides the basis for subsequent scientific demonstration (ἀπόδειξις ἐπιστεμονική), is what is really meant by the biblical term *faith* (πίστις), which characterizes the believer and leads properly and duly to the sort of knowledge (γνῶσις) that marks out the fully fledged disciple or Christian gnostic.[45] Like Plotinus, Clement espouses a modified version of Plato's philosophy, granting the senses a much more positive and reliable role as a stepping stone in the quest for knowledge[46] and a place among the principles of demonstration.[47] This "apparent compromise between rationalist and empiricist conceptualities"[48] notwithstanding, Clement remains true to the most distinctive feature of Platonism, namely the definitive gap in ontology and epistemology lying between the realms of sensation and reason.[49] True knowledge, he confirms, belongs properly only to the noetic sphere[50] and may be accessed only through a process of "unswerving abstraction" (ἀμετανόητος χωρισμός) from the objects of sense experience. This, he comments, "is the sacrifice which is acceptable to God. . . . For he who neither employs his eyes in the exercise of thought, nor draws aught from his other senses, but with pure mind itself applies to objects, practices the true philosophy."[51] As we shall see, Clement's endorsement of this dualistic framework generates some considerable problems for his efforts to elucidate a compelling Christian theology.

§5. Fleshy Texts and Spiritual Meanings

As a Christian theologian, of course, Clement is bound to make substantial appeal to Scripture as a source and primary authority, and he does not disappoint. Indeed, like Irenaeus, he is derisory in his dismissal of those who "selecting ambiguous expressions . . . wrest them to their own opinions . . . not looking to the sense, but making use of the mere words."[52] But the pages of Scripture direct the reader chiefly to events within the realm of human history, which, according to Plato, is "the object of opinion and irrational sensation, coming to be and ceasing to be, but never fully real."[53] This relegation of the empirical to a second order makes it difficult to attach ultimate redemptive or revelatory significance to particular objects and historical events in the way Scripture itself appears to do. To resolve the problem, Clement resorts to the sort of allegorical or typological exegesis of the text already familiar in the sort of Alexandrian Hellenic Judaism represented by Philo (and developed there for essentially similar reasons).

Thus, Clement contends, there are two levels of meaning to be identified throughout Scripture.[54] The sense "according to the bare reading"
(κατὰ τὴν ψιλὴν ἀνάγνωσιν)[55] is a literal sense pertaining to the realities of
the historical realm, and this is available to all, being graspable by simple
faith, just as a young child or someone struggling to master a new language can read according to the letter (πρὸς τὸ γράμμα ἀνάγνωσις)[56] even
though the sense of a whole word (let alone a sentence) may yet elude her.
Behind this, though, there is another hidden, mystical meaning, veiled by
the text rather than apparent on its surface, pertaining to realities located
in the noetic rather than the empirical world, and being apprehended
and grasped only by those whose mind has been specially purified and
illumined by God.[57] Thus the text of Scripture is symbolic and parabolic,
and must be subjected to a careful hermeneutic, its hidden meaning
(κεκρυμμένον) being constantly sought out beyond the literal or "fleshy"
(σαρκίνως) sense by those who would achieve true understanding.[58] Thus
Clement finds in Peter, to whom the Father in heaven rather than mere
"flesh and blood" has revealed Jesus' identity as the Christ (Matt 16:1),
a type of the Christian gnostic, one of those who do not get stuck at the
level of the literal meaning of the biblical text but rather "see through to
the thoughts and what is signified."[59]

Clement defines parable as "a narration based on some subject which
is not the principal subject, but similar to the principal subject, and leading him who understands to what is the true and principal thing."[60] The
suggestion of correspondence may remind us of the positive relation he
posits between phenonena and noumena, yet as so often in practice the
connection between literal and mystical sense in Clement's hands often
seems contrived rather than natural, manifesting the arbitrary encod-
ing of allegory rather than the organic connection generally associated
with symbolism. For example, where Plato provides us with the parable
of the cave in elucidating his epistemology, Clement (drawing and building directly on Philo's De Vita Mosis)[61] offers an instructive reading of the
High Priest's entry into the holy of holies which lays bare the shape of his.
Thus, he tells us, the veil that separates the external court of the Hebrew
tabernacle from the holy of holies signifies the division between the realms
of sense and intelligence, and the covering stretched in front of the five pil-
lars refers to the "barrier of popular unbelief" that keeps out those "who
think that nothing else exists but what they can hold in their hands."[62] The
true Christian gnostic, meanwhile, is to be found typified in the figure of
the High Priest himself, who passes through the veil from the sensory to

the noetic, ultimately achieving the glorious vision of God "face to face"[63] and putting off the sensory realm altogether, its being duly represented by the high priestly robe that is removed before entering the holy place.[64]

In both the form and content of this passage, then, grasp of the natural sense of the biblical text, like the empirical and historical realities to which it refers, is presented as a necessary stage on the ascent to understanding, but once the higher, mystical meaning has been grasped, it is supposed, the ladder can and should be kicked away, being no longer required and (here at least) having no very obvious or natural connection with the former. To continue to attend to it, in fact, would be to risk obscuring rather than illuminating the meaning that finally matters. A needful distinction between fact and significance, signifier and signified, once couched within the assumptions of the frameworks of Platonism (even those of the earlier rather than the later Plato), tends constantly and finally in this way toward their arbitrary separation, resulting in the loss of any enduring place for particular material or historical realities as either the site or the subject of redemptive meaning. The history of the reception of Scripture is, of course, well stocked with approaches to the text along allegorical lines, and portions of the biblical text itself either demand or encourage parabolic or typological strategies of interpretation as the way to access their natural sense (which, despite popular usage, is often anything but "literal"). Yet in schemes such as the medieval appeal to a "fourfold sense" of the text[65] the natural sense (whether parabolic, literal, poetic, or some other) is generally afforded a normative and permanent role in grounding strategies of interpretation, rather than being treated as a mere platform from which to leap precariously onto "higher" meanings seemingly remote and underived from the world of the text itself.

That a divinely inspired canon should generate multiple layers of meaning, and endlessly refresh its possible range of significance as it is read in many different cultural contexts and personal circumstances, might be expected rather than surprising and perceived as a blessing rather than a problem. Otherwise it is difficult to see how any text (let alone the text of Scripture in its presumed conjunction with "the Word of the Lord") could genuinely be new every morning in its salutary address. In this sense, it must be admitted, even the fourfold scheme and its counterparts seem rather conservative in their estimates and prescriptions. But such rich semantic potential and power cannot mean that texts can have no presumed limit to their interpretative scope, and encourages a more careful and responsible hermeneutic rather than a laissez-faire attitude in which more or less anything goes. When, therefore, both the interpretative approach and the proposed meaning are identifiably redolent of an ontology and epistemology quite alien to the world of the text itself (in this case, as so often over the centuries, that of Platonism in one or other of its forms), appropriate scrutiny is all the more urgent, lest the "mere words" be arbitrarily "wrested" in order to authorize or prop up assumptions and ideologies incommensurable with that world of meaning, and threaten to prohibit rather than extend its legitimate extension and regeneration via encounters with ever new contexts of reading.

§6. Logos, and the Soul's Divine Likeness

Endorsement of Hellenic frames of understanding necessarily has an impact on Clement's articulation of an incarnational Christology too. The typical dichotomy between, on one hand, an eternal realm of being and perfection and, on the other, the realm of material particulars in their submission to change and other conditions held to be incompatible with deity and anything approximating or analogous to it makes it difficult to take at face value the stark claim that God, in Christ, took "flesh" and made it his own. The point is incisively made in one version by the contemporary pagan polemicist Celsus, cited by Clement's pupil Origen: "God is good and beautiful and happy, and exists in the most beautiful state. If, then, he comes down to men, he must undergo a change, a change from good to bad, from beautiful to shameful, from happiness to misfortune, and from what is best to what is most wicked. Who would choose to change like that? It is the nature only of a mortal to undergo change and remoulding, whereas it is the nature of an immortal being to remain the same without alteration. Accordingly, God could not be capable of undergoing this change."[66] Other sets of qualities belonging properly either on one side or other of the line between the κόσμος νοητός and the κόσμος αἰσθητός might be cited in similar fashion, and it was, of course, the alleged incompatibility between them that lay behind the classic christological disputes of the fourth and fifth centuries, in the heat of which an emergent orthodoxy was duly forged.[67] Celsus, though, puts his finger nicely on the nub of the issue that was bound to make all suggestion of a genuine incarnation of God himself "foolishness to Greeks," namely that one whose proper state includes the quality of "immutability" cannot meaningfully *become* capable of appropriating or assuming new states, let alone become the personal subject of ones so unfitting for God as those entangled in the realm of materiality. Subscription to this premise a priori renders even the scrupulous formula of a hypostatic union of distinct natures problematic, for it insists that not even a divine hypostasis can bridge the gulf yawning between the eternity and history by making the properties of "flesh" truly its own, and leaves attempts to make sense of the incarnation bound to be redolent of notions finding expression classically in the theologies associated with names such as Arius, Apollinaris, and Nestorius.

There can be no doubt that Clement's intentions are orthodox enough, and he does his utmost to steer his Christology away from one or other logical conclusion demanded by the metaphysics he largely endorses. So, it is easy enough to trace statements unequivocal in their affirmation of the Son's economy in the flesh: Christ, he insists, has "openly become flesh"[68] in order to reveal "the Father's character to the five senses"[69] and so grant us the possibility of faith. Being "the fruit of the virgin"[70] he received "fleshly form" (σαρκὶ ἀναπλασάμενος)[71] and appeared "truly a man among the rest of human beings"[72] so that "God becomes a fellow-citizen with men!"[73] So far, so good, and Clement presses on to grasp the nettle presented by the murky depths of our fleshy existence in the world. Having thus become human for our sakes and wishing "in all points to be made like us,"[74] he affirms, Christ finally suffered and died for us as our "brother man," showing forth his great love for us.[75] Such an impressive array of avowals seems to indicate an unswerving commitment to the radical Christian notion of the full *inhomination* of God in the person of Jesus. And yet, as we shall see, Clement's anthropology on one hand and, on the other, his particular way of addressing the biblical theme of divine transcendence—both cast as variants of the Greek metaphysic we have already considered—prevent him from integrating this notion fully or allowing it determinative status in his understanding of God in God's relationship to the created order. The result is an account of Jesus' humanity that constantly undercuts its solidarity with our own, a model of salvation that in reality has little constructive to say about biblical focus on the passion or the death of Jesus for our sakes,[76] and a wider Christology which draws close to excluding God from the salvific economy altogether, drawing distinctions that leave God decisively on one side of a further χωρισμός posited within the realm of spiritual or "divine" realities, and the Logos (who, at least in some sense, "takes flesh") on the other.

Clement's writings predate those of Plotinus, but they are clearly drawn from the same basic pool of ideas as far as his anthropology is concerned. Human beings, he holds, are in this world essentially an unstable compound of two distinct (and in some sense antagonistic) elements, the spiritual and the physical, the rational and the irrational, a conjunction so unnatural and odd as to be appropriately likened to the Centaur of Greek mythology, the two parts, although bonded together, belonging properly in quite separate categories of existence.[77] Clement eschews any Manichean ascription of evil to the world of matter as such, emphasizing instead that the physical and ideal realms are "diverse" (διαφόρων) rather than "opposite" (ἐναντίων).[78] Clearly, though, he considers the realm of soul, mind, and ideas "better" (κρεῖττον)[79] than the world of material realities (a metaphysical rather than a moral judgment, but a judgment of value nonetheless), remaining unscathed, for instance, by the passibility of the latter[80] even though the mind/soul remains bound to the body until death releases it.[81] Indeed, the gradual withdrawal of the soul from the realm to which the body properly belongs, and its gradual severance from the body, is our lifelong task and education, enabling us to approach death (when occurs the final "dissolution of the chains which bind the soul to the body") as something welcome rather than to be feared.[82] At more than one level this is identifiably a message drawn from the same world as Plato's *Phaedo*,[83] not one evocative of the thought world of Scripture, and its conscription into Christian theology subverts much of what is most radical, religiously and metaphysically, in the Christian gospel, and drives Christology in a very particular direction.

For Clement, as for Plato and Plotinus, the spiritual part of our humanity belongs properly to the divine realm of intelligible realities and is not at home in the fleeting, constantly changing world of material phenomena. Like Plotinus, too, he subscribes to a threefold division of the human soul,[84] identifying the intellect (τὸ νοερόν), the irascible or emotive part (τὸ θυμικνόν), and the appetite (τὸ ἐπιθυμητικόν).[85] The latter two parts of the soul, Clement contends, are wedded unhealthily to the world of fleshly existence, the former being "brutal" and dwelling "close to insanity," and the appetite being prone to licentiousness and easy seduction. It is these parts of the soul, therefore, that require to be purified or redeemed, the intellect alone being entirely untroubled and free from pollution by materiality and its lower form of existence. Clement thus subscribes to a version of the Hellenic idea that the intellect belongs innately to the realm of divine realities, rooting this theologically, though, not in a concept of emanation but rather in the doctrine of humankind's creation in the image and likeness of God. Human nature, he argues, contains within its creaturely constitution "a certain fellowship with heaven," a divine spark that "though darkened by ignorance" is nonetheless capable of being fanned into flame and granting the soul, once purged of its earth-bound passions, a certain "likeness" (ὁμοίωσις) to God[86] or, more properly, the divine Logos, the archetype of whom the mind or logical faculty (ὁ λογικός) is an image,[87] this being accomplished through our being made "conversant with the contemplation of realities, and beholding the Father through what belongs to him."[88]

In Clement's hands the notion of our creation in the image of the Logos is intended to secure both an appropriate sense of God's otherness as Creator and an endorsement nonetheless of the popular idea of humankind's sharing, through participation in the realm of intellect and the Forms, in the sphere of what is divine. Thus, he insists, God has no natural relation to us, and Christians dare not suggest (as the author of various heresies do suggest) either that we are part of God or even that we share the same essence as God.[89] As we shall see duly, Clement's sense of God's radical transcendence is beyond dispute, leading him ultimately, in fact, to draw some novel distinctions with profound theological as well as christological implications. The only "likeness" to God we have is therefore an indirect one, likeness to the Logos who "belongs to [God]" and is thus able to mediate God's reality appropriately, being God's one true image in the world, and having in common with ourselves his belonging to the κόσμος νοητός (the substance of that "likeness," of which our creation in the image renders us capable). Clement is equally strong, though, in his emphasis on this latter relation, which is, in effect, a likeness of substance, a direct sharing in the key traits of the realm of eternal realities (Plato's realm of "being") of which the Logos (discarnate and incarnate) is the highest principle and exemplar. Thus Christ, in whom the Logos appears humanly on the stage of history, is a man who from first to last shows us that his humanity is, unlike ours (in the first instance at least), unscathed by either irrationality or passibility, the soul and its appetites (and so, too, indirectly, the body) in his case having been "rendered harmonious by reason in respect to the whole of life"[90] rather than assaulted by the irrationality and passion characteristic of the material realm of "becoming." Thus, he alone among humans may be said to be "perfect in all things at once,"[91] "like his Father God . . . sinless, blameless, and with a soul devoid of passion."[92]

§7. What Sort of Flesh?

The Integrity of Christ's Humanity

Clement is committed to the idea that in Christ we have to do with "God in a body of flesh."[93] But on closer inspection it must be admitted that he takes this body to have been quite unlike any other that we are likely to encounter; this is because of its indwelling by the divine Logos, the moral and spiritual qualities of whose nature necessarily bestow on it a unique character. Not only does Jesus' body not suffer any significant assault from the baser, more unruly physical urges tangled up with the commission of sin (being directed wholly by the disposition of the one who is himself the principle of rationality in the cosmos). It is set apart, too, Clement observes, even from the bodies of those few "Christian gnostics" who succeed fully in the quest for reason and holiness but who until death must yet submit to those remaining passions needful for bodily survival as such—the desire for food, drink, sleep, and so on. In the case of Jesus, though, Clement insists, "it were ludicrous to suppose that the body, as a body demanded the necessary aids in order to its duration," being sustained instead by "a holy energy," and his eating and drinking were merely cosmetic, "in order that it might not enter the minds of those who were with him to entertain a different opinion of him."[94] The qualities of the Logos being transfused through his whole humanity, just as Jesus' bodily existence was wholly directed by the dictates of reason, so too it shared curiously in other key traits of existence in the divine realm, so that Jesus was, whatever appearances might suggest, in reality "entirely impassible [ἀπαθής]; inaccessible to any movement of feeling—either pleasure or pain."[95] Whether Clement understands this to extend to physical pain is unclear, and he is not consistent in pressing the idea to its logical conclusion (which the Gospel accounts of Jesus' ministry make difficult),[96] but even a compromise of this sort posits a human experience far removed from our own and pares away the distinctives of existence in the flesh until they are so thin as to be all but transparent.

Rather than an economy aimed at the redemption of creation in all its fullness through its assumption into union with God, the impression in all this is of a shallow engagement with flesh aimed chiefly at a theophany (bodily appearance), the purpose of which is nonetheless to encourage and enable others to transcend and leave the trappings of materiality behind. The Logos assumes only as much of our human condition as is needful to perform this task of manifestation, and Clement can find no place for the incarnation as anything other than a temporary episode in the life of God. This much is clear in the passage already cited where Christ, the archetype of the Christian gnostic, is likened to the High Priest on the day of atonement, putting off his priestly robe as he enters the holy of holies, leaving behind all that characterizes the region of fleshly realities.[97] So, too, Clement notes, Scripture likens the descent of the Lord into the flesh figuratively to falling asleep, and Christ himself enjoins his disciples "'Watch,' as much as to say, 'Study how to live, and endeavor to separate the soul from the body.'"[98]

Given his anthropology, it would hardly be fair or correct to label Clement's account of incarnation "docetic." After all, the relationship he posits between the discarnate divine Logos and human beings is such that, by merely dipping his toe tentatively in the flesh rather than making fleshiness in its entirety his own, the Logos draws as close as is needed to show us the nature of "true humanity," since true humanity is itself finally to be had and to be seen not by the coming of God fully into the flesh but by the successful withdrawal and ascent of the human soul from it. And the bond of commonality between Savior and saved is contingent not on his appropriation of our condition but on our aspiration and achievement of his. "For the Word of God," Clement writes, "is intellectual, according as the image of mind is seen in man alone. Thus also the good man is god-like in form and semblance [θεοειδὴς καί θεοείκελος] as respects his soul. And, on the other hand, God is like man [θεὸς ἀνθρωποειδής]. For the distinctive form of each one is the mind by which we are characterized."[99] The difference between *Logos* and *logikos* is, finally, one of degree rather than kind, both belonging properly in the region of mind and spirit. In this sense, at least, Christ does not merely *appear* to be "divinely human"; he is the archetype of divine humanity and would be less rather than more so if he were to appropriate a deeper experience of material existence. For the same reason, Clement may be said to anticipate the later Christology of Apollinaris, who famously denied that the incarnation entailed the assumption by the divine Word of a human soul on the grounds that it was precisely the soul that was the source of sin, and in order to redeem us Christ must displace this sinful principle with an inner life dedicated from first to last to obedient devotion to God. The soteriologies are different, but both Clement and Apollinaris presume the same thing, namely that the ὁμοίωσις between divine logos and human mind/soul is such that the effective displacement of one by the other is perfectly natural and hardly constitutes any reduction of Jesus' true or full humanity.[100]

Clement's Christology, then, is well matched to his soteriology, the substance of which (despite his regular use of biblical terms and images to express it) is drawn from a world of assumptions and concerns rather different from those of the apostles and prophets and their articulation of the human circumstance, the nature of God's action to address it, and the character of the God who is gradually revealed in the process. In place of the story of the despoiling of creation by sin and the promise of its healing by and reconciliation with the God who has from the first purposed to dwell in its midst, Clement offers a familiar Hellenic alternative. Moral concerns lie at the heart of his redemptive narrative too, because within the Greek philosophical tradition knowledge and virtue are inseparable, and "it is impossible to attain knowledge by bad conduct."[101] But it is precisely with the attainment of knowledge (γνῶσις) of eternal divine truths that salvation is concerned, a mode of intellectual apprehension rendered impossible by existence in the body, and so demanding that (by grace rather than desert or natural inclination) "the soul is winged, and soars, and is raised above the higher spheres, laying aside all that is heavy, and surrendering itself to its kindred element."[102] The purity requisite for knowledge is achieved through discipline and a "crucifixion" of the passions,[103] but in Clement's version this is something rather different from the apostle Paul's exhortation to "live by the Spirit, and do not gratify the desires of the flesh."[104] The eschatological dialectic between unregenerate and regenerate or "Spirit born" (πνευματικός) humanity has been replaced by the Platonic dualism between "flesh" and "spirit" as such, and life in all its fullness entails not the redemption and making good of bodily passions but a form of "passionlessness" (ἀπάθεια) contingent on release from the material environment into which our bodies are keyed.[105]

For Clement there is a progression in salvation which reflects the hierarchical scheme in terms of which his anthropology and Christology are cast. It begins with the healing of our souls from the passions which beset them, for which we need a παιδαγωγός, one who will guide us by exhortation and example in the early stages of our ascent to a pure and "godlike" existence. It was for this reason, Clement affirms, that the Logos took flesh and manifested himself,[106] calling us to follow in his footsteps, which constitute the pathway to knowledge of God.[107] This, though, cannot happen by our own efforts alone. Since our mind is darkened by sin and ignorance, the bodying forth of word and example in Jesus must be accompanied by another redemptive approach, by the direct appeal of the Logos, "the first principle of all things,"[108] "a power incapable of being apprehended by sensation,"[109] but who, by virtue of the created likeness between them, the "understanding heart" being "made like the divine Word or Reason, and so reasonable,"[110] the Logos now "calls once again to heaven those who have been cast down to earth," and "through him alone, when he has risen within the depth of the mind, the soul's eye is illuminated."[111] As a man, then, Jesus serves as our example, pattern, and guide; as the divine Logos he directly instructs us (as our διδάσκαλος), drawing our minds ever further into a participatory union with divine truth.[112] This is the process that Clement refers to as the deification or "making divine" (θεοποιῶν) of human beings,[113] becoming the first to use this language in the Christian mainstream and granting it an identifiably Greek stamp from the outset. The Christian gnostic, he insists, is divine (θεῖος), God-bearing (θεοφορῶνν), and God-borne (θεοφορούμενος), indeed, "a god going about in flesh" (ἐν σαρκὶ περιπολῶν θεός),[114] having been "assimilated to God."[115] "When, therefore, he who partakes gnostically of this holy quality devotes himself to contemplation," Clement concludes, "communing in purity with the divine, he enters more nearly into the state of impassible identity [ταὐτότητος ἀπαθοῦς], so as no longer to *have* science and *possess* knowledge, but to *be* science and knowledge."[116]

§8. Radical Transcendence and the "Deity" of Christ

In all this talk of the Logos himself entering the region of the flesh as the man Jesus, and of the elevation and assimilation of our humanity to share in deity (θεότης) through realization of its created likeness to the Logos, there would seem to be little scope for accusing Clement of a failure to grasp or present the full divinity of Christ himself. Certainly, we can find places where Clement explicitly affirms the identity of the Logos as God. So, for example, he writes, "Nothing . . . is hated by God, nor yet by the Word. For both are one—that is, God" (ἕν γὰρ ἄμφω, ὁ θεός).[117] Yet a deep theological impulse (perhaps biblical and Hebraic in its provenance) leads Clement, having made this apologetic move in the direction of admitting θεότης to be participable by and commensurate with the qualities of human mind/soul, to make another countervailing move, this time one determined to underscore God's ultimate otherness with respect to creatures. To accomplish this swing of the theological pendulum Clement introduces a hitherto unknown emphasis on divine transcendence, pushing the idea in a direction that would subsequently become very familiar in both the philosophical and theological traditions of the East, and doing so in a manner that gives rise to questions about the direction in which his Christology seems most naturally to travel.

In our consideration of the theology of Plotinus (whose period of productivity, we recall, postdates Clement's own in Alexandria by several decades),[118] we saw that one of the features setting his thought apart from earlier forms of Platonism was its subscription to not just one but two drastic χωρισμόι, that between materiality and the intelligible realm being supplemented by another, arising within his account of God, between the radical transcendence of the One and the economic availability to and participability by human minds of Nous and the World Soul. This results in a tripartite scheme in which God belongs properly to the highest two tiers (that of "being" and that which lies radically "beyond being"), and humans to the lower two (those of "being" and "becoming") though caught up in a parabola of emanation, embodiment, and eventual return to their origin in the κόσμος νοητός, the divine realm of ideal and spiritual reality.

Clement, too, uses Plato's language of the One or the Good to refer to God. In fact, his own use of the term is more readily identifiable with that of Plato, seeming to denote the ultimate principle of the intelligible realm, and thus the highest object knowable by the human mind/soul. The gnostic's intellectual ascent to this "monad" is precisely the process of abstraction from the sensory region that we have already observed, stripping away the characteristics of bodily reality and even their ideal forms (depth, breadth, length, and so on) until there is reached the simple conception of unity (νοεῖται μονάς).[119] But Clement proceeds next to draw a careful distinction between God in God's economic condescension toward us on one hand, and God in God's eternal and immanent transcendence on the other; God as knowable to the human mind, and God as wholly beyond knowing or description; the God who is revealed and the God who lies wholly beyond revealing. Significantly, in Clement's version of it this distinction falls between "God" or the Father and the Logos/Son. "God," he insists, is "not a subject for demonstration, cannot be the object of science. But the Son is wisdom, and knowledge, and truth, and all else that has affinity thereto. He is also susceptible of demonstration and description."[120] Bear in mind again, this is not a distinction between the human Jesus and the divine Logos who takes flesh; it is a distinction drawn within the dynamics of God's own existence between the Logos/Son and "God" proper who is, Clement asserts, "beyond the One" (ἐπέκεινα τοῦ ἑνὸς), indicating that for him (unlike Plotinus) "the One" and "the Logos/Son" are one and the same.[121] We must, Clement insists, always take care to differentiate between the "essence" of God on one hand and God's power and works on the other. "The Son," he reminds us, "is the power of God, as being the most ancient Word before the production of all things, and his Wisdom . . . and the Son is, so to speak, an energy of the Father";[122] and his nature is the most perfect, being "nearest to him who alone is the Almighty One."[123]

Christian theologians have always felt bound to distinguish carefully that which may be known and spoken of God on the basis of revelation

from the fullness of God's reality as such, and most have been willing
to use the language of mystery and "unknowability" in this context. To
do otherwise would be hubris, failing to grasp the immensity and radical otherness of the reality to which the name "God" applies in Christian
theology, and failing to acknowledge the limited reach and inevitably broken nature of human language and ideas in naming and speaking about
God at all. No easy appeal to "revelation" can be supposed to overcome
this theological circumstance. In fact, as Karl Barth reminds us, the scale
and implications of the problem are itself known only in the event of revelation itself rather than a priori.[124] And yet, in the light of the claim that
God has revealed himself, that God has entered history humanly and
redemptively, the question may and must be asked about the *appropriateness* (rather than the adequacy) of whatever statements we make and are
called to make about God in making and unpacking this claim. May we
trust that such statements (God created the world out of the overflow of
his love in eternity, God is a holy Father, God took flesh and became one
of us in order to redeem us, God has promised to dwell in the midst of
creation, God has in Christ united our humanity to himself, and so on)
are appropriate statements to make of God, or not? Or must we admit that
God himself remains hidden, wholly unknown, wholly uninvolved in the
scheme of creation and its redemption?

§9. The Short Step to Arianism

Clearly Clement does not intend this. But the distinction he introduces
between "God" (in essence) on one hand and the sphere of action of the
divine Logos/Son on the other (the latter being the energy or power of
God and the one "nearest to him who alone is Almighty God"[125]) opens
up a gap between God's being and act which threatens to compromise the
force of any such statements. For now, we may admit that the divine Logos
is the subject of those various claims, having no need, strictly speaking,
to predicate such things of God himself, who, in essence, remains and
must remain "beyond" it all. Of course, Clement would insist, the Logos
is precisely the Word *of* God, and in fact he seems to have subscribed to
something like that distinction found earlier in the Apologists between
the immanent reason by virtue of which God himself is held to be rational (λόγος ἐνδιάθητος) and that active Logos which "realizes [God's]
purposes and reflects his will in creation"[126] (λόγος προφορικός). In a
fragment cited by Photius from Clement's lost work the *Hypotyposes*, this
twofold Logos is explicit: "The Son is called Logos like the Paternal Logos

[λέγεται ὁ υἱος ... ὁμωνύμως τῷ πατρικῷ λόγῳ] but this is not the one that became flesh. No, nor was it the Paternal Logos, but a certain power or emanation of his Logos that became reason and has been immanent in the hearts of men."[127] The fragment is disputed, but R. P. Casey notes its basic resonance with other, less precisely phrased passages elsewhere in Clement's writings.[128] And, despite Photius' use of the fragment to condemn Clement, the distinction between two logoi as such, Casey argues, need not in any event indicate an intention to sever the connection between the Logos/Son and the *ousia* of the Father, though it sets things up conveniently for such severing to occur in due course.[129] Nor need we doubt that Clement intends his description of the Logos/Son as "nearest to him who alone is Almighty God" as superlative rather than reductive in its force, an indication of something remarkable vis-à-vis the penetration of the human realm by divinity. But its force is, if taken at face value and when read alongside statements such as those noted above about the radical transcendence of the divine οὐσία, potentially the exact opposite. Just as Clement's subscription to the more traditional Platonic dualism between the realm of ideas and that of material realities results in a shallow "incarnation," thereby excluding the world of the body from salvation, so now his novel introduction of this second stark χωρισμός between God's essence and the realm of the Son/Logos and divine energy threatens to exclude the true God himself altogether from revelation, incarnation, and atonement, and to isolate God absolutely from any union with or participation by creaturely reality.

Clement's well-intentioned but ill-judged attempt to recalibrate a Hellenic metaphysic, and so protect the interests of a biblical concern to disentangle God from any natural or necessary relationship with his human creatures, introduces into Alexandrian intellectual culture a fault line with which theologians in particular would continue to struggle. Philosophically, as Bigg notes, this is "one of the most pregnant thoughts of the Second century. Clement," he writes, "has distinguished between the thinker and the thought, between Mind and its unknown foundation, and in doing so has given birth to Neo-Platonism."[130] Theologically, it opened up the way for a line of interpretation which would drive the distinction between God and God's Logos harder still, a line along which, as Casey observes, it was but a short (albeit a decisive) step to the Christology of Arius.

4

Deification

In chapter 3 we saw that the intellectual milieu of Platonism, far from suggesting a soteriology that would duly generate the christological orthodoxy of the fourth and fifth centuries (notions of salvation as "deification" naturally requiring some sort of fusion of divine and human natures in a single personal existence),[1] in actual fact made a properly incarnational theology difficult to accommodate at all. A fundamental antithesis between the spheres of spiritual/ideal and material realities was supplemented in due course by the projection of "the One," who alone is "fully divine" (αὐτοθεός), into a separate, radical transcendence, by comparison with which even the divine Logos might have to be viewed as a secondary, subordinate expression of divinity (δευτερός θεός)[2] belonging *within* the spiritual realm of being rather than lying *beyond* it (ἐπεκέινα τῆς οὐσίας). Within such parameters the claim that God himself has entered history humanly and in doing so redeemed not our souls alone but *our creaturely nature in its entirety* becomes exceptionally difficult to sustain. No doubt this is the claim that Christian theologians felt bound to commend to their pagan neighbors and to theologically aware members of the church alike. Those who, for apologetic reasons, did so by endorsing the prevailing intellectual climate, though, understandably found themselves struggling to make the claim stick, the ground rules of what might count as credible being distinctly unreceptive to any such idea from the outset. Incarnation of the sort borne witness to in Scripture would remain ἔθνεσιν μωρίαν (1 Cor 1:23),[3] being decidedly out of step with the sort of wisdom Greeks were either looking for or willing to recognize.[4]

Rendering Christian claims believable to the mindset of early-third-century Alexandria, therefore, was always going to be an enterprise in which both incarnation itself and the redemption bound up with it were at risk of shifting not just their center of gravity but their entire substance. So, despite what may have been his best intentions, we saw how, in Clement's hands, the gospel message tends repeatedly and all too easily to become the account of a less than fully divine Logos becoming less than fully human in order to liberate souls/minds to realize their inherent divinity—that is, their participation in the world of ideas of which the Logos himself was the type, the first and the highest instance.

§1. Theologizing in a Different Key

There were, though, other ways of engaging the gospel with Hellenism, ones that had rather different theological outcomes. Athanasius, Clement's eventual successor as bishop of Alexandria,[5] faced essentially similar cultural challenges, and his writings are seasoned with many of those same Greek terms and categories deployed by his illustrious predecessor, including his happy appropriation of Clement's description of salvation as θεοποίησις. And yet, apparent similarities and continuities notwithstanding, when reading Athanasius alongside Clement it is quickly apparent that we are in a quite different world of discourse. It is not that Athanasius does not wrestle with the intractable nature of certain Greek terms and the ideas commonly associated with them when conscripting them into Christian theology, nor that he does not himself from time to time fail to escape some of their less helpful connotations, especially in his less mature writings.[6] Overall, though, the atmosphere of Athanasius' theology is from the outset quite different from that of Clement. Here, rather than being permitted to draw with them their existing frameworks of plausibility, expectation, and significance, we find that the language and notions of Greek culture are situated within a fundamentally biblical vision, and their meaning modified abruptly wherever such relocation demands it. Athanasius' use of popular philosophical categories is measured and critical, and grows more cautious as his theology develops,[7] his explicit references to "the Greeks" being made more often than not in the cause of bewailing the incapacity of their systems to countenance any genuine immersion of God in the world and its history by taking flesh and becoming a human being.[8]

While, therefore, he echoes Clement respectfully as a predecessor from whom he has learned,[9] there is, even in Athanasius' relatively early work, no emulation of Clement's apologetic endorsement of Hellenic philosophy, baptizing it as God's covenanted way of preparing the Greek mind for the coming of Christ.[10] From the start, and throughout his writings, Athanasius' debt to the tradition represented by Irenaeus is equally apparent,[11] and it is this intellectual heritage, I suggest, that has the more profound and lasting impact on his theology, both in terms of its method and its substance.[12]

Whatever struggles he may have experienced, whatever lessons he may have learned, and however much he may gradually have adjusted his theological strategy, it is clear from the outset that Athanasius' concern is not with accommodating gospel claims to fashionable intellectual mores or canons of plausibility but with unashamed announcement "of the incarnation of the Word . . . which the Jews slander and the Greeks mock [Ἕλληνες . . . χλουάζουσιν], but which we ourselves adore."[13] Theology is primarily a function of "pious faith" (εὐσεβείας πίστει)[14] rather than a bid to secure intellectual acceptance, and there must be no failure to grasp the nettle or willingness to pull punches where this most shocking and outrageous of theological claims is concerned; for, Athanasius holds, piety itself will duly be nurtured and fed by a willingness to reckon with and expound rather than qualify "the apparent degradation of the Word" in his *inhomination* (ἐνανθρώπησις) for our sakes.[15] In his own exposition of it, certain emphases and points of clarity serve to differentiate Athanasius' incarnational theology from the more apologetic, qualified, and concessionary approach of Clement.

It is clear, for instance, that Athanasius sees no need to entertain any radical divorce between God himself and the world, and is thus not concerned in the least with treading gently around the claim that the Logos who takes flesh is to be identified as God himself. Indeed, his soteriology rests squarely on the recognition that it is precisely God, and no other or lesser being, who is personally involved with us as the man Jesus Christ. Again, whatever awkwardness and complexity the claim may entail, Athanasius is clear that the Word or Son of God is fully engaged with creation as a whole, not least that material dimension of it into which human bodies are naturally keyed, and in the incarnation becomes what we would most naturally term the "personal subject" of all Jesus' human experiences, spiritual and bodily. The "body" of Jesus, in fact, is not merely the vehicle for a revelation and redemption largely unrelated to it (let alone defined essentially in terms of opposition to it) but is itself the *object* of redemption through death and resurrection. For although he still subscribes to a version of Greek soul/body duality, Athanasius holds these much more closely together than typical Greek thinking permits, and his vision of the redemption of our humanity is always holistic and integrated. It is by appropriating and indwelling our "flesh"[16] and becoming, acting, and suffering *as a man* (there is no blanching here at the claim that the Logos/Word/Son becomes the subject of human suffering; rather, he indwells the body precisely in order that he may do so) that the healing, regeneration, and deification of our flesh and our souls alike occur. The *deification* of humankind, in other words, is precisely the obverse of the full *inhomination* of God himself,[17] reaching down to lay hold of our creaturely being and lifting it up to share in his own life and way of being.

In this chapter I consider how this incarnational focus and commitment plays out in the compound treatise *Contra Gentes/De Incarnatione* (*CG-DI*) and in Athanasius' three treatises *Contra Arianos* (*CA*). The former is the closest he comes to an apologetic work in the tradition of the Apologists or Clement and, I am presuming, represents an earlier and slightly less mature form of his thought than the latter,[18] which were written with specific intra-Christian polemical intent and a very precise christological and soteriological focus. Nonetheless, I contend that the theological vision of both is essentially continuous in its interlacing of the person and work of Christ.

§2. Deifying Creation

Idolatry and the Incarnation

In *CG-DI* Athanasius addresses himself to an individual reader (variously "friend" or "blessed one," and "true lover of Christ"),[19] though this may well be literary affectation behind which we should presume a wide intended readership. The single addressee reinforces, though, what I have already suggested, namely that we should treat *CG-DI* as a single work rather than two discrete treatises lumped together merely by convention. There is an underlying organic unity to the piece that may not be apparent at first glance and despite the evident differences of focus and tone between its two parts. Again, we should not be misled by the address to one who loves Christ as well as learning[20] to suppose that the work is purely a manual for Christian readers[21] nor, on the basis of its two distinct foci, that the first part is apologetic and the second catechetical.

Athanasius seems to recognize on one hand that the most persuasive apologetic device can often be the intelligent articulation of something in terms of its own proper logic (which will either commend itself to heart and mind or not), and on the other that believers will always benefit from well-reasoned responses to the challenges presented by unbelief and various pagan alternatives to Christian faith.[22] Thus, the burden of CG is certainly an "apologetic" exercise of sorts, directed in part against idolatrous beliefs and practices in pagan religion,[23] and in part against elements of Hellenic philosophy which Athanasius holds to be unreasonable (when measured by the canon of divine revelation),[24] or as bound finally to lend their reluctant support to Christianity rather than rejecting it.[25] But the ultimate canon of plausibility to which it refers again and again (explicitly and tacitly) in judging and weighing such things is the Christian story of God's coming among us humanly for the sake of our salvation—the very story which is subsequently spelled out at length in DI, which, for its part, continues to engage and dispute inter alia with the multifaceted "godlessness" of paganism. As Thomson suggests, therefore, the treatise as a whole is probably best understood as written for the benefit both of believers and the as yet unconverted,[26] albeit necessarily addressing each in a distinct register.

If we stand back and look at the larger trajectory of CG-DI as a single work, it becomes apparent that in Athanasius' hands denouncing idolatry and godlessness (ἀθεότης) is not merely a conventional apologetic gesture but part of an overarching theological and soteriological argument. To be sure, he draws on established literary traditions refuting the intellectual preposterousness of pagan idol worship and aspects of Greek mythology, some of which have their roots in Hellenic philosophical culture itself and others in the writings of his Christian predecessors and contemporaries.[27] Above all, though, the tone and content of Athanasius' response to idolatry is redolent of Christian Scripture, which he cites regularly,[28] and in condemning idolatry he situates it within a biblically derived narrative arc, linking it organically to the nature of the salvation effected by God by taking flesh. Significantly, it is in this context that Athanasius' play on θεοποίησις and its various cognates comes to the fore and from which it takes its proper sense. The besetting sin of humans, he insists from the outset, is precisely that of "deifying" creaturely things which ought under no circumstances to be treated as though "deity" (ἡ θεότης) were theirs, rather than belonging to "the true and real God, the Father of Christ" alone.[29] Glorifying creation rather than the creator, and ascribing divine status and honor inappropriately to various things (animals, natural phenomena, the works of human hands, human beings themselves),[30] those made in God's own image and likeness ceased to know God himself through the Word and instead became godless (ἄθεοι),[31] first reifying and then worshiping false gods (ψευδόθεοι).[32]

There is irony on a cosmic scale here, Athanasius suggests in his wider argument, since "deification" of two quite different sorts is to be found both at the root of the human problem and in the nature of God's glorious redemption of it. Whereas the sinful deifying and worship of mere creatures elevates them artificially and results in humans deviating and being cut off from knowledge of the one and only true God,[33] by way of response, the one and only true God himself lays hold of our creaturely humanity and makes it his own. His eternal Word and Son becomes human in a supreme act of divine condescension, so that our humanity and we with it might "be made divine."[34] In each case it is the sharing of creation in what belongs properly only to God that is envisaged, but the nature and mode of that sharing and the way in which it is accomplished are construed very differently indeed. The trajectories of the two circumstances are quite distinct: an overweening and blasphemous attempt to scale the heavens on one hand, and a radical, gracious, and costly coming down in order to lift us up to share in the life of God on the other. True "deification" is the contradiction and redemption of the chaos caused in the world by the sin of idolatry, and it occurs not by fanning into flame a divine spark latent within the human creature but by the *inhomination*, suffering, death, and resurrection of the eternal Logos himself, who returns to the Father bearing our creaturely nature with him. Thus, in response to our destructive attempts to make ourselves gods, God gives us to share in his own θεότης in a mode appropriate to our creaturely being by grace rather than by nature.

In all this, the proper identification and ascription of "deity" is precisely Athanasius' concern, and his emphasis fluctuates between the rigorous demarcation of boundaries (isolating and protecting what pertains to τὸν ἀληθινὸν καὶ ὄντας ὄντα Θεὸν alone) and a generous inclusion in which those very boundaries are gloriously breached. But the breach is by virtue of God's own desire and decision rather than any natural capacity or birthright of creatures, and it embraces not just our mind/soul but our humanity as a whole. There is thus little room for any dalliance in all this with the idea of essentially "divine" souls being released from the trammels of a material existence in order to return to their natural state, *revealing* their true "divinity" as those who issue from and belong to the realm of Logos, rather than being *made* "divine" (together with their bodies) through his incarnation. Any participation in that θεότης which is properly God's own, in other words, is precisely due to a θεο-ποίησις, a further creative act of the one who made us and who alone can make us share, *mutatis mutandis* (i.e., precisely as *creatures*), in his own life and way of being.[35]

§3. Identifying Logos

Like Irenaeus, therefore, Athanasius is concerned to insist that the world is the creative product of God himself rather than some gnostic or Platonic demiurge. There is, he insists, only one God, and this God is himself one, the true Father of Christ and the only Lord of heaven and earth, who called the cosmos into being out of nonexistence and fashioned it, and who alone rules over it.[36] This same God is, as the uncreated Creator,[37] "other than created things and all creation."[38] Indeed, God is, as Plato and Plotinus had borne witness, "above" or "beyond all created being" (ὑπερέκεινα πάσης γενετῆς οὐσίας) and so, by nature, beyond all creaturely thought and understanding;[39] and yet, in his very otherness God is not remote and, unlike the Neoplatonic One, has not left himself unknown in an inscrutable transcendence. On the contrary, God is, as the sole maker, sustainer, and orderer of all things visible and invisible, present to and fills all things, "containing and enclosing them in himself" even as he governs and guides them by his power.[40] And, albeit ineffable by nature, God has not left himself completely unknowable, but in his goodness and love generously opens himself to be known by his creatures, both through consideration of his works[41] and by drawing us into relationship with himself, thereby granting us not just biological life but the life of the one who is the source of all life (τὸ κατὰ Θεὸν ζῆν).[42]

Of course, Athanasius follows good biblical precedent in acknowledging that it is precisely through his Word or Son, who proceeds from the Father,[43] that God is present and known in this way.[44] But whereas for Plotinus (and for Clement) the distinction between God and the Logos provides a convenient way of disentangling the two, and so maintaining the gap between "the true God" and the messy world of finite creaturely existence, for Athanasius it is precisely a way of asserting God's own presence and activity in creation's midst, and insisting that God has himself transgressed the gap between himself and his creatures in the incarnation. The Word, he is adamant, is none other than God himself, and in the

Word, therefore, God himself has taken flesh and become human. Thus, "God exists, and is not composite; therefore his Word exists, and is not composite, but is the one, only-begotten, good God, proceeding from the Father as from a good source, who orders and contains the universe."[45] And again, "I mean the living and acting God, the very Word of the good God of the universe, who is other than created things and all creation."[46] In knowing the Word, therefore, we know God himself, and in encountering the Word we encounter God himself, for he is the very form of God's own condescension to created beings, in whom and through whom the Father creates and sustains and gives himself to be known.[47] So, "when thinking of the Word of God one must also think of his Father, God, from whom he proceeds and is therefore rightly called the interpreter and messenger [ἑρμηνεὺς καὶ ἄγγελος] of his Father."[48]

The passage from which this citation is taken is particularly instructive in considering the difference in emphasis between Athanasius and Clement in their doctrine of the Logos. Athanasius does not distinguish sharply here between a λόγος ἐνδιάθητος and a λόγος προφορικός (a Word immanent in God's being and an outgoing, active Word), a distinction of a sort which, we saw at the end of chapter 3, all too easily slides into a divorce, projecting God in his οὐσία (including his immanent reason) into a transcendence separable from and hidden behind the forms of the economy of creation and revelation. It was precisely such a distinction that permitted the radical transcendence which Neoplatonism predicated of the One, and which would duly compel the sort of Christology championed by Arius, denying that the Word who became incarnate was to be identified as God at all.[49] Athanasius gestures toward the distinction, but only in order to make the very opposite point. "If," he writes, "when a word is spoken by men, we . . . perceive by reasoning the mind which it reveals, all the more, by a greater and far superior effort of the imagination, when we see the power of the Word we form an idea of his good Father, as the Saviour himself says: 'Who has seen me, has seen the Father.'"[50] Far from differentiating "the thinker and the thought" so as to stress the transcendence and ineffability of the former,[51] Athanasius places his stress instead on the essential unity between them, and thus the integrity, authenticity, and reliability of the form in which the active and uttered Word is encountered and grasped by us. The Word of God (ὁ τοῦ Θεοῦ Λόγος) is precisely God the Word (ὁ Θεός Λόγος), the form that God's own self-communicative approach to creation takes, and he is thus the Father's "interpreter and messenger" *not* as a created third party external to the divine οὐσία but precisely as the Father's own Word,[52] one who coexists eternally with the Father, is "in" the Father and shares his very being,[53] as well as being "in" all things, visible and invisible as their Creator, "supporting them and giving them life by his will and providence."[54]

§4. Body, Soul, and the Gift of Life

In *CG-DI* Athanasius certainly trades on stock Greek ideas concerning the mind/soul, just as he concentrates his Christology mostly on the category of "Logos" as distinct from "Son," reflecting the language and milieu of the Greek context with which he was interacting,[55] and reflecting also his willingness to use contemporary philosophical ideas and even, as E. P. Meijering suggests, to attempt a theological synthesis between them and the heart of the *Regula Fidei* when doing so does not seem to threaten or contradict the latter.[56] Thus Athanasius affirms, in true Alexandrian fashion, human beings are composites of body and rational soul, the latter of which is the proper locus of our unique creation in the image and likeness of God (κατ᾽ εἰκόνα γὰρ Θεοῦ πεποίηται καὶ καθ᾽ὁμοίωσιν γέγονεν).[57] It is this, he indicates, that distinguishes us from all irrational animals and grants us alone within the scope of God's creation a share in the power of God's own Word, so that we "might be able to remain in felicity and live the true life of paradise."[58] The soul is rational, sharing in this quality of the Creator Logos himself, though Athanasius is again careful to emphasize the essential difference in the midst of likeness here: it is only "by participation" (κατὰ μετοχὴν)[59] and not by sharing the same nature (κατὰ φύσιν)[60] that the soul holds this likeness to what the Logos himself eternally is, he, as "absolute wisdom" (αὐτοσοφία),[61] standing over against those who are merely "wise" (σοφός), being himself the source and ground of all created wisdom.

While, therefore, the soul is "the road to God,"[62] a "shadow" (σκιά) of the Word himself within us,[63] rendering us "superior to sensible things and all bodily impressions" and capable instead of clinging "to the divine and intelligible realities in heaven,"[64] capturing their reflection like a mirror (κάτοπτρον)[65] and enjoying a dimension of life beyond the biological life of the body even while securely wedded to it,[66] Athanasius avoids any suggestion that all this is by virtue of a natural emanation from and return to God. Rather, he insists, it is an "added grace"[67] granted to those who, like the wider creation of which they are part, were called into being "out of nothing" (ἐξ οὐκ ὄντων)[68] and, apart from God's continuing goodness and mercy, are bound eventually to return to nothingness because of the corrosive effect of sin.[69] Furthermore, this grace of participation in the Word is a function and a vestige of our creation by and through the Word, who is none other than our Lord Jesus Christ,[70] the one who alone is the true Son and image of the Father. Yet, precisely because it is the moral and spiritual compass within our creaturely nature, through the correct alignment of which alone we enjoy knowledge of the Father, it is the soul too which (via the free will it exercises) turns away from its proper object and grants its attention and fealty instead to things "closer to hand" and unworthy of its ultimate desire and devotion,[71] thereby inventing wickedness and surrendering itself to the ruin of death.[72] Death, indeed, is not just a penalty imposed on those who transgress the commandment of God. Whatever the value of such metaphor, death, for Athanasius, is more properly the natural state of the soul (and its body) when it turns its back on the one who alone is the source of its life, and seeks the source and meaning of its existence instead in itself or other creaturely realities. Again, this is the very essence of the idolatry which Athanasius rails against, and the very opposite of the enjoyment of the "divine life" (τὸ κατὰ Θεὸν ζῆν) that God purposes for us and freely grants us by creating us in the image of his Word or Son.[73] Immortality, therefore, is not a quality of the human soul (or its body) by nature, but only by virtue of this superabundant divine gift of life in all its fullness or life "as God" (ὡς Θεός) in which the natural corruption of our creaturely nature is overridden, and we are invited to share in God's own life "by . . . participation in the Word"[74] (who again, we might remind ourselves, is none other than our Savior Jesus Christ).

The current reality of our circumstance, though, Athanasius insists, is very different. Because of sin, idolatry, and the transgression of God's law, God's human creatures have turned their backs on their Creator, eschewing, denying, and defacing whatever likeness to God was theirs to enjoy, reifying and deifying images of other sorts, and so returning to their natural state as mortal entities moving gradually back toward the nonbeing out of which their existence was originally and graciously summoned.[75] At this point Athanasius fuses epistemology and soteriology in a manner that draws biblical categories fully into play. It was by contemplating God and seeking knowledge of God, he indicates, that likeness to God and "eternal existence" should have been kept alive. Such "knowledge," though, has little to do with a gradual process of epistemic abstraction from the world of particulars, being much more about a practical knowledge of and faithfulness to the law of God, reflecting God's own moral and spiritual character. Having transgressed the divine commandment in paradise,

Athanasius muses, the unalloyed knowledge of God was complicated by the knowledge of good and evil, and humans (unable to resist the predations of evil) found themselves overcome and enslaved by death and corruption.[76] Thus the image and likeness of God in creation, and its capacity to reflect and echo God's own holiness, was ruined and gradually being obliterated by the "lawlessness" (παρανομία) of human sin,[77] and God's very purpose for creation thereby put at risk. This "absurd and improper" state of affairs[78] clearly could not be permitted to perdure, and so Athanasius' inquiry turns to the question of what it was fitting and necessary for God to do in order to redeem it. Given God's goodness and the mess sin had created, the short answer to this question, he suggests, is that the project of creation required a complete renewal in which its capacity to image God would be restored, communion with God reestablished, and the grip of death and corruption broken once and for all.[79]

§5. Christological Convictions and Soteriological Implications

It is here, at last, that Athanasius grasps the nettle of incarnation, notwithstanding the difficulties it creates for the Greek mind. Despite his presentation of it, his argument is essentially an a posteriori rather than an a priori one, seeking an understanding of salvation and its rationale that corresponds to the given *fact* (as he takes it to be) that God himself has entered history humanly, as one of his own creatures, in Jesus Christ. The structure, if not the precise substance and terms, of Athanasius' argument offers an instructive parallel to the one developed later in the Latin West by Anselm of Canterbury,[80] permitting the central claim of Christology to provide the question out of which soteriology properly arises (*Cur deus homo?*), rather than furnishing a contrived answer to soteriological questions asked and answered on other grounds altogether. If the image and likeness of God was to be renewed within the heart of our humanity, Athanasius suggests, then the one through whose agency we were created in the beginning and who is himself the very image of God would have to be involved again, and this was the Word or Son of the Father. But whereas the original creation was accomplished in such wise that the proper distinction between Creator and creature remained wholly intact, human souls being granted a mode of likeness to the Logos by way of creaturely "participation," this regeneration or renewal of humanity was to occur not by external fiat, but *from within*, the true image himself stepping over the defining χωρισμός between uncreated and created, fashioning an instance

of humanity for his own habitation, and etching that same image and likeness on it through the manner of his personal indwelling of it.[81]

So, Athanasius writes,

> the Word of God came to our realm; not that he was previously distant,
> for no part of creation is left deprived of him, but he fills the universe,
> being in union with his Father. But . . . he had pity on our race, and was
> merciful to our infirmity, and submitted to our corruption. . . . And lest
> what had been created should perish and the work of the Father among
> men should be in vain, he took to himself a body, and that not foreign
> to our own. For he did not wish simply to be in a body, nor did he wish
> merely to appear, for if he had wished only to appear he could have made
> his theophany through some better means. But . . . he, although powerful
> and the creator of the universe, fashioned for himself in the virgin a body
> as a temple, and appropriated it for his own as an instrument in which to
> be known and dwell. And thus taking a body like ours, since all were liable
> to the corruption of death, and surrendering it to death on behalf of all, he
> offered it to the Father.[82]

It was through this act of divine love and mercy too, therefore, that both
sin and its consequences (the subjection of our humanity to the power of
death and corruption) were undone and overcome,[83] this being in effect
simply the obverse of the restoration of the divine image in Jesus' own
humanity. And the whole economy, in both its retrospective and prospective aspects, required a total human action and passion from birth to
death, but one that extended in its scope beyond the limits of any single
member of the race to embrace all (since all were affected by sin and concluded under the sentence of death). When the Word himself came and
impressed his own image afresh on a humanity created and set apart for
the purpose, his sharing in "a body like ours" on one hand and the fact of
our relationship to him as our creator on the other sealed a union which
granted his actions and passion a universal status, enabling him first to
stand in for us at key points of our relationship with the Father, and second to communicate the power of his own renewed and incorruptible
humanity to us, breaking the hold and the power of death and the devil
over us and granting us "a happy and truly blessed life."[84] "Therefore," says
Athanasius,

> as an offering and sacrifice free of all spot, he offered to death the body
> which he had taken to himself, and immediately abolished death from all
> who were like him by the offering of a like. For since the Word is above all,
> consequently by offering his temple and the instrument of his body as a

substitute [ἀντίψυχον] for all men, he fulfilled the debt by his death. And as the incorruptible Son of God was united to all men by his body similar to theirs, consequently he endued all men with incorruption by the promise concerning the resurrection. And now no longer does the corruption involved in death hold sway over men because of the Word who dwelt among them through a body one with theirs.[85]

Such statements as these suffice to make it clear that for Athanasius salvation is not about the liberation of essentially "divine" souls from the bonds of base materiality, nor accomplished by the soul's ever-increasing and intensified contemplation of a Logos whose incarnation is only ever an awkward, incomplete, and temporary accommodation to the incarcerated state from which it must begin its journey. Athanasius' vision is at once more splendid and more biblical. Salvation, he insists, is nothing more and nothing less than the restoration and completion of what God, in creation, had purposed and begun, and it has to do with purging corruption and establishing the image of God (and that sharing of God's life that it grants) as a reality across the whole of our creaturely nature—spiritual, moral and bodily. And this is achieved not by kindling into flame a divine spark latent in our humanity but smothered by the trappings of bodily existence, but by the Word of God himself immersing himself to the hilt in the world of the embodied souls, making it his own, reinscribing his own image on it and so lifting it up to share with him in the life of eternity. The "deification" of humanity, therefore, is utterly contingent on the "enhumanization" (ἐνανθρώπησις) of God the Word/Son and his desire to unite us with himself and his life as participants in his own image, through which our access to his Father is also ensured.

§6. Redeeming Materiality

The centrality of the body (σῶμα) in Athanasius' account of redemption is clear from the unashamed emphasis he places on the promise of bodily resurrection as the focus of Christian hope and joy, "as firstfruits of which [the true Son of God] raised up his own body and showed it as a trophy over death and over death's corruption by the sign of the cross."[86] Christians, he insists, do not fear death.[87] But this is not because it comes, as it did for Socrates, as the soul's welcome escape from the body, but because in Jesus' resurrection from death we have God's pledge that our whole humanity, currently mired in corruption, will not perish but share in that eternal or divine life for which its creation was always intended—with God dwelling in its midst, and it being drawn into God's own existence by virtue of its union with the Son. So, it was no mere pedagogical utility or fleeting theophany when the Word took flesh and "put on" (ἐνδύειν) bodily existence, but the means whereby bodily existence itself should be purged of corruption and death, and "having put on immortality, might then rise up and remain immortal."[88] The corruption that had occurred, Athanasius observes, "was not outside the body, but was involved with it."[89] Notice, though, how the solution he infers from this is very different from that encouraged by his Hellenic backdrop. There is no suggestion that an essentially discarnate Logos indulges in a merely fleeting and partial liaison with the world of the body in order to facilitate our souls' final release from it. Instead, bodily existence as such is laid hold of, the Word thereby "extending himself in all things,"[90] in order to transfuse it (body and soul, things visible and invisible) with his own life. Bodily existence as such, in other words, is to be regenerated rather than shunned, and this involves its assumption, indwelling, and owning by the one who himself created it in the beginning. The logic here is exactly that of the later patristic maxim that "whatever is not assumed (in the incarnation) remains unredeemed," and it is the redemption of the body and all that pertains to it which Athanasius is concerned to secure from any attempt to deny it or reduce its significance. His reason for doing so, we may presume, is not an a priori aversion to the idealism of Greek thought but his belief that in actual fact in Jesus Christ our "flesh" in its entirety (body and soul) was laid hold of by God and, not least in the bodily resurrection that followed the self-offering to death of the cross, made good and made new.

For this reason, Athanasius will have no truck with any suggestion that the Word, being God, ought not to have touched the realm of material existence at all (μὴ σώματος ἄψασθαι), operating instead from a safe, "hands-off" distance, or at least keeping his level of involvement to the barest minimum.[91] Of course, he acknowledges, the Word of the Father is incorporeal (ἀσώματος) by nature, and it is due to the Father's mercy and goodness alone that he put on bodily existence (σῶμα) and became our Savior.[92] Furthermore, having created a bodily existence for himself (as Jesus of Nazareth), the divine Word's personal indwelling of it was such that he was not enclosed or circumscribed by it but continued, as God, to contain and to sustain and to rule over all things (just as, while present to the universe as a whole as its creator, he is not and cannot be contained within it).[93] Nor, Athanasius assures us, should we be concerned that the holy Word of the Father might have been polluted by laying hold of our flesh in its corrupt condition, any more than he was or could be tainted and taken captive by death. On the contrary, his presence in the body, existing as a man (ὡς ἄνθρωπος), had the very opposite effect, sanctifying the body, purging it of corruption and filling it with his own life.[94] And the body that he took and made his own (τῇ τοῦ σώματος ἰδιοποιήσει)[95] was no mere semblance but a body like ours, shared in common with all those "liable to the corruption of death" (albeit itself pure and unalloyed by the transmission of sin)[96] so that he could surrender it to death on behalf of all, and so, by offering it to the Father, overturn the hold and influence which death had on it and establish the life of God himself in its place.[97] The biblical imagery of sacrifice and offering lies at the heart of Athanasius' understanding of what occurs in Christ, recognizing, as he does, the convergence and transformation of various strands of Old Testament imagery, understanding, and expectation in the Son's inhomination. He echoes the theology of the fourth Gospel, noting that the one who was himself the creator of all things has come and tabernacled among us, dwelling in our midst in a holy temple which he fashioned for the purpose (his body), and offering his body up to death and to his Father in order to cleanse it and bestow eternal life on it. The incarnate Son, in other words, is temple of life, holy of holies, priest, and sacrificial offering all at the same time,[98] and it is amid this cluster of images that the secret of our redemption is finally to be sought, for it was in and through this sacerdotal or liturgical action (concentrated in but not limited to the cross) that Christ put an end to death, opened the gates of heaven, and bore us up in his body into the presence of God.[99] Clearly, whatever the word "body" means for Athanasius, it includes the materiality of our existence, the physical frame by which we are keyed into the cosmos. The question is whether, given the shape of Athanasius' Christology and the direction of his soteriology, it must finally connote more than this.

§7. Did the Logos Keep Body and Soul Together?

The question of whether or not the incarnation involved the Word of God assuming a human mind/soul was one that would arise explicitly during Athanasius' career in association with the Christology of the Syrian bishop and theologian Apollinaris.[100] When it did, he was apparently happy to answer in the affirmative, and on explicitly soteriological grounds. So, a council convened and presided over by Athanasius at Alexandria in 362 insisted, "The Saviour had a body neither without soul [ἄψυχον], nor without sense, nor without intelligence [ἀνόητον]," since "the salvation effected in the Word" was not "a salvation of body only, but of soul also."[101] While it has been suggested that these crucial clauses may have been insisted on by others at the council rather than Athanasius himself, the fact remains that he placed his seal of approval on them, and he echoes them elsewhere in his later writings.[102] Nonetheless, precisely how he understood them remains contentious. Frances Young, for instance, suggests that he may have taken them to mean no more than that the body of Christ was endued with rationality and "soul" by the presence within it of the indwelling Logos, himself the uncreated archetype of these elements of our creaturely nature.[103] In his earlier works, to be sure, including CG-DI and CA, the language Athanasius uses to describe the incarnation leaves the question of Jesus' human soul much less clear, leading most scholars to suppose either that it was not an issue he had grappled with directly or even that his views on the matter prior to 362 were essentially consonant with (or at least tacitly sympathetic to) those propounded unashamedly by Apollinaris and duly pronounced heterodox by the wider catholic consensus.[104]

In CG-DI Athanasius' characteristic incarnational vocabulary juxtaposes the personal identifier "Logos" with the general noun "body" (σῶμα), and can refer more or less in the same breath to the "embodiment" (ἐνσωμάτωσις) of the Word as well as his "enhumanizing" (ἐνανθρώπησις).[105] So, he tells us, in Christ the eternal Word of the Father "took" a body like our own,[106] "came to" and was subsequently "with" or "in" a body,[107] made the body his own,[108] "put the body on" and "clothed himself" with it as a covering,[109] appeared in his human body,[110] suffered and died courtesy of his body,[111] dwelt in the body as in a temple,[112] and used the body as an instrument (ὄργανον) in the task of fashioning our redemption.[113] The consistent conjunction of Logos with "body" in this manner can certainly be read as though Athanasius presumes the assumption of a less than complete humanity in the incarnation, the body being merely a physical covering (ἔνδυμα) in which a divine agent clothed himself, the thinking, willing, imagining, and feeling of Jesus thus being directly those of God himself rather than those of a man whose interior life had been laid hold of and was being conformed to God's character in a manner that involved its modification, growth, and development. At the same time, though, Athanasius can refer (sometimes in the same passage) to the incarnation as the Word's taking a body in order to become, be, and act/suffer humanly, "as a man among men," possession and "use" of a body immersed in the world of the senses naturally being part and parcel of this.[114] Of course, Athanasius reminds us, he himself was "not merely a man but God" (μὴ εἶναι ἄνθρωπον μόνον, ἀλλὰ καὶ Θεὸν);[115] yet it was nonetheless as a man (ὡς ἄνθρωπος) that he came among us and submitted himself to death.[116]

The christological expression of *CA* is also varied. Here, again, the juxtaposition of the terms "body" or "flesh" with verbs having "Logos" as their subject is very common, though the alternative "Son" enjoys greater prominence than in the earlier work. Other terms are also commonly used, though, and instances can be classified helpfully in terms of two key uses of verbs rather than the attendant nouns: verbs indicating the act of "assuming" or "taking" on one hand, and uses of the verb "to become" on the other. First, there are familiar statements concerning the Word's appropriation of flesh or a body, though Athanasius can also refer to what was appropriated as "humanity" (ἀνθρώπινον)[117] and even simply "that which is ours" (τὰ ἡμῶν).[118] The act of appropriation itself, meanwhile, he describes variously as the uncreated Logos "assuming," "taking," "putting on," "bearing," "being in," "being clothed in," and even "putting around himself" (περιτίθημι)[119] this hitherto foreign, creaturely mode of existence; for it was precisely by putting on created flesh (τὴν κτισθεῖσαν σάρκα) at the will of his Father and dwelling in it, Athanasius affirms, that he established the new creation of God.[120] Second, therefore, Athanasius uses the verb γίνομαι ("to become") in order to flag the fact that incarnation involved the Logos in a gracious act of condescension, *becoming* something that hitherto he had not been, something quite other than what he was by nature in his eternal life as God. Typically, what the Word is said thereby to have become is ἄνθρωπος—a human, or a man,[121] and henceforth what he does, says or suffers as Jesus is via the integrity of this new enhumanized existence, which is to say precisely *humanly* (ὡς ἄνθρωπος).[122]

Athanasius is especially concerned to insist that what occurs here is that the Word or Son *becomes* a man as distinct from having "come into" a man,[123] since the latter suggests a divine possession or cohabitation akin to the Spirit's indwelling of believers, a model which at a single stroke surrenders what Athanasius takes to be the heart of the gospel's radical claim, namely that it is God himself who is the grammatical or logical subject of all statements about Jesus. When Jesus acts and suffers, that is to say, it is God himself (the Word) who acts and suffers directly, albeit humanly, in a manner proper to what he has now become rather than what he eternally was and is. To suggest otherwise is, Athanasius sees, to skirt around the scandalous identification of Jesus as God (Θεός ὡς ἄνθρωπος to be sure, but Θεός nonetheless) and so sever the nerve of the gospel itself.

Significantly, in describing this radical new departure for God Athanasius also juxtaposes γίνομαι with the noun "flesh" (σάρξ, never σῶμα).[124] This, of course, simply echoes the Johannine prologue, but Athanasius also references wider biblical connotations of the term, "it being the custom of Scripture," he writes, "to call man by the name of flesh."[125] "Flesh," then, can refer both to something that the Word assumes and makes his own and to that which, in doing so, he becomes (such instances being equivalent to "human" or "a man"). If its reference is sometimes to the material aspect of human nature alone, therefore, elsewhere it arguably denotes our humanity as a psychosomatic whole,[126] or at least whatever Athanasius understands becoming "human" to entail.

George Dragas proposes an analogous (not identical) breadth of range for Athanasius' use of σῶμα (body) in CG-DI[127] whereby, he argues, it has a holistic rather than merely a partial reference to our creaturely nature, inclusive of our human psychology and spirit as well as bone, sinew, and other self-evidently "fleshy" elements. Thus, he argues, "the distinction of ἄνθρωπος from σῶμα, too, should be understood as the distinction between that which the Logos becomes in himself and that which becomes a possession of his."[128] Whether this claim is correct or not lies beyond the scope of our consideration, though it no doubt merits rather more careful exegetical attention than it has generally received. For our purposes we may simply note its consonance with the wider pattern we have observed, namely that in both texts Athanasius uses various anthropological terms in more than one way, and clearly feels neither awkwardness nor contradiction in holding that in the incarnation the uncreated, immortal, and impassible Logos of the Father both "takes flesh" and, precisely in doing so, himself actually "becomes human," this being what had to take place if we were to be "deified" via a glorious exchange of attributes, prerogatives, and relationships.[129]

This, we might note, makes it awkward to slot Athanasius' thought too neatly or conveniently into a Hegelian struggle between "Logos-sarx"/"Logos-soma" and "Logos-anthropos" models of the sort which scholars such as Alois Grillmeier (following in the nineteenth-century footsteps of F. C. Baur) have proposed as the pattern whereby classical incarnational theology evolved.[130] But, presuming that Athanasius' Christology as a whole made good sense at least to him, the complementarity (and sometimes interchangeability) of σάρξ, σῶμα, and ἄνθρωπος as key terms in his theology does not yet determine their meaning. Does "becoming human" entail the Word appropriating a "flesh" or "body" possessed of its own creaturely psychology as well as biology? Or might "human" in this context refer perfectly well to a creaturely physical frame indwelt in this particular instance by the divine Logos (as archetype of the *logikos* human mind/soul)?[131]

§8. Transplant or Regeneration? The Soul and Salvation

Significantly, unlike his contemporary Apollinaris, Athanasius nowhere denies that the incarnation excludes the appropriation of a human soul, nor makes any soteriological play of the claim that the Logos displaces such a soul.[132] Apollinaris, we recall, would insist that it was a necessary condition of the redemption of our humanity that the soul in it (which was the seat of sin and the cause of death) should, in the Savior, be excised and replaced by the sinless obedience of which the eternal Word himself alone was capable.[133] No such claim ever surfaces in this form in Athanasius' writings and, as we have already noted, when faced it is explicitly denied in his writings from 362 onward where the mind/soul is spoken of as the object (together with the body) of the Word's redeeming economy and hence, by implication, an essential part of that which is assumed in order to be transformed or "deified." This is a rather different soteriology, where salvation occurs precisely by divine appropriation, healing, and regeneration from within rather than the surgical removal of the offending organ. And the suggestion, therefore, is that a psychic displacement or transplant of the sort envisaged by Apollinaris would not actually redeem our humanity, leaving its mind/soul essentially in the same fallen condition, the Word's undoubted natural capacity for obedience and holiness having pushed it aside rather than being worked out in and through it in a regenerative manner. This is the soteriology and Christology unfolded much more explicitly a generation later by the Cappadocians and captured conveniently in Gregory of Nazianzus' (c. 330–c. 389) familiar maxim concerning the scope of the incarnation: "Whatever is not assumed is not healed" (τὸ γὰρ ἀπρόσληπτον, ἀθεράπευτον).[134] If an argument for Athanasius' tacit supposition of a human soul in the incarnation is to be mounted, it is in terms of his subscription in these early writings to an essentially similar soteriology that it might best be attempted.

If we do not presume a priori (as, for instance, Dragas does) that "body" and "flesh" are terms which Athanasius expects to be understood in such a manner as unambiguously to convey "full humanity" rather than mere material or biological existence, we are left asking why, if he is in fact *not* an "Apollinarian before Apollinaris," and if the human soul is indeed

a "serious theological factor"[135] for him on soteriological grounds, Athanasius is so coy about the whole business, apparently avoiding any and all
explicit allusion to the human psychology of the Savior.

§9. A Chalcedonian Interlude

First, we should remind ourselves of something that is too often either
overlooked or misunderstood: there is a careful logical distinction to be
drawn between psychological makeup (possession of soul, mind, spirit,
or whatever) and personal identity (the answer to the question *whose* soul,
mind, or spirit are we talking about?). In the terms of later christological
formulation designed precisely to clarify this, the first is a matter of οὐσία
or "nature" (that totality of our physical and psychical makeup which
as human beings we all possess) and the other of ὑπόστασις or "personhood."[136] The rendering into Latin of ὑπόστασις by *persona* (and the subsequent history of the latter and its cognates in Western thought) has often
led theologians (especially in the modern era) to suppose this to be a psychological category rather than a purely metaphysical one, presuming its
close equivalence to notions of "personality," ego, or self-consciousness.[137]
As E. L. Mascall observes, it is easy enough, "in virtue of the fact that it is
only in consciousness that the person comes to perceive itself, to draw the
false conclusion that person and consciousness are simply identical."[138] In
the context of classical Christology, though, they most certainly are not,
and "the integrity of Christ's human nature ... depends on the fact that person or hypostasis is a metaphysical entity and not a psychological one."[139]
Hypostasis, in the thought world on which the fifth-century theologians
drew in formulating the so-called doctrine of hypostatic union (or the two
natures doctrine) was not even an exclusively anthropological category,
referring rather to the "inherently unmultipliable and incommunicable"
aspect of a particular object or thing that makes it what *it* is that nothing
else is (so that even two identical widgets on a factory production line are
each possessed of their own hypostasis).[140] The *hypostasis* of something,
Rowan Williams observes, is thus "a subject beyond all its predicates ...
the unique ground of all its predicates, or, as you might say, the 'terminus'
of its predicates."[141] Even the word "subject" here is capable of misinterpre-
tation, so we should be clear that it refers to a logical or grammatical and
not a psychological "subject" (as in "subjective" or "subjectivity").

  In the case of what we now, happily or otherwise, call human "persons," of course, the distinction between οὐσία and ὑπόστασις is easy
enough to draw in terms of the way different questions are typically

formulated: "nature" (as an identifiable set of qualities or predicates) answers the question "what?" (what sort of thing is it that we are dealing with), whereas "person" (the ground or terminus of some particular set of predicates) pertains to the question "who?" Thus, a soul, mind, consciousness, ego, or personality are all, as psychological constituents, things that human beings *have*, just as surely as we have Achilles tendons, elbows, eyes, and body hair. They are part of our "nature," whereas persons are those who *have* such things, the peculiar metaphysical entities or nodes around which clusters of qualities coalesce and to whom they identifiably belong. And in the context of classical Christology, therefore, the adjective ἀνυπόστατος means simply "lacking in independent existence,"[142] a reference to the fact that the *hypostasis* of Jesus' humanity is precisely and always that of the Logos himself, apart from whom there *is* no man Jesus to be reckoned with. Where Jesus is concerned, that is to say, the answer to the question "who?" or "whose?" will always be one that affirms his identity as the eternal Son or Word come among us humanly. Despite its unfortunate rendering via the Latin *impersonalitas*, therefore, ἀνυπόστατος is *not* equivalent to ἄψυχος or ἀνόητος. It does not mean that "Jesus had no human personality; on the contrary, it allows us to say unequivocally that his experiences were of precisely the same order as ours."[143]

§10. Athanasius' Alexandrian Emphases

(a) Avoiding Arianism

The careful distinction between what in the incarnation pertains to the category of "nature" and what to hypostasis or "person" was forged only a century or so after Athanasius composed *CG-DI* and *CA*. The theological concerns behind it, though, are already to be found in the fourth century, and not least in Athanasius' writings. His particular christological concern (unsurprisingly, given his Alexandrian context and the dispute with Arius that flared up there) was to insist absolutely on the identity of the one incarnate as Jesus Christ with the eternal and uncreated Logos of the Father. In other words, using the later terminology of the Chalcedonian Confession, the ὑπόστασις that we must reckon with in Jesus is not an independent human "person" but precisely the Word of God who "took to himself a body and lived as a man among men" (ὡς ἄνθρωπος ἐν ἀνθρώποις ἀνατρέφεται).[144]

The Arian habit was to draw attention to things predicated unashamedly of Jesus in the Gospels which, they held, could never be predicated of God (dependence on the Father, experiencing fear and doubt about his vocation, developing and growing in wisdom, experiencing ignorance, and praying to God, among others), and to conclude that the one of whom such things were said could not be "the Most High God" at all (not ὅμοιος κατ᾽οὐσίαν), but a lesser being altogether (albeit a highly exalted angelic one), a "First Creature" who, falling on the creaturely side of the gap between God and creation, would be capable of incarnation without theological contradiction.[145] For reasons we have already considered, Athanasius was concerned at all costs not to permit any distinction to be drawn between Jesus and God so far as ὑπόστασις was concerned, the identity between them being the most vital and scandalous thing to be reckoned with in the "good news." His response, therefore, was constantly and consistently to differentiate between those things that might and should be predicated of the Word/Son by virtue of his eternal existence as God on the one hand, and things which may and must properly be said of him in the incarnation, namely as the man Jesus. In other words (again borrowing the later, more precise terminology), Athanasius distinguishes painstakingly between what is true of the "person" of the Word himself (as one who properly and eternally shares the Father's "divine nature") and what is true of him only (but properly) because he has "taken flesh" and has thereby now added a whole new human, creaturely dimension ("human nature") to his personal existence as the Son.

Thus, Athanasius argues, when Scripture speaks of Jesus suffering and dying we should not leap to the Arians' conclusion, for "[The Logos] himself was harmed in no respect, as he is impassible and incorruptible and the very Word and God" (Αὐτολόγος ὢν καὶ Θεός).[146] Such things, he insists, are not said of him *as the Logos*, but because of the flesh or body which he took and made his own. He assumed and bore human flesh along with all its attributes,[147] and "on account of this the properties of the flesh are said to be his, since he was in it."[148] Thus, Athanasius affirms, such things *are* therefore properly predicated of the Word himself, "because the body which ate and was born and suffered was no one else's but the Lord's [οὐκ ἑτέρου τινός, αλλὰ τοῦ Κυρίου ἦν]; and since he became man, it was right for these things to be said of him as a man [ὡς ἀνθρώπου λέγεσθαι], that he might be shown to have a true and not an unreal body."[149] Paradoxically, therefore, while we may say that in all this it is God who suffers, we may only say this of him *humanly*, holding in our mind at all times the fact that this immersion of himself in our humanity does not deny or contradict who or what he is eternally. It is due to "the human economy [ἡ ἀνθρωπίνη οἰκονομία] . . . that he undertook for our sake,"[150] and does not affect or impair "the substance of the Word" (τῆς τοῦ Λόγου οὐσίας) himself[151]—that is, that "nature" which is his properly and eternally. Therefore, Athanasius continues, at the death of Jesus on the cross "the whole of creation was confessing that he who was known and suffered in the body was not simply a man [οὐχ ἀπλῶς εἶναι ἄνθρωπον], but the Son of God and Saviour of all. For the sun turned back, and the earth shook, and the mountains were rent, and all were terrified; and these things showed that Christ who was on the cross was God" (τὸν μὲν ἐν τῷ σταυρῷ Χριστὸν Θεὸν ἐδείκνυον).[152]

§11. Athanasius' Alexandrian Emphases

(b) Avoiding Nestorianism

In all this careful differentiation, Athanasius' chosen way of expressing things entails him in predicating of the "flesh" or "body" assumed by the Logos experiences which are certainly not ones ordinarily ascribed to the body as the soul's material counterpart in dualistic anthropologies. Thus, he tells us, fear[153] and ignorance[154] as well as hunger and pain may be predicated of the Word only because they belong to the "body/flesh" that he appropriated and made his own. We have already reckoned with the possibility proposed by Georges Voisin, Dragas, and others of reading these terms psychosomatically (i.e., as a reference to our creaturely nature as a whole rather than our material frame alone),[155] and it is undoubtedly one of the weaknesses of interpretations of Athanasius along Apollinarian lines instead that in order to do so they are compelled to ascribe to him a certain amount of nonsense. So, for example, in one of the most influential pieces of scholarship on the subject, Marcel Richard accuses Athanasius of a "gros malentendu" in this regard,[156] while Grillmeier refers to "Athanasius' remarkable procedure of making the 'flesh' of Christ the physical subject of experiences which normally have their place in the soul."[157] If, though, we prefer the wider interpretation of "flesh" and "body," and take at face value Athanasius' claim that, "bearing our flesh, [the Word] became man, and hence he so acts and speaks,"[158] it still seems incumbent on us to inquire why he is not more explicit and straightforward in his language, ascribing the psychological experiences of the incarnate Lord to the human soul which (on such a reading) he assumed him to have. After all, would not such explicit ascription have better served his theological intent? And can we account theologically for what appears to be a deliberate and wholesale avoidance of it, without giving ground to the construal of him as someone for whom a human soul in the incarnation was in these works either a matter of indifference (Grillmeier) or theologically problematic (Richard)? I believe we can, and although doing so cannot prove anything decisively one way or another, it at least sends us back to the texts more confidently, armed now with more than one way of reading them, and hoping to determine which one makes the better overall sense of his argument.

As I suggested above, the overriding christological concern for Athanasius was that of asserting the identity of Jesus as the eternal Logos, insisting that there was only one "person" (ὑπόστασις) to be reckoned with in the incarnation, and that Jesus' words, actions, and experiences were thus properly the words, actions, and experiences of God himself, albeit belonging to him only by virtue of his having made our "flesh" or nature his own, and not balked at any of its properties or affections,[159] or its situation vis-à-vis God himself as creature,[160] so that such things are not "to be understood of his Godhead"[161] and "do not touch him according to his Godhead."[162] This identification of Jesus with God himself was breached in theologically disastrous ways by the Arian insistence that the "Logos" in question was not in fact God at all but a created Creator, a supreme angelic spirit who, while highly exalted, was nonetheless qua creature capable of involvement with and immersion in our humanity in ways that the Most High God himself could and would not deign to be. But it would be just as severely breached, Athanasius realized, by any suggestion that the eternal Word, rather than himself becoming a man by creating for himself a humanity like ours (and so joining us to himself by sharing fully in what was ours), instead were held merely to have descended on a man possessed of his own independent ὑπόστασις, "indwelling" his humanity as a sort of occupying presence, as the Holy Spirit is said in fact to come and indwell the lives of believers. This sort of christological duality, too, despite being framed differently, would compel (or enable) us to distinguish sharply between the identity (ὑπόστασις) of the one who speaks, acts, and suffers as Jesus, on one hand, and the one who indwells or occupies his humanity (but may readily be subtracted from it without its integrity being lost), on the other. But "when the flesh suffered," Athanasius insists, "the Word was not external [ἐκτὸς] to it; and therefore is the passion said to be his."[163]

Although so-called "Logos-anthropos" Christologies are more typically associated with the province of Asia Minor, their basic pattern was not wholly unfamiliar to Alexandrian Christianity, and is in fact

approximated to quite clearly in the theology of one of Athanasius' com-
peers, Origen, whose resort to the thought world of Hellenism was more
pronounced and more enthusiastic than Athanasius' own. Origen had
sought valiantly to explain how it was that the eternal Logos of God came
to be "enclosed within the limits of that man who appeared in Judaea,"
and in doing so had appealed to an essentially Hellenic theory of the preexistence of human souls as spiritual entities (τὰ λογικά).[164] The Logos,
he had argued, "conveyed invisibly a share in himself to all his rational
creatures, so that each one obtained a part of him exactly proportioned to
the amount of affection with which he regarded him."[165] One of these created spirits, through the exercise of free will, surpassed all the others in its
affection, being "attached with a warmer love to the author of its being"[166]
than any other, and was so closely (and uniquely) united to the Logos as
to become one spirit with him, so that it could itself legitimately be spoken
of as the Son of God, the Power of God, the Christ, and so on.[167] What
Origen had done here was to draw on an apostolic premise (Paul's suggestion in 1 Cor 6:17 that "anyone united to the Lord becomes one spirit
with him") and fuse it with current speculation about the nature of the
human soul in order to account for the presence of the Logos humanly in
Jesus. We need not doubt the "orthodoxy" of his intention in doing so, but
what results is in effect a Christology which, in order to avoid predicating
human experiences of the divine Logos directly, ascribes them instead to
a preexisting (and thus independent) human soul from whom the Logos
may conveniently be distinguished at relevant points. If the distinction is
pressed, this quickly and easily slips into a theology of the Word's "adoption" and indwelling of an exemplary human soul, a degree Christology
grounded in the same sort of union with the Logos (i.e., one of affection
and will) which all believers may aspire to and attain.[168]

While we may applaud the unashamed acknowledgment that the
incarnation was indeed characterized by fully human experiences on
Jesus' part, the potential theological consequences become awkwardly
apparent when, for instance, Origen deals with questions about the psychological anguish and suffering involved in the incarnation and especially the passion. Whose experiences are these? Unlike Athanasius,
Origen refers them directly and without hesitation to Jesus' human soul in
order to avoid predicating them of the Logos who, he insists, "suffers nothing of the experience of the body or the soul."[169] Taken together with his
insistence on the preexistence of Jesus' soul, though, rather than affirming
the full humanity of the Logos (which is no doubt what Origen intends),

this tends inevitably toward disentangling the two at all the key junctures, leaving the Logos personally unscathed by things which are now attributed instead to "the man whom he assumed."[170] Absent later conceptual clarification of what in the incarnation pertains properly to the category of ὑπόστασις and what to οὐσία, such a suggestion was difficult to avoid, for personhood is in practice bound up inseparably with psychology. It is, as Mascall suggests, "only in consciousness that the person comes to perceive itself,"[171] and to ascribe experiences to the human soul while denying that they can be predicated of the divine Logos is thus always likely to suggest the existence of two distinct ὑπόστασες to be reckoned with in the incarnation, the one being merely united to or closely associated with the other, rather than one ὑπόστασις of whom two quite different sets of qualities and experiences may and must properly be predicated.

Such a suggestion, whether tacitly entertained or explicitly made, is something that Athanasius cannot countenance, being concerned above all to affirm the divine Logos or Son as the personal subject of the human existence and experience of the Savior from beginning to end. Nothing was to put at risk this fundamental christological insight—the identity of Jesus as none other than God himself present among us humanly—for it both transformed the significance of Jesus' words, actions, and passion, and laid an axe to the roots of all ontological dualisms that would isolate God from his creatures in remote, inaccessible transcendence, leaving us to deal instead with one or another reified intermediary such as a Platonic demiurge or the Arians' "First Creature." The Origenistic notion of a preexistent human soul involved in the incarnation was one Athanasius was to dismiss explicitly at the end of his career, in *Ad Epictetum*.[172] The question which may legitimately be asked, though, is whether, given this overriding concern, and given the lack, for now, of any agreed way of clarifying Origen's presumed point and so avoiding a proto-Nestorian "two sons" Christology, we might not reasonably expect Athanasius already in *CG-DI* and *CA* to be wary of identifying himself explicitly with a foregrounding of the human soul of Jesus in accounting for the fear, grief, ignorance, and other "psychological" aspects of the incarnation, choosing instead to ascribe these to the "flesh" or "body" which the Logos assumed and made his own. It seems to me that we might, and that his consistent use of σάρξ, σῶμα, and ἄνθρωπος in the manner described above makes better sense if interpreted in this light as quietly inclusive rather than exclusive of ψυχή where relevant.

§12. Draining the Serpent's Venom

Regeneration from Within

Are there, then, good grounds for preferring an inclusive rather than an exclusive reading of these terms? As I have already suggested, the answer seems to me to lie in the logic of the sort of soteriology to which Athanasius adheres. That "the whole man, body and soul alike, has truly obtained salvation in the Word himself"[173] makes no sense at all unless the "flesh" which the Word assumed consisted of all that needed saving, namely both body and soul. Furthermore, the way in which Athanasius understands salvation as having taken place in these earlier texts appears to entail the presence of a human pyschological subject (mind/soul/will), not just as the passive object of salvation, but rather as a part of our nature appropriated, conscripted, and actively involved in the fashioning of salvation itself.

Christ, we recall, is the Logos who alone can recreate that which he originally created in the beginning. Now, though, he creates not ex nihilo but by laying hold of and restoring that which had fallen into sin and corruption. Again, he does this not by remaining at a distance from what he had made, as in the beginning, but by laying hold of it in a wholly new manner, assuming it and making it his own, namely by himself *becoming creature* for us, so that by the union of nature established we might be *recreated*, renewed in him and in his likeness.[174] For if Christ "was not *created for us*," Athanasius writes, "we are not created in him; and if not created in him, we have him not in ourselves but externally; as, for instance, as receiving instruction from him as a teacher. And, it being so with us, sin has not lost its reign over the flesh, being inherent and not cast out of it," whereas in truth he became one of us, "that by his dwelling in the flesh, sin might perfectly be expelled from the flesh, and we might have our mind free."[175] He comes in "created flesh" as a man and at the Father's will, "that whereas the first man had made it dead through the transgression, he himself might quicken it in the blood of his proper body, and might open *for us a way new and living*, as the Apostle says, *through the veil, that is his flesh*."[176] This expulsion of sin from Adamic flesh occurs, again, not by some external fiat, but by the Word doing in the flesh what we did not and could not do, fulfilling the law and, bearing our sins in his own body, offering himself to death on the tree, so making payment of the debt or ransom price which sin had incurred and,[177] having raised himself from death, offering himself afresh to the Father, making expiation (ἱλασκόμενος) to God on behalf of all.[178] The resonances with the Irenaean theology of recapitulation here are so strong as to be palpable,[179] and the differences from earlier Alexandrian accounts difficult to overlook with impunity.

In all this, Athanasius insists, the entire creation is reconciled to God *in* the Son of God himself, since all died in his death,[180] and all were sanctified and redeemed from sin and death in him.[181] The Creator himself having come down and been created for us as a man, he duly becomes for us not just our righteousness,[182] but the new creation of our humanity itself,[183] carrying his own "flesh" up to stand before his Father.[184] But in doing so he collected together "all the tribes of Israel" and opened a new way into God's presence for them,[185] so that the heavenly powers are not surprised to see us, one body with him, entering their realm.[186] Despite the desire of some scholars to trace here the legacy of Platonist ideas of "universal humanity" and the like,[187] the allusion to Israel tells us instead that we are back in the world of Athanasius' widespread appeal to the imagery of the Hebrew cult and the typology of the incarnate Logos as the High Priest in particular. In ancient Israel, he reminds us, the High Priest was a figure who clothed himself with special garments and entered into the holy of holies in order to make sacrifice for the people, mediating between them and God. Here, he argues, the ministry of the Son of God himself was foreshadowed, who took earthly flesh as his priestly vestment, thereby gathering "the tribes" in his person so that as High Priest he might duly offer himself to the Father on behalf of all, cleansing all from their sins in his own blood, and drawing near to the Father not for his own sake, but for others,[188] thus making a faithful and enduring sacrificial offering for all.[189]

In a study far more deserving of attention than it has generally received (being significantly at odds with prevailing currents of interpretation both in its own day and since), Melville Scott draws attention to the fact that for Athanasius, Christ's priestly "offering" on the cross seems to be merely a focal point in which the significance of a whole life and ministry of atoning self-offering is vitally concentrated.[190] Furthermore, "Christ did not come to assert the inherent sanctity of the flesh, but to crucify the flesh,"[191] a process wrought through a life of obedient struggle in which sin was denied and expelled by active obedience, and our humanity reforged in God's own image and likeness, as God's own character is worked out through a victorious conflict with sin and corruption in and through the Word's own humanity, reaching its climax in Jesus' death on the cross. It is in this sense, above all, Scott suggests, that "atonement" occurs not just in a particular act or moment of the Son's incarnate economy, but in the very action and event of incarnation itself, as our humanity and God are "reconciled" not just in an external relational transaction (whether legal or personal in nature), but *actually* and *ontologically*, being coordinated and correlated fully with one another in the person of the one who is himself "God," but is so *humanly*. That humanity which is God's own, in other words, is laid hold of by the Word not in some materially and spiritually neutral state, let alone in a condition already predisposed toward God, but in that very condition needful of redemption, to be regenerated and rendered "at-one" with who and what God eternally is only by his manner of indwelling it from birth to death, resurrection and ascension.

In support of his case Scott cites the following lengthy extract from *CA*:

> [God] sends his own Son, who becomes Son of Man by taking created flesh, that, since all men were under the sentence of death, he, being other than them all, might himself for all offer to death his own body; and that henceforth, all having died in him, the word of that sentence might be accomplished (for all died in Christ), and that through him might therefore become free from sin and from the curse which came upon sin, and might truly abide for ever, risen from the dead and clothed in immortality and corruption. For, the Word being clothed in the flesh . . . *all the venom of the serpent began utterly to be drained from it; and if any ill effect began to grow from the impulses of the flesh it was cut away; and, together with these death, the consequence of sin, was removed* as the Lord himself says, "The prince of this world cometh, and findeth nothing in me," and "For this end was he manifested" as John has written, "that he might destroy the works of the devil." But when these had been destroyed from the flesh, we were all set free by reason of our kinship to his flesh . . . and we shall no longer from henceforth dread the serpent, for he has been brought to naught, having been smitten by the Saviour in the flesh, and having heard the words "get thee behind me, Satan."[192]

For Scott, passages such as this one provide clear indication that Athanasius understands the sanctification and regeneration of our humanity as the result of a struggle in body, mind, and soul with its propensity to sin, of "actual resistance to temptation, not as the necessary result of the presence of the Divinity" as Apollinaris supposed.[193] In fact, where Athanasius differs from the soteriology of Apollinaris is not in his judgment that the human soul is corrupt and the source of sin, but in the understanding of how, in Christ, this circumstance is duly addressed and the soul (together with the rest of our nature) made good, being restored in the image of the Word himself. For Apollinaris, strictly speaking *this does not occur*, the Word himself substituting himself for the fallen soul of Jesus, and so guaranteeing a sinless and holy existence. The soul, in other words, is here effectively replaced rather than restored or renewed. For Athanasius, though, Scott maintains, the fallen and disfigured human soul itself is laid hold of, becoming the human soul of the Word, and through the Word's appropriation and indwelling of it, it is, by a fully human wrestling with and expunging of sin, bent back into shape through a sustained act of obedience, love, and devotion to the Father. "Christ fought our battle," Scott writes, "and only because he fought our battle did he win our victory."[194]

This concurs with the seriousness with which Athanasius takes the notions of Christ's obedience (which, as we shall see in a later chapter, is a hollow christological category where it is taken to be automatic rather than hard-won),[195] his offering of himself (and with himself our humanity) to the Father, his insistence that this offering was to remit a nontransferable debt,[196] and the pneumatological indicators that Christ received the Spirit in order to adapt our humanity and open it up to the Spirit's life and work. Indeed, he writes, "when the Lord, as man, was washed in Jordan, it was we who were washed in him and by him. And when he received the Spirit, we it was who by him are made capable of receiving it."[197] And again, "when the Lord came on earth, there was a necessity that he should not refuse to be called inferior to the Spirit, in respect of his manhood, as he really was. . . . For since man's nature is not equal of itself to casting out devils, but only in the power of the Spirit, therefore as man he said, "But if I through the Spirit of God cast out devils."[198] None of this is consonant with the claim that the incarnation involved the replacement of a human psyche by the divine mind and will of the eternal Word, being suggestive instead of the healing of that psyche through its personal identification with the Word and his renewal of it from within by offering it in obedience to the Father in our stead and on our behalf, drawing it into his own life, bestowing on it and opening it up to the impulse of the Spirit of holiness,[199] refashioning it in his own image, and so lifting it up (and us with it) into the Father's presence as a creaturely temple where God and humanity finally dwell together as one.

This seems to be the sort of soteriology lying behind the insistence of *Ad Antiochenos* and the statement of *Ad Epictetum* 7 that "the whole man, body and soul alike, has truly obtained salvation in the Word himself."[200] That we have traced its presence already in *CG-DI* and *CA* makes it difficult, surely, to suppose that the question of Jesus' human ψυχή was ever a matter of theological indifference to the author of those texts,[201] and more reasonable to interpret his christological formulations as intended tacitly to include rather than exclude the appropriation of a soul like ours, its being vital to that redemption of our nature which occurred *in* Christ, rather than merely being performed *by* him.

§13. Incarnation as Deification

Our concern in these opening chapters has been with the scholarly suggestion that it was the apologetic adoption of essentially unbiblical models of salvation as the divinization or deification (θεοποίησις) of our humanity which provided the main impetus for the emergence of the Christology that eventually triumphed as "orthodoxy" through the conciliar statements of councils at Nicaea, Constantinople, Ephesus, and Chalcedon.[202] My argument has been that this suggestion correctly identifies an organic connection between Christology and soteriology but often misrepresents both the soteriologies concerned and their attendant Christologies, and so gets the connection between soteriology and christological orthodoxy wrong.

In chapter 3 we considered the sort of soteriology that came to prominence in the so-called Catechetical School in Alexandria in the third century, noting its consonance with the "philosophical theology" of the Neoplatonism which developed at the same time, in which the deification of humanity consists in the divine soul's purification from immersion in the material realm, and its ascent to full contemplation of truth, being naturally capable of this through its essential likeness to the divine Logos. Christologically, though, we saw how within the theological schema envisaged, neither the full deity of the incarnate Logos nor his human integrity is finally possible to affirm, let alone the union of God with our embodied human condition. Rather than leaning naturally in the direction of a doctrine of hypostatic union, in other words, this theology is one which, owing to its entanglements with Greek cosmology, ontology, and epistemology more or less renders it impossible to take seriously any of the core components of that doctrine. Athanasius' willing appropriation and use of the language of salvation as θεοποίησις at the culmination of his argument in *CG-DI* and repeatedly in *CA*[203] presumes a very different understanding of the term, and of its christological concomitants. It is, I suggest, an understanding consonant with, and a serious theological development of, the flirtation with such language to be found in Irenaeus' doctrine of recapitulation, according to which salvation ultimately involves our creaturely nature "passing into God" or being "promoted into God"[204] courtesy of God's having joined himself to it in the economy of the incarnation.

Athanasius takes great care to differentiate between two very different modes of sharing or participation in God. First, the Word or Son shares fully and properly in God's very being, as the Father's "proper Word and radiance," whereas we, as creatures, are by nature "foreign and distant from God."[205] And yet, he insists, when the Word takes our creaturely flesh upon himself, he knits us into himself "not according to the substance of the Godhead; for surely this is impossible; but according to his manhood . . . since we are like him according to the flesh."[206] In doing so, Athanasius maintains, "he himself has made us sons of the Father, and made men gods by himself becoming man."[207] Our "participation" in God, whereby we are "made gods," is, in other words, precisely a participation in the *incarnate* Son who, being joined to us already as our Creator, has subsequently united himself to us more completely by the brotherhood of our created nature.[208] When the Son makes our humanity his own, furthermore, by virtue of the union established we too are adopted and drawn in to enjoy his unique filial relation to God as Father and, being "knit into the Godhead" by sharing in the same Spirit as anoints the human Son himself,[209] and duly sharing in his life of self-offering to the Father, this υἱοποίησις is what our deification in Christ finally means.[210] And, Athanasius argues, "if all that are called sons and gods, whether in earth or in heaven, were adopted and deified *through the Word* [διὰ τοῦ Λόγου υἱοποιήθησαν καὶ ἐθεοποιήθησαν], and the Son himself is the Word," then "it is plain that through him are they all, and he himself before all, or rather he himself only is very Son, and he alone is very God of very God."[211]

This is the fact of the gospel as Athanasius sees it: the eternal Word or Son of the Father, who is himself Θεὸς ἀληθινός ("the true God"), has become one of us in order to heal our humanity from sin and death and draw it into the life of God himself. In this he "deifies" it, granting it to share in the Son's eternal relation of love for the Father and the Father's reciprocal love for the Son in the power of the Holy Spirit. It is this remarkable vision of salvation that drives Athanasius' implacable opposition to Arius, whose proposed compromise with Hellenism (especially its queasiness about God getting his hands dirty by direct involvement with creatures) puts it at risk. For the participation we have been granted in the incarnation (our θεοποίησις), Athanasius insists, lies not in likeness to any mere "First creature" or δεύτερός θεός (secondary god) but, astonishingly, sharing in the inner life of the Creator of heaven and earth himself, and in the bringing to fulfillment of his original creation. And for Athanasius, I have argued, the gift of this participation is ours *only* because the true God, in the person of his Word or Son, appropriated and made his own a humanity like ours (in both body and soul), lifting it up by his personal indwelling of it, expunging from it the power of sin and the curse of death, and establishing it within the life of God as a temple in which God and humanity may dwell together at one.[212] But it *is* ours, because God's "being" consists precisely and most fundamentally in the communion enjoyed eternally by Father, Son, and Holy Spirit, and the "owning" of our humanity by which the eternal Son becomes the human Son, drawing it fully into this same nexus of relationships in God *is*, therefore, its establishment within the life, the "being" of God himself, in which we now share indirectly, by the gracious adoption which the Word's assumption of and identification with our "flesh" thus entails.

This rich vision disintegrates at a stroke if the Savior (*in* whom and not merely *by* whom salvation is wrought) either is not identified as himself "God with us," or is not understood to be "one who in every respect has been tested as we are, yet without sin." We can see, then, both how this soteriology is indeed inextricable from Christology (for here the person of the Savior is in some clear sense *identifiable with* his work rather than the mere condition for its completion) and how it concurs happily with that model of incarnational theology which eventually emerged through the debates from Nicaea to Chalcedon.

Far from being an essentially Hellenic and unbiblical model of θεοποίησις, though, this seems rather to be one unfolded through reflection on the magnitude of biblical claims about Christ and the way in which, read in their canonical context, intimations of his true identity affect theological understanding of all that he does and says and suffers and its significance for us. It is Christology, in other words, that here initially determines the shape and substance of soteriology, and not vice versa. There is, as we have seen, a more Hellenic notion of "deification" at large among the Christian theologies of Alexandria, but, far from being one that either reflects the concerns or dictates the shape of subsequent christological orthodoxy, in reality it renders it wholly untenable, and is, I suggest, more truly the progenitor of the several "heterodoxies" in the teeth of which that orthodoxy was duly forged and maintained.

II

Reconsidering the West

5

Satisfaction

"Here is my servant, whom I uphold,
my chosen, in whom my soul delights;
I have put my spirit upon him."[1]

"Almighty God, our heavenly Father, who of thy tender mercy didst give
thine only Son Jesus Christ to suffer death upon the cross for our
redemption; who made there (by his own oblation of himself once offered)
a full, perfect, and sufficient sacrifice, oblation, and satisfaction, for the sins
of the whole world."[2]

Words and images may typically enter the flow of theological tradition
bearing a particular and fairly clearly defined meaning for those who lay
hold of them. But meanings are never precisely fixed, and in the case of
words appropriated and applied to the mysteries of God's being and action
in particular, given meanings are necessarily broken and made new. They
must be adjusted and adapted to refer to the realities of one whose ways
are not as our ways, and who, even as he gives himself and his purposes
to be known, constantly eludes our attempts to pin down and define.
Furthermore, within the imaginatively diverse ecology of talk about salvation, meaning quickly accrues to core words and images as they are variously fused with or set in counterpoint or apposition to, and so modified
by, others held to be equally significant in their purchase on the matter.[3]
And, of course, meanings shift and evolve too as we translate words and

images from one societal context to another, and as whatever secular, non-theological significances they may have shift and evolve courtesy of current social mores.

In Western liturgy and theology, the language of "satisfaction" is of ancient and widespread standing, though, for reasons just indicated, its force and connotations are likely to vary (perhaps quite significantly) from one context of use to another. In our own day, once we step outside the specifically theological context, perhaps the primary use is one that we might identify as *aesthetic*. We derive satisfaction, we typically say, from that which gratifies some desire, satiates appetite, or delights our sensibility. Satisfaction is obtainable, too, from the accomplishment of some demanding or challenging task that we have set ourselves, typically one that requires of us the acquisition and successful performance of some new skill set, resulting in a pleasing outcome. To be "satisfied" in such instances means to be happy or content with the state of things, albeit they might conceivably be better yet or improved on in future. In each case, too, the condition of "satisfaction" refers to a sort of pleasure or sense of well-being linked directly to the fulfillment of a perceived lack or absence, or the transcendence of some hitherto presumed limit in our range of experience. What is at first glance a quite distinct, secondary category of use pertains to our capacity to meet the obligations, demands, and expectations placed on us by others within various sorts of relationship, as, for instance, when we meet the terms and conditions of some binding agreement, or make adequate reparation or remuneration for some debt (financial or of other sorts) incurred in our dealings with others. Here again, though, the connotation is of something essentially *positive* done or accomplished, the analogy being indicated by the typical use in each case of the language of "fulfillment," albeit with slightly different resonances in each case.

Despite its secondary status in contemporary usage, the soteriological use of "satisfaction" and its cognates has rather more obviously to do with the latter category than the former, at least as regards its initial appropriation and development by the theologians of the Christian West. And yet, if we take seriously God's entrustment of the good news to the vagaries and potentialities of human language, and if we are willing to follow the traces of meaning associated with this word down the trajectories of its varied use, we may find that our understanding of the atonement is refreshed and reinvigorated rather than simply clarified (as though there were one original and authorized meaning to be had, and the theological task were to identify, isolate, and reinstate it). What gives God "satisfaction," in other words, may turn out to be something more and other than the first theological users of the term were able to appreciate.

§1. Tertullian and the Theology of Penitence

It is generally supposed that the language of satisfaction entered the theological lexicon courtesy of some unashamed borrowing from the technical vocabulary of Roman jurisprudence. Tertullian of Carthage (c. 150–c. 225 CE), a lawyer before he was a theologian, is mostly credited with the responsibility. It is not in his treatment of the work of Christ, though, that Tertullian's most substantial contribution to the development of that doctrine's vocabulary is to be found,[4] but in his practical and moral treatises, where the relationship between God and the Christian disciple is configured in terms of categories borrowed from the vocabulary of Roman private law, central to which were the technical terms *meritum* and *satisfactio*. Franks (following Hermann Schultz's classic treatment of the subject)[5] notes that, in the believer's relationship with God understood along these lines (i.e., as structured around divinely ordained prescriptions and obligations), in general terms merit is won through obedience or compliance (*solvere*), while noncompliance incurs a state of debt (*debitum*) that must somehow be dealt with. More precisely and properly, though, meritorious performances are those that are *nonobligatory*, reaching identifiably beyond the demands of *solvere* to works of moral and spiritual supererogation (patience, penance, fasting, virginity, martyrdom, and others).

The arithmetical and pecuniary connotations of the imagery at work here suggest that, by the avoidance of sin and the performance of supererogatory works, one might gradually build up a surplus of merit in one's standing with God, and naturally invite the question about the transferability of this surplus to the accounts of others in order to pay off their debts. The idea that certain persons of particular holiness—notably those who had died as martyrs—might indeed be in a position to redeem the sins of others in this way seems to have been current in Tertullian's North African context.[6] Indeed, it is precisely in rejecting this suggestion that Tertullian himself comes closest to suggesting an understanding of the work of Christ cast in the same terms: "Let it suffice to the martyr to have purged his own sins," he writes. "It is the part of ingratitude or of pride to lavish upon others also what one has obtained at a high price. Who has redeemed another's death by his own, but the Son of God alone? . . . For to this end had he come, that, being himself pure from sin, and in all respects holy, he might undergo death on behalf of sinners."[7] By inference, the suggestion here is that Christ (and *only* Christ) in his obedient life and supererogatory death has accrued a surplus of merit sufficient to pay (satisfy) the debt which sinners owe.[8] If Tertullian himself shies away from applying this schema directly to the atonement, the notion of Christ's life and death as a *satisfaction* of demands implicit in the divine-human relationship nonetheless enters the bloodstream of Western theology here and crops up more explicitly in accounts of Christ's death among Tertullian's successors.

If Christ's merit were indeed reckoned as transferable to sinners in such a manner as to cancel our debt before God, then for Tertullian it is at the moment of our baptism that this transaction occurs. It is in his discussion of initial repentance and the implications of *post*-baptismal sin, though, that his own use of this legal image is unfolded. Such sin, he insists, places the sinner once more in breach of the terms of God's legally binding demand on us, incurring a second, threatening, and urgent debt to be dealt with. In this circumstance, Tertullian insists, a sinner must "*per delictorum poenitentiam . . . domino satisfacere.*"[9] Given the subsequent course of Western soteriology, it is tempting to interpret this as meaning that it is through bearing the penalty (*poena*) due for our repeated failings that God is duly satisfied, whether that punishment be understood to be borne by us or absorbed within the scope of a vicarious infliction already borne by Christ. Yet while the compound notion of a "penal-satisfaction" certainly appears prominently in later Western theologians, it is less obviously apposite in terms of the metaphor which Tertullian initially frames.

According to Schultz, in the world of private jurisprudence from which Tertullian's picture is borrowed, *satisfactio* is understood not as a punishment incurred and suffered due to the failure to meet some obligation but rather as *an alternative means of discharging* that debt in a manner that the claimant finds agreeable (i.e., which is "satisfactory" to redress the circumstance and restore the relationship to equilibrium). Here, then, "satisfaction," as Franks observes, has no organic connection with the notion of a punishment inflicted and borne by way of desert but "has affinity rather with *solvere,*"[10] being in effect a subspecies of merit. *Aut solvere aut satisfactio.* Either we meet our obligations in the way specified by contract, or we meet them in some other manner which is pleasing to the claimant. Otherwise, *poena* is the proper legal outcome. In the case of satisfaction as in the case of *solvere,* therefore, the performance is an essentially meritorious one, something positively offered (and worthy of

offering) rather than passively borne or inflicted. The *poenitentia* involved
in the case of postbaptismal sin, therefore, is (according to the logic of Tertullian's chosen analogate) better translated and understood as involving
an active "penitence," the reparation or making good of an offense, and not
a punishment exacted. By extension, too, therefore, applied to the atoning
life and death of Christ the metaphor of satisfaction understood thus suggests something of positive value (meritorious) offered to the Father by
the incarnate Son in recompense for humankind's failure to comply with
his demands, and not an act of retributive justice meted out by an impersonal justice, let alone one borne by an undeserving victim in our stead.

Insofar as this is correct, we might say that the logic of satisfaction
here draws rather closer to the spirit of the biblical and liturgical language
of sacrifice—the voluntary offering of something pleasing in God's sight
and his nostrils—than to the judicial imagery of a capital penalty exe-
cuted on a hapless victim.[11] It must be admitted, though, that Tertullian's
handling of the image is not altogether free from penal connotations, its
distinct suggestion of something meritorious (originating in God himself, and so pleasing to him)[12] being offset by his indication that what the
"abolition of former sins"[13] effected thereby requires in practice are acts
of self-abasement and self-inflicted chastisement (*castigatio*), the inner
disposition of penitence being accompanied and further enhanced (*com-
mendet*) by outward signs of *mortificatio*.[14] All this is perfectly consonant,
of course, with the Christian awareness that what pleases God and brings
life often involves deliberate curbing of the sinful impulses which "come
naturally" to our fallen nature—a "putting to death" of "self" or "the deeds
of the flesh" as Paul's imagery has it. It would be consonant, too, with any
attempt to apply Tertullian's language to the circumstance of atonement,
where it is by laying hold of our nature and putting to death in it whatever
resists and is hostile to God's will that Christ regenerates it, and offers it
up as a holy sacrifice which "satisfies" (is pleasing rather than displeasing
to) his Father. Yet, while Tertullian speaks of *poenitentia* as the meritorious product of a self-discipline which honors God, he can also refer to it
as appeasing God,[15] and thereby avoiding eternal punishment by a form of
plea bargaining, as it were, settling for a lesser sentence here and now, and
imposing and executing it ourselves.[16] It is but a small step from here to a
view in which external acts of *poenitentia* are understood less as the sacramental expression of penitence and more as a kind of "penance" in which
sins are paid for by the individual sinner via forms of self-inflicted *poena*.

John McIntyre, in a forthright rebuttal of Franks, ascribes the presence of such penal overtones in Tertullian to the existence of a more complex pattern of usage in Roman legal vocabulary than Schultz's study admits. Granted that in *private* law "satisfaction" may refer to meritorious performance which constitutes an alternative to punishment, nonetheless, he maintains, in Roman *public* law the same term can and often does bear straightforwardly penal connotations. What Schultz (and Franks in his reliance on Schultz) fails to acknowledge, he argues, is that both forms of legal practice are relevant for interpreting Tertullian, whose view of "satisfaction" is consequently one capable of understanding it either as a meritorious offering or as a quasi-penal self-infliction, toggling between them without any sense of awkwardness.[17] Perhaps this is so. Perhaps, too, McIntyre is correct in urging us not to follow Franks' commission of the "fallacy of origins," encouraging us to suppose instead that Tertullian's peculiar meaning is properly to be sought not in the canons of Roman law at all but in the presumably long-established practice of confession to which he refers and to which he now applies the term, a practice in which ideas of meritorious offering and penalty may already have been juxtaposed and counterpoised.[18] Yet it is of the essence of metaphor that its meaning resists easy definition via either of the associational contexts to which it now belongs, and that its use transforms both, its fittingness consisting precisely in its ability to trespass between and modify their respective sets of expectations.[19] If McIntyre is correct about the pattern of the word's use in Roman legal vocabulary, and if (we have no evidence other than Tertullian's own) there was an established practice of confession in which notions of merit and penalty were already held in tension, then we can see that Tertullian's coining of the metaphor of satisfaction was judicious;[20] but it remains true that our primary attention should be paid not to either of these putative contexts but to the ways in which Tertullian himself uses the term, and that, as we have seen, is with a clear suggestion of something meritorious accomplished in God's sight, albeit something which might otherwise (or perhaps, paradoxically, *also*) be construed in penal terms.

Where the theology of a sacrament of confession and reconciliation is concerned, the fluctuation or slippage between these two strands (the penitential and the penal) may be deemed problematic in various respects. Both strands, though, must surely be permitted their proper place in any attempt to reckon with the fullness of the atoning work of Christ. The imagery of law and the penal execution of justice cannot, after all, be avoided if we are to grapple seriously with apostolic testimony of the meaning of

Christ's death on the cross, whatever else may yet need to be said. Within such attempts, furthermore, it is likely that each of these images will be subject to some cross-fertilization with the other, and with others laying claim to proper theological attention—victory, sacrifice, healing, ransom, reconciliation, liberation, justification, sanctification, and the rest.[21] It is important, though, to attend to images in their own right as well as in their mutually modified state, for only thus can we hope to discern the distinctive contribution of each, and appreciate how it might help us to qualify and, in its turn, be qualified by the connotations of others.

Such careful consideration is, I believe, particularly apt and important in the case of the image of Christ's work as a "satisfaction," since the distinctive connotations and contribution of this image have too often been subsumed without remainder within various forms of penal imagery, being focused wholly on the death of Jesus by judicial process on the cross, and presenting him (in one convenient formulation of the matter) as "bearing what we could not bear" rather than "offering what we could not offer."[22] This tendency is apparent even among Tertullian's immediate successors, who quickly lost sight of any connotations of meritorious offering within a covenanted relationship and tended to subsume the image within (rather than allowing it to complicate or modify) an essentially penal and impersonal account of things. Hilary of Poitiers (c. 315–c. 367 CE), for example, clearly senses and wrestles with the problem. Reflecting on the presumed axiom that God, by nature, cannot suffer or die, he emphasizes that the passion and death of the incarnate Son are voluntarily undertaken, and "will make amends by fulfilling a penal function" (or, perhaps, "by satisfying the demand for punishment"), yet not in such a way that the Son suffers the perception that he is actually being punished.[23] Here *satisfacere* is apparently already removed from the logic of persons, and refers rather to the proper fulfillment of abstract legal prescriptions contingent on law-breaking; yet Hilary knows that it cannot be right to say that Jesus was "punished" by God (even though he may have borne a penalty), and he grasps the importance of insisting that his submission to death was valuable inasmuch as it was voluntary rather than coerced, deserved, or natural. Ambrose of Milan (c. 339–397 CE) is also faithful in holding in play more than one image, including that of satisfaction, but in his hands, too, the latter falls into place within a pattern primarily penal in its overtones. Christ underwent death, he writes, "that the sentence might be fulfilled, and that satisfaction might be made to the judgment [*satisfieret judicato*]: the sentence was the curse pronounced upon sinful flesh even unto death."[24]

There can be little doubt that the mainstream appropriation of *satis-factio* in Western atonement theologies has continued in this vein, under-standing by it a variant of or a synonym for penalty bearing. When, in the early sixteenth century, Thomas Cranmer deployed it in the Eucharistic liturgy of his prayer book, for example, it is likely that both he and those who were duly formed by the liturgy had some such notion of a "penal-satisfaction" in mind. My argument is not that penal imagery has no place in atonement theologies or their liturgical expression but that if and when the language of satisfaction is effectively collapsed into penal language, its distinct contribution is occluded, and its capacity to qualify and modify other images (including ones of penalty bearing) is denied to the detri-ment of a wider and more adequate account of the matter. What is inter-esting is that the same theological mainstream has typically laid claim to the endorsement and support of the theologian who has offered the most developed account of Christ's death in terms of the imagery of satisfac-tion, Anselm of Canterbury (1033–1109 CE). In doing so, I believe, they both misunderstand and misrepresent him. In the next part of this chapter, therefore, I offer a reading of Anselm's classic *Cur Deus Homo?* ("Why the God-Human?") with the aim of clarifying his exposition of the atonement in these terms. I then trace connections with an account of the work of Christ which, despite being largely sidelined, overlooked, and also misun-derstood, I consider to be the natural heir to his key insight: John McLeod Campbell's (1800–1872) presentation of the atonement as centered on the "vicarious penitence" of the incarnate Son of God. I do so not in order to promote this strand of soteriological reflection as the most adequate or "truest" view but simply to keep its distinctive contribution seriously in play as one among a number of complementary angles of approach in our attempts to apprehend a reality the fullness of which must by definition always elude us, and as affording at the very least an important corrective to the unqualified advocacy of Christ's death in terms of a certain sort of "penal substitution."

In what follows I hope as far as possible to allow both theologians to speak for themselves in such a way as to demonstrate both divergence and convergence in their thinking about the atonement. Of the many lit-erary witnesses and advocates on whose services one might call in such an undertaking, only a small handful have been selected, partly because limitations of space would not allow otherwise, but also because views expressed on the matters in hand are so diverse as to muddy the waters rather than facilitating a clear view of our subject within a small compass.

§2. Anselm

The Satisfaction Made by the *Deus Homo*

Anselm's approach to demonstrating the necessity for and nature of the atonement is essentially similar to the method he pursues in other works, and is referred to already in the *Praefatio* as his determination to proceed in this case *remoto Christo*—"leaving Christ aside, as if nothing had ever been known of Him."[25] As McIntyre shows, this is an approach which brackets out of consideration certain core elements in the pattern of Christian believing, precisely in order to demonstrate how the logic (*ratio*) of the remaining pattern requires the missing pieces for its integrity or completion. Such an approach "discovers that certain propositions, accepted at the beginning . . . by both the believer and the unbeliever, logically imply conclusions accepted by the believer and denied by the unbeliever."[26] The initial propositions, McIntyre observes, are neither theologically neutral "first principles" nor the sort of explicit *articula fidei* to which unbelief can by definition grant no assent. Rather, they include things which, in a particular intellectual context, faith is able to affirm on the grounds of their having been "thought together with" the truths of the gospel (the constructive task of theology in every age, and which generates the larger "pattern of Christian believing"),[27] and which, at the surface level at least, overlap or coincide with things held within the "patterns of unbelief" (though as one digs and unpacks them further, differences will soon appear in their significance precisely owing to the respective patterns within which they are situated and "made sense of").[28] The "initial propositions" may also include, though, specifically theological elements of the Christian *credo* which, for the purposes of the argument, Anselm's opponents "are prepared to grant while they deny certain other articles of faith."[29] But even these theological premises, McIntyre notes, will not be "pure" from the alloy of the contemporary intellectual environment. The task of constructive theology alluded to above can proceed only by "relating the *fides* to the concepts, categories and beliefs of the contemporary *intellectus.*" Again, many of these concepts, categories, and beliefs will be ones shared at least at first glance by belief and unbelief, the divergences of understanding becoming apparent only once their situation within different patterns of understanding are reckoned with. In both instances, therefore, McIntyre concludes, "What St Anselm does is to indicate that some contemporary concept[30] which has several possible meanings, one of which is presumably employed by his opponents, has a specifically

Christian meaning which is just as valid as the others and the employment of which enables his argument to proceed with conviction."[31]

In *Cur Deus Homo*, as McIntyre notes, "it is the existence of the God-man together with the atoning value of His Death which constitutes the *intelligendum* or the *probandum* of the work, the x, the logical necessity of which is implied by the a, b, c, d accepted by the critics of the faith."[32] Whence, then, are these "agreed" propositions derived? As already noted, the image of *satisfactio* is at the heart of the case Anselm builds; but what connotations does the word bear as he picks it up and uses it? It has been held that the source of Anselm's imagery lies in the feudal obligations of Teutonic society, patterns of social order which would have been familiar to his interlocutors, and thus a convenient ground from which to argue.[33] Others have held that, his use of nonbiblical terms and categories notwithstanding, the substance of Anselm's presentation of the atonement is already to be found encoded in the pages of Scripture.[34] Others still have supposed that, despite his use of social analogies, the meaning of Anselm's terms is perhaps better understood by situating it within the long flow of the medieval church's system of sacramental confession and the penitential theology which undergirded it.[35] According to this last view, in other words, *satisfactio* in *Cur Deus Homo* is best understood as meaning whatever it meant in that tradition, which stretched, as we have seen, all the way back to Tertullian and beyond.

None of these suggestions seems satisfactory in isolation, yet each of them may have some part of the truth. As noted above, constructive Christian theology will always need to relate the tenets of its *credo* to current thinking, and in doing so it will modify any terms that it chooses to use, whether biblical or secular in origin. Secular parables used to speak of divine realities can no longer mean whatever they originally meant. Biblical and traditional ideas, meanwhile, explored by integrating them with a wider fabric of things believed to be true, and translated into contemporary terms and images come, in the Spirit's hands, to mean more and other than they originally meant—continuous, but nonetheless more and other. This means that no rigid reduction of Anselm's meanings to the logic of any of these several sources is likely to bear much fruit, for it fails to recognize the extent to which his thought is generative of new and distinct meaning, *theological* meaning determined above all not by its etymological roots but by the unique divine circumstance to which Anselm here applies his mind.[36]

The relationship between *Cur Deus Homo* and the penitential theology of Tertullian is, I think, particularly interesting and suggestive. As McIntyre observes, the eight hundred years or so that separate the two theologians perhaps preclude the idea of any great influence exerted on Anselm's thought by Tertullian, or even permit us to list him as a primary source.[37] As David Hogg reminds us, "We do not know how well, if at all Anselm was acquainted with Tertullian's writings or of anything written by subsequent authors who picked up on his idea of satisfaction." Certainly, the language of satisfaction passed through many theological hands in the intervening centuries, and will have been handed on to Anselm in a form Tertullian himself may or may not have recognized. And yet, Hogg suggests, "while the links may not be direct, the conceptual similarity is such that, however convoluted the flow of information may be, there is sufficient correlation to warrant a case for continuity."[38] This, I think, is correct. For while Anselm's development of the notion within the context of a theology of the atonement bursts the old wineskins of anything Tertullian might have understood by it, the tantalizing thread of similarity and suggestion remains in Anselm's insistence, as we shall see, that the *satisfactio* offered by the incarnate Son to the Father is essentially a matter of meritorious offering, and has nothing to do with penalty bearing.

The question that Anselm sets himself to attempt to answer in *Cur Deus Homo* is "for what reason or by what necessity did God become man, and by his death, as we believe and acknowledge, restore life to the world, although he could have accomplished this by means of another person, whether angelic or human, or simply by an act of his will?"[39] It is to the *ratio* and the *necessitas* of the incarnation and the cross, therefore, that he directs our thought.

The short answer to this question, of course, is that it is human sin that has necessitated these drastic measures on God's part. Yet much more than this must be said if we are to grasp why and how the divine economy is related to our human plight. Sin, Anselm tells us, is best understood as a failure to render to God that which is due to him from every creature. The Creator-creature relationship he suggests, is not unlike that between ruler and subject, and everybody knows that subjects owe certain dues to their human overlords. If these are not properly rendered, then a situation occurs in which the honor of the Lord is at stake, and his justice compromised. In such a circumstance, it is expected that some reparation proportionate to the damage done will be made, plus something extra to compensate for the offence caused, or else the Lord is likely to exact some form of punitive measure instead. Furthermore, the extent or value of the compensatory payment will be determined by the place in the social order of the one wronged or offended.[40]

In the case of God and his creatures, Anselm explains, "The will of every creature must be subject to the will of God.... This is the debt which angel and man owe to God, so that no one sins if he pays it and anyone who does not pay it, sins. This is the only and the total honour which we owe to God and which God exacts of us.... A person who does not render God this honour due him, takes from God what is his and dishonours God, and this is to commit sin."[41] In fact, however, no one renders this due to God, and thus all *are* in a state of sin, a state of being severely in God's debt with the final demand for payment due. "As long as [man] does not repay what he has plundered," Anselm continues, "he remains at fault. Neither is it enough merely to return what was taken away, but on account of the insult committed, he must give back *more* than he took away.... Thus, therefore, everyone who sins must pay to God the honour he has taken away, and this is satisfaction, which every sinner must make to God."[42]

To make matters even worse, it becomes clear that we can do absolutely nothing even to begin to repay the original debt which we owe, let alone make extra compensation. Owing God all that we are and have already, even if we cease from our sinful ways, our obedient lives cannot be considered as repayment of our outstanding debt, let alone as a compensatory satisfaction for the offense caused to God.[43] Yet even if we did not owe all this to God, and supposing that we did have something to offer which was not already God's by right, whatever we had could never be enough to repair the enormous damage done by our sins. For reparation is to be made over and above the corresponding offense, and offense is to be measured in accordance with its object, in this case, God himself. "Therefore," Anselm reasons, "you do not make satisfaction if you do not return something greater than that for whose sake you were bound not to commit the sin."[44] "This," remarks Boso, Anselm's hypothetical interlocutor, "is a very crushing thought"!

Given that all this is the case, what is God to do? Humankind is trapped by its own sins into a terrible plight, the only way out of which is for some payment to be made. God cannot forgive us without such a payment, his honor having been compromised. "To remit sin in such a way would be the same as not to punish it. And since to deal justly with sin (without satisfaction) is the same as to punish it, then, if it is not punished, something inordinate is allowed to pass."[45] So, then, God must either punish the sinner, *or else* receive full satisfaction from the sinner, in which case forgiveness and restoration may follow. Yet we have seen that what is owed by the sinner is too great. It seems that punishment, and not forgiveness, must be the plight of mankind.

Here it is that Anselm finally arrives at the all-important answer to his opening question. For satisfaction to be made, and punishment avoided, he insists, what is required is "someone to render to God, for the sins of man, something greater than everything that exists outside of God . . . [for this to be possible] it is also necessary for [this person] to be greater than everything that is not God. . . . But there is nothing that surpasses all that is not God but God himself. . . . Therefore no one but God can make this satisfaction. . . . But none ought to make it but man. Otherwise it would not be man making the satisfaction."[46] "It is necessary that one and the same person be perfect God and perfect man to make this satisfaction. For no one can make the satisfaction unless he is truly God, and no one has the obligation unless he is truly man."[47] Hence the necessity and reason behind the incarnation.

What, then, is the payment, the *satisfactio* which Christ makes, and which atones for human sin? Anselm tells us: "None other than Christ ever gave to God *by dying* anything he was not at some time necessarily to lose, or paid what he did not owe. He, however, freely offered to the Father what he would never have necessarily lost, and he paid for sinners a debt he never owed himself."[48] Thus, having lived a life in which he made perfect payment of his dues to God, living always in perfect accordance with the divine will, Christ freely offered his life up, not as we do, as something owed due to sin, but as a freely given gift. Thus he acquired merit, and put God in his debt. What could God give to him that did not already belong to him? Anselm asks. Nothing. Yet it would be improper for this great deed to go unrewarded, so God agreed to transfer the infinite merit accrued by Christ to those for whom he came and died. Thus the satisfaction owed by humankind to the divine honor is made, and we are forgiven our sins.

Several things require to be noted at this juncture.

(1) It is true enough that Anselm's presentation of the atonement is one in which the focus is ever on the *death* of Christ. Yet the way in which he sets things out forces us to concede that, taken in isolation, the death is utterly empty of saving significance. It is precisely because it follows on from a life of perfect human obedience that this death possesses its super-erogatory character, and thus its significance for others. Christ satisfies and makes reparation for others by a transfer of merit, yet this merit is

not secured by his death alone but rather by that death viewed within the context of his whole life, in which all that was owed to God was rendered to him. If Anselm's theology is cross-centered, therefore, it certainly is not so to the exclusion of an emphasis on the whole life of the incarnate Son of God as an obedient rendering of that which was due to God.

(2) Christ satisfies, both in his life and his death, therefore, not by "bearing that which we could not bear" but precisely by "offering that which we could not offer." The cross is viewed here not as a penal measure borne but rather as a meritorious giving up of that which was not demanded of the giver. Again, we must tread carefully here, for while, like Tertullian, Anselm does indeed present punishment and satisfaction as alternative outcomes of sin,[49] it is clear that (like Tertullian again) the distinction between what each of these amounts to lies not so much in what is done or suffered as in a fundamental difference of disposition and relationship. "Either the sinner freely pays what he owes," he writes, "or God takes it from him against his will. It may be that a person by free choice shows due subjection to God—either by not sinning or by making reparation for sin—or it may be that God subjects him to himself, against the person's will. . . . And in this matter, we must observe that just as man, by sinning, plunders what belongs to God, so God, by punishing, takes away what belongs to man."[50] Where the sinner is concerned, therefore, since he cannot "pay what he owes" by dying (his death itself being already factored into his ever-accumulating debt), death is experienced as punishment, whatever his life amounts to being taken from him like the few remaining personal effects of a bankruptcy. This logic does not apply to Christ, who alone is able to offer his life up to death meritoriously (due to the prior perfect offering of his life). In each case it is death which is experienced. But the distinction between the modes of *satisfactio* and *poena* remains as a vital marker, and we must stress again that for Anselm it is quite clear that the cross is no punishment: how could it be, when Christ's whole life is one long self-offering to God?

(3) Significantly, for Anselm we ought not even to say that the death of Christ on the cross is something which God wills or demands. We must distinguish, he insists, between Christ having done something under the requirement of obedience on one hand, and his enduring what happened to him without obedience requiring it *because he persevered* with that obedience on the other.[51] Christ freely endured death, therefore not by giving up his life out of obedience, but by obeying a command to preserve justice, in which he persevered so unwaveringly that he (willingly) incurred death

as a result. The cross, then, is not something that Christ submitted to in direct obedience to God but rather something to which he was submitted as a direct result of his obedience to God in a world where such obedience is bound to lead to hostility, violence, and death.

The differences between Tertullian's use of the imagery of merit and satisfaction in the context of penitential theology and Anselm's deployment of the same terms in constructing a theology of atonement are admittedly marked. Both acknowledge the possibility of something meritorious in God's sight. For Tertullian this includes acts of a supererogatory nature, and for Anselm the death of Jesus falls precisely into this category, being something not demanded of him within his relationship to God as divine lawgiver. Whereas for Tertullian, though, such acts are always personal and nontransferable, Anselm pushes the image further, suggesting that Jesus' merit, being the summit of a life lived completely in accord with the obligations covenanted between God and humankind, and being offered by one who himself is God (and whose life is thus of infinite value) are capable of transfer between him and us, and alone sufficient to cancel the debt incurred by our sin (just as our sin, being against God himself, incurs an infinite debt beyond our payment). Whereas, for Tertullian, *satisfactio* consists in acts of supererogatory merit worthy of pitting against the commission of postbaptismal sin, Anselm insists that everything that we are and have and are capable of offering, past, present, and future, are already owed to God; only a life fully and freely offered to him in its completeness, and then handed over to God voluntarily, can accrue supererogatory merit. For both, though, satisfaction constitutes an alternative to penalty bearing—for Tertullian, within the believer's individual relationship with God, and for Anselm, in the relationship between the one who substitutes himself for us, and us in our relationship with God. Merit, therefore, is contingent on obedience and voluntary self-offering, and merit sufficient to cancel the debts of humankind on the infinite value of the self-offering of the one who is himself the Father.

§4. McLeod Campbell

The Vicarious Penitence of the Incarnate Son

It might have been helpful to rehearse here some of the historical background to the circumstances of McLeod Campbell's ministry and writings.[52] As it is, however, we must be content to remind ourselves that Campbell attained a certain notoriety by having been deposed from the ministry of the Church of Scotland in 1831 for allegedly preaching in a manner "contrary to the Holy Scripture and to the Confession of Faith Approven by the General Assembly of the Church of Scotland."[53] This episode has inevitably affected the interpretation of Campbell's writings, disposing some readers against a balanced or objective hearing what he has to say. Yet in fact the homiletic proclamations for which he was deposed (and the doctrines contained therein, namely the universality of the atoning work of Christ and the doctrine that assurance is of the essence of Christian faith)[54] are today virtually forgotten, attention being focused rather on the content of his magnum opus written much later in life, *The Nature of the Atonement*. In this his more developed work, Campbell does not make any radically new departures, but develops his earlier thoughts, and elucidates them with particular polemical intent, setting himself over against the austere Calvinism of the New England theologian Jonathan Edwards. Thus, his key themes are once again the universality of the atonement (although he considered himself no universalist), its unconditional nature (although he was certainly no antinomian), and a criticism of the presentation of atonement in terms of a penal substitution in which Christ, on the cross, is punished for the sins of the world.

My objective here is not to present a comprehensive sketch of Campbell's theology but simply to draw attention to points at which what he actually says seems to challenge the standard interpretations. In particular I suggest that, while in certain respects his soteriology is remote from that of Anselm, there are nonetheless some surprising and significant similarities which hitherto have been overlooked or ignored by the commentators. I attend briefly to four points of Campbell's theology, drawing both on the early published sermons (the "heretical" material for which he was deposed from his charge) and *The Nature of the Atonement* of 1856, seeking to draw out his characteristic emphases and so clarify the heart of his theological concern.

(1) Notwithstanding the testimony of numerous writers on the history of the doctrine of the work of Christ, there can be no question that McLeod Campbell affirms the need for an atonement in which the divine wrath (his term) is dealt with, and that he sees this atonement as something that has been wrought by Christ for us. In other words, he does not, as has sometimes been suggested, adhere to an Abelardian or Socinian model of atonement, or "moral influence theory" in which "the real atonement takes place when, with the same attitude and response of Christ's perfection, obedience is seen in us."[55]

Campbell is utterly opposed to any suggestion that God might forgive human sin by some arbitrary edict of divine will. Indeed mere clemency or mercy in God would not be sufficient to calm the troubled hearts of those awakened to the reality of their sin but only the clemency or mercy which is "presented to them in connexion with the sacrifice of Himself by which Christ put away sin, becoming the propitiation for the sins of the whole world."[56] Thus "when it is argued," he writes, "that the justice and righteousness of God and his holiness, and also his truth and faithfulness, presented difficulties in the way of our salvation, which rendered for their removal an atonement necessary, I fully assent to this."[57] There is, due to our sin, a gulf between God and us which must be bridged if we are to be reconciled with our maker and forgiven by him. How, then, are we to think of this as having been achieved? "The Gospel declares," says Campbell, "that the love of God has not only *desired* to bridge over this gulf, but *has actually bridged it over,* and the atonement is presented to us as that in which this is accomplished."[58]

Thus the atonement is something that God does, and not something that we do. It is the product of his prevenient love for sinful humankind, and not something which humans bring to placate an angry and otherwise unforgiving deity. Indeed, "if we could ourselves make an atonement for our sins, as by sacrifice the heathen attempted to do, and as, in their self-righteous endeavours to make their peace with God, men are, in fact daily attempting, then such an atonement might be thought of as preceding forgiveness, and the cause of it. But if God provides the atonement, then forgiveness must precede atonement; and the atonement must be the form of the manifestation of the forgiving love of God, not its cause."[59] This key theme of Campbell's theology disintegrates in the very moment that it is conceded that what atones for our sins springs from us ourselves (albeit in response to a prior manifestation of divine love) and not wholly from God. The fact that, as 1 John 4:19 proclaims, "we love because he loved us first" is thus a description not of the dynamics of atonement for Campbell but rather of our response to the prevenient, unconditional, atoning, and forgiving grace of God. It is God, then, who provides the atonement, and in Christ that he has done so.

Not only does Campbell insist on the objectivity of the atonement as something wrought by God in Christ on behalf of sinners, he also insists on the gravity and weight of human sin. Thus, while his characteristic stress ever falls on the nature of God as love, and the relationship between God and God's human creation having been revealed to us as essentially filial rather than legal, he is nonetheless also quite emphatic concerning the fact that the God who reveals himself in the incarnate Christ is one who punishes human sin and cannot tolerate it. The love of God in Christ is not a benign tolerance but rather a holy love. Most important still, of course, it is a forgiving love, yet this forgiveness is a costly thing for the one who secures it.

Thus, he writes, "the sufferings of Christ teach you these things concerning God, that God loves sinners, his enemies—that God's holiness rejects and his righteousness punishes sin, *though* he loves and *while* he loves those whom he punishes."[60] God's heart is revealed by the Son to be that of a Father who loves and forgives his children, yet this love does not override the justice which makes atonement necessary. "Christ," Campbell insists, "when made a curse for us, showed us, that however much God loved us, and however much his pronouncing this curse was consistent with actually loving us, this curse, unless exhausted in Christ, would have continued upon man for ever."[61] It is the measure of God's Fatherly love that he has done all that needed to be done for us to be freed from the curse in sending his only begotten Son to Calvary for our sakes.

(2) If, then, the atonement is something wrought for us by God in Christ, and if this same God is a God who cannot tolerate sin but must deal with it justly, how are we to understand the nature of this atonement? What comes to pass in order to secure it? There are many elements in Campbell's answer to this question, but here my purpose is simply to note that, in all that he says on the matter, he speaks clearly (and, in relation to the points outlined above, consistently) of Christ's death as a bearing of our sins, and as a bearing or dealing with the righteous wrath of God.

"The wrath of God against sin," Campbell argues, "is a reality, however men have erred in their thoughts as to how that wrath was to be appeased. Nor is the idea that satisfaction is due to divine justice a delusion, however far men have wandered from the true conception of what would meet its righteous demand."[62] Thus, he continues, "Christ, in dealing with God on behalf of men, must be conceived of as dealing with the righteous wrath of God against sin, and as according to it that which was due."[63] For Campbell there is certainly more to be said than that Christ, in dying on the cross, met the demands of divine justice and thus fulfilled the sentence of God on human sin. Yet he does not deny that this is so. Indeed, he sees it as an integral part of what he calls the "retrospective" aspect of Christ's atoning activity, the dealing with God on behalf of humankind in relation to our sinful past. In saving us from sin the incarnate Son submits to the sentence of the law[64] and exhausts its requirement, leaving nothing more to be done. Indeed, for faith in the atonement to be engendered, "it is . . . necessary that the death of Christ, as *filled with divine judgement on sin,* shall commend itself to the conscience."[65] "Christ, making an offering for sin, has taught us God's condemnation of sin—Christ *willingly* submitting to make himself an offering for sin, showed he was of one mind with the Father, that that love was a delighting in that very thing in God's character which led to the curse of the law. It *pleased* Christ to be bruised. This was the mind of Christ. What an awful and glorious testimony to the Father's righteousness in the punishment of sin has the Son thus given! How different from man's testimony in regard to sin is this condemnation of it in his flesh—this putting his seal to the righteousness of the curse, by bearing it himself in his own body."[66]

It pleased Christ to be bruised, bearing the righteous curse of God in his own body, that we might not have to bear it. The cross, insofar as it is the submission of the Son of God to the verdict of "guilty" pronounced by the Father on the human race, and the willing submission to the sentence passed in relation to that verdict, is absolutely necessary to the atonement wrought by him. The atonement certainly entails more than this for Campbell, but it does not entail any less.

(3) Campbell has no complaint, therefore, about the idea that God's nature demands an atonement for the sins of humankind, nor the apostolic suggestion that this atonement was wrought on the cross where the demands of the divine justice and wrath were fully met. Yet at times (and this is particularly true of *The Nature of the Atonement*) he is so vehement in his polemic against contemporary presentations of atonement in terms of a penal substitution that he appears at points to be distancing himself from these biblical images and embracing a model of atonement which is less clearly focused on the death of Christ, and thus makes less of the sufferings of Christ as having atoning value. To interpret Campbell in this way, however, is to misunderstand him, and is only possible if careful attention has not been paid to the whole text of his work. If we are to understand him properly, then we must consider that which for him is the key issue, namely the *nature* of the sufferings which Christ bore and which, Campbell believes, endues them with their atoning worth. It is in this, as we shall see, that, despite the eight centuries and many other things which distance them from one another, his thought draws close to the key insight inscribed in Anselm's exposition of the *ratio* of atonement.

Campbell approaches the atonement with a conviction that the only way to understand it properly is to allow it to be viewed in its own light. In other words, his starting point is not some a priori definition or model (biblical or otherwise) of what atonement ought to consist in but rather the complex reality itself, namely what God has *actually done* in his Son to atone for the sins of the human race, as that is unfolded in the whole canonical witness of Scripture. Thus, while he allows his understanding to be informed by the Old Testament categories of guilt, divine wrath, sacrifice, and so forth, he also recognizes the fact that such biblical institutions can be just as much a hindrance to our theology as a help if they are not viewed afresh from the New Testament perspective wherein their fulfillment and culmination are to be found, and where they are inevitably transformed through their convergence and application to concrete reality. In modern parlance, he employs a christological rather than a chronological hermeneutic to the whole text of Scripture. Thus, rather than interpreting the fact of Jesus' death on the cross in terms of the rich inheritance of Jewish ideas about atonement alone, he also takes into consideration the ways in which the reality transcends the expectation, insisting that only when this is done can the full significance and nature of what actually transpired be grasped or apprehended.

This hermeneutical procedure leads Campbell, like Anselm (though with different theological outcomes), to place enormous weight on the identity of the one who goes to the cross for us. The significance of the cross is transformed for him by the radical acknowledgment that it occurs within the very life of the triune God, as the Eternal Son offers himself up to death to the Father in the power of the Holy Spirit so that sins might be forgiven. This having been seen, the cross takes its place as the climax of the self-giving economy of God, the pouring out of the incarnate life of the Son in obedience for our sakes. Were we to consider the phenomenon of the cross in isolation, abstracting it from its context in this selfless and (properly speaking) *kenotic* movement in God's life, then we might interpret it in many ways, basing ourselves solely on the sacrificial and judicial conceptuality familiar enough from the Old Testament, or perhaps borrowing images and ideas from social institutions familiar within our own context. Once we have perceived the staggering truth about the cross, however, then the way in which we employ any such conceptuality must always be tempered and informed by this new insight. Again, the old wineskins will not hold the new wine; the identity of the one who atones for our sins forces us to engage in a process of reinterpretation and reevaluation which will rupture and transform all analogies, if we are to arrive at a truly *Christian* doctrine of atonement.[67]

In particular, Campbell registers surprise at the way in which the Calvinist theologians of his day failed (in his view) to think through some of the radical implications of the central Christian doctrines of incarnation and Trinity for their understanding of the atonement. Abstracting the passion of Christ from this larger matrix of his incarnate life and ministry, these theologians transform it altogether, and focus too narrowly on certain empirical aspects of it. "What I have felt," Campbell writes, "and the more I consider it, feel it the more—is, surprise that the atoning element in the sufferings pictured, has been to their minds *sufferings as sufferings, the pain and agony as pain and agony.*"[68] "My surprise is," he continues, "that these sufferings being contemplated as an atonement for sin, *the holiness and love seen taking the form of suffering* should not be recognised as the atoning elements—the very essence and adequacy of the sacrifice for sin presented to our faith."[69] In other words, the discontent which Campbell feels with contemporary expressions of the atonement in terms of a penal substitution is not that they should focus on the sufferings of Christ but rather that they should focus on the physical anguish and sufferings of the Savior as *physical anguish and sufferings alone,* and should interpret them as essentially punitive, identifying in this the atoning element. "It is not a question," he writes, "as to the fact of an atonement for sin. It is not a question as to the amount of the sufferings of Christ in making atonement. It is not a question as to the elements of these sufferings. . . . The question . . . is this: The sufferings of Christ in making his soul an offering for sin being what they were, was it the pain as pain, and as penal infliction, or was it the pain *as a condition and form of holiness and love under the pressure of our sin and its consequent misery,* that is presented to our faith as the essence of the sacrifice and its atoning virtue?"[70] In other words, when we view the cross within the context of the life of Jesus, the incarnate Son of God, and when we consider the dynamics of this man's relationship with God, and when we remember just who this man is, does the category of punishment by physical infliction provide us with an adequate or helpful interpretation of what takes place on the cross? The answer, to Campbell, is clear enough. "It was the spiritual essence and nature of the sufferings of Christ, and not that these sufferings were penal, which constituted their value as entering into the atonement made by the Son of God when he put away sin by the sacrifice of himself."[71]

Thus it is not that Christ does not deal with the divine "wrath" or that his death is unimportant in his doing so, but the *identity* and the *disposition* of Christ himself in making his sacrifice compels Campbell to draw a distinction between "being punished" in our place on one hand, and that which Christ actually does and experiences on the other. The oft-misunderstood terminology of "vicarious penitence" which he uses to describe Christ's atoning work is not of his own devising but is drawn from his engagement with the theology of Edwards. If sin is to be properly satisfied for, Edwards writes, "there must needs be either an equivalent punishment, or an equivalent sorrow and repentance."[72] When we look to the life and death of Jesus, Campbell argues, what we actually see is a life lived out in absolute oneness of mind with the Father. The incarnate Son enters into our broken and fallen humanity, and views it *from within* with the same eyes as God. Throughout his ministry he has to struggle with the temptations to which it is subject, and to encounter the darkness which is the consequence of its sinful state. Throughout all this his tacit cry is "Father, not my will, but yours be done," and his death is a final amen to the righteous judgment of God on humankind, sealing the sentence of God, by submitting himself to that which it demands, and so perfecting the atonement which he has to make, not for himself, but precisely for others.

When we see all this, Campbell asks, can we really view this death, in isolation from the rest, simply as a moment in which this man is punished by God, being inflicted with physical pain and death? Is this not to miss the very point of it, namely that it is the supreme moment of self-offering to God on the part of this man, and has its proper place only within the overall context of this whole life of obedience and sacrifice? This, he insists, is not to lessen the awfulness and darkness of the cross but precisely to *heighten* it, seeing its true pain as consisting in the awfulness of divine wrath viewed from the perspective of one whose life has been lived in utter oneness of heart and mind and will with God. Furthermore, it is to see that this suffering is not restricted to Calvary but begins from the moment that one who sees things from such a God-perspective enters fully into our human situation. Things that may appear trivial to us might be an unbearable burden and pain to one with eyes to see and ears to hear, and such suffering of the consequences of sin must be recognized as an integral part of the sacrificial self-offering of the Son. But to return to the cross: what takes place there, Campbell argues, is the perfect confession of human sins by *the only one who could see things in such a way as to make that confession at all.*[73] And this confession is made not in order to avoid the consequences but precisely in the act of embracing these consequences in all their awfulness, "meeting the cry of these sins for judgement, and the wrath due to them, absorbing and exhausting that divine wrath in that adequate confession and perfect response on the part of man,"[74] uttering "a perfect Amen in humanity to the judgement of God on the sins of man. Such an Amen was due in the truth of things."[75]

In comparison with this, Campbell argues, the concentration on physical infliction as physical infliction, on death as death, seems to have missed so much. "We may find cases where the physical infliction and the indignities offered have been as great or greater, but how shall we calculate the infinite difference that the mind in which Christ has suffered has made?"[76] Thus, while death in itself, considered purely as human death, could not atone for sin, "*death filled with that moral and spiritual meaning in relation to God and his righteous law* which it had tasted by Christ and *passed through in the spirit of sonship* was the perfecting of the atonement."[77] In and through it, not only were the demands of divine justice satisfied and the price of human rebellion against God fully paid, but they were satisfied and paid in a voluntary submission to death in which a human mind and will and soul were manifestly and uniquely at one with the righteous divine verdict on the human race. "Seeing it to be impossible," says Campbell, "to regard suffering, of which such is the nature, as penal, I find myself forced to distinguish between an atoning sacrifice for sin, and the enduring as a substitute the punishment due to sin—being shut up to the conclusion, what he suffered was not—because from its nature it could not be—a punishment."[78] It is for this precise reason that, in response to Edwards' formulation of the matter, he suggests that in fact a "perfect sorrow and repentance," properly understood in the terms outlined above, might well be a more helpful category in interpreting the nature of Christ's atoning work.

For Campbell, then, Christ, in his death as in his life, makes the perfect response to God's judgment upon our humanity, a concurrence of heart, mind, soul, and body with the perspective afforded by the Father's own holiness, one which we were and are called to make, but are utterly unable to make. He makes this response in our stead, and in a manner that pleases the Father, even though making it means his willingness to suffer and to die.[79] Consequently, for Campbell, even in the midst of the darkness of the cross, the Father's verdict upon Christ must remain that of the baptismal narrative: "This is my beloved Son, in whom I am well pleased."[80] The cross opens up no awful division in the Trinitarian life of God. The Son, willingly embracing and enduring the consequences of the divine wrath on human sin, does that which delights the Father even though it grieves the Father's heart that it should be necessary in the first place. And the death of Calvary, therefore, has its significance precisely as an organic culmination and perfection of a life whose moral and spiritual value as a complete self-offering to God is already the atonement (the perfect at-one-ment of God and his human creature), and in which God's glory is finally manifest in human form. Here, Campbell captures well the Johannine paradox of the "lifting up"[81] of Christ, the abject weakness and suffering of the Son in which God's glory is nonetheless manifest and his name hallowed.

§5. Satisfaction, Sacrifice, and Sonship

In a lecture on "The Kingdom of Christ" delivered in 1841, Alexander John Scott, a contemporary of Campbell's, fellow Scot, and personal friend, writes, "[Christ] says, 'Henceforth I call you not servants, but I have called you friends.' This is the meaning of *spiritual*. To do a thing because I am commanded, without entering into the principle, motive or spring of it—that may be service; to do a thing, entering into the principle of it—that is the spiritual obedience of a friend or son. . . . Now, in reference to our standing towards God: what God, because God is love, has commanded me to do, this if I do, because some measure of God's love is in my heart, I do it as His friend; this if I do merely because God has commanded me, without any degree of sympathy with God in my heart, I do it as a servant."[82] In this distinction lies something close to the heart of Campbell's understanding of what it is that "atones" between God and humankind, what it is that God looks for from his human creature and finds, initially, only in Jesus, though purposes it for all, namely, not just the consistent performance of certain sorts of deeds (and avoidance of others), but their performance as the outward expression of an inner reality which concurs and resonates with God's own heart and mind, which reflects or echoes God's own way of seeing the world and shares in his desires and purposes for it. That such is found only when the one who is not just obedient servant but loving Son takes flesh and so "bodies forth" that which belongs first to God but which he longs and delights to see embodied in his creatures, is also at the heart of Campbell's essentially filial understanding of the atonement and the wider pattern of redemption he sees as issuing from it.

Anselm, whose commendable desire for order rather traps him within the entailments and logic of his chosen metaphor, has relatively little to say about what Campbell refers to as the "prospective" rather than "retrospective" aspects of atonement—that is to say, what it is that Christ saves us *for* as distinct from what he saves us *from*.[83] His account, shaped as it is by a desire to attain systematic and aesthetic unity and consistency,[84] is bound, insofar as it succeeds, rarely to break out of the legal and contractual ethos of the image with which he begins and on which he builds. Yet, within the self-imposed limitations of his approach, he, too, captures the key insight with which I have been concerned in this chapter, namely that—whatever more we may wish to say—atonement is about something *offered* to God which God finds intrinsically valuable, and its value lies in some way precisely in the mode of its being offered. Satisfaction comes from the provision of whatever "satisfies" God, and where this is concerned what Scott calls "entering into the principle" or "spiritual obedience" is the heart of the matter. That Anselm would have been happy, in another context, to have this construed as contingent on Christ's filial relation to the Father, or further unfolded in terms of our own redemptive participation in that filial relation, we need not doubt.

If we return, at this juncture, to the suggestion I made earlier, that words and images drawn into the service of theology may sometimes do more work than those who first appropriated them intended, and that in doing so, as we explore the traces of meaning accruing to them from time to time, they may cast fresh and unexpected light on the realities of which they were conscripted to speak, what might be said in this regard of the image of "satisfaction"? I draw this chapter to a close by offering some reflections on this question, both drawing on what we have seen thus far and proposing some further theological connections and routes of exploration—in particular, the suggestion that if we allow the image of satisfaction to guide us, then the heart of the atonement contains a *liturgical* impulse and movement which links it far more directly with the dynamic and substance of the life of the church than we often suppose, and, without losing sight of the importance of the category of "substitution," nonetheless makes talk of our "participation" in Christ's self-offering for our sakes more meaningful and grounded than it has sometimes appeared to be.

To begin, and to sharpen the issue, we might refer again to the Johannine enigma of an apparently God-forsaken suffering which is somehow to be acknowledged as the manifestation of God's glory in human form, the very thing in which God's name is hallowed. How can this be? Is this claim not just as disturbing to our sensibilities and theologically suspect as the idea that what sets the moral and spiritual order of the universe to rights is the infliction by God of an infinite amount of pain and suffering per se on an undeserving victim, that what "satisfies" his divine grievance over human sin is being able to mete out an equivalent amount of physical pain, in accordance with some arcane and deeply troubling calculus? How could anything like that truly be "satisfying" to God?

But just what is it, we might ask, that glorifies God? If, as the psalter suggests, God is glorified by the starry heavens and the rising and setting of the sun, the snowcapped mountains and green valleys, the birds and beasts and insects, as well as by human beings, then what common element can we discern which serves to glorify him in all this creaturely diversity? For an answer to this question we might refer back to the narrative of creation in the priestly account in Genesis 1 and the repeated refrain "And God saw that it was good."[85] In this divine judgment upon the world we may identify a basic sense of "satisfaction," of contentment with what has been made, the perception within it all of a goodness or rightness which directly reflects the goodness of its divine fashioner. God enjoys his creation. It issues not from any sense of lack or incompleteness in God but from an overflow of his fullness and joy. And, having expressed himself creatively, he stands back and views it with a deep sense of satisfaction. It is indeed something "good." And it is its essential goodness, its correspondence to God's creative intent and purpose, its reflection of God's own nature and character, which serves to glorify God. It is this which gives God joy and pleasure as he surveys it.[86]

In the case of the mute and inanimate creation, of course, this "goodness" has no specifically moral content. But in the case of the human creature this dimension enters decisively into the picture. The heavens may well declare the glory of God simply by their natural majesty and wonder, but when the psalmist turns to humankind just a few verses later it is to a consideration of the perfect law of God that he directs our thoughts, and reminds us that human thoughts and words (and, we might suppose, actions) which are pleasing to God are those which are blameless and free from the rule of sin.[87] Humans are distinct from the natural order not only or primarily by virtue of their articulateness or rationality but supremely inasmuch as they are moral beings who are called to reflect not just God's majesty and wonder but above all his holiness. Humans are distinctively moral creatures. Mountains may glorify God by their awesome and rugged beauty. The planets and stars may glorify him by their majesty and by their reliable conformity to the laws of nature, which he has woven into the fabric of the universe. Animals may glorify God by their diversity and beauty and their correspondence to his divine fashioning in and through the evolutionary process. But in the case of humans alone the categories of cause or law or process will not suffice. Here for the first time we encounter a further factor which comes closest to the heart of God's own being: moral action. Thus the command comes to them as to no other creature, "Be holy, for I am holy."[88]

How, then, is God glorified in his human creature? The key lies, surely, in the opening phrases of the one piece of dominical liturgy which we have: "Our Father in heaven, *hallowed be your name*. Your kingdom come, your will be done on earth as it is in heaven."[89] God's name is hallowed not by our telling him how great and majestic he is, legitimate and important though such verbal expressions of praise may be. God's name is hallowed rather by human activity in which his own holy love is reflected and reciprocated from the side of the creature, in his will being done "on earth as it is in heaven."

Holiness, understood not in merely aesthetic terms, but as absolute moral reality and authority, is characteristic of all that God is and does, so that his love, while fundamental to his nature, is precisely *holy* love. When this same God creates, what he creates is marked by a moral, as well as a physical and natural, order. Morality is woven into the very warp and woof of the universe as a direct reflection of God's own moral nature. And what God finds supremely "satisfying" in creation (or in history as its extension through time) is the reciprocation of his own holy love from the creature's side, a response which humans alone among his creatures are suited to render. Thus it is precisely the offering of holy love back to God which, in humans, glorifies him and hallows his name. What he desires most, and enjoys most, in his creation is not its staggering beauty, or its physical complexity and intricate ecosystems, but this reflection of his own inner nature, the rendering back to him of love in holiness from humankind, created in his own image and likeness. It is for this that he longs, to share and to enjoy this with another that he created at all, and this which he is determined to find.

Yet creation, and the worship which it sets in process, is an act which takes place as an overflowing of the Trinitarian life of God himself. That which the Father makes and declares that "it is good" he makes in and through his Word or Son, and in the power of his own Holy Spirit, which permeates it and holds it in existence from moment to moment. Thus to be a creature is to exist within this set of triune relationships, and to be a fully human creature is to relate to God as Father through the Son, in whom we live and move and have our being, and in the life-giving and life-sustaining power of the Spirit.

In creation, in other words, what we are dealing with is the calling into existence of a created other in order to echo and share in the overflowing of that uncreated love and joy which echoes through eternity, and which is the Father's love for the Son and the Son's love for the Father in the Spirit. Creation is drawn into a dynamic of worship and adoration which is both logically and "temporally" prior to it, a dynamic which is the eternal Trinitarian *koinonia* of God, Father, Son, and Holy Spirit, in which each person reflects perfectly the being and character of the others in a supreme perichoretic[90] paean of praise.

If there is one place where the essence of worship and atonement are closely linked in Christian theology then it is in the deployment of the metaphor of sacrifice in relation to each. In old Israel it was impossible to isolate either the idea or the reality of atonement from the context of worship, for atonement lay explicitly at the very heart of the cultic life of the nation. The annual bearing of the nation's sins into the holy place on the shoulders of the high priest and the ritual shedding of blood which signified the covering of those sins was a focal point in the liturgical life of the covenant people before God.[91] Here, in this sacrament of divine grace, both God's holy anger in the face of sin and his merciful acceptance of the sinner found expression. "The effect of atonement was to cover sin from God's eyes, so that it should no longer make a visible breach between God and His people. . . . Sacrifices were not desperate efforts and surrenders made by terrified people in the hope of propitiating an angry deity. The sacrifices were in themselves prime acts of obedience to God's means of grace and His expressed will."[92] For Israel, then, worship and atonement were integrally linked at the very deepest level. A substantial part of her worship was concerned precisely with the mode of atonement for sin prescribed by God. Atonement was, she believed, a present and ongoing reality.

If the gospel accounts of Jesus' own reflection on his forthcoming death are to be taken at face value, the category which he most often employed to make sense of it was that of sacrifice. At least we must admit that it was so in the faith of the early Christian community. Jesus' death is construed (to cite just one example) as the sacrificial offering which secures forgiveness of sins for many, and in which the establishment of

God's new covenant with Israel is ratified (Matt 26:26–27). This particular instance is helpful for our purposes, focusing attention, as it does, on the notion of covenant as the social, political, cultic, and theological context for the language of sacrifice in relation to Jesus' death. It is within the context of God's choosing of Israel as a special people, of course, that the demand to holiness emerges in the specific form of *torah*.[93] Israel is to be a priestly people, a holy people whose holiness reflects that of Yahweh. In this she is to be representative rather than exclusive of the nations, and, ultimately, of the creation as a whole in its common calling to hallow God's name. The covenant is established by the grace of election, and the obligations of covenantal existence are clearly spelled out in the law's precepts. Yet Israel is representative of humankind in another, more tragic, sense also, in that, from one generation to the next, she fails to fulfill the covenant from the human side.

It is within this situation of election, covenant, and failure that the distinctive understanding of sacrifice within Israel arises. As a divinely furnished sacrament of grace, a means of atonement for that sin which otherwise threatens to render her relationship to God impossible, sacrifice enabled Israel to continue within the covenant. But this was a provisional arrangement, and the fullness of Israel's hope lay not in the existing imperfect covenant with its sacrificial provision but in the decisive eschatological action of God himself in establishing a new covenant in which the relationship would finally be perfectly fulfilled from both sides, the law being engraved no longer on stone but on the flesh and blood reality of human life. This expectation corresponds to the divine promise of the covenant formula, a formula which, we might suppose, contains as much God's promise to himself as to Israel, "I will be your God and you shall be my people."[94]

The prevalence in Western theologies of atonement of forensic and legal metaphor (under which the language of sacrifice has all too often simply been subsumed) has, as I have already suggested, encouraged an essentially passive notion of Jesus' death. The cross is something which happens or is done to Jesus, either by the Jewish and Roman authorities, or else by God. Whatever the specific merits or difficulties attaching to forensic imagery, I wish to suggest again that by teasing the language of sacrifice out from entanglement with it an aspect of Jesus' death which is otherwise too readily obscured comes to our notice, namely its nature as ethical action.

In the ritual symbolism of sacrifice, as prophetic denunciations of the mere ritualism sometimes associated with it make clear,[95] what is manifest is the self-offering of the participant. The offering up of something of supreme value betokens that complete offering of self to God which is the proper response of humanity to his gracious initiative in creation and election. As we have observed, Israel, like the church, repeatedly failed to make this offering in practice in her daily life. But here, sacramentally (and in the case of Israel proleptically), it was shown forth and treated by God as made. Without this ethical aspect the symbolism of sacrifice was quite empty of meaning. Sacrifice, one might say, was no *ex opere operato* manipulation of God, but a sacramental covering of the people's sin by the sign of that reciprocal holiness in which God's name is truly hallowed in his creature and covenant partner.

The image of "satisfaction," so often construed in primarily mercantile or forensic terms, can enrich and deepen our appreciation of what is at stake here, I suggest, precisely by permitting the aesthetic and moral connotations accruing to it some play in the theologial context. We certainly cannot overlook or underplay the darkness of the crucifixion, and the words of Jesus "My God, why have you forsaken me?" must be allowed their full weight. But when we consider the ethical dimension of the cross, its place as an active embracing of the divine will, as an aligning and reconciling of divine and human consciences in the person of the human Son of God, we must also, as I suggested earlier, recall those other words, spoken first at the baptism and then again at the transfiguration, and recalled, surely, in the judgment uttered by the centurion in Mark's gospel precisely in the face of this dark event: "This is my beloved Son, in whom I am well pleased." It is precisely because Jesus embraces the awfulness of God-forsakenness willingly, as a homologation of the divine judgment on human sin, and because he does so as a man, from the side of fallen and broken humanity, that his death (of a piece with his life) is genuinely and supremely "satisfying" to the Father. It is the love, the reciprocal holiness, the worship implicit within this action which heals and perfects a broken humanity, and thereby invites again the ancient divine judgment "it is good."

The New Testament metaphor of sacrifice, I think, enables us to lay hold of this sense in which worship lies at the heart of the atonement. The attitude of Jesus in his death, its relation to his entire life of obedient service wrought through moral struggle, its nature as a perfect confession of God's holiness, is bound up with its value as an atonement which covers the sin of humankind. Not only is the atonement a "payment" for the history of human sin. It is at the same time much more. It is precisely the point in human history where an actual reconciliation or at-one-ment of God's life and ours is to be identified. In the particular history of Jesus of Nazareth, the history of the covenant, and thereby of creation itself, is both overturned and paradoxically fulfilled. The old Adam dies as he must, and the new humanity is established in his place. But the old dies only as he offers himself to death willingly, and thereby fulfills his creatureliness, subverting the order of sin and death, and introducing a new order of holiness, being raised up into a new existence in the power of the Holy Spirit.

Viewed within its proper christological context, of course, what we must say is not that here at last God finds a human who makes the long-desired response of faith and holiness which fulfills creation and atones, but that God himself has here finally acted to fulfill his covenant promise to Israel : "I will be your God, and you shall be my people." In the humanity of God himself we find the perfect atonement and *koinonia* between God and humankind which is the writing of the law on tablets of flesh and blood, and the *telos* of creation in which God is perfectly glorified.

Outside the former parish church of St. Paul's in Worcester there is a startling crucifix commissioned earlier this century by the then parish priest Geoffrey Studdert Kennedy. What is striking is that the dying Christ, instead of hanging limply on the tree with head downcast, is gripping the cross, visibly embracing the death which it entails, and has his head thrust heavenward, a look of triumph and doxological joy on his face. In this telling image, and the alternative reading of the cross which it provides, the whole complex of theological motifs treated in this chapter are bound together. In death, as in life, Jesus offers to his Father the perfect response from the human side of the Creator-creature relation. But what he thus does humanly is nothing less than an earthing at the level of the human of a relationship which he enjoys eternally as God with the Father in the Spirit. He is the Christos, the anointed one, whose human life glorifies the Father, in whom the Father is well pleased, and who, even in his submission to death in solidarity with sinners, satisfies his Father in a perfect sacrificial offering of himself. He who has received the Spirit from his Father here offers the same Spirit back to the Father in love and praise (cf. Matt 27:50 and John 19:30, where the absence of a possessive genitive at least creates a suggestive ambiguity), reproducing the inner Trinitarian holiness among human beings, and thereby bringing the divine self-realization in creation to a glorious, infinitely satisfying fulfillment.

§6. Satisfaction, Worship, and the Trinity

What I have suggested thus far is that both creation and atonement manifest what might be called a "liturgical" character. But if this is so, then the matter certainly cannot stop there. For God's purpose in creating and redeeming is not to establish a new covenant, a new creation, the boundaries of which might be reckoned identical with those of the particular history of the man Jesus of Nazareth. Christ is what he is and does what he does not to the exclusion of others but precisely in order that others might be redeemed and drawn in to share in this new reality. If so, then the worship which we offer to God as the church is fundamentally related to the twin "liturgies" of creation and atonement, related not simply as cause and effect, stimulus and response, or prerequisite and postlude, but because *they are fundamentally the same sorts of thing.* I certainly do not intend in saying this to suggest that Christian worship has any capacity to atone for human sin, nor that it somehow supplements the atoning value of Jesus' self-offering. What I mean is simply that the very thing which, when Jesus does it, atones for the sins of the world is nonetheless the precise thing that we are each called to do, both as creatures and as participants in the covenant—namely to make that response of reciprocal holiness which hallows God's name, even when what this entails is the putting of self on the cross. This is our *telos* as creatures.

But there is more to be said even than this. For the whole point about Jesus' perfect self-offering to God is that it obscures and displaces our sinful failure to make this offering. This does not mean that we are no longer called to make any response but rather that in making it we no longer do so in isolation from his perfect offering of it on our behalf. What we offer, the response which we make to God, is offered and made in the closest possible union with Christ's offering and response, the offering of God's own Son in the flesh. The church's worship is offered "through Christ" not simply in the sense that his atoning death makes it possible for us to approach God in worship but because, being of the same essential kind, our offering and his are fused together, the imperfections and partiality of ours being lost in the perfection and completeness of his. The call to worship, to "be holy," therefore, is not the call to make an independent response to what God has done in Christ, but rather to share actively in that hallowing of God's name which he has offered and continues to offer in the flesh on our behalf.[96] Atonement lies at the very heart of Christian worship, therefore, inasmuch as in worship we share actively in what Christ is and does in atoning for us. It is the church's hallowing of the Father's name which does not and cannot take place apart from the presence in its midst of the one whom the writer to the Hebrews calls our *Archiereus*, our High Priest, who offers to the Father an atoning liturgy in his life and death in our place and on our behalf.[97]

This realization has some very practical and pastoral consequences. First, the fact that our every act of worship is "covered by" and united with the one perfect human response of Jesus, in whom the covenant is perfected and fulfilled, lifts from our shoulders the burden of responsibility of feeling that, God having done all that he has for us, we must now make an appropriate and fitting response. For we know ourselves to lack the moral resources needed to make any such response. If we try to make it we fall into one of two traps: either that of self-righteousness (having persuaded ourselves that we have after all succeeded in making it) or guilt and fear (because in truth we know that our outward words and actions very often veil a sinful, weak, and inadequate inner response which we hope will remain hidden from our fellow Christians). But God knows that we are not able to bring to him the sort of perfect holiness which hallows his name, to conform our lives at every point to his life and will. And his command "Be holy" is a call simply to bring ourselves just as we are, both good and bad, and to unite our offering with Jesus' once-for-all offering of worship on the cross and his ongoing worship of the Father in our midst as the great High Priest. Our worship is precisely a sharing in his worship, through the presence of the Creator and Redeemer Spirit among us. If we once lose sight of this fact, if the linkage between our response to God and that wrought by the same Spirit in Christ is broken, then it will not be long before guilt and fear come to characterize all that we do in the sanctuary, as we don the veneer of liturgical purity and respectability together with our Sunday best, and prepare to participate in the great conspiracy of silence in the church.

Secondly, there is in many quarters a nervousness about bringing all that we have and are to God as a sacrifice of praise. For we are only too aware of our limitations, of the way in which our gifts and skills and our creativity are tainted by sin in one way or another. Thus we are uneasy about bearing such things into God's presence as a fitting tribute. We prefer to adopt an essentially passive stance in worship whenever possible, allowing the minister to preach the word, to administer the sacraments while we, somewhat timidly, make our approach to God and wait to hear him speak to us or to bless us in some way. The model of worship here, that is to say, is one in which the chief dynamic is directed from God to humanity. Now this, of course, is rooted in a very important half-truth—that all that we are and possess and do falls short of that which is truly fitting as a response to God. But it is only a half-truth. And we must set it firmly in the new context created by Christ's atoning offering of himself *which was a human offering of a complete and perfect humanity to God.*[98]

If worship and atonement are essentially linked to creation, as I have argued, and if Jesus offers what he offers precisely as a priest of creation, thereby fulfilling the vocation of humankind as a whole within the created order, then the call to worship is a call not to an essentially God-humanward event but to an event in which there is both a humanward and a Godward dynamic, both of which are decisively focused in Christ's person and the activity of the Spirit there. Here, in union with the human Son of God, we offer to God a sacrifice of praise which represents the goodness of his creation, all that we are and have as his creatures: gifts of music, drama, dance, administration, practical skills, personal skills; all of these, our created humanity in all its fullness (and not our financial gifts alone!) we bring to the Lord in an act of complete self-dedication and praise. Of course these things are tainted with sin; they are not unblemished. Yet, offered together with the offering of the one who is the only true Lamb of God, they form an acceptable and pleasing sacrifice to our Father in heaven. We offer them in solidarity with Jesus and his offering; our offering of them is enabled and undergirded by the very same Spirit with whom he was anointed, and who enabled and undergirded his once-for-all response for us. Thus they are offered only in and through the transforming realities and power of both the cross and the Spirit. But they are offered. We do not hold them back from God, afraid that they may not be good enough for him—as if anything that we have to offer could be, apart from its assumption and redemption in Christ. To continue to view worship instead in terms of an ultra-Protestant "sit up, shut up, and listen up!" model is surely to ignore and to deny on one hand the essential connection between this weekly congregational event and the liturgy which is the rest of our lives, and on the other its nature as an active sharing by the Spirit in the priestly humanity of God himself.

For, finally, Christian worship is a thoroughly Trinitarian event. Rather than construing it as the point at which a grateful humanity offers its response to a gracious creator and redeemer, or else as the point at which God acts and we allow ourselves to be acted on, not wishing to obtrude our sinful humanity and thereby to defile the event, we must learn to construe worship as the point at which the church shares actively in an ongoing event within the life of God, as the Father pours out the Spirit of sonship on those who, together with the one true and eternal Son, respond in holy love and joy, liberated from their fears and inadequacies by the healing presence of Christ in their midst and the redemptive anointing of the Holy Ghost who transforms our dross into riches. Here the dynamic of interpersonal love and glorification, which may be identified eternally within the triune life and which we find earthed in a once-for-all manner in the history of the man Jesus, is reflected and echoed abroad within the church, as individual men and women are taken up by the Spirit and given to participate in that liturgy in which all creation declares the glory of God.

6

Substitution

Within the Christian West there have been widely differing interpretations of the precise nature of salvation and its implications for humankind. At the time of the Reformation in particular, disagreement as regards the proper meaning of key scriptural terms such as "grace," "justification," and "sanctification" was a major cause of division between Rome and the emergent Protestant churches. Were these primarily to be understood within an "objective" or "subjective," an "extrinsic" or "intrinsic" frame of reference vis-à-vis believers themselves? Was the redemption of our humanity, that is to say, something wrought wholly by God *for us*, or something into which the quality of our own human action and capacity must be factored (something done *in us* and perhaps in some sense even *through* and *by us*)? Might it be possible to hold these together, granting each due emphasis in a manner that avoids engaging in a soteriological zero-sum game?

Protestant views, taking the Reformers' decisive lead, have traditionally sought to emphasize the fact that from beginning to end salvation is the work of God. To this end it has stressed the objective nature of redemption, as something resting not in the least on the believer's own capacities but only on the salvific work of Christ in his obedience unto death on the cross. Grace, it typically insists, consists primarily in the fact that God "imputes" Christ's righteousness to others, not that they are made righteous in themselves. Consequently, the emphasis has tended to fall on the

151

retrospective aspect of redemption, this being readily appropriated within an essentially extrinsic schema, being seen, for example, as a transaction completed in our stead by a third party.

The Catholic criticism of this view has generally been that such a stress on objectivity robs salvation of much of its existential import in a manner which is wholly unbiblical. Thus, for example, Louis Bouyer[1] provides a penetrating and enduring critique of what he takes to be the Protestant approach. "The Word of God," he maintains, "categorically proclaims a grace that is a real gift; a justification by faith that makes man really just."[2] Over against this, he suggests, the *iustitia* of the Reformation appears to be merely a legal fiction, a change in God's attitude or legal disposition toward us rather than a change in the being of Christians, and as such unworthy of the repeated indicatives of the New Testament concerning the redeemed state of those who are in Christ. Catholicism has instead emphasized the reality of "grace" at work in the life of the believer, seeking to take fully seriously the prospective dimension of redemption, the active participation of men and women in the new humanity established in Christ, the role of the sacraments in the nurturing and deepening of this subjective reality; in short, the fact that grace does not leave us essentially unchanged but gives us new life, such that we can be spoken of as really *iusti*, and even as sharing in the life of God himself. Yet reciprocally this emphasis has often seemed, to Protestant minds, to endanger the complete sufficiency of Christ's once-for-all redemptive ministry, and to rate rather too highly the redeemed status of the individual, forgetting that humanity is yet sinful and stands with Adam under the condemnation of the cross.

In spite of the increased levels of mutual understanding to which various formal conversations and scholarly studies have sought to bear witness amid the thawing ecumenical environment since Vatican II,[3] it would be wrong to give the impression that differences between the two traditions are in reality more apparent than actual, or that theological consensus may be had simply by adjusting emphases or clarifying the force of contested words and their meanings. There would seem to be a residual and basic difference of understanding concerning the status of the believer (as regards what he or she is held to *be*) in relation to the alleged accomplishments of God's saving engagement with us in Christ and the Spirit. Is the believer, in other words, as the result of incarnation and atonement, truly and basically righteous (*iustus*) or sinful (*peccator*)? Do we really possess *iustitia* as Christians, or is the grace that we proclaim more appropriately pictured (in Martin Luther's vivid image) as a cloak decorously obscuring the sight and smell of a rotting corpse lying beneath it? Is the church, in the familiar binary of popular theology, best thought of as a society of saints or a school for sinners?

Arguably, both Catholic and Protestant formulations of the matter struggle adequately to overcome this duality not because of what they each affirm but because of the framework within which they seek to affirm it, one that tends in practice to differentiate sharply between the person of Christ and his work, and defines salvation as humanity's direct and immediate participation in certain "benefits" procured by the latter.[4] The question thus arises as to the precise nature of these benefits, and by what means we might suppose ourselves to be drawn within the scope of their influence and efficacy (or not). It is in this context that the dilemma between "objectivity" and "subjectivity" inevitably emerges and a choice between them seems to be necessary. If we seek, on one hand, to insist on the finished work of atonement accomplished by God for us, then grace is easily reduced to an external forensic relation, the *iustitia* of a third party which covers our sinfulness but in which we have no actual part or participation. If, on the other hand, we seek to do justice to the evangelical indicatives concerning believers, then we may interpret grace chiefly in terms of a supernatural transubstantiation of our humanity, an "infused righteousness," leading us both to play down the total substitution of Christ in our place (doing what we cannot do) and perhaps to place too much weight on the significance of our own moral and spiritual capacity and too little on the empirical reality of our abiding sin and incapacity. Within the anthropocentric and pragmatic paradigm I have alluded to, there does not seem to be any way of being faithful to both aspects and of affirming that the human person reconciled to God in Jesus Christ is genuinely (in another Lutheran phrase) *simul iustus et peccator*. Ironically, both points of view may be described as extrinsicist in their accounts of grace. One makes grace something external to our being, while the other tears it away from its ontological moorings in the humanity of the Savior. In doing so, I suggest, both ultimately rob his humanity of its true mediatorial significance.

The polarity between objective and subjective is not one that we find reflected in the New Testament's account of salvation. Here, in apparently paradoxical fashion, the believer is spoken of at one moment as a sinner, entirely dependent on the forgiving love of God, and at the next as someone unequivocally *iustus* and *hagios* in Christ. And here, perhaps, we have stumbled across a key to the problem. For the New Testament speaks rarely if ever of any relationship of the believer to some commodity called "grace"; what it emphasizes is a relationship with the Savior. The gift and the Giver are never separated. Jesus does not simply proclaim the gospel or fulfill the preconditions of some external transaction courtesy of which it holds true and applies to our case; he is himself its substantial content. The believer does not receive *salvation*, indeed, but *Christ*. If the longstanding disequilibrium in Western soteriology is to be resolved, what would seem to be required is a paradigm shift in which the highly influential schema of divine-human relationship proposed and systematized by the Roman lawyer Tertullian is deconstructed,[5] and the organic connection of atonement and redemption to the person of the Savior himself recognized. We need, in other words, to consider the questions of grace and justification again from a strictly christological perspective, asking not "What do I gain from grace?," as if the latter were some independent quantity or commodity earned and made available by the effective performance by Jesus of some "work" external to its actual substance, but "Who am I in Christ? And on what basis?"

In the preceding paragraphs I have used the term "Protestant" with my fingers crossed; for while it is true that much (perhaps even most) Protestant theology has operated within the sort of scheme alluded to above, there have been those in every age since the Reformation who have recognized its limitations and resisted its implications, pursuing instead a soteriology more fully integrated with the shape and substance of Christology. The purpose of this chapter is to suggest that the French Reformer John Calvin (1509–1564), despite the way in which he has often been interpreted, is one such, and that revisiting aspects of Calvin's soteriology may thus be worthwhile for theological conversations designed to go back behind long-established and entrenched divisions in pursuit of more ancient, catholic, and biblically founded insights.

§1. The Incarnation as the Regeneration of Our Humanity

In the discussion of Calvin that follows, certain distinctions are drawn that might helpfully be noted in advance. First, there is the distinction to which I have already alluded, between the retrospective and prospective aspects of atonement. The terminology is anachronistic in its application to Calvin,[6] but the substance of the distinction itself is identifiably present in his writings. Second, there is a clear distinction between that which Christ has done "for us" (substitution) and that which he does

"in us" (participation). The main reasons for identifying and thus label-
ing these parallel distinctions in advance is a somewhat equivocal use
in Calvin of the more familiar terms "justification" and "sanctification."
On occasion, "sanctification" is used by him to refer to that which Christ
does "in us" through the power of the Spirit at work in our lives.[7] There
are many instances, however, where "sanctification" is spoken of as having
been worked out *for us*, apparently in reference to the prospective aspect
of salvation. So, Calvin writes, Christ "has put on our flesh and consecrated it as a temple to God the Father and has sanctified himself in it to
make atonement for our sins."[8] This is, as we shall see, an important part
of Calvin's conviction that "the whole of our salvation is not to be sought
anywhere else than in Christ."[9] Finally, there is the important familiar dialectic between that which we are "already" and that which we are "not yet."
Precisely how these various ideas hold together in Calvin's exposition will
become clearer as we proceed.

As far as Christology is concerned, Calvin places himself explicitly
and firmly within the tradition of Chalcedonian orthodoxy, both in the
letter and the spirit. Furthermore, the pattern of his Christology is determinative for his soteriology. All that he has to say concerning humanity's
relationship with God is directed by this reality, and none of the models
of redemption to which he refers is allowed to trespass outside the interpretative context established by it. Who Christ is makes all the difference
for interpreting the meaning and significance (for us and for God) of what
he does.

Thus Calvin is unequivocal in his affirmation of the full divinity of
Christ. The incarnation involves no compromising of the Son's godhead:
"When it is said that the Word was made flesh, we must not understand
it as if he were ... changed into flesh, but that he made choice of the virgin's womb as a temple in which he might dwell. He who was Son of God
became the Son of Man, not by confusion of substance, but by unity of person."[10] More important still, perhaps, is the seriousness with which Calvin
takes the full humanity of the Savior. In spite of what might be referred
to as his Alexandrian emphasis on the divinity of Christ, there is no corresponding tendency toward monophysitism. Not only does Calvin insist
on the integrity of the humanity of Christ in his life and death, he will
accept no lessening of its integrity even after the ascension. "Those fanat-
ics," he says, "who imagine that Christ has now put off his flesh because
the days of the flesh are said to have passed are talking nonsense. It is one
thing to be truly man, even though endowed with a blessed immortality.

It is quite a different thing to be subject to the human trials and infirmities which Christ underwent as long as he lived in the world but has laid aside now that he has been received into heaven."[11] Clearly, then, Calvin will subscribe to no kenotic reduction of the Savior's *humanum* in glory. The incarnation is no temporary episode in the life of God but rather a permanent involvement in the human situation, albeit one in which the human condition itself is decisively transformed.

The reasons for this orthodox christological insistence are, I believe, profoundly soteriological ones. There can be no denying of Christ's divinity, no shedding of his flesh, no dissolving of the hypostatic union, precisely because for Calvin these are not mere prerequisites or conditions of our enjoyment of *something else* which is salvation. Calvin discerns a salvific meaning in the humanity of the divine Saviour which makes a nonsense of any attempt to interpret salvation in wholly extrinsic terms. Indeed, there is for him, as we shall see, a very real sense in which Christ's humanity, taken up into this personal union, *is* the salvation of the human race.

At the outset of the *Institutes* Calvin declares his central point of reference in theology to be "the simple knowledge of Christ only, for in that the whole gospel is really included. Thus, those who teach anything but Christ wander into forbidden territory."[12] In hamartiology and anthropology, therefore, Calvin's starting point is not some general experience of the plight of humankind but the person of the Savior, complete with all that he offers to us. Total depravity does not mean that we are absolutely incapable of doing good, as has so often been suggested. On the contrary: "It is certain that in this degenerate and vitiated nature some remnant of God's gift still remains; whence it follows that we are not perverted in every part . . . but since the contagion of evil has run riot through every part, nothing free from all defilement will be found in us."[13] Yet this radical portrayal of humanity's fallen state is arrived at not on the basis of self-examination or the judgment of others but rather by looking to the grace of God in Christ, and extrapolating back in order to fathom the extent of the human condition. The salvation wrought in Christ, Calvin believes, involves a total renewing and remaking of human nature, such that it can be described as a "rebirth," a description which must not be given a purely spiritual reference: "By the term 'born again' [Christ] means not the amendment of a part, but the renewal of the whole nature. Hence it follows that there is nothing in us that is not defective; for if reformation is necessary in the whole and in each part, corruption must be spread everywhere."[14] In this way Calvin's insistence on "total depravity" reflects a concern similar to the patristic contention that "what is unassumed (by God in the incarnation) remains unhealed." Common to both is a procedure which begins with the radical grace of God made concrete in the incarnation of Christ (itself already understood as the *substance* and not merely the necessary *means* of the salvation being wrought by God), and comes only a posteriori to its theological anthropology. What Christ *does*, in other words, is interpreted consistently in the light of who he *is*.

Far from the doctrine of total depravity in Calvin being an accurate measure of his opinion of humanity, therefore, it would be better treated as a reflection of the breadth and richness which he perceives in the salvation wrought in Christ—the refashioning of a humanity fallen away from God, and the bestowal of all that God wishes humanity to have and to be. In his concentration on the person of the Savior, in other words, Calvin takes seriously what we have referred to as both the retrospective and the prospective aspects of redemption. "The Son of God," says Calvin, "became man in such a manner that he had God in common with us."[15] This paradoxical statement lies at the heart of Calvin's understanding of grace. All that Christ does, he does humanly, as a man (though not merely a man) who has a human relationship with his Creator. Indeed, his *human relationship* with the Father is central to the salvation of others. How, then, does Calvin understand this as having been worked out?

It is hardly necessary to demonstrate the presence of retrospective motifs in Calvin's theology. He takes fully seriously the language of the New Testament concerning Christ's death and suffering as a bearing of the consequences of humanity's sinfulness, employing to the full the range of available biblical imagery. Thus, for instance, he frequently connects the cross with the sacerdotal language of temple sacrifice. "What else," he asks, "*was* the death of Christ but a sacrifice for the expiation of our sins?"[16] Elsewhere the negative and dark imagery of penal suffering (forensic and household) is employed. Christ, we learn, "underwent in mortal flesh the judgement of God";[17] indeed "he underwent the horrors of hell in order to deliver us from them."[18] "The destruction of our sins by Christ was necessary," Calvin writes, "in order that Christ might restore us to the Father's favour. This could be accomplished only be his suffering in our place the punishment which we were unable to endure."[19] Such examples might easily be multiplied many times over. The essential thrust of them all is the same, namely that an important part of the salvation of humankind involves dealing with human guilt, putting to death the old humanity, the payment of our debt; whatever the conceptuality employed, the direction is essentially a retrospective one, a negating of the negatives of our life before God, bringing us back into a condition of innocence, purity, or solvency, removing the stains that pollute and defile us, and whatever claims the law, the debtor's court, or the executioner may once have had on us.

Yet this is far from being the whole picture as Calvin presents it. Alongside the retrospective dimension of salvation, he also demonstrates a clear vision of and concern with its prospective substance. Atonement does not consist simply in a judgment borne, a debt paid, or the nonreckoning of sin and guilt. The wider context is God's positive purpose, the establishing of humanity in a wholly new relationship with God, the exaltation of humanity to a previously unknown glory. In short, in Calvin's own words, humankind is given to share in the sonship of Christ, for, "becoming Son of Man with us, he has made us sons of God with him; . . . by his descent to earth, he has prepared an ascent to heaven for us; . . . by taking on our mortality, he has conferred immortality upon us; . . . accepting our weakness, he has strengthened us by his power; . . . receive our poverty unto himself, he has transferred his wealth to us; . . . taking the weight of our iniquity upon himself . . . he has clothed us with his righteousness."[20] Far from leaving our humanity essentially unchanged, therefore, the glorious exchange involves a radical transformation of our being. Retrospective and prospective "go together as if tied by an inseparable bond, so that if anyone tries to separate them, he is, in a sense, tearing Christ to pieces. Accordingly, let the man who aims at being justified by God's free goodness, through Christ take note that this *cannot possible be done* unless at the same time he lays hold of him for sanctification."[21]

Yet here we approach an apparent difficulty in Calvin, and it concerns the objective/subjective or for us/in us distinction that provided our point of departure in this chapter. We find many places where Calvin insists that salvation in all of its aspects is complete and finished in Jesus Christ, and as such depends in no way on our cooperation or involvement. "Since," he says, "we see that every particle of our salvation stands thus outside of us, why is it that we still trust or glory in works?"[22] Calvin's emphasis on the objectivity of salvation is everywhere apparent. The terms "substitution" and "imputation" are ever in his mind, and it becomes clear that this extends to every aspect of our relationship with God, prospective as well as retrospective. Thus, he argues, Paul in his letter to the Colossians "teaches that *all* parts of our salvation are placed in Christ alone, that they

may not seek *anything* elsewhere."[23] Again, this would seem to be the sense
in which Calvin speaks of grace in terms of Christ's offering to us his own
body, "for in his flesh was accomplished man's redemption; in it a sacrifice
was offered to atone for sins an obedience yielded to God to reconcile him
to us; it was also filled with the sanctification of the Spirit; finally, having overcome death, it was received into the heavenly glory."[24] All this has
been accomplished *for us* in the one man Jesus Christ. The humanity of the
Savior is the place where God has worked out our salvation, and all that he
wills to do for humankind he does, in the first instance, in this one man. If
Christ has become the "old man" in order to be put to death for us, so too
he is the "new man" who has recreated our broken and fallen humanity,
taking it up into a life of obedience and loving sonship, living out this life
in our stead, sanctifying our flesh, and offering it to the Father for us.

It is this "for us" that Calvin perceives to be the very heart of the gospel. Nothing is left undone in the saving purpose of God for his creature.
Nothing is left for us to complete, for there are no conditions attached to
this *charis*. It has all been worked out for us, Calvin insists, in our substitute Jesus Christ. The bitter cup of God's wrath has been drained to the
dregs, and the new humanity has been established in his person. Yet it is
the same "for us" that is so problematic. If Christ has done everything for
us, has substituted himself for us at every point, in what sense can there
then be a real participation of humanity in the grace of God? If Christ has
not only died for us, but has in a real sense lived out the life of sonship for
us, how does this benefit us? Does it not exclude us precisely from that
which we are told Christ came to give us? Is not the charge of extrinsicism,
of a fictitious grace, shown to be appropriate if we must speak not of *our*
faith, love, obedience, righteousness, and so forth, but of Christ's alone?

This would indeed be the case if "substitution" or "Christ for us" were to
be the final word. It is, for Calvin, the *primary* word, yet it is not all that is to
be said. For there are many occasions when he makes it quite clear that we
must also speak of a real participation of believers in this redeemed humanity, or of salvation at work *in us*. The salvation which Christ works out is a *real*
salvation, and is given to those who are in need of it in a *real* sense, and not in
some fictitious manner. Thus he writes that Christ "did not enrich himself
for his own sake, but that he might pour out his abundance upon the hungry
and thirsty,"[25] and insists that as Christians "we know that being sanctified
by the Spirit of regeneration, we *are being made* new creatures in order that
we might live to God."[26] It would seem to be quite groundless, therefore, to
accuse Calvin of positing a grace with which leaves humanity unchanged.

§2. The Disagreement with Osiander

How, then, are we to see these two emphases as being held together? How is it that Calvin can insist simultaneously on both the objective nature of our redemption complete in the one man Jesus Christ and its presence as a transforming existential reality in our lives? If there is nothing left undone in Christ, how can there be any further scope for grace in our lives? Must we not assume that what Calvin means by substitution is in some sense different from the way that term is generally interpreted?

In seeking to answer this question, Calvin's dispute with the Lutheran theologian Osiander proves instructive.[27] The accuracy of Calvin's presentation of the views of Osiander matters less for our purpose than his arguments refuting what he believed those views to be. In short, according to Calvin, Osiander "has clearly expressed himself as not content with that righteousness which has been acquired for us by Christ's obedience and sacrificial death, but pretends that we are substantially righteous in God by the infusion both of his essence and of his quality."[28] There are two related issues here: first, that the only "righteousness" which Christ bestows on us is intrinsic to us (i.e., a quality of our being), and second, that it is *divine* and not human righteousness that is infused into us in this action of grace. Calvin is strongly opposed to both propositions.

Osiander's motive seems to have been the admirable one of seeking to take seriously the fact that grace imparts a real salvation to humanity, and that this in some sense involves us in a union with God, or a sharing in the divine life. These are, I think, both propositions to which Calvin assents. It is to the way in which they are interpreted by Osiander that he objects. On one hand, Calvin cannot allow that there is any "mixing" of our humanity with divinity. This is to trespass beyond the christological boundaries stated by Chalcedon ("without confusion, without change, without division, without separation")[29] and to assert a divinizing of Christ's human nature of a sort which has no biblical warrant whatever. Thus Calvin insists that "even though Christ, if he had not been true God, could not cleanse our souls by his blood, nor appease the Father by his sacrifice, nor absolve us from guilt, nor, in sum, fulfil the office of a priest . . . yet it is certain that he carried out all these acts *according to his human nature.*"[30] It is the *human* righteousness of Christ which is given to us in grace, and through which we are enabled to approach the throne of grace. Salvation is, for Calvin, a remaking of human nature as part of the promised new creation, not some blurring of the infinite qualitative difference between Creator and creature.

Yet, given that this is *what* we received, Calvin cannot subscribe to Osiander's view of *how* we receive it either. Osiander, he says, "laughs at those men who teach that 'to be justified' is a legal term; because we must actually be righteous. Also, he despises nothing more than that we are justified by free imputation."[31] It would seem that here Calvin is concerned to defend at least a certain sort of extrinsicism. His main criticism of Osiander's understanding of justification is that it robs the Christian of all assurance. In focusing primarily, indeed solely, on the righteousness which is intrinsic to our individual being, he neglects that all-important element of substitution, of "Christ for us" that Calvin believes to be an irreducible element of the gospel. "No portion of righteousness sets our consciences at peace until it has been determined that we are pleasing to God, because we are entirely righteous before him."[32] If the only righteousness that Christians can be said to possess is that which is manifest on the empirical level in their daily existence, then what sort of assurance or peace are they likely to enjoy? No, says Calvin, rather "this is a wonderful plan of justification that, covered by the righteousness of Christ, they should not tremble at the judgement they deserve, and that while they condemn themselves, they should be accounted righteous *outside* themselves."[33]

It will not do, however, to accuse Calvin of extrinsicism because he says these things. It is true that he teaches quite unashamedly the idea that salvation is, in the first instance, a matter of substitution. It has taken place in the one man Jesus Christ for us, and this precisely because we were and are not capable of doing it for ourselves. So, God's self-substitution for us in his incarnate Son is precisely the element of gift or grace to which the gospel bears witness. Yet when he uses the terms "substitute" and "imputation"—terms whose subsequent history has often done little to commend them—Calvin clearly does not intend them in an entirely exclusive sense. On the contrary, he argues, "we do not . . . contemplate Christ outside ourselves from afar in order that his righteousness may be imputed to us, but because we put on Christ and are engrafted into his body—in short, because he deigns to make us one with him. For this reason, we glory that we have fellowship of righteousness with him." Imputation, therefore, is not a matter of fiction, but a real sharing or fellowship in the righteousness of this particular human being. It is, first and foremost, external to us, yet it really belongs to us because of the union which we have with Jesus. What is his has become ours. Thus, Calvin argues, "you see that our righteousness is not in us but in Christ, that we possess it only because we are partakers in Christ; indeed, with him we possess all its riches."[34] Calvin's point is that the "for us" of substitution does not exclude us or leave us unchanged. It is an inclusive rather than an exclusive concept. Indeed, there is an important sense in which it must be said that we *were in him* when he wrought our salvation for us. So, Calvin writes, humankind "was united with God in the person of one man, because all men are made up of the same flesh and the same nature."[35] Christ is our substitute, yet not in any sense which excludes us or leaves us remote from the reality of grace, but rather in such a way that we are implicated in all that he does and has and is. First and foremost, this is complete for us in his humanity; yet just as Calvin thinks in terms of humankind having been "in Christ" through his inclusive substitution, so too he emphasizes the reality of "Christ in humankind," or that active participation of believers in him which is the work of the Holy Spirit, the flowing of the sap from the stock of the vine to the individual branches. And the key to all this is pre-cisely Calvin's grasp and foregrounding of the organic union (a "fraternal alliance of the flesh") established between the one man Jesus and all other members of the human race when the Word took our flesh and made it his own, drawing it into his own life as the Son.

Calvin refers to all this as the "marvellous exchange" that has taken place in the incarnation itself, effecting a radical change in our circum-stance: "That he being made with us the Son of Man, hath made us with him the sons of God; that by his coming down into earth, he hath made for us a way to go up into heaven; that putting upon him our mortality, he hath given us his immortality; that taking on him our weakness, he hath strengthened us with his power; that taking our poverty to himself, he hath conveyed his riches to us; that taking to him the weight of our unrighteousness, wherewith we were oppressed, he hath clothed us with his righteousness."[36]

§3. Self-Substitution in Life as in Death

Calvin's theology of substitution, we might say, is a theology of the perfect tense. That is, in speaking of redemption he is referring to a present state which results from a past action. This is true with reference to the *whole* of redemption, and not merely its retrospective aspect. In the first instance the language of redemption refers to the reality of the vicarious humanity of Christ; he is the one man who stands in the place of all others before the Father. This is substitution. Yet the language of redemption has a second-ary reference whereby it applies to us, and in so doing it remains in the perfect tense. We are already sanctified, obedient, righteous, perfect sons and daughters of God. This is a present reality which rests decisively on a past action; yet we have not yet moved beyond the scope of the language of substitution in saying it, for what we are now we are only "in Christ." That is to say, the secondary reference of such language derives its significance wholly from its primary reference to the one who exists and acts and suffers as our substitute. We *are* these things only because he is and has and holds these things for us. They belong to us only inasmuch as we are united to his flesh and engrafted into his body, but *as* we are and *because* we are united to him, as and because we have our true being and our identity no longer in isolation but only in and through our union with him, so these things do genuinely belong to us. And we share them with him both as they are complete in him and as, gradually, they work themselves out in us and we become that which, in him, we already are.

There is, therefore, yet a third application of the language of redemption in Calvin, which derives its significance wholly from these other two. This is couched in the present and future tenses and often the imperative mood. Here it is that Calvin speaks of the ongoing reality of regeneration in the lives of individual Christians, a reality which looks to the future for its culmination and toward which we proceed in the life of discipleship. But this latter use of redemption language, or the language of grace, is never separated from the other two and is always subordinate to them. This is not to deny its importance in any way but rather to recognize that the sanctification which we "put on" in the Christian life is (a) something which we *already* possess, and (b) not a reality separate from Christ but rather a participation in Christ, a result of *Christ* in us.

In this Calvin is faithful to the familiar theological dialectic between the "already" and the "not yet," which has a perfectly good christological as well as an eschatological application. The danger of taking the latter seriously at the expense of the former is precisely the danger of extrinsicism, of failing to do justice to biblical statements insisting that as believers we are *already* participants in the perfection of the new humanity. The equal and opposite danger is that of failing to take fully seriously the *not yet* aspect, and looking into the depths of one's own being to detect the reality of the new, regenerate humanity. This is the danger which Calvin detects in Osiander. That Calvin falls into neither trap is clear enough. So, for example, he writes of Christ that "engrafted into him we are *already*, in a manner, partakers of eternal life, having entered the kingdom through hope. Yet more: we experience such *participation in him* that, although we are still foolish in ourselves, he is our wisdom before God; while we are

sinners, he is our righteousness; while we are unclean, he is our purity . . .
while we still bear about the body of death, he is yet our life."[37] Yet none
of this can make any sense until the central theme and premise of Calvin's
theology is grasped, namely union with Christ and participation in him.
Only this can prevent the eschatological dialectic from collapsing into one
error or the other. It is *in Christ* that we are already redeemed, insofar as
we are implicated in his humanity. In ourselves we are gradually becoming what in him we already are, and this is the work of Christ in us, but we
are not yet there. Nevertheless, the center of gravity lies in what we are in
Christ rather than what we are in ourselves. The dominion of sin over our
lives is ended, although the experience expressed by the apostle Paul in
Romans 7 remains only too familiar.[38] Only thus can the *simil iustus et peccator* of Protestant Christianity be prevented from collapsing either into
an extrinsicism which turns grace into a legal fiction, or a different kind of
extrinsicism which cuts grace loose from its moorings in the person of the
Savior. Both instances effectively short-circuit the mediatory role of Jesus'
humanity in our dealings with the Father.

Instead of this Calvin sketches a theology in which both substitution
and participation are central, and in which both rest on the saving union
which God has established between this man and others. Here we begin to
see the salvific significance Calvin ascribes to the Savior's humanity. Far
from being of merely instrumental value, it is itself the very substance of
salvation, Christ's making us "participants, not only in all his benefits, but
also in himself."[39] It is the whole humanity of the Savior which he offers
to us to "clothe our nakedness," and our sharing in grace is none other
than a sharing in this humanity through our union with Christ. Indeed
"when the apostle defines the Gospel, and the use of it, he says that we are
called to be partakers of our Lord Jesus Christ, and to be made one with
him, and to dwell in him and he in us; and that we be joined together in an
inseparable bond."[40] Union with Christ, therefore, is not simply a necessary aspect or precondition of the gospel; in all that matters it *is* the gospel.

§4. Atonement, Union, and Participation

Union with the substitutionary (or vicarious) humanity of Christ, and participation in this same humanity: these are the twin aspects of redemption
in Christ as Calvin perceives it. Owing to our saving union with Christ, all
that he has and all that he does now belong to us, and vice versa. But even
this does not express the wonder of the "marvellous exchange" as Calvin
sees it; for the whole truth is that, because we are united to Christ, all that

he *is* becomes ours, while he takes what is ours upon himself. What he does and what he has depend entirely on who he is—the obedient, loving Son of the Father loved by the Father and in the closest fellowship with him. And even this is not something which he withholds from us. To be sure, he alone is the true and eternal Son. Yet he gives us to participate in his filial status. "The chief of all God's promises is that by which he adopts us as his sons and Christ is the cause and root of our adoption. For God is Father only to those who are members and brothers of his only-begotten Son. Everything comes to us from this one source."[41] "Christ possesses this name by right, in as much as he is by nature the only Son of God. But he shares this honour with us by adoption when we are ingrafted into his body."[42]

Because we are united to the humanity of Christ, then, we are united to the human Son of God and are given to share in his human sonship. Thus in Calvin's theology, Paul van Buren concludes, "God's love for men is none other than the Father's love for the Son,"[43] or as Calvin himself writes, "We may safely conclude, that since by faith we are engrafted into [Christ's] body, there is no other danger that we shall be cut off from the love of God; for this foundation cannot be overturned—that we are loved because the Father has loved him."[44] Our union with the humanity of Christ is such that we share in his human relationship of love and obedience to his heavenly Father, empowered by the Holy Spirit and in the reciprocal love which flows from the Father's heart to him. In other words, we may say, our union with the man Jesus is in itself a union with God. It is so because in the very person of Christ the gulf between God and humanity has been bridged. The Son of God has taken our humanity and has "joined" it to his eternal divinity, healing it from its broken state, and conforming it to his creative will. He has put to death the old sinful humanity and has raised up a "new humanity" in its place, living out a life of fellowship and sonship *in his own humanity,* in relation to the Father and the Spirit. As Calvin affirms, "The difference between God and man is very great, and yet in Christ we see God's infinite glory joined to our polluted flesh, so that the two become one."[45]

This is atonement as Calvin understands it: that our "polluted flesh" should be taken up and united to the eternal Son, who is *homoousios* with the Father. At-one-ment between God and humankind *has* taken place *in* the person of Christ. The hypostatic union itself is an atoning union, as God takes our flesh up into the very life of the Godhead, and, purging it of all that separates it from him, establishes it in the filial relationship of the Son to the Father in the Spirit, thus making it his humanity. We are, in this event, not "divinized" but rather established and vindicated as truly human, sharing in the new humanity of God himself.

"It was necessary," Calvin argues, "for the Son of God to become for us 'Immanuel' . . . in such a way that *his divinity and our human nature might by mutual connection grow together.*"[46] It is in this sense that we may say that the incarnation *is* the atonement. God and our humanity *have been* reconciled in their personal union in Christ, as Jesus sees with God's eyes, wills God's will, feels what God himself feels, and lives accordingly. The relationship of correlation between Creator and creature has been restored and renewed. "Atonement," therefore, is not simply a consequence of something that Christ does, and which pertains to us individually and independently of him. Nor is the incarnation to be considered a mere prerequisite of some atoning act or other. The two things stand and fall together, for they are in reality one and the same. In Jesus Christ who is Son of God and Son of man, the union between God and us, which is our "highest good,"[47] has been reforged. Jesus' humanity and his divinity coexist in closest fellowship in his person. None of this is to deny the absolute importance of his death or his obedience, or of anything else which he does. But it sets these firmly within the context of the outworking of atonement which *begins* with the baby in Bethlehem and ends in the glorious resurrection of the Last Adam from the death which he died in our place, and in whose vicarious humanity we now participate in the power of the Spirit.

What this brief study of Calvin's theology shows us is that when grace is interpreted from a christological perspective, being seen not as the *tertium quid* either of an external divine decree or an infused substance but rather as the self-giving of God himself for us and to us in the person of Christ, the dilemma which has so long plagued Western Christianity is able to be transcended. For the question of whether "grace" is objective or subjective to the believer presupposes a framework in which the mediatory capacity of the Savior's humanity is circumvented. When it is realized that Jesus mediates not as some third party to the dispute but as the one *in whose very person* the two estranged parties are brought together and reconciled, then the focus of questioning must alter. For then we realize that the privilege which we are given is not restricted to the possession of "benefits" earned for us by some external transaction in which Christ is the main agent, but rather that we have been adopted into the relationship which the incarnate Son has with the Father in the Spirit, namely into the very Trinitarian life of God himself. This is ours by virtue of our union with Christ, apart from whom we have and we are nothing.

7

Mediation

§1. Getting Things in Order

To reflect on the theme of Christ the Mediator is above all to reflect on the relationship between the answers to two distinct but properly inseparable questions: Who is Jesus? How are we to think of his agency as the one who saves us? Both questions are capable and desirous of quite a wide variety of answers, at least if we would be faithful to the biblical source materials in the way that the Westminster divines insist we must, and themselves certainly seek to be. What the apostles offer to us is a rich tapestry of different images for salvation and Christ's involvement in procuring it, most (but by no means all) of which are borrowed from the social, political, and religious life of the nation of Israel. Not all appear to be equally significant or central to an understanding of the gospel to be sure. It does seem to be the case that some serve as what we might call controlling metaphors in relation to which others are to be made sense of or qualified. Each is modified as it is taken up into the complex network of images and significances surrounding the mystery of the person of Jesus, and it is vital, therefore, that they are understood in the light of the reality to which they refer us, as well informing our understanding of it. None, we should constantly remind ourselves, is in any crude way identical with the reality to which it points us, and presumably one reason for the diversity of metaphors used is precisely that none was deemed adequate in itself to refer to the complex

167

reality of what God has wrought in Christ for the salvation of sinners. There is an important complementarity to be discerned in the variety. Part of the task of the theologian is to handle this resource of apostolic images and, in offering an interpretation of salvation for his or her own context, to discern the relationships of order and priority and mutual qualification pertaining among them, and how each is itself qualified in its application to the person and work of Christ. This is a vital and sensitive task, and for our purposes it is important to inquire into the possible distorting effects either of exalting any one set of images at the effective expense of others with an equal biblical claim to serious attention, or allowing one set of metaphors rather than another to serve in a controlling manner as supplying the framework within which all others considered are made sense of.

In order to pin the issue down a little more definitely I want to look at the eleventh article of George Wishart's translation of the First Helvetic Confession of 1537:

Of Jesus Christ and That is Done by Hym

This Christ, the very Sone of God, and very God and very man also, was made our brother, at the tyme appoynted he toke upon him whole man, made of soule and body, hauynge two natures unpermyxte and one dewyne person, to the intent that he shoulde restore unto lyfe us that were deed, and make us aryse of God annexte with him selfe. He also after that he had taken upon him of the immaculate Virgin, by operacion of the Holy Goost, fleshe, whiche was holy bycause of the union of the Godhed, which is, and also was lyke to our flesh in all things excepte in synfulnes : And that bycause it behoued the sacrefice for synne to be cleane and immaculate, gaue that same fleshe to death for to expell all our synne by that meanes. And he also, to the entent that we shuld have one full and perfecte hope and trust of our immortalitie, hath raysed up agayne fro death to lyfe his owne fleshe, and hath set it and placed it in heauen at the ryghte hande of his Almighty Father.

And there he sytteth our victorious champion, our gyder, our capitayne, and heed, also our hyghest bysshop in dede, synne, death, and hell, beynge victoriously ouercome by him, and defendeth oure cause, and pleadeth it perpetually untyll he shall reforme and fascion us to that lykness to which we were create, and brynge us to be partakers of eternall lyfe. And we loke for hym, and beleueth that he shall come at the ende of all ages to be our trewe ryghtuous just Judge, and shall pronounce sentence against all fleshe, whiche shal be raysed up before to that judgement, and that he shall exalte the godly aboue the heauens, but the ungodly shall he condempne bothe body and soule to eternal destruction.

> And as he onely is oure mediatour and entercessour, hoste and sacri-
> fice, bysshop, lorde, andn our kynge; also do we acknowlage and confesse
> hym onely to be our attonement and raunsome, satisfaction, expiacion, or
> wysdome, our defence, and our onely deliuerer: refusyng utterly all other
> meane of lyfe and saluacion, excepte thus by Chryst onely.[1]

As Reformation summaries of an apostolic account of Christ's saving
person and work go, as well as being among the earliest this has surely to
rank among the best, both in terms of the comprehensiveness of its coverage and, perhaps more importantly, the way in which it weaves the various images together and locates them in relation to one another. I cannot
help feeling as I read through chapter 8 of the Westminster Confession
or the relevant questions and answers of the Larger Catechism that the
theological tone is subtly but significantly different, and less satisfying. It
is not so much that the coverage is more restricted (a quick comparison
reveals things in each that are not in the other, but they are few) as that its
primary focus is a different one. To paraphrase Groucho Marx, it is like
some people's piano playing: all the right notes are there, but in the wrong
order! And it has an impact on the music.

Westminster's typically Reformed use of the image of Mediator as
the primary designation of Jesus points us straightaway to the particular
family of images which serve in a controlling capacity in the Confession's
theological approach to the relationship between God and humankind;
namely, those surrounding the theme of covenant. It is here, if we are
to identify any source of unease with Westminster's presentation of the
mediation of Christ, that we must attend. Not that there is anything
wrong as such in making significant use of the covenant metaphor. Its centrality to the biblical presentation of God's relationship to his creatures
is not to be doubted. But we must probe an issue which chapter 8 of the
Confession itself invites us to probe. How is the logic of the christological
orthodoxy faithfully reiterated in article 2 related to the logic of mediation and, indeed, to the theme of God's covenant? And what difference, if
any, does the first make to our understanding and exposition of the other
two? My suggestion is that it must. For it seems to me that a Christian
understanding of the relationship between God and humankind must be
informed above all not by the theme of covenant first and foremost but by
the central reality to which the Bible as a whole may reasonably be said to
point us, the place where God himself is most closely related to humanity, namely the inhomination of his own Son to dwell in our midst in the
Spirit's power. How God is related to his creature here, I suggest, must

guide our thinking about the divine-human relationship in all its wider aspects and qualify any other metaphor which we wish to deploy. Here, then, I am staking a claim to an alternative hermeneutical strategy to that which I perceive to be operative in the Westminster documents. Mediation and covenant must not furnish the framework within which we make sense of and accommodate the biblical imagery pertaining to incarnation, but vice versa.

§2. The Logic of Mediation

I want to step back now from the particulars of Christian theology and ask a question about the category of mediation as it is used more broadly. What does this word convey for us or for our unchurched family, friends, and neighbors? After all, if we would find the word used, then our newspapers are just as fruitful a source as our Bibles or manuals of seventeenth-century theology. And if we are to continue to make use of the language of mediation then it is imperative that we are aware of its wider resonances and significances outside the exposition of the gospel message.

The *Concise Oxford English Dictionary* defines "to mediate" as, first, to "form connecting link between; be the medium for bringing about (result) or conveying (gift etc.)," and second, to "intervene (between two persons) for purpose of reconciling them." So, in the broadest possible terms, a mediator is simply someone who brings two parties or groups together in some way. This may (most often will) involve, however, the additional connotation of facilitating the reforging of a broken relationship, whether personal, legal, political, commercial, and so on. A mediator may, for example, be one who persuades and then enables alienated parties to begin to talk to one another again in a family row, an industrial dispute, an international incident, or whatever. Or he may act chiefly as the representative of one party in making an indirect approach to the other—an intermediary. He may take a very active role in the cementing of the relationship, brokering the terms of some agreement acceptable to all parties. He may even stand surety for, or make good from his own resources, the deficit arising from some hitherto broken contract, in order to facilitate the continuation of a relationship otherwise in serious jeopardy. Doubtless we could furnish further variations on the theme, but these will suffice as a general picture.

In order to act as mediator in these various possible contexts, presumably a person must usually be possessed of some qualities or experience that renders him or her particularly suitable. Sometimes, apart from whatever natural skills or training in diplomacy he or she may possess, what will matter above all is the mediator's status as a neutral third party. Where the rival interests of different groups are at stake, and where trust is perhaps in short supply, the mediator must be able to talk to both sides with a guaranteed even-handedness arising from the fact that his own personal interests coincide with neither set, and to operate with a disinterested objectivity, appealing only, perhaps, to certain agreed principles of justice or fair play. In other cases, what matters more than such neutrality is precisely a certain level of *belonging* to both groups, and an ability to draw on an insight which spans the divide between them—an ability to see things, as it were, from both sides and to translate the highly charged signals which that fly back and forth, and so foster increased mutual understanding. Possessed of these and other possible sets of skills or qualities, someone may be chosen to step into the political, commercial, or personal breach and attempt some sort of accommodation. But, let us note at this point, this step and what follows it consist solely in the execution of a task or the fulfillment of an office to which the person has been appointed. At the end of the crisis or the meeting or the day or the week, that person can step out of the breach again and lay the office aside with impunity like a garment. Mediation is a job that mediators do and which, no matter how committed to it they may be, and no matter how involved they may become in particular cases, they can stop doing while yet continuing to be themselves. Who they are, their personal background, qualities, experience, and so on, may be more or less closely related to equipping or qualifying them for the task, but the task of mediating as such is logically distinct from their personal identity and being. They could pack up tools and go off to do something quite different instead. Most of our use of the language of mediation probably has to do with this sort of thing.

If we reflect on a different circumstance, however, we may see that there is at least another way in which mediation might be supposed to occur. Think of a pair of lovers each belonging to quite distinct racial or national groups which happen to be in the midst of a vicious and prolonged conflict. The meeting of the two, their falling in love, and the development of that love duly bears the fruit of a deep mutual insight. Gradually each comes to think to some extent as the other thinks, to see the world through the other's eyes, to speak the other's language, to indwell the other's world. Each comes to acquire a "second first language" in terms of the broadening and modification of their outlook. Now, we might well suppose that each of these would be equipped with just the sort of skills, knowledge, experience, and so on which might be highly useful in any negotiations between the two warring factions. Both are likely to have developed the capacities to render a message from their own side into terms which the other side may hear, understand, and accept. Conversely, each will be possessed of the requisite connoisseurship required to read signals coming from the other side. Considered individually, then, each is well fitted for the task or office of mediator.

Yet surely we must say more than this. For considered now not separately but together, in the union of their mutual love, there is an important sense in which the two of them actually *constitute*, by who and what they are, a conciliation between the estranged tribes. The love which defines who and what they are together, that is to say, is precisely an *example* of the healed rift, the mutual coexistence of hitherto estranged parties which is sought. It is not simply a skill or quality which equips them to do some further thing, or an instrument which effects something else which we may call mediation. The love in which they are united *is* a mediation between the two groups. Together, considered as a relational unity, they are actually a realized instance of the desired mediation. The hitherto estranged groups actually meet, adjust, and conform to one another's ways of being and thinking and doing in the world in the midst of their very existence as a couple wedded together by love. Were they not each from different groups, or were they not truly united in love, then this would not be the case. But, being who and what they are together, they cannot in fact cease to mediate between their respective tribes. Only by ceasing to be who and what they are together could this occur.

A further example suggests itself in our use of language, and specifically in the process which we call translation. As George Steiner reminds us, translation is, in effect, an activity of linguistic mediation, bearing the freight of meaning across the borders which divide our speech, a bringing together of the senders and receivers of signals in a bid for a reconciliation of meaning. Those who would engage in the task must first equip themselves for the office of translator by acquiring, in addition to their own native language, sufficient skill and insight into another to enable them to have a foot in both linguistic camps, to straddle the border, bringing together two distinct linguistic groups and effecting an exchange of goods. There are, though, some who by virtue of their upbringing actually already belong to more than one such linguistic set. Steiner, himself multilingual, reflects on this phenomenon whereby, from his earliest memory, the world around him was describable simultaneously in three different ways, none of which seemed to be any more or less satisfactory or primitive than the others. "It was habitual, unnoticed practice for my mother to start a sentence in one language and finish it in another. At home, conversations were interlinguistic not only inside the same sentence or speech segment, but as between speakers. Only a sudden wedge of interruption or roused consciousness would make me realize that I was replying in French to a question put in German or English or vice versa."[2] The result of this polyglottally induced triple-audition was to provoke something of a crisis of identity: "In what language am *I*, suis-*je*, bin *ich*, when I am inmost? What is the tone of self?"[3] For our purposes it is Steiner's profound inability to answer this question which is most relevant. The point is simply that, at the core of his personal being, Steiner identifies no one linguistic allegiance but finds three streams of language completely intermingled. The mediatory activity which we call translation, therefore, is one which he finds himself unable to engage in consciously precisely because the semantic convergences which it entails are already there, part and parcel of who he is and his way of viewing and mapping the world. He cannot *not* do it. It simply happens as a natural consequence of his personal makeup. He cannot see a horse without knowing it simultaneously as *ein Pferd* and *un cheval*. He is, as it were, one person subsisting in three distinct linguistic worlds.

All analogies are limited; and unless we wish to be charged respectively with Apollinarianism and Nestorianism (and perhaps much worse besides) we had best admit the limitations of these before going much further. Their sole function here is to indicate a genuine distinction between mediation as an office which someone may either fulfill or not, without ceasing to be who and what he or she otherwise is, and a distinct sort of mediation which is, we might say, actually constituted by, or internal to, who and what someone actually is. The reason for drawing the distinction at all is simply that it seems to me to be highly pertinent in the context of considering the way the notion of mediation is modified in the biblical tradition, to which I now return.

§3. Christology, Mediation, and Covenant

The story which the Bible tells about the relationship between God and humans is, of course, in large measure a story of estrangement and reconciliation. The God of the Bible creates and calls his creatures into fellowship with himself. He creates in love and with the purpose of enjoying the creatures' reciprocal love. Yet the love which God seeks from the human side is not just of any sort but the reflection of his own, in P. T. Forsyth's phrase,[4] "holy love." In the face of the fall of human beings into sin and wanton Godlessness, however, God's love is not quenched but burns ever more fiercely in a determination not to allow evil to despoil that which he has made and adjudged to be good. Hence, in the purposes of his gracious love, he calls Israel out of the sinful mass of humanity in order to live in fellowship with him, to be his people in the world, and as such to carry forward his creative and redemptive purpose in history, to be a bearer of the promise not to the exclusion of others but precisely in their behalf that they too might in due course hear and receive and respond to God's gracious and holy call to life.[5]

It is in this context of Israel's self-understanding as a people chosen and called by God that the biblical language of covenant or *berith* arises. While it is generally supposed that the provenance of the metaphor lies in ancient Near Eastern suzerainty treaties (reinforcing Israel's conviction that Yahweh and no other was her true King—a theme which was to find powerful restatement in seventeenth-century Scotland!), what matters theologically is less the structure of the supposed original than its modification to fit the nature of Israel's peculiar circumstance. In particular we should note that the establishment of the covenant is uniformly presented as lying in Yahweh's choosing and promising. Indeed, the sole foundation of the covenant is his promise and subsequent faithfulness to it. The promise itself is quite unconditional, and while it makes equally unreserved demands on Israel, it is rarely suggested that the relationship between her and Yahweh will itself be put in jeopardy by anything she does, and in fact her (in practice repeated) failure to live up to the demands of the covenant does not lead to this conclusion. While the characteristic form of the covenant formulae, therefore, is certainly two sided: "I shall be your God, and you will be my people," and "You shall be holy, for I the Lord your God am holy," and so on, these are primarily understood as promises and commitments on God's own part, referring to states of affairs which he himself will duly bring to pass, before they are understood as imperatives designed to transform Israel's way of being God's people in the world. Thus the context for the giving of the law to Israel is the objective context of God's grace in establishing, sealing, and maintaining the covenant relationship regardless of Israel's initial worth or her subsequent sin. The law furnishes the people with a clear indication of what it must mean for them to live as God's chosen people in the world. Furthermore, it indicates the likely consequences of failing to abide by this pattern. But the context for the law is promise, and Israel's keeping or failing to keep it can neither establish nor dissolve the covenant relationship itself. As Walther Eichrodt notes, "The majesty of divine love shows itself in this, that God alone has the power to dissolve the relationship, yet never makes use of it."[6] The distinction between the logic of covenant and of promise is thus quite a difficult one to draw. The covenant in its purest form is properly "a proof of Yahweh's love as this seeks to awaken the responsive confidence and love of men,"[7] although the danger of a slide into a legalism which inverts the order of grace and *torah*, and is obsessed with the exact observance of mutual rights and duties, was always latent in the metaphor.

Insofar as Israel knows of a theology of mediation, of course, it is within the institutional structures of her covenanted life under Yahweh, and is embodied in three figures in particular: the prophet, the priest, and the king. Each of these figures in the national life acts in some way either to bring God before the people, or the people before God, or both. The prophet brings God's Word to the people. The priest both interprets the ceremonial and moral law of God authoritatively on one hand, and officiates in the cultus, especially in the offering of sacrifice, on the other.[8] On the Day of Atonement in particular, the high priest stands in God's presence and makes an offering on behalf of all twelve tribes for the expiation and covering of their sins, in a divinely ordained means of maintaining the covenant in spite of Israel's failure to live within the terms of its obligations.[9] He is thus a representative figure on the part of God before Israel, and on the part of Israel before God. The king, too, has a twofold representative function. On the one hand he is Yahweh's regent, and stands in the nation's midst as a visible and tangible symbol and agent of God's rule, administering justice in God's behalf and protecting the nation from forces which would threaten to disrupt its covenanted life under God.[10] On the other hand, the king is also Yahweh's subject, and stands shoulder to shoulder with his subjects as one who must be faithful in keeping the covenant.[11] As the so-called Deuteronomic History of the books of 1–2 Samuel and 1–2 Kings makes plain, however, his actions are more than merely personal in this regard. When the king is obedient, the nation flourishes. When he departs from God's law and its faithful administration, the nation is cast into a downward spiral. The reality of Israel's life under God was, as the Old Testament text makes quite clear, often an unholy mixture of recalcitrance, waywardness, disobedience, and bad faith. The one who had called Israel, who had delivered her from captivity, and brought her into the land flowing with milk and honey, was variously ignored, rejected, and betrayed. And yet his heart and his promise remained constant. And out of the midst of the continual chastisement and exile which marks her repeated falling from grace, Israel's hope for God's future begins to be formulated. Chief among its themes is the expectation of a time when God's covenant with his people will be renewed and established forever, when the law will be written in human hearts rather than tablets of stone, when the Spirit of God will be poured out and the demands of the covenant finally fulfilled from the human side. And in the midst of this hope there emerges a concomitant expectation that all this will be accompanied by the appearance of an anointed instrument of the covenant, a messianic mediator who will bear this salvation in his train, equipped to do whatever needs to be done for its procurement.

Reformed theology's penchant for the category of mediator (μεσίτης, which, as such, appears relatively rarely in the New Testament; given the Old Testament background it is interesting to ask what the reasons for this might be) to refer to the redemptive significance of Jesus is thus far from arbitrary. It draws directly on the apostolic perception that in Christ's person and ministry we find a fulfillment of this entire long history of foreshadowing and promise. In him the kingdom of God is brought near, and the new covenant inaugurated. All God's promises are yea and amen in him. But the ways in which Jesus is presented in the apostolic texts posit significant discontinuities as well as continuities between the forms of the promise and the perceived substance of its fulfillment in Jesus. In particular, while the bilateral structure of mediation is preserved, nonetheless the notion of an intermediary will no longer hold, either in the God-humanward or the human-Godward direction. Jesus is no mere representative or go-between, elected and equipped to fulfill a symbolic or pragmatic office. He is, on both sides of the relationship between the distinct parties in the ancient covenant, God and Israel, the real thing, the genuine article in person. And, in the very paradoxical and ambiguous state of affairs which New Testament reflection on the question of his identity discloses and begins to unfold, it must be said that these two distinct parties are actually brought together in the constitution of his own incarnate person.

Thus, for example, Jesus is a prophet like unto Moses, one who discloses God to the people in a way hitherto unknown and unexpected. But he is not just a prophet: he is the very Word of God himself present in the midst of his people, and he makes God known not just by what he says and does but also by what he is, the image of the invisible God. God is known here not indirectly but in a curious way directly. "You have heard it said . . . yet I say to you . . ." The Word here has become flesh, rather than simply conscripting flesh into his service. At the same time, though, as a human being Jesus must himself hear and respond to the Word which his Father speaks. So, too, he is the Davidic messiah, the king who comes to establish the kingdom and to rule in it. Unlike any king before him, however, Jesus is no mere regent, no intermediary between the true king and his subjects. He is Israel's true king in person, having taken flesh and now dwelling among his subjects with an authority quite unlike any other they have ever encountered. Like all the kings of Israel, though, Jesus is one who not only must administer the law but must himself fulfill its precepts as the primary subscriber to the covenant. And again, this, unlike any king before him, Jesus does perfectly, both fulfilling the law and himself duly bearing the judgment which human breaking of it incurs, taking the responsibility for his people's sins on himself. He is Israel's God and king; yet, having crossed over the boundary which creation and covenant equally suppose, he becomes one of his own subjects, and is in his perfect keeping of the covenant the true Israel. Again, Jesus is the High Priest who offers sacrifice to God to expiate our sins. Yet, unlike any other priest before or since, he is also at once the one who offers *himself* as a spotless offering pleasing to God, and the God who is pleased to receive this worship. The symbolism of Israel's cultus is torn wide open as the wholly unlooked-for happens, and God himself steps in to make from the human side that offering which from the divine side he looks for and is well pleased to receive. In the mystery of Jesus' person as (to borrow the later terminology which Westminster endorses) one person subsisting in two distinct natures, God and humanity meet and dwell together and have their respective modes of being conformed perfectly to one another.

Here, then, we have to do with a mediation of a sort which is qualitatively distinct from that found in Old Testament foreshadowing. If we choose to keep our focus on the category of covenant, then what we must surely say is that in the apostolic perception the covenant between God and Israel (now revealed to be an open rather than a closed covenant, and one which embraces the gentiles also) has been fulfilled and established on a rock-solid foundation by the self-substitution of God for sinful human beings. The ancient covenant promise "I shall be your God and you shall be my people" finds its first ever (although not its last) fulfillment in the person of this man whose life is precisely a reflection of and a reciprocal offering back of God's own holy love from within the sphere

of the human, the side of sin. Hence his very life is from the first to the
last moment both a transforming and a reconciling segment of human history. Transforming because in it he does from within the conditions of
our fallen state what we can and do not do ourselves, healing our nature
through a victorious struggle from its hitherto seemingly incurable corruption. Reconciling because his human life is in its entirety, and not just
in the death which is its necessary climax, a bringing together of God and
humanity, a coexistence in which God looks on his creature and is well
pleased, and the creature relies from moment to moment on the gracious
and loving sustaining and guidance of his Father in heaven. This could
by definition be true of no other human person. It is the peculiarities of
Jesus' personal circumstance, his unique identity as the personal presence
of God in human form, the dynamics and constitution of his person as
these are falteringly expressed even in the neat formulae of the fourth and
fifth centuries, that not only enables but actually obliges us to think of
things in this way. Jesus is the fulfillment of the covenant from both sides
in all that he is and does. What he does is vital to his identity, and cannot be abstracted from who he is, of which it is an unceasing expression.
He is the point in human history at which God and humankind are truly
reconciled, where God looks for and finds the perfect response to his own
nature as holy love. This is the deeper meaning of Paul's statement that
"God was in Christ reconciling the world to himself." The reconciliation is
actually *in Christ*; it is not some state of affairs external to Christ himself,
brought about by things which he does and which he is equipped to do by
virtue of his being on one hand fully God and on the other fully human,
these being, as it were, qualifications or prerequisites for the task or office
of which he has to acquit himself. All God's promises are yea and amen in
him, and nowhere else. He is the site, the locus, the reality of reconciliation between God and humanity. He is not only "God with us" but also,
and in the same incarnate integration of divine and human existence, "us
with God," granting us access to his Father not just by what he does, but
in his company, together with him, in his name, in union with him, or,
in Paul's terse phrase, simply "in him." Mediation, then, is not just something which he does (although of course it entails him in doing much) but
something which, in the specificities of his personal identity, he embodies
in himself.

There is a further vital dimension to the New Testament's handling of
the themes of covenant and mediation which we must reckon with before
moving on. Not only are these Old Testament categories seen as taken up

into and fulfilled in the incarnate appearance of God as man, they are also consistently subordinated to another set of categories deemed to merit a more ultimate controlling influence on our understanding of God and salvation. The life of Jesus in the anointing and empowering of the Spirit is not finally to be understood in terms of the category Christ but rather that of Son. Jesus' relationship to his Father in heaven, his reception of and response to the Spirit's anointing are held to be revelatory of a pattern of relationships which, while they are earthed here in a human life, nonetheless precede that life in the eternal being of Israel's God. The Son of God becomes a human Son in order that the Spirit of sonship might also in due course be poured out on others, and they come to share in that which he eternally is and enjoys in his fellowship with the Father. This is the insight which, as we have seen in earlier chapters, various among the Greek fathers expressed in terms of the so-called wondrous exchange formula: He became what we are in order that we might come to share in what he is. Here the logic of Trinity, incarnation, and salvation are woven inextricably together. The deepest truth which Jesus reveals to us about God by making his own secret identity known to us enfolds within it the truth about God's redemptive intent for us. It is knowledge which, as we receive it, has self-involving force.

So, however we are to continue to make sense of the language of covenant and its attendant categories, it must be in terms of this ultimate truth about God and salvation that we do so, and not independently. Perhaps this is why the christological category of mediator is so rarely used in the New Testament, having been effectively eclipsed or subsumed by what were recognized to be more basic truths about God's own character and his relationship with his people. Certainly, it is notable that the Epistle to the Hebrews, in which the category is arguably most obviously present, opens with a lengthy reflection on the sonship of Christ, thereby locating what it has to say about his priestly and royal ministry and fulfillment of the covenant within an explicitly filial framework. The point is not, therefore, that the imagery of the covenant may now be set aside but rather that the reality to which it refers us in Christ and in ourselves is perceived to be more akin to a personal and filial, rather than a legal, political, or commercial, relationship. The symbol of sonship must be granted theological priority over those of covenant and mediation. Eichrodt notes how already in Israel's faith as expressed in the Old Testament the image of God as Lord of the covenant certainly does not enjoy exclusive attention. It is never isolated from a wider network of images which serve to qualify and modify it: father, husband, redeemer, shepherd, and so on. "Hence," he writes, "Israel is made aware from the beginning that Yahweh is never the hard 'creditor,' relentlessly exacting the conditions of his covenant, but that his claim to honour rests on the fact that he owns the title *'erek 'appayim*" (the compassionate and gracious one).[12] With the final and full revelation of God as Father, Son and Holy Spirit in the person of Jesus, the qualification and modification becomes even more necessary and more marked. For now it is believed that to call God Father, together with his Son and in the empowering of the Spirit of sonship, is to utter that which is more fundamental and appropriate than to think of him as Lord of the covenant.

§4. Christology, Mediation, and Covenant Theology

In this final section of the chapter I want to consider how the sort of theology which unfolded in the Westminster documents relates to all this. I don't want to fall into the alluring trap of making sweeping statements about covenant theology which have subsequently to die the humiliating public death of a thousand qualifications. I do, though, want to locate Westminster within a wider theological pattern, and to indicate how within that pattern there are different possible emphases and insights, some of which concur very well with the model of mediation which I have ventured, and others which have the practical effect of subverting it entirely. So, I shall allude in what follows both to Westminster itself, and to other examples of the covenant tradition.

First, I do think it is entirely fair to suggest that the Confession inverts the order of priority between filial and covenantal imagery in its understanding of Christ's mediation. It is, of course, entirely orthodox in its subscription to the doctrine of hypostatic union, and takes pains to relate the various elements in that doctrine to an understanding of Christ's office as Mediator. But Westminster (unlike the First Helvetic Confession, the Heidelberg Catechism, Calvin's French Confession of 1559, the Scots Confession of 1560, the Thirty-nine Articles of 1563, and other comparable Reformed documents) locates the incarnation within a semantic context created by a discussion of God, election, and the divine-human relationship for which its influence cannot be deemed decisive.[13] It is not the first Reformed confessional text to do so,[14] but it is distinctive in its thoroughgoing deployment of the metaphor of covenant for the purpose. In his (in some respects generalized and unduly jaundiced) account of covenant theology, Perry Miller notes how among its exponents the theme of covenant acquired the status of the key for understanding the entire history of God's dealings with humankind, "a scheme including both God and man within a single frame, a point at which, without doing violence to their respective natures, both could meet and converse."[15] The opening phrases of chapter 7 of the Confession locate it fairly and squarely within such a view: "The distance between God and the creature is so great, that although reasonable creatures do owe obedience unto Him as their Creator, yet they could never have any fruition of Him as their blessedness and reward, but by some voluntary condescension on God's part, which He hath been pleased to express by way of covenant." It then goes on to unfold the distinction between and logic of the so-called covenants of works and grace respectively. But surely it is not the framework of *covenant* to which Christian theology is obliged to turn in seeking a point at which, without doing violence to their respective natures, and by virtue of divine condescension, God and humanity meet, but the event of the incarnation? Of course it is not necessary to drive a sharp wedge between the two, but the hermeneutical relation between them is vital, as I have already argued here. God and humanity have entered into a union which goes far beyond that afforded by the logic of covenant, and we must understand the latter in the light of it, and not vice versa. I say more about the theological consequences of the inversion of this relationship later, but next I want to inquire as to what factors may be supposed to have made the covenant concept particularly attractive to the Westminster Assembly as a basic framework for understanding and articulating divine-human relations.

The political context in which the Confession was drafted can hardly be deemed irrelevant. Covenant theology predates the meeting of the Assembly by more than a century, of course,[16] but the specific circumstances which led to the English Parliament convening an Assembly at Westminster at all lent to this particular biblical metaphor a sharper than average bite. In his book *The Covenants of Scotland*, John Lumsden traces no less than thirty-one covenants in the political life of the nation between the Dun Covenant of 1536 and the Children's Covenant of 1683.[17] The extent to which the emergence of covenant as a key theme in the Reformed tradition influenced the political use of the concept in Scottish life, and to which that use itself reciprocally furnished a hermeneutic which affected Scottish theology, is a fascinating topic careful consideration of which lies far beyond the scope of this chapter.[18] That the two uses of the term were utterly intertwined, just as political and religious developments were themselves tangled up on both sides of the border, is beyond serious doubt. That the nature of contemporary political covenants had a shaping impact on the substance of the use of the idea in Puritan theology seems to me to be equally clear, and to be part, at least, of the reason for the willingness among covenant theologians (including those at Westminster) to embrace a model of the relationship between God and the elect in which it was openly and unashamedly admitted that there were "conditions" to be met on both sides. Political agreements were inevitably of just such a sort, and not least the Solemn League and Covenant of 1643, which was in large measure responsible for the Assembly being convened at all.

The shaping impact of political thinking might also be traced in another facet of the covenant scheme, namely its practical effect on the doctrine of God. The Confession, as has often been noted, resounds with a deep sense of God's sovereign majesty, a sovereignty manifest, as the early chapters remind us, in his complete self-sufficiency, his deserving and demanding of utter obedience from his creatures, his disposing of all that happens in his world, his freely choosing to shower love and grace on some regardless of their lack of worth and to condemn others, and so on. Since the medieval period and the emergence of nominalism such a stress in Christian theology was rendered even more potent by a voluntarist doctrine which construed God as absolute will, unconstrained even by his own nature, and hence inherently unpredictable. In his discussion of the covenant theme in Old Testament theology, Eichrodt notes how one of its key functions is to banish the specter of arbitrariness and caprice which haunted pagan religion, thereby creating in Israel's piety an atomosphere of trust and security.[19] With Yahweh she knew just where she stood, both in terms of his promise and the demands which it made on her. We should not forget that the political struggles of the English Civil War were largely a reaction against the longstanding model of absolute monarchy to which Charles I aspired, and from which the subscribers to the Solemn League and Covenant were determined to keep him. Given the persistent stress in Reformed theology on God's absolute sovereignty and freedom, and given the insecurity and unease which reflection on the idea of divine caprice tends naturally to engender, it may well be supposed to have been unsurprising for the theologians at Westminster to turn to a metaphor which effectively transformed God from an absolute to a constitutional monarch in a single stroke, at least so far as the elect were concerned. In himself God is and remains of course utterly free, and under no obligation to do anything for anyone. But he has, in the covenant of grace, placed himself under constraints and entered into a relationship in which, so long as the conditions are kept from the human side, believers may be entirely confident of his beneficence toward them. Thus the theme of covenant in a peculiar way renders God, as well as the believer, accountable for his actions while yet managing to preserve the doctrine of his absolute freedom in the background. Hence Tyndale: "If we meek ourselves to God, to keep all his laws, after the example of Christ, then God hath bound himself unto us, to keep and make good all the mercies promised in Christ through all the Scripture."[20] This sort of thinking undoubtedly could and did lead some more enthusiastic articulations of the scheme into apparent un-Reformed excess. "You may sue [God] of his own bond written and sealed," one such informs us, "and he cannot deny it."[21] But we must never overlook the doctrine of providence and secondary causality, which, in the best exponents of the covenant scheme, immediately served to rob what otherwise sounded like contractual language of its offense. It is not "spiritual commercialism"[22] precisely for the reason that, if the elect bear the fruit of "repentance, faith and the diligent use of the outward means whereby Christ communicates to us the benefits of his mediation," which the answer to Q. 153 of the Larger Catechism refers to us as "requirements" of the covenant, this is a matter of that disposing of their wills by grace of which the Confession speaks in its opening sections.

This leads us to a further theological circumstance which very likely commended the covenant scheme to the Assembly's theologians, namely the need to steer a careful course between the twin errors of Arminianism and antinomianism, both of which were in plentiful evidence in England at the time.[23] What was required, therefore, was "explicit grounds on which to plead the necessity of 'works,' but to discover them without sacrificing the absolute freedom of God to choose and reject regardless of man's achievements."[24] This covenant theology managed to do by furnishing explicit grounds both for moral obligation and individual assurance. The elect could not presume upon God's grace precisely because the terms of the covenant of grace could not be breached. It was not supposed that any could actually keep the moral law in this life, but that believers would strive to do so and would manifest due faith and repentance was a necessary corollary of their being in covenant with God at all.[25] On the other hand, as we have already seen, these aspects of a believer's life are the product not of his own effort (and hence meritorious) but of God's grace at work in his life. God himself, in other words, supplies that which he demands and underwrites the covenant which he has made.

Samuel Rutherford's treatise *Christ Dying and Drawing Sinners to Himself*,[26] which issues from the period of his involvement in the Assembly's debates, is a classic example of this theology. So, for example, he makes the classic charge against the antinomianism of John Saltmarsh and others that it confuses justification (that which God does for us in Christ) with sanctification (that which God does in us). In this context he rejects Saltmarsh's claim that Christ repents, obeys the law, or is sanctified for us, except in the uncontentious sense that "Christ by his grace worketh *in us* repentance, and new obedience, and mortification, and the change of the whole man."[27] Rutherford's fear is that talk of Christ's obeying in our stead will lead straight to the conclusion that we need therefore not obey for ourselves. Hence the need for sanctification in the believer is effectively displaced. In this case, he notes, "my walking in holiness cannot be rewarded with life eternal, nor have any influence as a way, or means leading to the kingdom," whereas, in fact, while God himself grants the power of obedience, he has ordained such obedience needful to attaining this "reward." Saltmarsh's claim has been that the source of assurance for the believer is to look to Christ's obedience, penitence, holiness, and so on, which God has wrought in the flesh of Jesus. This need not entail a rejection of a subsequent working of these same qualities in the believer himself. It may simply be an insistence on the complete self-substitution of the Son of God for us in our relationship with God, veiling our weakness and inadequacy at every point with his perfect new humanity. But Rutherford rejects the suggestion, insisting that the source of Christian assurance is not in Christ's obedience, precisely because that is *in Christ* and not *in us*, and thus can furnish no evidence of *our* interest in it.[28] The gospel itself, he tells us later in the same volume, reveals only the terms on which we may be saved; it is the efficacy of the gospel in particular lives that tells us whether or not we actually are.[29] In response to Arminianism, on the other hand, Rutherford appeals simply and consistently to the doctrine of the irresistable grace by which God draws us to himself and establishes in us genuine newness of life. Hence there are "Evangelicke conditions," and among these "Faith is the condition of the Covenant of Grace, and the only condition of Justification, and of the title, right, and claim that the Elect have, through Christ to life eternal. Holy walking, as a witness of faith, is the way to possession of the kingdom."[30]

In all this, then, what Rutherford does in effect is to insist that, while God's covenantal relationship with humans is conditional, it is nonetheless God himself who is responsible for the fulfillment of those conditions in us. In other words, contrary to the theology of mediation which I espouse in section 3 of this chapter, it is we rather than Christ in whom the covenant is finally fulfilled by God's Spirit. The doctrine of second-ary causality and a sophisticated compatibilism enabled the theology to both have its theological cake and eat it in this respect. But, as the tone of covenant theology's statements repeatedly confirms, while the *theoretical* difference between it and Arminianism may well be enormous, in terms of *practical* piety it might make little difference. Philosophical determinism is ever beset by the problem that it is impossible to live as if it were true, and this is just as much the case in the matter of faith, repentance, and walking in holiness as elsewhere. The sting in the tail, therefore, is that, despite the best intentions of the model and the protests of some of its adherents,[31] believers are finally urged to look to (God's working in) the quality of their own faith, repentance, and holiness in order to confirm the truth of their particular participation in the covenant. That what many found when they did so failed in any way to furnish such assurance is hardly surprising.

Antinomianism arises when Christ's self-sanctification for our sakes is deemed to be entirely substitutionary. If it is not thought of in this way, however, and if there is a due insistence that what God has done *for us* through the Spirit in the humanity of the Son he subsequently begins to do *in us* by that same Spirit—if, in other words, the intrinsic and organic connection between substitution and participation is affirmed, then antinomianism is rendered impossible. *Neonomianism*—a new legalism—on the other hand, is what arises theologically when substitution and participation are separated, so that what God has done for us in the "work" of the Son is understood to be logically and ontologically separable from (rather than the organic root of) what God subsequently does in us by the workings of the Spirit. No self-respecting covenant theologian would make such a claim, least of all Rutherford, for whom the theme of the union of the believer with Christ was paramount. Nonetheless, my closing suggestion is that covenant theology tends naturally and inevitably, by virtue of some of the things it *does* affirm, in precisely this direction.

Specifically, its subordination of the logic of incarnation to that of covenant results in an understanding of Christ's mediation in terms of an office through the acquittal of which he certainly *establishes* the covenant of grace (purchasing "benefits" for the elect both by his passive and his active obedience) but does not actually *fulfill* it from the human side in his own person. This covenant is *fulfilled* by each particular person who is drawn into it by God's irresistible call and the disposal of their will through the Spirit. The covenant is certainly fulfilled by God from first to last, yet his promises are, we might say, *yea* in Christ, but only actually *amen* in us via the Spirit's individual disposing. But this, for reasons indicated, seems to be incapable in the final analysis of furnishing adequate grounds for assurance, a disposition which, while it may not be what Christians may expect to experience at every moment, was nonetheless what Martin Luther was seeking and found when, wrestling with the text of Paul's Epistle to the Romans, he accidentally sparked off the Reformation. To that extent, for any theology worthy of the epithet "Reformed," it must surely be deemed proper rather than alien to Christian faith as such.

If, on the other hand, we think of the covenant relation between God and humans as fulfilled once and for all and completely in the person of Jesus in a total self-substitution of his perfect new humanity for ours, and if we insist, at the same time, that our union with him (established thereby) can only result in a work of his Spirit in us which, while it is not the fulfillment of the covenant, is nonetheless a vital consequence of our identification with him in his fulfillment of it for us, then assurance and a grounds for Christian obedience can and must be held properly together. For then it is precisely the fact that Jesus has done everything for us which on one hand obliges us to respond in faith, repentance, and obedience and on the other sets us free to do so in a manner unhindered by fear and despair. Fear and despair, we should note, will otherwise arise naturally enough from the sense of personal inadequacy and failure which those who view their humanity in the light of Christ's own are bound to have, leading to the all too familiar suspicion that we may not have believed hard enough, repented with sufficient earnestness, or obeyed thoroughly enough to fulfill the conditions of the covenant. It is this familiar experience that fuels a certain sort of attitude to the regular practice of "confession" in sacramental traditions, and the weekly "altar call" still evident in some evangelical congregations at which many if not most of those responding and "going forward" will typically have been Christians for many years, nonetheless feeling the need to "repent" again and more satisfactorily. There is, let it be said at once, nothing wrong as such either with regular confession of our sins (whether directly to God in personal prayer or, for Catholic believers, through the sacrament of reconciliation) or with initiatives of renewed repentance, except when they are motivated by a sense of some legal condition needing to be met in order to satisfy God and render him gracious, rather than the gratitude and devotion consequent on discovering that God is *already* gracious, already loves us more than we can imagine, and longs for nothing more than our return to him. And if Christ has fulfilled the covenant in our place, if he *is* the fulfillment of the covenant from God's side and, as our brother, from ours, then there can be no further talk of conditions needing to be met; there can only be the joy of discovering that, included in him, all that is his is already ours to share, and the excited expectation of what that may and must mean for us as his new life is communicated to us by the Spirit.

Of course, things are not quite so neatly resolved as this. One might reasonably ask, for example, whether there is any consistency in looking only to Christ and his reconciling of our humanity to God in himself if, according to the doctrine of double predestination and a covenant made only with the elect, what is to be done in Christ is in no sense undertaken *for all*, and might not, therefore, finally prove to have been for *us* at all? Did Rutherford not have a point, therefore, when he insisted that assurance can only be had, if it can be had, by seeking evidence of our sharing in Christ *in ourselves*? Calvin himself, we have seen, embraces the inconsistency rather than resolving it,[32] and refuses the sort of resolution that Rutherford chooses. Within the covenant tradition itself Fisher handles it by indicating that the slightest desire for assurance, sorrow for sin, or even asking the question about how to get a gracious God shows that we are indeed chosen in Christ and that "his fulfilling of [the] covenant is imputed" to us.[33] Thus he both denies what Rutherford insists (that before someone may turn to Christ he or she must first have "been with child of hell" in a law-induced self-despair and repentance)[34] and insists on what Rutherford, for fear of antinomianism, explicitly denies—that the viler the sinner the more he or she should be urged to come to Christ.[35] For it was precisely the love of vile sinners that drove God himself in Christ to take on himself our flesh, purging and purifying from the vilest of our sins and stains, offering it to his Father, and handing it back to us as a gift for us to enjoy and participate actively in. It is in apprehension and grateful receipt of the humanity of Christ as "gift" (and grace) in this sense that true faith and repentance consist, and they are the product of gladness rather than despair. For then and then alone, obedience will be genuine, being motivated by love and gratitude for the one who has given his all for us and in our place at every point, rather than by guilt or fear or an essentially selfish religious concern to secure "eternity" by a lonely struggling with our own sin, seeking (but almost certainly failing) to prove to ourselves that we can identify ourselves in the minor premise of Reformed theology's "practical syllogism,"[36] showing "sufficient fruits and evidences of a true and lively faith," as Westminster has it, and thereby of our eternal election. The tension remains, though, and while not all theological tensions are ones capable or desirous of resolution, the model of mediation that I have explored in this chapter, grounded as it is in the ontology of the person of Christ (and interpreting the language of "covenant" in terms of it rather than vice versa), lays down some fundamental challenges to any attempt to limit its scope, and so problematizes the Reformed premises around which covenant theology in the tradition of Westminster is structured.

8

Sanctification

§1. Jesus' Death and the Hallowing of God's Name

Treatments of "sanctification" in Western theology do not typically focus on the cross. This, though, is to the detriment both of our understanding of what occurs on the cross and our theology of sanctification (which otherwise far too easily and too quickly loses touch with the heart of what occurs there). One significant exception to such doctrinal balkanizing is the Scots congregationalist theologian P. T. Forsyth (1848–1921), with whose thought we are chiefly concerned in this chapter. I seriously doubt whether Forsyth had more to say on any topic, or returned more frequently to any facet of Christian faith, than the cross. There can hardly be a book or an article within his extensive corpus in which some reference or allusion to it is not made, and in most it dominates page after page, whether the ostensible theme be the doctrine of God, the church, ethics, the sacraments, society, or whatever. All is concluded *sub specie crucis*. Thus a chapter on Forsyth's theology of the cross opens itself to the temptation of becoming a chapter on his theology as a whole, a temptation I resist. Our focus is on Forsyth's theology of atonement in particular, at the core of which lies the conviction that the most apt rubric for the foot of the cross and the wider shape of human life alike is the petition Jesus taught his disciples to pray: "Father . . . Hallowed be Thy Name."

Even this more narrowly defined field, however, presents a significant challenge to the assiduous scholar. For while the larger body of Forsyth's theology lives and breathes only as it is supplied with oxygen by the capillaries which lead ultimately to and from its heart in the crucified Jesus, it is, nonetheless, virtually impossible to isolate any comprehensive or coherent system from the living body of his thought even about this most central of concerns. The occasional and ex tempore nature of many of his works and his frequently passionate and rhetorical style defy such cold and calculating analysis. He himself refused the attempt to map the complex logical connections which lay tacit in his theological unconscious, thereby presenting any would-be commentator with the challenge of attempting to do so for him. Again, I resist this temptation, partly because it has been attempted by others, and partly because even this task would occupy more time than the confines of a single chapter can reasonably afford.

An alternative approach might have been to seek to trace the development of Forsyth's thinking about the cross through the forty years or so of his publishing career. But if my reading in the field has convinced me of anything it is that, while there is certainly some development to be charted, in broad terms his understanding changed relatively little from the mid-1880s until the time of his death in 1921. There is change of emphasis and expression to be discerned, but little, I think, of theological substance. There was, of course, that one determinative change of direction which saw him part company with the Ritschlian theological education he had received in Göttingen and which during his early parish ministry shaped his preaching decisively. The one significant piece dating from this period of his life, a sermon preached in his first charge in Shipley, Bradford, in 1877, titled "Mercy the True and Only Justice," reads like a manifesto for the very theological liberalism which he was to attack so fiercely in later years, and is hardly recognizable as the work of the same man. By the time of the appearance of *The Old Faith and the New*, in 1891, the theological Rubicon had clearly been crossed, and Forsyth was already engaged in that programmatic recanting of the Liberal Protestant gospel which was to occupy him for the rest of his life. Somewhere, in the decade which separates these two pieces of writing, Forsyth had undergone something resembling a conversion experience, a profound discovery of the moral reality of his circumstances under God, a transition, as he himself would have it, "from a Christian to a believer, from a lover of love to an object of Grace."[1] It was a transition which was to color all that followed and to drive it with an existential passion.

The way from love to grace lay across a deep chasm of natural human resentment and theological repentance, a chasm bridged only at one point, across which Forsyth himself had stumbled, and to which he henceforth sought to lead his readers and fellow travelers—namely the cross of Christ and all that it signified. Across the ravine lay a "strange new world" in which this same cross dominated every horizon, and which Forsyth spent the rest of his life seeking to map and to describe for the benefit of those who had not yet been there for themselves.

In this chapter, then, I touch briefly on some of the more significant landmarks in Forsyth's account. I look first at the ultimate interpretive key for making sense of the cross—the moral order; second, at the necessity for an atonement arising out of this context; and third, at the place of the death of Jesus within this atonement, and just what this reveals to us about the nature of the atonement itself.

§2. The Ethical as the Ontological

Perhaps the most striking facet of the universe as viewed through the eyes of an "object of grace" is its irreducibly moral structure. There is, according to Forsyth, a "moral order" which is just as surely woven into the fabric of God's creation as that other "order" which is investigated by the natural sciences. Indeed, in terms of the status of our knowledge, the moral must be said to be more ultimate and more reliable than either the physical or the intellectual.[2] With more than a century and a half of the back and forth of the philosophical quest for epistemic certainty in his sights, Forsyth insists that it is in the practical reason alone, and not the pure, that real authority is to be had,[3] and that the moral order, unlike the physical, lays hold of us through the organ of conscience in a direct manner, rather than being at best an inference (however trustworthy) from data rendered by our sensory apparatus.[4] As fundamentally moral beings we find ourselves engaged more naturally and immediately with this stratum of reality than with the bodily world of our spatial and temporal intercourse. Forsyth does not develop this latent dualism but he is quite adamant that, whether we recognize it or not, ultimate reality is moral[5] and the questions which really matter concerning human life are moral questions. "The last reality," he writes, "is a moral reality . . . it has to do with a moral situation."[6] "The last reality, and that with which every man has willy-nilly to do, is not a reality of thought, but of life and conscience, and of judgment. We are in the world to act and to take the consequences."[7] "That is the final human question—how to face the eternal moral power. What is it making of us? What is He doing with us? What is He going to do? That is the issue of all issues."[8]

This conviction that as human beings we inhabit a moral, as well as a physical, universe and not a multiverse, that a universal and objective moral structure is given to our experience just as surely as the "laws" of gravitation and thermodynamics, that our actions and their consequences are plottable within a moral and not just a physical framework of cause and effect, is a function of Forsyth's supreme emphasis on the holiness of God, a holiness which, as Forsyth protests in the face of certain contemporary uses of the term, consists not in some aesthetic quality, the sublime and mysterious remoteness of a snowy alpine peak,[9] but in absolute moral authority[10] and a passionate and unswerving opposition to sin and evil in all its forms. It is holiness, and not love (at least, love only in the distinct form of *holy* love) which is most fundamental to God's nature. That this same God should invest his creation with so direct a reflection of his own being, then, ought not to surprise us unduly. To say "ultimate reality is moral" is in effect to say God is holy love.

It is interesting to note that, while the theme of the *imago Dei* finds little explicit treatment or development in Forsyth's theology (a fact which reflects his relative neglect of the doctrine of creation as a whole), it is here if anywhere that the idea enters in, as he refers repeatedly to conscience not just as that in humans which keys them directly into the moral order and in and through which God addresses them, but as something which both share in common. "What is the atonement," he asks, "but the 'satisfaction' of the conscience—God's and man's—the adjustment, the pacification, of conscience, and especially God's?"[11] Reconciliation is not, as the Ritschlians would have it, a matter of two hearts making up, or of an adjustment in which humans open themselves and their lives to God, but a matter of two consciences making good.[12] Our conscience would demand a satisfaction for our sin, says Forsyth, even if God did not,[13] a fact of our moral psychology "the root of [which] is really in God's, who so made man in his image that the transgressor's way is hard."[14] Conscience, Forsyth observes elsewhere, may be thought of as the moral nature of God in the constitution of human beings.[15]

This perception of the moral as the real, the ethical as the ontological, finds further expression in Forsyth's description, contra Hegel, of the ultimate cosmic and eschatological scheme of things not as the self-realization of *Geist* but of the Holy in history. "The great object of things is not the self-expression of the Eternal in time," he writes, "but His self-effectuation as holy in a Kingdom."[16] "Holiness is the eternal moral power which must do, and do, till it sees itself everywhere."[17] In biblical terms this is articulated in the command of the Lord to Israel, "be holy, for I am holy" (Lev 11:45), a command , Forsyth insists, expresses a concern proper to the very nature of God, and without the satisfactory resolution of which he cannot rest. Thus we might say that the realization of effectuation of the kingdom is that alone which can "satisfy" God. Certainly, as we shall see, the sense in which Forsyth applies the term "satisfaction" to the atonement is determined by this specific framework of understanding. In an important sense, as we shall also see, this self-realization, for Forsyth as for Hegel, ultimately entails self finding itself in the other: although in this case it is not in the realization of any latent principle within the other, but of God's self becoming the other in the kenotic act of incarnation, and "realizing" his own holiness *in* the other through atoning action.[18] This could be achieved, Forsyth notes, "only by bringing to practical effect an answering and trusting holiness on a world scale amid the extremest conditions created by human sin."[19] If one wanted a concise statement of Forsyth's understanding of just what was achieved in the atonement one would have to search long and hard to find a better formulation than this.

God's nature as the Holy, then, of which the moral structuring of reality and the moral constitution of human beings as those who exist under its jurisdiction are but created reflections, or expressions, is the supreme concern which underlies and drives all existence toward its goal, God's and ours. It is that with which God himself is, and must inevitably be, chiefly concerned,[20] and it is the question which is set uncomfortably over against each of us as we live our lives: just how do we stand here? What will be our fate or our destiny? All in all, the text inscribed on the portals of God's universe (and the one which Forsyth never tires of citing) is "Hallowed be Thy name."[21]

When all this is borne in mind it is hardly surprising to find Forsyth suggesting over and over again that the liberalism of his theological youth, with the rather naive, sentimental, and optimistic account of the nature of the moral relationship between God and humanity which it proffered, must be abandoned as a dangerous substitute for Christianity of the apostolic and evangelical sort. To get it wrong *here* was inevitably to get it wrong throughout. And get it wrong Forsyth believed they had: not only the theologians, but the whole ethos of the age was, he suggested, one caught up in a crisis of moral direction and authority which made the intellectual despair of the eighteenth and nineteenth centuries seem trivial by comparison. Having all but lost any sense of God's holiness, the age had lost sight of its moral bearings, and lost sight, above all, of the reality of the human situation as one of guilt and liability to judgment and wrath, terms which Forsyth never shies away from, although the meaning with which he invests them is somewhat sanitized, or at least refined, by comparison with their use in the Protestant orthodoxy of earlier centuries.

To some extent, Forsyth argues, what his generation faced was the problem of Christianity having to be rescued from its own moral success.[22] After more than a millennium of the saturation of society by Christian moral precepts and attitudes, "man's devilry" had become well disguised, overlaid by a thin but effective veneer of moral respectability and social norms. Too many generations had been "born good,"[23] born and baptized into the church with its moral code and expectations. The boundary between the redeemed and the unredeemed, grace and nature, had become difficult to discern. Compounded by a theology which viewed God in essentially aesthetic rather than moral terms and presented Christianity as "just human nature at its best" and the kingdom of God as "just our natural spirituality and altruism developed,"[24] the net result was a complete and utter loss of perspective on the reality of the human situation. "So much of our religious teaching betrays no sign that the speaker has descended into hell, been near the everlasting burnings, or been plucked from the awful pit. He has risen with Christ . . . but it is out of a shallow grave, with no deepness of earth, with no huge millstone to roll away."[25] Again, "it was not Galahad or Arthur that drew Christ from heaven. It was a Lancelot race. It was a tragic issue of man's passion that called out the glory of Christ. It is a most tragic world, this, for those who see to the bottom of it and leave us their witness to its confusion, as Shakespeare did in *Hamlet, Lear* and even *The Tempest*."[26] Needless to say, Forsyth does not consider the tragedians of the literary world to have had the final say. The gospel, he insists, is precisely the story of the *transformation* of the human tragedy into God's great *commedia*.[27] But the actual moral situation of the race, considered apart from Christ, is one of tragic dimensions. In order to see things as they really are we must recapture a due sense of God's holiness, or lay hold of the moral order with its absolute demands, and consider ourselves in its light. The starting point for such a reevaluation must be the cross of Christ, because "we only learn the Christian measure of our sin when we see what the sin of our sinful race means for Christ."[28]

There can be little doubt that in all this we hear Forsyth speaking powerfully from the depths of his own personal experience. Yet he is not merely insisting that all Christian experience should be like his. He fervently believes the realization of guilt and its accompanying factors to be proper to the experience of salvation,[29] and believes that in objective terms all humans are united at this one point at least—that all have breached that moral order which must not be breached,[30] have challenged the very holiness of God, and thereby stand liable to judgment. "Love in the face of sin," he writes, "can only assert itself as holy love; but that means as stung and wounded love. But assert itself it must . . . by really judging and subjugating once for all the unholy thing everywhere, killing it in its eye, and replacing Satan's Kingdom by the Kingdom of God."[31] To fail to face up to the reality of this situation, to pretend that it is otherwise than this with God and human beings, is to fail to take seriously enough either sin or (therefore) grace, and to fail to do justice to the reality of moral personality in either God or humanity.[32]

Two further elements in Forsyth's thinking about the place of the moral are worthy of brief mention before we turn our attention to the atonement.

First, while he sets human existence clearly within the framework of a universal and objective moral order, and while he speaks of conscience as that aspect of our nature which is keyed directly into this order,[33] as our bodies key us, *mutatis mutandis*, into the physical order, Forsyth entertains no optimism about the ability of humans by virtue of natural capacities to grasp what is the good in any given context, let alone to do it. In fact there is a manifest tension in his thinking here. On one hand he can speak of conscience as speaking to us of the moral order,[34] as a moral power within us yet in a sense other than us,[35] as the Word of God within us,[36] yet on the other he immediately qualifies this so as to undermine any of the moral optimism which so characterized the liberal accounts in the wake of Kant (most of which were far more optimistic, it must be said, than Kant himself). "We must take man in his actual historic situation," Forsyth writes, "and if we do this the so-called natural conscience does not exist. It is an abstraction; and what exists is the historic product, the sinful conscience."[37] Here we hear a theme which is sustained throughout his theology. The relationship between the natural and the redeemed, between nature and grace, is one not of continuity and evolution but of radical discontinuity and revolution. Redemption comes, when it comes, to each of us as a crisis in which we discover ourselves to be called into question. The "natural" response to the gospel message, therefore, is not one of welcome but of rejection:[38] the drawing near of the holy in human form to the sinful results in his crucifixion. And in a sense it is ever thus.[39] We are not merely wayward or naughty children but prodigals. We need not to be improved or developed but put to death and recreated.[40] In Forsyth's own inimitable rhetoric, God's reconciling revelation "does not come to grout the gaps in nature, not simply to bless nature, but to change it, to make a new earth from a new foundation in a new heaven."[41]

So much so is this the case that, Forsyth insists, we are not even capable of perceiving the need for the atoning work of Christ, let alone of responding appropriately to it, apart from the power of that work itself acting on us. "The death of Christ," he writes, "had to redeem us into power of feeling its own worth. Christ had to save us from what we were too far gone to feel."[42] "Before the revealing act is complete we must by the act be also put in a position to receive it and appreciate it. The word must not return void, else it is but a sound. The circle must be closed for the spark."[43] The message of the cross, we might say, creates its own point of contact.

Second, Forsyth speaks frequently of the moral order in such a way as to differentiate it from the moral condition of humankind as that is evident at the empirical level. He refers to "the real world unseen,"[44] a mystical or hidden realm in which the kingdom is already a reality,[45] the holy has already achieved self-realization through the ministry of Christ. "It is," Forsyth writes, "a solemn and fortifying thought that interior to all space, time, and history there is a world where God's name is perfectly hallowed, His will fully done, and His Kingdom already come."[46] This hidden realm is the world of the "real," as opposed to the world of the "actual,"[47] and the purpose of God is that what has been achieved in reality should now be "followed up and secured in actuality." It is tempting to lose patience with such talk, asking irritably where precisely this other world is to be found, and supposing it to be some quaint rhetorical way of asserting something which is better couched in eschatological terms. But, to return to our starting point, we must recall that for Forsyth the moral order is the most ultimate reality, being, as it were, the extension of God's moral personality into the creaturely realm. Hence what he seems to be insisting here, and it is a view which his doctrine of atonement goes on to develop, is that in Christ something happens in the historical sphere which yet has meaning and value discernible only when we cast our gaze beyond that sphere; that Jesus' saving activity, rooted as it is in history, was not confined to the theater of the human story, but, supremely at the point of the cross, has its deepest meaning only within the telling of God's story.[48] Something happened there which, whatever its impact on humans, and whatever its historical consequences, had

decisive consequences for God himself, "establishing the kingdom" in the
very life of God which is the moral order, bringing the Holy to an effective
self-realization which must subsequently work itself out more widely in the
historical realm. What we have here, then, is something akin to the eschatological tension between the "already" and the "not yet" in the New Testament theology of the kingdom, in which the "already" is understood as
referring to an adjustment made within the very nature or life of God, and
the "not yet" to its eventual actualization in the human sphere.

§3. Atonement

Justice the True and Only Mercy

Let me embark on this section with a lengthy citation:

> Judicial punishment can never be inflicted simply and solely as a means to
> forward a good, other than itself, whether that good be the benefit of the
> criminal, or of civil society; but it must at all times be inflicted on him, for
> no other reason than *because he has acted criminally*. . . . He must first of all
> be found to be *punishable*, before there is even a thought of deriving from
> the punishment any advantage for himself or his fellow-citizens. The penal
> law is a categorical imperative; and woe to that man who crawls through
> the serpentine turnings of the happiness-doctrine, to find out some con-
> sideration, which, by its promise of advantage, should free the criminal
> from his penalty, or even from any degree thereof. . . . If justice perishes,
> then it is no more worth while that man should live upon the earth.

The words are not those of Forsyth but of Kant, cited by F. H. Bradley in his
essay on "the vulgar notion of responsibility."[49] The sentiments, however,
express admirably Forsyth's attitude toward the relationship between
human sin and divine judgment, argued in the face of what had come to
be an unspoken assumption of the theology of his day, namely that punishment, where it existed, was acceptable only if reformative rather than
retributive, and that God was of such a sort as had no final *need* to exact
judgment on sin, but could simply forgive it in a supreme act of voluntaris-
tic mercy. For Forsyth, judgment, and thereby atonement, is an absolute
necessity as the basis for reconciliation between God and humankind.[50]

This insistence rests on Forsyth's assertion of the moral order as
the real. This order, he insists, is objective and universal, and is not to be
tampered with. It is not a bylaw arbitrarily imposed and therefore readily
suspended;[51] it is an eternal and unchangeable ordinance the demands of
which must be met.[52] It inheres in the very nature of reality, is as much a

part of the fabric of the universe as the molecular structure of hydrogen or the force of gravity, and cannot be set aside or indeed broken without the moral structure of reality being placed at risk.[53] Thus, when its laws are broken, restitution must follow; holiness, says Forsyth, must assert itself in the face of evil, must *heal* itself.[54] In more traditional soteriological terms, sin creates a situation of guilt, and judgment must follow, otherwise the structure of our existence, and with it the very meaning of what it is to be human, begins to disintegrate. In Kant's words, "If justice perishes, then it is no more worthwhile that man should live upon the earth." "The dignity of man," Forsyth insists, "would be better assured if he were shattered on the inviolability of this holy law than if for his mere happy existence it were ignored."[55] God, he suggests, is more concerned for our dignity as his creatures than for our happiness[56]—or, again, the chief concern of the Holy is to find his holiness reflected and reciprocated in his creature. God, therefore, could not waive his moral order but must honor it,[57] for the guilt of humanity is no mere matter of private and personal affront but rather of a public justice,[58] a public truth, in which God must safeguard not his own honor or his own feelings, but truth itself. It is in this sense, I think, that Forsyth insists that the cross is the *crisis* of the moral universe:[59] he plays on the underlying Greek meaning, but exploits the ambiguity of the English word to the full. The judgment is a crisis point because without it, apart from it, the very nature of things would be put at risk. The cross, as the point where God's judgment is effective once and for all, is thus the moral Armageddon of the race,[60] the longed-for Day of the Lord, the Last Judgment,[61] which safeguards the moral soul and future of humanity, reorganizing the very structure of the universe at its most real level.[62]

But we must not lose sight in all this of what, for Forsyth, is the most significant fact of all. Since, as we have already seen, the moral order is really nothing other than the holy nature of God viewed in relation to and expressed within the fabric of his creature, to say that the moral law is eternal and inviolable is not to set some third entity over against God and the universe but precisely to say that it is God's holy being which necessitates judgment, that the cross is a crisis for God as well as for his creature, and that in a profound sense it actually safeguards God's own existence, since it deals with that which puts his very being under threat. Forsyth is not afraid of such strong language or such radical conclusions. "The holy law," he writes, "is not the creation of God but His nature, and it cannot be treated as less than inviolable and eternal, it cannot be denied or simply annulled unless He seems false to Himself. If a play on words be permitted in such a connection," he adds, "the self-denial of Christ was there because God could not deny Himself."[63]

Sin is the death of God. Die sin must or God. Its nature is to go on from indifference to absolute hostility and malignantly to the holy; and one must go down. There is no compromise possible between the holy and the sinful when the issue is seen from the height of heaven to the depth of hell, and followed into the uttermost parts of the soul. And that is the nature of the issue as it is set in the cross of Christ. It is the eternal holiness in conflict for its life. In the Son of God the whole being of God is staked on this issue. It is a question of a final salvation both for man and for God.[64]

Such statements make it quite clear that for Forsyth the atonement is not a matter of any arbitrary vindictiveness, or of addressing some sort of abstract legal code. It is a matter of God's satisfying the law of his own being,[65] of meeting conditions internal to his own nature, of preserving his own life in the face of threat to it. Of "doing justice" to himself as well as to his creature. The cross, then, as the focus of his own atoning activity, is in a profound sense crucial for God's own existence.[66] Far from being unnecessary to the redemption of the race, or being merely an incidental visual aid or stimulus to human response, the death of Jesus on the cross was, quite literally, the most necessary thing in the world. For the redemption of the race was at the same time the self-rescue of God from a potentially fatal circumstance.

Nothing could be further from all this than the Ritschlian account which Forsyth himself had advocated with zeal in that early sermon of 1877. From the mid-1880s onward, and with increasing vigor as the years passed, he stood its title on its head and insisted that justice, the self-realization of the Holy in the creature, the establishment of the kingdom, is the true and only mercy, as well as the only possible course of action for a truly holy God.

Atonement, then, we should note, is addressed first and foremost not to the moral or legal status of individual human persons, nor to that abstraction of atonement theologies "the human race," but to the objective and universal moral order within which all humans "live and move and have their being." Only secondarily, and as inhabitants of this same order, do particular persons come into consideration, a fact which Forsyth never tires of emphasizing. Viewed thus, he writes, "the work of Christ was ethical, final and positive. It was something which had a completeness of its own before human experience, and apart from it."[67] Thus Forsyth sets himself apart from what he would have considered the unduly anthropocentric emphasis in much contemporary atonement theology, which insists on asking *first* about the significance of the atonement for, and its impact on, the actual here-and-now existence of particular people. Thus, for example, Paul Fiddes objects to traditional juridical interpretations of the cross because their narrow focus on the historical event of Golgotha, while furnishing an account of salvation in terms of the supposed release of individuals from debt or guilt, cannot adequately explain how we are *actually* released from the power of sin in our lives, an aspect of experience which is therefore generally treated as a second and separate stage in God's saving work, a distinct activity of regeneration, rather than an integral part of atonement itself.[68] Forsyth, on the other hand, because he sees atonement primarily not as a matter of either the status or the experience of individual persons but an adjustment of the cosmic order of things which thereby inevitably has universal implications (just as surely as if the molecular structure of oxygen were to be adjusted tomorrow), presents both aspects under the one rubric of the self-realization of the Holy: first, in the order of reality, and secondarily, as that "reorganization of the universe" works itself out in actuality and history. On the distinction between objective and subjective atonement, let us only mention briefly here that it is a distinction which Forsyth dislikes and prefers not to use. Its terms presuppose an anthropocentric focus, whereas Forsyth's focus is ever on God's purpose of the establishing of his kingdom in human history, and the cross of Jesus as the surety both to humans and to God of the completion of that goal.

§4. The Death of Jesus

The Self-Realization of Holiness in the Sphere of the Human

How precisely, then, does the death of Jesus on the cross fit into this scheme of things and realize, as Forsyth suggests, this divine purpose? First we must return to the language of the cross as the judgment of God upon human sin. In the light of the cross, Forsyth insists, we must confess that we live in a saved world precisely because we live in a judged world.[69] In the cross we see "a work historic yet timeless and final" in which "the absolute and irreversible judgment was passed upon evil. There, too, the judgment of our sins fell once for all on the Holy One and the Just."[70] "God," writes Forsyth, "must either inflict punishment or assume it. And He chose the latter course, as honouring the Law while saving the guilty. He took His own judgment."[71] Again, "God must either punish sin or expiate it, for the sake of His infrangibly holy nature."[72] Thus Forsyth is content to employ all the dark imagery of the forensic metaphor, of Christ's death as a curse, a bearing of the wrath of God, an exhausting of the punishment due to human sin. Yet he makes a decisive distinction which qualifies this language: Christ's death may be described as *penal* because it relates directly to that which we could only experience as punishment, namely the consequence of our sin in its collision with God's holy nature. But God did *not* punish Christ on the cross.[73] It is only a sense of personal guilt which transforms the experience of that which is the consequence of human sin into punishment, and Christ, in experiencing death, knew no such guilt. Thus while "it was the punishment of sin that fell on Him,"[74] he did not experience it as punishment, and his Father cannot be thought to have been angry with him as he bore it.[75]

In fact the precise opposite was true. It was because Christ voluntarily submitted in obedience to the death of the cross, because he placed himself in the way of his own judgment and acknowledged it as righteous in his bearing of it, that this same death has the atoning value which redresses the moral order of the universe. Thus, in a supreme paradox, the attitude of the Father toward his Son on the cross was simultaneously one of enormous grief and pain and one of great joy and delight.[76] What it never is, is an attitude of anger. Forsyth anticipates Moltmann here in a profound passage from *God the Holy Father*: "Love, loss, fatherhood, motherhood, wifehood, widowhood, home, country, and the heroisms that renounce these are . . . embalmed forever in the heart of the infinite Father, once bereaved on His Son, and the Eternal Son, once orphaned of His Father."[77]

This leads us directly to the question of the nature of satisfaction in God. Forsyth employs the Anselmian terminology but interprets it consistently within the framework of his idea of the overall divine purpose as the self-realization of the Holy. Satisfaction, therefore, is no mere matter of an excess of merit obtained through supererogatory obedience, although Anselm's model is in many ways closer to Forsyth than traditional theories of a penal exaction. Rather, satisfaction is almost an aesthetic quality: it is that which God feels when he finds himself in the world through the presence of a reciprocal holiness. It is divine self-fulfillment in relationship with a holy other.[78] It is the satisfaction of a job well done, a sense of well-being, a delight. It might be supposed to be (although Forsyth, to the best of my knowledge, never makes this comparison) that which God felt at the creation when he saw that "it was good." It is certainly that which God expressed at the baptism of his Son in whom he was well pleased. For

Forsyth, this self-same attitude extends all the way to the cross, and, having ruptured its darkness, manifests itself in the resurrection.

This understanding of satisfaction in essentially positive, rather than negative and retrospective, terms finds a parallel in Forsyth's description of judgment. Judgment, he argues, is no mere matter of inflicting a punishment upon sin: viewed in terms of the larger scheme of things, it is "the actual final establishment of righteousness upon the wreck of sin."[79] In referring to the death of Jesus as the decisive judgment of God, therefore, Forsyth intends us to understand this moment as the decisive invasion of the kingdom of this world by the kingdom of God, of the arena of sin and evil by the presence of an unprecedented and radical holiness. "There is only one thing that can satisfy the holiness of God," he writes, "and that is holiness"[80]—holiness offered, of course, from the human side. "The holiness of love's judgment must be freely, lovingly, and practically confessed from the side of the culprit world."[81] The ancient word to Israel, "You shall be holy as I am Holy," must be fulfilled. Only in this is there genuine satisfaction for a holy God. And its achievement, the establishment of the kingdom, of righteousness, from within the sphere of sin, by God himself, is the judgment of God upon sin.

It is for this reason that Forsyth repeatedly insists that the atoning thing in the death of Christ was obedience rather than suffering and death per se.[82] It was the voluntary *submission* to suffering and death, and the acknowledgment of them as the righteous judgment of God upon human sin which was the holy, and therefore the satisfying, thing. Christ's death was no mere death, but rather death as "a decisive moral achievement,"[83] the homologation of God's judgment upon human sin,[84] the adjustment of God's conscience and man's,[85] and thereby the renewal of the image of God in humanity and the establishment of the kingdom of God. God, Forsyth writes, "must satisfy His being's law. And he did so by uniting with that law the concrete reality of history in the life, passion, and death of Jesus Christ."[86]

In other words, the death of Jesus had atoning significance not in and of itself as death, nor even as the punishment due to human sin (note that for Forsyth it is such, although interestingly he does not pursue the question of *why*), but rather in that *knowing* it to be such, Christ willingly submitted to it, and thereby sealed a perfectly holy life which alone could constitute an adequate satisfaction to a holy God. In him, we might simply say, reverting to more biblical language, the covenant promise is fulfilled: You shall be my people and I shall be your God. Reciprocally, the motif which runs through Jesus' life as the Son beloved of his Father is "Hallowed be Thy Name." It is as the concrete expression and climax of a life driven by that same concern for God's holiness, or, viewed differently, as the climax of God's entry into the life of the other in order to find and to realize his own holiness there, that the cross of Calvary has satisfying and atoning significance. It was simply "the enthronement of the Holy in the arena of human experience, under the conditions of a historic situation concrete with the soul of the race."[87] Christ, Forsyth writes, "set up the Kingdom in his own person and work."[88]

This, then, is the judgment of the world, a judgment which asserts itself not merely negatively in punishment "but positively in righteousness; so that judgment is not a terror but a hope, and the day of the Lord is not convulsion and catastrophe, but creation, a new heaven and earth, wherein dwell the peace of righteousness and assurance for ever."[89]

In closing, I want simply to hint at the direction which Forsyth's thought takes from here. For, of course, the question remains to be answered concerning the nature of the relationship between this decisive moment of history and the history of our experience, this new creation and established kingdom and the still convulsing and catastrophic world in which we live. For there can be no question of God resting content with a judgment, an atoning holiness, a new creation manifest in Christ and Christ alone. If there is a distinction to be drawn between the real and the actual they must, nonetheless, not be allowed to drift apart into a dualism which denies redemption to the historical, and leaves Forsyth's God open to the charge that he is concerned with his own holy being to the exclusion of the sort of passionate concern for the creature of which the New Testament speaks so clearly. No such dualism is permitted to open up in Forsyth's theology. Christ's death has its final value, he affirms, only when its effect in us is taken into account.[90] Indeed, Christ's response to God on the cross is not one which excludes us, but in which our response is already present, latent in the power which pours out from the cross itself, the power which itself directly creates and generates our holiness.[91] "Whatever we mean, therefore, by substitution," he writes, "it is something more than merely vicarious. It is certainly not something done over our heads. . . . It is a matter not so much of substitutionary expiation (which, as these words are commonly understood, leaves us too little committed), but of solidary confession and praise from amid the judgment fires, where the Son of God walks with the creative sympathy of the holy among the sinful sons of men."[92] Christ, he notes, "is not only the pledge to us of God's love, but the pledge to God of our sure response to it in a total change of will and life."[93]

In some sense, in other words, the "objective" aspect of the atonement in Christ is precisely the vanguard, the firstfruits, the security of the ultimate return, the "subjective" realization of holiness in us, the historical or eschatological manifestation of the kingdom in the world. Only then will God truly be satisfied. Only then will his joy be complete. Only then will God have done justice to himself, and to his decision to create.

This is the question to which Forsyth addressed himself brilliantly in one of his latest and best-known books, *The Justification of God*, or, in his own preferred title, simply *Theodicy*. I end by citing at length from this book and thereby providing an anticipatory hint of Forsyth's vision of a universal restoration, a realization of what has already been secured in reality in *actuality*,[94] the manifestation of God's kingdom on earth, the realization of holiness not just in Christ's life, but in ours, when God will be all in all:

> There never was such a fateful experiment as when God trusted man with freedom. But our Christian faith is that He knew well what He was about. He did not do that as a mere adventure, not without knowing that He had the power to remedy any abuse of it that might occur, and to do this by a new creation more mighty, marvellous, and mysterious than the first. He had means to emancipate even freedom, to convert moral freedom, even in its ruin, into spiritual. If the first creation drew on His might, the second taxed His all-might. It revealed His power as moral majesty, as holy omnipotence, most chiefly shown in the mercy that redeems and reconciles.[95]

> There is an Eye, a Mind, a Heart, before Whom the whole bloody and tortured stream of evolutionary growth has flowed. . . . And in the full view of it He has spoken. As it might be thus: "Do you stumble at the cost? It has cost Me more than you—Me who see and feel it all more than you who feel it but as atoms might. . . . Yea, it has cost Me more than if the price paid were all Mankind. For it cost Me My only and beloved Son to justify My name of righteousness, and to realise the destiny of My creature in holy love. And all mankind is not so great and dear as He. Nor is its suffering the enormity in a moral world that His Cross is. I am no spectator of the course of things, and no speculator on the result. I spared not My own Son. We carried the load that crushes you. It bowed Him into the ground. On the third day He rose with a new creation in His hand, and a regenerate world, and all things working together for good to love and the holy purpose in love. And what He did I did. How I did it? How I do it? This you know not now, and could not, but you shall know hereafter. There are things the Father must keep in His own hand. Be still and know that I am God, whose mercy is as His majesty, and His omnipotence is chiefly in forgiving, and redeeming, and settling all souls in worship in the temple of a new heaven and earth full of holiness. In that day the anguish will be forgotten for joy that a New Humanity is born into the world."[96]

9

Revelation

In the mid-twentieth century a distinguished British theologian spoke of
the loss of concern for the recovery of the historical Christ as the most
distinctive and determinative element in modern Christology. The theologian was Donald Baillie, whose book *God Was in Christ* (to which generations of apprentice British theologians and teachers of theology since
have owed a quiet but substantial debt) was published in 1948.[1] Things
have undoubtedly moved on since those words were written, but, as so
often in theology, the passage of time sees underlying concerns remain
only to resurface in new forms, and we may safely permit Baillie to pose
the question which this chapter seeks to address, and to do so in both general and specific terms.

§1. Was the Word Made Flesh in Vain?

In general terms, Baillie's concern in 1948 was with a trend in Christology toward a practical (if not a theoretical) Nestorianism:[2] in other
words, an effective separation of Jesus (the man from Nazareth whose
mummified remains two centuries of historical-critical archaeology had
attempted to uncover in the impure textual sand of the Gospels) from the
divine Word with whom the gospel and faith allegedly have to do. Baillie
acknowledges that such dualisms were in large measure a reaction to the
poverty of the nineteenth-century quest for the Jesus of history and its

eerily proto-postmodern outcomes. No matter, then, that the most expert
critical attention to the sources available had rendered only a bewildering series of identikit images having in common at most the fact that they
looked remarkably unlike the figure portrayed by the evangelists. Faced
with this veritable identity parade of "fully human" figures from the imagined past, Christian faith need not despair when the real Jesus of history
repeatedly refused to step forward. For faith as such, it was now insisted,
is not and could never be contingent on the results of historical scholarship. Its roots lie elsewhere, in (in Martin Kähler's phrase) a *sturmfreies
Gebiet*, an invulnerable area. History and belief do not belong within the
same sphere of influence and consideration. Fact and faith, whatever the
positive relation between them may be held to be, must constantly be disentangled in order for faith to be liberated from historical skepticism and
theology properly oriented toward its true object. Historical study can
neither render nor falsify faith. Faith is not rooted in the conclusions of
the historian, but in an encounter with the living God, a phenomenon of
which the historian as such knows and can say nothing at all. That "the
Word became flesh" need not be questioned, but *faith's* proper concern
is ever with the divine Word who addresses it in the here and now rather
than the historical "flesh" which he once became. Therefore history cannot become the basis of constructive theology (which has to do precisely
with the concerns of faith). There is, then, a sort of reciprocal epistemic
kenoticism operating here: the Word of God, in giving himself for and to
us, empties himself of all that is proper to him as God and assumes the
form of a contingent and corrigible datum of historical research; while we,
for our part, empty ourselves of the felt need or the possibility of knowing
this datum in any clear or unambiguous manner, content for our Christian faith and our theology to rest instead on less intellectually secure but
nevertheless genuine foundations.

Baillie's judgment on this christological trend and its consequences
for Christian faith and theology is harsh. There is, he argues, "no stability in a position which accepts to the full the humanity of Christ but has
no interest in its actual concrete manifestation and doubts whether it can
be recaptured at all; which insists on the 'once-for-all-ness' of this divine
incursion into history, but renounces all desire or claim to know what it
was really like."[3] Far from securing the doctrine of incarnation from the
acids of criticism (as Baillie supposes this approach might be intended
to) such a bracketing off of the Jesus of history in order to concentrate
on a logically distinct Christ of faith actually stultifies it and constitutes

its effective abandonment. In such a scenario the Word does not really "become flesh" at all, we might say, but hovers above the level of the flesh, at least in all those respects which are significant for faith. To those who advocate such an approach the question must be put whether "Christ lived for nothing, and the Word was made flesh in vain" since the particular shape of this enfleshing is held to be either unknowable or irrelevant or both.[4] In either case the logic of incarnation as such is seriously eroded. Baillie's call in the middle of the twentieth century was thus for a Christology which took with renewed seriousness the question of the significance of Jesus' humanity, the precise form and content of the Word's enfleshed existence under the conditions of history, for faith and theology, without collapsing back into the sort of optimistic romantic historicism which first launched the quest on its fateful voyage. In broad terms, Christian New Testament scholarship has heeded his call, the advent of the so-called third quest being the most recent and potentially fruitful initiative in this direction.

This brings us to the more precise focus of this chapter, namely to inquire into the significance of the humanity of Christ in Karl Barth's theology of revelation, with particular reference to his development of that doctrine in the 1924 Göttingen lectures in dogmatics and the first volume of the *Church Dogmatics*. If justification for this particular line of inquiry be sought, then three main considerations may be advanced in mitigation: First, Barth is the systematic theologian in whose writings the themes of Christology and knowledge of God find their most serious and extensive treatment in the twentieth century. Second, his treatment of these themes is, of course, one which tackles head-on the very issue which Baillie raises: the peculiar place of the *humanitas Christi* in the mediation of our knowing of God. Third, and not entirely unrelated to the preceding, while Barth is not the sole culprit he is prominent among those on whom Baillie's sights are firmly fixed.[5] Thus, Baillie writes, in its severe reaction to the failure of the Jesus of history movement, Barth's "theology has become so austerely a theology of the Word that . . . it is hardly a theology of the Word-made-Flesh."[6]

This is a serious charge indeed if it can be made to stick. That there is certainly a question to be answered is indicated by the essentially similar charge laid at Barth's door (or, perhaps, skillfully wrapped around a rhetorical brick and thrown through his window) some thirty years later by Richard Roberts, in relation to Barth's handling of the relationship between time and eternity.[7] After a marathon overview of the *Church*

Dogmatics, Roberts offers the following judgment on its complex theo-logic: "Wherever the content of revelation and its time draws close to the reality common to humanity, ambiguity results because the 'reality' of revelation must both affirm and deny, recreate and annihilate at the same moment." But, "if the God of the orthodox Christian Gospel is prized apart from the structures of contemporary human life" in this way, Roberts concludes, "the ontological dogma of the Incarnation loses its roots in the shared and public reality of the world in which we live; it hovers above us like a cathedral resting upon a cloud."[8] The point here is essentially similar to Baillie's. If Barth's *Logos* truly becomes *sarx*, the particular way in which the "becoming" or the union between the two is consistently construed in his theology nonetheless risks reducing it to the point where it loses all purchase in the real world, thereby robbing it of genuine redemptive and revelatory force, and finally robbing theology of both its theme and its form as talk about God.

In what follows I explore what truth there may be to such charges. Unsurprisingly, the evidence is far from unambiguous. Yet I believe the ambiguity to lie in the critical *reception* of what Barth says rather than being inherent in what he says. The latter is certainly marked by *dialectic*, but this is not the same thing. Therefore I side neither with Roberts' spirited attack nor with Graham Ward's attempted careful defense of Barth from the standpoint of a Derridean philosophy of language.[9] As both Roberts and Ward recognize, it is with Barth's espousal of the so-called "analogy of faith" that the capacity for ambiguity arises. One suspects, however, that any attempt to make sense of this analogy in terms of a general philosophy of language or anything else, however well intentioned, would provoke a thundering denial from Barth himself. The point is (as Roberts certainly sees but Ward may not), for Barth, the *analogia fidei* is and must be sui generis and arises precisely and only as a result of the very particular conditions of human speech about God, conditions which can by definition apply to no other object of human knowing and speaking. Behind this device, therefore, there lies a very particular ontology of divine-human relatedness, an ontology which is itself decisively shaped and informed by the structure of Chalcedonian Christology. It is, in effect, an analysis of the linguistic implications of believing that when God becomes human his presence in the world is to be understood and confessed in terms of the transcendental category of "hypostasis," and does not involve any mixing or modification of either creaturely or Creatorly "natures." It is this dialectic at the level of being which renders the concomitant dialectic at the level of speaking, and to subsume the *analogia fidei* under any wider linguistic pattern is thus precisely to miss its primary point.

I suggest that one key to a more sympathetic reading of Barth than either Baillie or Roberts is able to offer lies in inquiring not just into the implications of the fifth-century epithets "unconfused" and "unchanged," which his theology certainly reinforces, but also into the other two Chalcedonian epithets, "undivided" and "unseparated," which his explicit embrace of the two natures doctrine equally implies. What, in other words, does it mean for Barth to say that the humanity of Jesus is inseparable from the presence of the Word in the world? Or (by inference) that the "flesh" of this particular historical man cannot legitimately be excluded from the picture where our knowledge of God is concerned? Barth makes both these claims, yet they are not ones which sit comfortably with the supposition that he dehistoricizes revelation or sees the humanity of Jesus as in any sense incidental to it. Is there, then, inherent and irresolvable ambiguity here? If there is, then it must be said that this is not so much a problem with Barth's theology as such as it is one which he shares with the ancient architects of Chalcedonian theology and perhaps with Christian theology as a whole in the mainstream of its attempts to make sense of the mode of God's presence in the man Jesus of Nazareth and the implications of this for our thinking about his relatedness to creation more widely. I hope to suggest, though, that Barth's interpretation and deliberate deployment of Chalcedonian categories is far from ambiguous, and that attention to his use of the categories "hypostasis" and its Alexandrian elaboration "anhypostasis" in particular furnish a consistent and coherent pattern within which to locate and make good sense of his various statements.

§2. Eutyches Resuscitated? Revelation and Barth's Theological Turn from the Subject

Consideration of the wider theological context within and in response to which Barth's distinctive theological emphases developed makes his persistent leaning toward a dualism between the divine and the human, the infinite and the finite, the eternal and the temporal easier to appreciate. Baillie's appeal to the failed history of the quest in this regard is relevant but scarcely adequate. The bid to secure faith by uncovering the facts about Jesus was only part of a much broader and more complicated pattern of theological development in the nineteenth century, a pattern in which Barth discerned the danger of a thoroughgoing blurring and even loss of the proper boundaries between Creator and creature, God and the realm of the "flesh." Thus Baillie's quip, writing in the christological wake of that century, that "Eutyches . . . is dead, and he is not likely to be as fortunate as Eutychus in finding an apostle to revive him!"[10] was and is only partially true. To be sure, it is unlikely that a crudely docetic account of Jesus will ever escape unscathed again (although it is worth noting Stephen Sykes' insistence that just what "full humanity" means in the case of Jesus is a question demanding investigation rather than a topic for dogmatic extrapolation from our own experience of being human).[11] But there is more than one variety of monophysitism, and the nineteenth century may be construed from another angle precisely as a breeding ground for a form of Eutychian error in which, in one way or another, the divine was constantly brought down to earth, and the created (at least in some of its aspects) exalted and celebrated as *homoiousios* if not *homoousios* with it.

The Romantic idealism which discovered God lurking in and under every leaf, stone and organism, and which interpreted history itself as a mode of divine self-expression or self-realization, is only the most explicit (and for that reason arguably the least pernicious) form of this. There were lots of other versions of it, ways in which theology was led (as Barth believed) to abandon its own proper object (God himself) and to shift its attention to and to locate its own ultimate source and possibility within some aspect of the sphere of nature, history, the phenomenal, "the flesh." It was not in Hegelianism alone that there was, in effect, an adoption of the incarnation of the Logos as a metaphysical principle rather than a contingent fact. The essential unity between God and the world was a truth as widely adhered to in one form or another as it was subversive of the doctrine of revelation in anything like its traditional versions. By the late nineteenth century the most significant streams of Christian theology had either quietly pushed this doctrine aside and substituted for it some other (more "natural") basis for their endeavor, or else had refashioned the concept in ways which served effectively (if not intentionally) to relocate it within the sphere of human (natural) rather than divine (supranatural) possibilities. Into the first category we may place Kant's concerted bid to limit the range of reason in order to make room for faith and Schleiermacher's appeal to a general and innate human God-consciousness as both the basis and the object of theological reflection. Into the second must go many of Barth's Ritschlian teachers, who eschewed the notion of religion being rooted in any general human capacity whatsoever and insisted instead on the positive and particular revelation of God in the historical person of Jesus, yet in doing so they tended mostly to identify the content of that revelation directly with historically locatable phenomena (the teaching, or the moral and spiritual example, or the personality of Jesus to cite just a few familiar instances). Thus "revelation," whatever its ultimate source, was effectively reduced to those this-worldly phenomena from Jesus' life which remained once the vultures of academe had picked over the corpus of the New Testament.

As a mature teacher of theology, Barth adopted the habit of having his students begin by reading Feuerbach. For, in Feuerbach's accusation that talk about God is, in the end, only talk about humanity, Barth identified the most complete and telling judgment on the nineteenth-century theological project. For all the varied emphases which may be identified, the chief characteristic of that project was in one way or another to seek to found religion, and the theological reflection which attaches to it, on some aspect of a human nature and experience which *belongs to history and may be understood within its terms*. We should note that the largely precritical appeal of Protestant Orthodoxy to possess an inspired and "inerrant" biblical text and of Roman Catholicism to an "infallible" human magisterium fared little better in this respect under Barth's scrutiny. In all these ways, Barth believed, theology had effectively already capitulated to Feuerbach's charge and had left itself no way of locating its final source in a God whose reality and activity utterly transcend the sphere of the human. It was in the task of reaffirming this essential difference that Barth immersed himself.

The only way to secure what must be secured here, Barth insisted from his earliest writings, was from the outset to be unequivocally clear about the proper logic of theological statements (i.e., their claim to speak *about God* and not about some dimension or feature of the human), and this in turn would mean being quite clear about the conditions under which alone such speech is possible. Christian faith and speech are essentially response and not essentially source. God produces faith, and not vice versa. It is this concern which lies behind Barth's relentless appeal to the category of revelation and his particular way of interpreting what is involved in revelation. The account which he offers of the doctrine, therefore, is a properly postcritical version of it.

It is important to note that this issue of the vital differentiation of God from the world is not an issue about God's presence within or immanence to his creation but rather about the mode of this presence. Barth, as is apparent from first to last in his writings (and not least his account of revelation), believed God to be radically present and active in the world through the agency of the Spirit, but, equally, to be so transcendent of the world he fills with his presence that it would be mistaken and dangerous to point to any part of the created cosmos (physical or spiritual) and identify it with or as being "like" God. The alternative to Romantic pantheism and the Liberal Protestant identification of "divine" principles and virtues enfleshed in human nature and culture was certainly not deism. Rather, it was a more subtle and theologically adequate differentiation of modes of divine presence and absence.

That one might or ought properly to think and speak of a perichoretic penetration of all created things by the God who calls them into existence and sustains them is not a problem for Barth. Transcendence is not a spatial or temporal category but an attempt to articulate the wholly and holy otherness of the God in whom we live and move and have our being. But this general presence of God to the world, precisely because it is the presence of the transcendent and wholly other God, is not accessible to human knowing and experiencing. It is transcendent with respect to the objects of human experience and cognition. Barth had certainly learned from Kant that God cannot be treated as if he were just another phenomenon within the sphere of human knowing. Thus "we have to admit that we cannot see, hear, feel, touch, or either inwardly or outwardly perceive the one who reveals himself, not because he is invisible or pure spirit, but because he is God, . . . the subject that escapes our grasp, our attempt to make him an object [Objekt]."[12] Again, "God does not belong to the world. Therefore, he does not belong to the series of objects [Gegenstände] for which we have categories and words by means of which we draw the attention of others to them, and bring them into relation with them." The implication of this is clear enough: in general terms "it is impossible to speak of God, because he is not a 'thing,' either natural or spiritual."[13] God, precisely because he is God, is not a possible object of human knowing or speech. This is not, we should reiterate, because God is remote or absent from the world but because his mode of presence within it is one of radical transcendence.

Thus, Barth eschews every form of what he refers to as "Christian Cartesianism,"[14] namely the assumption that the possibility of a human knowing and experiencing of God is one which either is or ever becomes "man's own, a predicate of his existence, a content of his consciousness, his possession," that it rests at some point decisively on something located within and accountable for in terms of the potentialities of natural and historical existence. To think thus is to have missed the point about God entirely. But, of course, in order to grasp the point about God, in order to grasp any point about God, there must already be some knowledge or experience of God actualized in the human sphere. This is the careful irony of Barth's insistence that knowledge of God is impossible: we can only know that it is (ordinarily) impossible because in actual fact the possibility of it has (surprisingly and extraordinarily) been established and realized. This is no a priori anthropological analysis, then, but an a posteriori reflection on the implications of the fact that and the way in which God has actually made himself known.[15]

For Barth, knowledge of God is both impossible and possible for particular human beings, but the impossibility and possibility do not exist on the same level. In general terms, and in terms of natural human capacities, knowledge of God is wholly impossible, yet God's own capacities transcend and bracket this truth without invalidating or even modifying it, calling forth faith and acknowledgment from the side of the particular creature in an event every bit as miraculous as the virgin conception and the resurrection with which Barth repeatedly compares it.[16] Should the miracle, the enabling, the determination of our existence in the creation of faith cease from God's side, then the truth of our natural incapacity would remain unscathed. Faith and obedience, which are an integral part of what Barth intends by the word *revelation*, are the granting by the Spirit of a "capacity of the incapable," a capacity called into being ex nihilo and held in being by God in accordance with his own choosing.

§3. Crossing the Boundary?

Epistemic and Hypostatic Union

The "radical de-divinization [*radikale Entgötterung*] of the world, of nature, of history"[17] which Barth commends is thus not at odds with the claim that God may be and is actually known and experienced in the world, but is in fact established by this claim. "Revelation and it alone really and finally separates God and man by bringing them together. For by bringing them together it informs man about God and about himself, . . . it tells him that this God (no other) is free for this man (no other). . . . The man who listens here, sees himself standing at the boundary where all is at an end. . . . The revelation that crosses this boundary, and the togetherness of God and man which takes place in revelation in spite of this boundary, make the boundary visible to him in an unprecedented way."[18] What is at issue, then, is not the *fact* of God's knowable presence and activity in history, but the question of the *mode* of this presence. And here, Barth is quite clear, we have to do with a distinct mode of presence which is not general but specific, not available to all everywhere and always but only to some in particular

times and places. "Always in all circumstances the Word of God is reality in our reality *suo modo, sua libertate, sua misericordia.* Consequently,
it is present and ascertainable only contingently—again, *suo modo.*"[19] The
revealing presence of God in the world in the mode of his Word is, in other
words, a matter and a function of God's election, a matter of contingency
at both the divine and the human levels.[20] Thus revelation as such is "not a
condition [*ein Zustand*], not an opening through which any Tom, Dick or
Harry may look into heaven, but a happening [*ein Geschehen*]."[21] God does
not render himself into the epistemic custody or control of humanity in
general. Indeed, even in the case of those to whom he *does* reveal himself,
God does not do this but remains from first to last the *Subjekt* as well as the
Objekt in the knowing relation which is established. His mode of presence,
Barth constantly insists, is never direct but always indirect.[22] It is a pres-
ence which is paradoxically both immediate and mediated, and in which
God is both known and yet remains hidden in his proper transcendence.
We must not misunderstand the mode of his presence. There is, at the level
of the flesh, no fixed and unambiguous *Offenbarheit* to which the few any
more than the many may turn and lay claim.

From the first edition of *Der Römerbrief* (1919) onward, a singular
concern may be identified in Barth's writing on the theme of revelation:
namely, to give an account of the reality of this happening or event in
which the proper (and vital) distinction between God and the world is
maintained at every point. God is known in the midst of historical existence. That, as we have seen, is the miracle. But in the midst of this miracle
God remains the one who is wholly other than us, and we, for our part,
remain human.[23] The radical boundary between God's existence and ours,
between the uncreated Lord and the creature, is, that is to say, in some
sense transcended in the event of knowing, yet without any concomitant
loss or compromising of either God's identity or ours. Furthermore, the
one who does not and could never belong to the world of "objects" locates
himself within that world, giving himself over to us as an *Objekt* of our
knowing, yet doing so (crucially) in such a manner that he remains in control (*das Subjekt*) of this knowing from first to last. How, then, are we to
think of this? How can it be *possible* for God genuinely to be known *in* the
world without yet being *of* the world? What must happen in order for this
to be possible?

The answer to these questions, Barth realized, lay somehow in the
christological insistence that in Jesus God himself has "taken flesh" and
entered into the sphere of creaturely existence which is also the sphere

of human knowing. The boundary which separates God's existence from ours may ordinarily be an absolute barrier to our knowing God, but it is no obstacle to God himself in his freedom and his desire to cross the line and make himself known to us.[24] For this to be possible he must assume a knowable form, and this he has done in Jesus Christ. God has entered the world of our conceptuality,[25] become an object of our knowing,[26] put himself at our epistemic disposal. God, in other words, has become a part of the world of phenomena within which human knowledge ordinarily arises. Thus, Barth inquires, what if God, the one who as such even in his immanence within the world can never ordinarily be an object of human knowing "be so much God that without ceasing to be God he can also be, and is willing to be, not God as well. What if he were to come down from his unsearchable height and become something different. What if he, the immutable subject, were to make himself an object [*sich selbst zum Objekt machte*]."[27] In this case God would be present in the world in a new and distinctive way, and in such a way as to be accessible to ordinary human modes of perception and knowing. It is in this sense that the incarnation is the primary condition for the objective possibility of God's self-revelation in the world. The Word has "become flesh."

Yet this unqualified profession of divine inhomination raises more questions than it answers, and Barth was well aware of the convoluted history of its interpretation, not least in ways which would betray rather than secure the points he deemed to be so vital to a healthy reorientation of theology in the modern period. Specifically, there are ways of thinking about the *Menschwerdung Gottes* in the modern period which amount in practice to a mild monophysitism, and thereby compromise all that Barth was seeking to safeguard. To begin with (and arguably most seriously) such monophysite trends put at risk the boundary between God and creation itself, a boundary which Barth insists is reinforced rather than transgressed in the crossing of it from above by the Word. They risk the location of "revelation" as such (and thereby the ultimate basis and source for human talk about God) within the sphere of history and the human, and thus hand Feuerbach the keys to the kingdom. They risk the loss of faith's and theology's proper nature and object (namely a sharing in communion with God himself) and settle instead for a two-dimensional "knowing" which terminates at the level of familiarity with a figure in history or a character in a story. In Barth's own terms, by mistaking the veil of the flesh for that which it veils, such approaches fail to inquire into what really matters, and shut themselves off from the possibility of the veil becoming an open door.

Finally, by thinking of revelation in terms of a revealedness at the level of the flesh, such monophysitisms fail to account for the particularity of revelation as a function of divine election, and for the activity of the Spirit in the creation of faith and obedient response to the divine Word. Thus the bare assertion that God has taken flesh and entered our world as a human being is necessary but crudely insufficient to account for the actual mode of God's revelatory presence and activity. The nature and implications of this "assumption" and "becoming" would, Barth perceived, need to be pinned down much more precisely.

As early as the *Göttingen Dogmatics* (1924)[28] Barth came to see that this modern set of theological problems had its ancient counterpart, and that the classical doctrine of hypostatic union espoused at the Council of Chalcedon in 451 offered resources to enable him to make sense of the peculiar claim that in Jesus God "becomes not-God as well" and, through this "secondary objectivity" and the creation of faith by the Spirit gives himself to be known by men and women of his choosing. The precise function of the "two natures" doctrine (in the incarnation there is one "hypostasis" to be discerned subsisting in two distinct "natures") was to insist on the personal presence of God in a particular human life while yet differentiating the content of that life at every tangible point from God's own existence as God. Within this context the term hypostasis (the rendering of which into Latin as *persona* and subsequently the English "person" is only partially helpful depending on the precise connotations of its particular use) serves as a transcendental category. It is deliberately differentiated from the category "nature." In other words, "hypostasis" is not a predicate of nature, either God's or ours. Rather, it is, in Rowan Williams' words, a category referring to "a subject beyond all its predicates . . . the unique ground of the unity of its predicates, or, as you might say, the 'terminus' of its predicates."[29] Hypostasis is not something which someone (God, Jesus, or us) *has*; it is precisely the grammatical subject (as we might say) who *has*, possesses, or is characterized by the various predicates of the relevant "nature" (including, we should note, personality, mind, and consciousness with which the category is frequently confused, as in the numerous ill-targeted objections so often found in contemporary christological works against the category anhypostasia).

We can see how this finely tuned categorial distinction suited Barth's purposes perfectly. God becomes the man Jesus, yet this becoming entails the addition of a human level of existence ("nature") to who and what God eternally is, an existence which thus remains logically distinct at every point from his divine "nature." The logic of divine becoming in the incarnation is a logic of addition (that is, the addition of humanity) to God's eternal existence, and does not entail the predication of either loss or change to God's nature as Creator. Thus the mode of God's presence in the world in incarnation and revelation is certainly not one which renders God as such available for inspection or apprehension by human knowers. God enters the world and is present within it "hypostatically" while yet remaining utterly distinct from it by nature. In apprehending the man Jesus, we do not as such and without further ado lay hold of God. We are, after all, beholding God's *humanity*, which serves, as Barth repeatedly reminds us, as much to veil God (*kata physin*) as to render the possibility of his knowability (*kat' hypostasin*) in the world.

To repeat, then: since "hypostasis" is a transcendental category rather than a predicate of either divine or human natures as such, there is nothing of God's *nature* present phenomenally. It is not "God" as such, but rather God as/having become "not-God" who/which is present in the world and available to the normal channels of knowing. God is both present and yet hidden in the flesh of Christ. Revelation is both immediate and mediated, for while God is truly "in Christ" God also transcends and does not "become" the *humanitas Christi* (which is yet also the *humanitas Dei*). The inhomination of God is thus not itself revelation, according to Barth, but simply the condition for the objective possibility of revelation. To be sure, revelation needs a physical event, a genuine presence of God in the sphere of phenomena, but revelation itself is and must be much more than an epistemic event at this level, for revelation is a knowing of God himself in his nature as God, and the God who is known transcends his own humanity.[30]

The self-objectification of God for our sakes in Jesus Christ, therefore, is not the terminus but only the starting point and the vital means for God's self-disclosure to his creature. In order for this same human form to become transparent with respect to God's own being there must be a corresponding reception, hearing, and response within the human sphere.[31] Faith and obedience, as the form of all true human knowing of God, are a gift bestowed by God in the event of revelation itself. Here too, though, we are dealing not with a permanently bestowed condition of receptivity and response but with a capacity created in the happening of divine self-giving. God, through the creative agency of the Spirit, draws us into communion with himself, and in doing so lifts us up beyond the limits of our own natural capacity into the self-transcending circle of the knowledge of

God. Faith, that is to say, as and when it arises is not a capacity which we bring to and with which we meet and respond to God's revelation: faith is itself the form which that revelation assumes within the reality of historical existence. No satisfactory account can be given of its possibility in purely human or historical terms. Apart from God's creative and redemptive act it has no existence. It is, we might say, anhypostatic, and enhypostatic in God's revelatory drawing of people to himself.

In the event of revelation, therefore, the proper boundary between uncreated and created, infinite and finite, eternal and temporal, God and humanity, is crossed from both sides. In the words of a Scottish liturgy, "[God] has made his home with us that we might forever dwell in him." But the nature of God's incarnate presence among us and of our corresponding being in his presence is one in which the boundary itself is not transgressed or called into question. God's becoming is not to be identified at the level of nature but is hypostatic. Correspondingly, our knowing, which begins with the humanity of God in Christ, is indirect and mediated but is one in which we are enabled to transcend the natural limits of our knowing by an act of the Creator Spirit from above and are opened up to commune with God himself. In doing so we are not deified or supernaturalized, but our humanity is drawn into a creaturely correspondence with the reality of God. Revelation is thus not a phenomenon within the world but an event, happening, or action in which, through our knowing of certain this-worldly realities, we are drawn into a relationship with a reality lying beyond this world altogether.

§4. Analogy, Correspondence, and the Historicity of Revelation

In this final section we effectively return to the question with which we began, namely, does the humanity of Jesus really matter in the event of revelation in anything more than the purely formal sense that we have identified? That is to say, given that we need a phenomenal stepping stone in order to make cognitive contact with the God whose reality utterly transcends the realm of phenomena, does the actual shape or content of the phenomenon itself matter very much? Or can Christian faith, to which in some sense the figure of Jesus must be deemed central, rest easy where questions about what this Jesus was actually like, what he did and said, what happened to him, and so on, are concerned? Approaching the same problem from a different angle, we might inquire whether, in order to support a Christology at all, God's presence in Jesus must make (and be seen to make) some empirically identifiable difference at the level of the flesh. As James Mackey observes, a Jesus whom historical research uncovered as the first-century equivalent of a used car salesman might be supposed to pose problems for the claim that in and through him God was present and is made known. We might be less grotesque (and less jocular) in our example and say, simply, without sliding into docetism, that it seems likely that Jesus was someone who stood out identifiably from the crowd in ways which made people stop and wonder. This is not at all the same thing as saying that "revelation" could be read off from his facial expression or was contained in his teaching and actions: it is simply to suggest that the most likely starting point for Christology (as the Gospels themselves indicate) was a question about Jesus, a question which arose naturally enough from simply having been in his presence or even hearing the stories told about him by those who had.

This, it must be admitted, is where the two natures doctrine is vulnerable if it be adopted as a satisfactory christological framework in and of itself—not, to my knowledge, that this doctrine has ever encouraged notions of a profligate and morally dubious Jesus, or even a dull Jesus easily overlooked. But in itself it does not offer any clear framework for identifying and evaluating what in positive terms it might mean for the flesh that here God is in it. This, of course, was not its purpose. It was purely a formula of careful analytic differentiation, intended to ascribe christological statements to the relevant level of discourse: statements about Jesus' humanity on one hand, and those pertaining to him as God on the other, holding on meanwhile to the principle of hypostatic identity which holds both levels inseparably together. In order to serve this purpose adequately, though, its interest in the humanity of Jesus tends ever toward the general and the shared, that "humanity" which all humans indwell rather than the particular human character of the man from Nazareth. Furthermore, in its constant careful segregation of Jesus' "human" from his "divine" predicates, this doctrine shifts attention away from the role of the humanity of Jesus in revealing God to us. For, if everything that may be said of the man Jesus can and must properly be ascribed to the category of his human nature, and as such radically differentiated from what is true of him "as God," then there is no very strong basis for supposing what we see in Jesus' character and actions as a man is also to be true in some sense also of God, or to be a reflection or function of his secret divine identity (the sort of thing which is true of God when God is "enfleshed"). Whether we point to Jesus' goodness, his love, his table-fellowship with sinners, his hunger, his fear, his suffering, or whatever, the two natures scheme furnishes no basis for assuming or arguing that some (and not others) of these human characteristics are directly related to the fact of his being "God with us." In each case the response must be strictly the same—these things are true of him *humanly,* and do not pertain to his existence as God. This is a response which, taken alone, rather short-circuits the revelatory capacity of his humanity as such.

As we have seen, Barth does not think of revelation as such as in any way containable within the humanity of Jesus, yet we may still ask whether the suitability of that humanity to refer us beyond itself in the event of revelation in the way which Barth envisages is not related in any way to its particular shape. Flesh and blood may not reveal God to us in and of themselves, but is the relation between the flesh and blood which God actually assumes and the purpose for which he assumes it arbitrary? If God is so wholly other and there is no natural analogy between him and anything at the level of the human, is it anything more than a matter of sheer caprice for God to "reveal" himself in the man Jesus rather than, say, Ivan the Terrible or a dead dog? If we suppose it to be so, then, of course, the question of what Jesus was really like ceases to be of any serious significance and (in a way reminiscent of Bultmann's appeal to the singular moment of the cross) we are liberated to let the fires of history burn: all that is needed is the bare assertion that God entered hypostatically into union with our humanity once (a claim famously, and in terms of its subsequent interpretation unfortunately, made by Kierkegaard).

There are elements in what Barth has to say on this theme which certainly lean in this direction. Thus, for example, he insists that the form of revelation is related to its content not simply by a relationship of difference or otherness but actually by contradiction.[32] Elsewhere he is less vigorous in his efforts to overthrow the idea that knowledge of God's nature could be translated into flesh-and-blood terms by virtue of a general *analogia entis,* and alludes simply to the essential ordinariness of Jesus as a man among men. The alternative suggestion is delightfully captured in a claim in one of Gerard Manley Hopkins' sermons that, since we know that God is beautiful, Jesus himself must have been the incarnation of physical beauty: "Moderately tall, well-built and slender in frame, his features straight and beautiful, his hair inclining to auburn, parted in the midst, curling and clustering about the ears and neck."[33] Barth, who generally preferred to take his cue from Isaiah's "he had . . . nothing in his appearance that we should desire him," was quite clear that this was not what it meant to claim that "the fullness of the Godhead dwelt in him bodily."

Yet while Barth demurred on every possible occasion from what he took to be a theologically unhealthy interest in and focus on the humanity of Jesus as such, and even once insists that theology must finally dare not be too christocentric (*etwas weniger christozentrisch*)[34] since it is with God and not with Jesus that it is finally concerned, he nonetheless also eschewed any form of docetic lack of interest in Jesus, his character, teaching, actions, and passion. Christian thought about God, he insists, and much else besides must be decisively shaped by what it finds at this point, rather than importing preconceived notions from elsewhere.[35] Similarly, while he insists that revelation is an event, a happening, and not a body of truths or principles which may be codified and systematically applied (in philosopher John Macmurray's terms, it is a matter of "personal" rather than "abstractive" knowledge), nonetheless Barth is absolutely clear that there is a vital conceptual and verbal component in revelation, and he has no time at all for the sort of nebulous, noncognitive encounter with infinity much beloved of post-Schleiermacherian trends in theology. The following citation suffices to make the point: "Faith and obedience vis-à-vis revelation stand face to face first of all with this historical, self-explicating revelation, or else they do not stand before revelation. It would be a comfortable conjuring away of the offence but no more and no less than the conjuring away of revelation itself, if we were to say that we will cling to God himself but will have nothing whatever to do with all the astonishing things that are linked to our being able to cling to God himself. Faith means not only believing in God but also believing in this and that. To put it with all the offence that it involves, it means believing in the Trinity, or in the NT miracles, or in the virgin birth. And obedience means not only uniting our own wills with God's but, for example, keeping the ten commandments."[36] And so it continues.

It is not, then, that the objective form in which revelation comes to us is unimportant but simply that it is not sufficient and is not in itself the object of our knowing of God—it is merely its creaturely and phenomenal vehicle. And from the above and many other similar passages it is clear that the particular content of this divine self-objectification is non-negotiable. Talk about God is demanded of us by God's address in Christ and the Spirit, and the terms in which we are to engage in *Nachdenken* and *Nachreden* are mapped out for us by a consideration of the man Jesus within his proper context in the history of Israel. With specific reference to Jesus himself, while Barth will have nothing to do with any idealizing of his humanity, he is also content to admit that there is that about it which reflects the unique presence of God, which is its secret. Thus, for example, "In becoming the same as we are, the Son of God is the same in quite a different way from us; in other words, in our human being what we do is omitted, and what we omit is done. This Man would not be God's revelation to us, God's reconciliation with us, if He were not, as true Man, the true, unchangeable, perfect God Himself. . . . How can God sin, deny Himself to Himself, be against Himself as God? . . . Therefore in our state and condition He does not do what underlies and produces that state and condition, or what we in that state and condition continually do. Our unholy human existence, assumed and adopted by the Word of God, is a hallowed and therefore a sinless human existence."[37]

So, then, there is little mileage in maintaining that the enfleshing of the Logos makes little or no identifiable difference to the flesh itself in Barth's Christology. It clearly does. But it is important to grasp the *nature* and the *source* of the difference which it makes.

Jesus' humanity is not different because it is (to use a misleading phrase) "the incarnation of God"—that is to say, the rendering or replication of what God is, scaled down conveniently to the dimensions of our historical existence. To think thus, Barth supposes, is to risk obscuring the essential otherness of God and to encourage the sort of speculative scaling of the heights of heaven rooted in a general "analogy of being" which he so disdains. In *this* sense, he insists, *finitum non capax infiniti*. The presence of God in Christ is under the mode of the hypostatic becoming of the Word who becomes, precisely, not-God, and not "micro-God." What we do *not* have in the *humanitas Christi*, therefore, is a representation or icon of the divine *ousia* under the form of human *ousia*. Rather, what we have is the hypostatic presence of God among us humanly, and in such a way as to reconcile our fallen and estranged flesh to God, renewing and transforming the flesh until it corresponds, in terms proper to its own "nature," to who and what God is in his. This, then, is the primary reason for Jesus' humanity being essentially other than ours: not that it is a snapshot of God, and made over to "look like" God, but rather that it is the firstfruits of a new, redeemed humanity in correspondence with God. When God speaks his Word into the realm of flesh, we might say, it results not in an echo, but precisely in a reply, a response from the side of the creature to the Creator's call. In other words, attention must be granted here in Christology to the *enhypostatic* as well as the *anhypostatic* aspect of incarnation.

The eternal Word of God becomes the particular man Jesus, born of Mary and Joseph, and it is precisely in his particularity and not in spite of it that his universal significance, his concrete fulfilling of the covenant between God and humankind, is to be identified. It is precisely here that the particularity of Jesus' humanity as reflected in the gospel stories of his life and ministry can and must be accommodated, therefore; for we cannot begin to answer the question, What does it mean to be the man who corresponds to God, who fulfills the covenant from the human side? by speaking in general terms (in terms of the general category "human nature") but only by retelling those same gospel stories, making sense of them out of their Old Testament background, considering the ways in which Jesus lived, the particular things which he did and said, and allowing these to issue their own very particular challenge to us as their outlines overlap, cross, and conflict with the patterns of our own particular lives.

It must be admitted that Barth's Christology suffers from a relative lack of development in this respect. For reasons having to do largely with his absolute determination to avoid all forms of subordinationism, he fails to develop the model of divine self-communication as inherently relational, a relationality which in Jesus embraces humanity into the network of its own rich dynamics, and witnesses God not just as a human *speaker* of the Word but also as its *hearer* and *respondent* from the human side. Although the basic milieu for nurturing such an Antiochene emphasis are clearly all present in Barth's theology (he repeatedly affirms the radical assumption by God of a "complete" humanity even in its "fallen" state and, as we have already seen, tends toward an insistence on the relation of radical otherness between the two "natures" of Christ), his own inclinations at this point are nonetheless finally in an Alexandrian direction, ever insisting on the hypostatic identity between Jesus and God and stressing the essential *Einigkeit* within the *Dreieinigkeit Gottes* so that it is hard for him to accommodate any developed focus on Jesus as a person who is a respondent to the Father and the Spirit.[38]

To return to our main point: if we ask on what basis Jesus' humanity is able to serve as a fit vehicle or medium of God's self-disclosure, then, following Barth, we must say several things: First, that like all flesh in the first instance and in and of itself, it has no capacity to do so at all. It is only as God is present to and active within it, not just hypostatically as the Word but also as the indwelling Spirit who creates human response, that it acquires any such capacity, being lifted up "from above" to a self-transcending correspondence to God's own being and activity. Thus it is not because it is "supernatural" or in some sense "like God," but insofar as Jesus' is a truly natural human existence which corresponds to the nature and will and calling of the God who is wholly other than it *even in this correspondence*, that the flesh of Christ functions in a revelatory (or perhaps protorevelatory) way. Of course we may infer certain things about God on the basis of what we apprehend at the level of his humanity: that he is capable of becoming what he becomes (*Infinitum capax finiti*) and that he wills to become this for our sakes. This in itself suggests certain things about God's character, things which we can only make sense of in terms of human characteristics such as love, faithfulness, and so on. Furthermore, within the assumption by the Son and adaptation by the Spirit of our sinful humanity into faithful correspondence with God, we may consider that we have reason to suppose certain analogies between Jesus' human character and his character as God to exist. When Jesus forgives and accepts sinners and outcasts, for example, we may reckon that this tells us something of who God is and what God is like, and that this is part of the purpose of God's becoming human at all. And, so long as we do not slide into any easy generalization of such particular claims (so that Jesus' hunger and tiredness lead us equally to predicate these traits of God), we may be right to suppose this. But the extraordinary human love, faithfulness, forgiveness, and so on of Jesus do not "show us" God directly, rather they point beyond themselves to the reality of God; and the nature of this "pointing beyond," and the precise points at which it does and does not occur, are not knowable in isolation from the relationship of faith in which we are properly related to God himself. The particular form of Jesus' humanity as "sanctified flesh" is vital in this task, but it is very definitely penultimate rather than ultimate.

A similar logic can and must be applied, of course, to the subsequent adaptation and determination of those to whom God speaks and discloses himself through this self-objectifying economy. Here, too, there is both a fully human and a fully divine presence and activity to be discerned. There is, that is to say, a union and mutual indwelling of human and divine in the event of faith,[39] a union not now of natures at all but of activity. Here, there is no hypostatic assumption by the Word of the flesh. The relevant flesh here, that is to say, is ours and not his. But the Spirit is present and active from first to last in our flesh, taking *our* broken, fallen, and alienated humanity and lifting it up way beyond any "natural" capacity which it might be supposed to have and rendering it *capax infiniti*. This capacity never belongs to us as such: rather it is the fruit of (a function of) a relationship in which we are held from above by the Spirit from moment to moment.

This leads us to a vital point about the way in which our language and conceptuality function in revelation (for language and conceptuality there must be, as we have seen). The substance or reality of what we "know" as we commune with God himself cannot be captured or communicated adequately in language itself. Another way of putting this formally is to say that the *modus significandi* of our analogical predication can never be specified, a fact of which Aquinas, it must be said, was fully aware. Were it able to be specified, then the analogy would not be necessary in the first place. Yet speak of this reality we can and must, and in doing so Barth is clear that we are constrained by faithfulness to the conceptual tools furnished in God's self-objectifying in Christ. In other words, we allow the story of Jesus and its wider context in the story of Israel to shape the pattern of our thinking, speaking, and testifying. But in doing so we are constantly aware that our words are merely "knocking at the gates" of the truth which we seek to express.[40] The dialectic between God's existence and ours (including our language and its ordinary semantic range) remains and is never resolved. That our thinking and speaking should, as it were, overreach themselves or transcend their natural range and in some indefinable sense refer appropriately to God, this again is entirely a matter of God's adoption and adaptation of that which pertains to the flesh. In the event of revelation, the moment in which the veil of the flesh is rendered transparent, we "know" how our language refers because we are in relation with that to which it refers (a relation which, contrary to much post-Wittgensteinian analysis, is not entirely mediated by language; we frequently know more than we can say). That we cannot say it is part of what it means to recognize that God remains mysterious and wholly other, a fact which becomes more and not less apparent as we are drawn closer to him.

All this, then, is the force of the so-called analogy of faith of which Barth was so fond of speaking. In the event of God's own personal self-disclosure, both the media and the recipients of that disclosure are lifted up beyond the limits of their natural capacities and established within an epistemic triangulation the third term in which is God himself. Thereby God is truly known and may properly be spoken of. But in the knowing, God remains mysterious: the mystery is never fathomed but rather indwelt.

§5. Was God in Christ?

So, was God "in" Christ? Is revelation "historical" in any sense? Does the castle ever rest on terra firma, or remain suspended tantalizingly but largely irrelevantly in the clouds? What we have seen is that, for Barth, revelation is not a thing, a condition or an aspect of some nature, but rather a relationship between the reality of God and our created world. As such, "revelation" can and could never be apprehended or laid hold of at the level of nature or history although, as we have seen, it certainly is apprehended from within nature and history (where else could it be if it is actually to reveal anything to anyone?). The attempt to lay hold of revelation "in" the phenomena of fleshly existence is, to use one of Barth's own images, like trying to scoop the moon's reflection from the surface of a pond.[41] It is to mistake the historical coordinates of revelation with a relation or event which embraces and yet necessarily transcends them. God "touches" history and the flesh in the hypostatic becoming of the Word and the creative indwelling of the Spirit—but never *kata physin*. There is, we might say, no physical contact, but a divine relating to us which is proper to the integrity of God's own nature and which creates, calls into being ex nihilo, a reciprocal relating from our side. So revelation is historical in the sense that it happens within history, embracing and transforming particular features of created, fleshly existence. But it is *not* historical in the sense that its happening can be accounted for in terms of the normal cause-and-effect processes of nature and history. That it happens at all is pure miracle. It is in the world but not of it. Apart from God's action "from above," it has no being, no independent existence or reality. As a reality in the world, therefore, it is, to use a christological metaphor, *anhypostatic*. Were it not so, it would not really *be* revelation at all; we would not be knowing God but one of the many surrogates which, as Feuerbach saw, humans are prone to gather or fashion from the world of objects and to throw up toward the clouds from below to see which, if any, will stick. The loss of any genuine sense of transcendence (and thus of a proper understanding of immanence) in much contemporary theology suggests that the problems which Barth faced are just as live in the early decades of the twenty-first century as they were at the outset of the twentieth, and that the emphases which he adopted and the categories on which he drew in addressing these problems thus merit our continued theological consideration.

10

Filiation

The term "deification" is one generally associated with the theology of the Christian East, though it also has an established history and plentiful advocates in Catholic thought.[1] For the most part Protestant theologians, not least those in the Reformed tradition, have been severe critics rather than advocates of the theology of deification. Where it has been given serious consideration at all, the theme has generally been treated as an unbiblical skeleton in the Christian closet, owing more to the classical philosophical schools than to the apostolic gospel. As an historian of doctrine, T. F. Torrance (1913–2007) knew better than this, having learned the term's meaning (as he would choose to define it) from such luminaries of the patristic tradition as Irenaeus of Lyons, Athanasius of Alexandria, and the Cappadocians. The contention of this chapter is that, despite his own solidly Reformed roots, in Torrance's own theology what we witness is a transformation and convergence of Eastern and Western soteriological motifs, such that the account of salvation which he offers is itself, at the last, best captured in its fullness by the term "deification."

At first glance this may indeed be a contentious claim. To begin with, it must be admitted that, while he commends consideration of it to Reformed Christians, Torrance expresses some reticence about the term "deification" itself, finding it to be a less than adequate rendering of the Greek terms *theosis* and *theopoiesis*.[2] For one thing, the term is easily

misunderstood, not least in the wake of currents in modern Western theology which have proposed the inherent "divinity" of the human spirit
and transmuted the gospel into a call to realize this essentially divine
nature. The resurgence of similar monistic motifs in so-called New Age
spiritualities and philosophies of the late twentieth and early twenty-
first centuries grants such caution even more warrant. As we shall see,
nothing could be further than all this from the meaning of the term as
Torrance understands it. Yet, despite his reluctance to use the language
of deification without constant qualification and clarification of the
peculiar sense it bears in his thought (words, he never tires of insisting, must always be interpreted in accordance with the reality to which
they refer us, and not vice versa), given Torrance's own perception of the
nature of salvation and the way in which he situates this vis-à-vis other
core doctrines, no other term is finally adequate to the task of classifying
his thought. The best way to demonstrate this is by offering a whirlwind
exposition of the shape of Torrance's understanding of the locus and
nature of salvation and its relationship to the doctrines of the Trinity
and the incarnation in particular.

A brief exposition of the inner logic of Torrance's soteriology is
problematic. In part this is because of the fundamental unity of Christian theology as he himself perceives it, and his refusal to treat any given
doctrine in isolation, abstracted from the complex web of relations in
which it finds its proper place. In his thought there is, as it were, a "perichoretic" indwelling of doctrines in one another, so that in attending
to any one, one finds oneself immediately in the sphere of influence of
several others without any awareness of having migrated. There are also
issues of ontic and noetic priority to be reckoned with in approaching
particular parts of this dogmatic whole. In some measure, too, the problem lies in Torrance's literary contribution, which, despite its expansive
nature, lacks (and resists) a single sustained systematic expression of
the whole. One is thus compelled to draw on a variety of sources and
to harden the edges and pin down the location of concepts and the relationships between them that he himself was sometimes content to leave
less than entirely clear. The dangers of inappropriate overdetermination
must always be borne in mind in any such undertaking.[3] What follows,
therefore, must be treated as a provisional and partial account, suited
only to the specific task of indicating how Torrance's theology might
best be read as one which embraces the theme of salvation as the deification of our humanity.

§1. Identifying the Doctrinal Center of Gravity

The immediate doctrinal locus for the doctrine of deification is generally provided by theological anthropology, its advocates mostly choosing to earth it ultimately in the soil of humankind's creation in the image and likeness of God. Torrance's approach is quite different. While a theology of our creation *kat' eikona* certainly forms a significant part of the backdrop to his discussion, it does not occupy center stage and is not permitted independently to set the parameters in terms of which salvation is made sense of. As we have just seen, for Torrance doctrine maps a complex web of relationships between different aspects of the reality which is God's relationship to the world, and within this web as he sees it the doctrines of creation and of humanity, while not unimportant, are nonetheless more remote from the center of this particular conversation than some others. Thus it is the doctrines of the Trinity, incarnation, and the deity of the Holy Spirit which supply the matrix for the articulation and development of his account of salvation as *theopoiesis*, the "utterly staggering act of God in which he gives himself to us and adopts us into the communion of his divine life and love through Jesus Christ and in his one Spirit, yet in such a way that we are not made divine but are preserved in our humanity."[4]

We should note that Torrance's soteriology is certainly one in which the theme of salvation as the redemption of human beings from guilt and the judgment due to sin (imagery characteristically under- rather than overplayed in Eastern theology) is not neglected but finds a central place.[5] The human dilemma is at root that of alienation from God as a direct result of sin, and of perpetual enslavement to a nature determined by its fallen condition. Thus for Torrance "sin" is more (though never less) than a moral, let alone a forensic reality; it is the state in which our humanity exists, a basic fact of our ontology understood in relational terms (as those whose primary reality is constituted by personal relationship to God and to others). Correspondingly, salvation is presented in familiar terms, as an "atonement" wrought in Christ's humanity whereby sinful humans may, despite their sin and alienation, have access to the Father and enjoy fellowship with him. The existential breach caused by sin is bridged by Christ's atoning work; humanity is reconciled to God. Yet the way in which Torrance construes this redemptive activity of Christ sets his presentation of the matter apart from much atonement theology in the Protestant tradition. The fundamental point of contrast lies again in his refusal to understand the logic of reconciliation in terms of what he himself calls "external relations"[6] but rather as an ontological reality established within the very depths of human being by the whole course of Christ's incarnate history, from the conception in the womb of Mary to the ascension to the Father's right hand.

Protestant theology has typically dealt with the notion of atonement in one of two ways, both of which are characterized by Torrance as cast in terms of external relations between God, Jesus Christ, and the human race. The distinguishing feature has generally been the ascription of either a judicial or else an ethical nature to these relations. In either case, atonement is construed fundamentally as a transaction between various parties where, as a result of some atoning action which Christ performs, the status of the parties relative to one another, or to a divinely instituted legal code and its sanctions, is adjusted.[7] The relations are "external" because there is a tacit denial here that any change is effected at the level of our human "being" (that being the perceived emphasis of the Roman doctrine of an "infused righteousness") but only at the level of our forensic or moral standing before God. Hence the classic Protestant insistence that believers are best thought of as forgiven or reconciled sinners, rather than "saints" who have, through some mystical transformation of their inner being, been "made holy."[8] Furthermore, the atonement is, in all these cases, perceived to be external to the being of God rather than located at the heart of it.

Again, Torrance sees things rather differently. Rather than embracing the classic Protestant account of imputation (in which God agrees to treat those who are not righteous as though they were) he argues for an understanding in which, while moral and forensic language finds its proper place, atonement is nonetheless grasped as an ontological fact, something wrought within the depths of human nature as such. In the atonement, he insists, human being, the reality of human existence as we find it in the world, is really and actually reconciled to God. Fallen and debased as it is, our humanity is laid hold of and refashioned in a supreme re-creative act of the Spirit, being bent back from the warped and twisted shape it has assumed, into the form which it was always intended to have within the teleology of divine creation. Atonement, therefore, is not merely retrospective (looking backward to the brokenness of sin and death) but prospective, having as its outcome the fitting of our nature to share in that close personal communion with a Holy Father that is its proper eschatological destiny. On this understanding, then, the word "atonement" does not refer to a mere modification of legal or moral standing but to a root-and-branch transformation of our humanity in its entirety, "reconciling" it to God by drawing it into a lived correlation with the shape of God's own life. To use the seminal biblical metaphor so beloved of Torrance himself, in this correlation the covenant between God and Israel (and Israel on behalf of humanity) is finally fulfilled from both sides.[9]

§2. Atonement and Revelation

This summary account provokes at least one obvious question to which readers will demand an answer. Refusal to provide an answer to it immediately is at least faithful to the experience of reading Torrance's own work, and before answering it, therefore, I want to draw attention to another key theme which lies, unusually, at the center of Torrance's soteriology rather than elsewhere in his theology, namely, his account of revelation and the participation of human beings in knowledge of God. Other theologies might place this logically prior to the stuff of dogmatics proper, as part of the prolegomena in which the necessary conditions for theology are described. For Torrance, too, theology (and the faith of which theology is a product) can arise only because God has made himself known, and in this sense an account of revelation has a determinative place in our theological epistemology. Like his mentor Karl Barth, though, Torrance sees that (1) paradoxically theological prolegomena must really always be the last word rather than the first (since we should always describe our mode of knowing a posteriori, in the light of the actual engagement with something, rather than allowing a priori considerations to provide a prescriptive template) and (2) when we chart our knowing of God we discover that the shape of this "knowing" itself is part of the substance of dogmatics rather than a mere condition for it. We have already seen how various dogmatic fields overlap and interpenetrate, and this is precisely what we find to be the case here.

In short, salvation, according to Torrance, can finally be described as the drawing of men and women by the Holy Spirit to share in the self-knowledge of God. Since this description lends itself unhelpfully to various forms of gnostic or rationalistic interpretation, it demands immediate qualification. Drawing on a distinction borrowed from the philosopher of science Michael Polanyi, Torrance makes it clear that the saving knowledge spoken of here is not of the abstractive sort (the sort of knowledge that consists chiefly of data and might be recorded in written form or looked up on Google) but *personal* knowledge, the sort of knowing that occurs when (as we say) we "know" another person or people, rather than when we "know" the square root of 897.6, or the date of Shakespeare's

birth, or the Ten Commandments.[10] To say that we are granted participation in the self-knowledge of God, therefore, is not first and foremost to say
that we know some otherwise hidden and inaccessible things *about* God,
for instance that he exists in the threefold form of Father, Son, and Holy
Spirit. This, in Torrance's own terms, is a second-order mode of knowledge, the informational product of reflection on a first-order encounter.
Such things (the things we might loosely refer to here as "doctrine") are
generated by and secondary to the more important and fundamental way
in which we know God, namely by enjoying fellowship with the God who
is Father, Son, and Holy Spirit, as God approaches us and draws us into
the circle of his own self-knowing. Knowledge *of* God in this sense renders knowledge *about* God, and not vice versa. And for Torrance, precisely
because God *is* threefold ("triunity" refers appropriately not just to the
shape of our knowing but to the shape of what is known), and because
of the pattern of the divine economy in history (in which the eternal Son
"takes flesh"), this same personal knowing arises in the distinctive form
of a sharing by the Spirit's power in the eternal relationship which the Son
has with the Father, and doing so from the Son's perspective.

It is clear, then, that here the theology of "revelation" (God making
himself known to human beings) is, when viewed from a certain angle,
necessarily a theology of redemption too. Since, for Torrance, the description of *how* we know cannot properly be disentangled from the concrete
particulars of *what* we know ("the object determines the mode of knowing"), treatment of it involves a carefully articulated account of how we
are lifted up by the Holy Spirit into personal communion with the Father
through union with the Son.[11] In effect, the doctrine of our "knowledge"
of God entails a doctrine of adopted sonship, and this in turn entails a
description of our sharing (at a level appropriate to human creatures)
in the inner life of the divine Trinity since, Torrance emphasizes, "the
Father/Son or Son/Father relationship *falls within the very being of God*."[12]
Hence we are already in territory where the language of "deification" or
participation in God seemingly lies close to hand, but there is a vital component as yet to be added.

For human beings to share in the inner life of God requires that they be
at one with God and not in a state of alienation from him. "Requires" here
does not refer to some arbitrary condition imposed by God, of course, but
simply describes the logic of the circumstance: we cannot both be reconciled to and alienated from God at the same time, and sharing in the Son's
communion with the Father is fundamentally a reconciled state. Torrance

links this specifically theological point to a wider epistemological observation: "All genuine knowledge," he writes, "involves a cognitive union of
the mind with its object, and calls for the removal of any estrangement or
alienation which may obstruct or distort it."[13] Where our knowing of God
is concerned, the relevant obstruction is caused by our sin, and thus in
order for God to make himself known to us in the relevant sense this sin
must be dealt with and the existential breach which it has opened up fully
healed. Again, the theologies of revelation and salvation overlap.[14] Indeed,
Torrance's way of putting the matter suggests their spheres of influence
are concentric: God reveals himself in atoning acts. To know God is to be
reconciled to him as the Spirit lifts us up, effecting a "cognitive union with
him in which our whole being is affected by his love and holiness. It is the
pure in heart who see God."[15]

§3. Subject, Object, and Incarnation

The question which naturally arises at this point, though (now with more
force than ever), is just how this view of things differs from the traditional
Catholic notion of justification via an infused quality of righteousness,
a change effected by grace in the very depths of the sinner's own being
which fits him or her for the life of grace. Has Torrance not departed
radically from the distinctive Reformation emphasis on atonement as
an objectively wrought and finished work standing over against the sinner as the source of his or her confidence before God? Must we suppose
now that the epithet "justified" does indeed refer to some subjective condition of sinners, rather than referring sinners outside themselves and
beyond any worth and capacities identifiable in themselves for assurance?
The answer is a resounding negative, but in order to see how and why we
need to reckon with a further distinctive element in Torrance's soteriology, namely his fusion of the claim that atonement is ontological rather
than extrinsic, with an appeal (at first sight rather odd) to the category of
substitution.[16] Yes, he insists, God has indeed laid hold of our humanity
and, through the anointing of his Spirit, has refashioned it, justifying and
sanctifying it, and finally lifting it up to share in the dynamics of his own
triune existence, but the locus of this saving activity is not to be identified
in the particular lives of believers but rather in the unique history of the
one man Jesus Christ.

    In the personal history of Jesus, Torrance maintains, the eternal Son of
God himself assumed human nature and lived out a life of human sonship
before his Father in the power of the Holy Spirit, healing and sanctifying

that nature from its sinful disposition, bending it back from its warped existence into alignment with God's creative purpose for it, bearing it in humility to the cross in order to judge it and pay the price for human sin, and finally raising it up in a glorified state on the third day and exalting it to the Father's right hand.[17] In all this, our fallen nature is transformed "from within" and rendered capable of sharing in the divine life, but it is so "vicariously," the refashioning of our humanity having occurred "for us" in our substitute and representative, Jesus Christ. Furthermore, the reconciliation here occurs from both sides at once, God moving toward man, and man moving reciprocally toward God within the constitution of a single personal existence.[18]

As is immediately apparent from this, for Torrance the doctrines of the incarnation and the atonement are utterly inseparable. There can be no proper understanding of the "work" of Christ apart from an equivalent grasp of his person, precisely because his person is, in a profound sense, identical with the substance of his work. Atonement is not an abstract quantity that follows on from something that Christ does. It is what Christ *is*, namely, one in whom God and humanity exist in a reconciled relationship and in accordance with God's purposes in creation and covenant. Thus Jesus "does not mediate a revelation or a reconciliation that is other than what he is, as though he were only the agent or instrument of that mediation to mankind. He embodies what he mediates in himself, for what he mediates and what he is are one and the same. He constitutes in his own incarnate Person the content and the reality of what he mediates in both revelation and reconciliation."[19] In Jesus Christ, in other words, we actually see God and humanity at one, coexisting in fellowship in a harmonious unity of will and activity within the dynamics of the incarnate Son's life. In this sense, for Torrance, the hypostatic union of natures should not be construed as something timeless and static, but precisely as an atoning personal history in which the life of God and man meet and are conformed to one another in the Son's constant love for and self-offering to the Father.[20] Mediation, therefore, the bringing together of God and man, is not just a role which Jesus performs but something involved in the very dynamics of his personal being as the incarnate Son.[21]

Of course this was an at-one-ment forged only through the most profound struggle with the inherent propensity of our fallen nature toward sin and death. Thus "reconciliation was a creative as well as an atoning act of God accomplished in the ontological depths of human existence and its desperate condition under divine judgment, in order to redeem mankind from bondage and misery, sin and guilt, and to regenerate human nature, raising it up from its lost and corrupt condition into union with the divine Life embodied in Jesus Christ and exhibited in his resurrection from the dead."[22] This is an understanding of atonement which broadens the focus of our attention out from the death of Jesus on Calvary and insists that the latter is the logical culmination and natural symbol of a whole life in which sin is judged and put to death and obedience offered freely and gladly to the Father. In fact, in fusing the doctrines of the incarnation and atonement, Torrance eschews the habitual limiting of either to particular moments in Jesus' history (the virginal conception and the crucifixion respectively) and insists on approaching them as interlocking dimensions of the Son's engagement with the flesh in its historical entirety. Thus "the incarnation includes the whole life and activity of Jesus Christ culminating in his resurrection and ascension, while the atonement begins from his very conception and birth when he put on the form of a servant and began to pay the price of our redemption."[23]

Undergirding this model of salvation is Torrance's affirmation of the Nicene *homoousion* as applied both to the Son (in his divine and human natures respectively) and to the Spirit. On one hand Christ is and must be consubstantial with the Father as regards his divinity. It is precisely because the Son of God is not related to God externally, as all creatures are, but rather belongs to the eternal being of God that he is able both to make God known to us (he himself is the very personal presence of God in our midst) and to reconcile our humanity to God by assuming it and living out his life of divine sonship from within it. On the other hand, Torrance's ontological account of reconciliation also demands that Christ should be *homoousios* with us as regards his humanity, sharing to the full in our human condition. If he took our flesh in order to renew it from within, then that which he assumed must of necessity have been humanity as we know and experience it, under the damaging and terminal effects of sin, bound by the power of sin, caught up in the gradual downward spiral that leads to judgment, destruction, and death. Thus, Torrance insists, what the Son of God assumed must have been precisely what in theological terms we call "fallen" humanity, and not some neutral or pre-fallen substitute for it. What he fashions for himself in the virgin's womb is thus precisely humanity in that condition which needs to be redeemed. To be sure, having assumed it, Christ lives out a "sinless" existence within it; this, indeed, is the heart of the redemptive activity itself. But unless Christ had taken to himself our corrupt and sinful nature, his sinless and obedient life before the Father would not have been "atoning," would not have possessed the reconciling and renewing force which they do in fact possess. This is Torrance's understanding of the patristic dictum that "the unassumed is the unhealed,"[24] a claim which makes sense only within the sort of ontological model of atonement with which he works.

Jesus Christ, then, is both the man who is reconciled to God in the very depths of his own personal being, and the God who, as man, thereby reconciles others in and to himself. But in what sense, we may ask, is this latter claim actually true? If, notwithstanding the ontological nature of atonement it is also substitutionary and objective to us, if Christ's particular humanity rather than ours is the locus of God's regenerative and redemptive activity, then in what sense can it be maintained that we are actually reconciled or healed in the process? Are we not simply confronted here, as it were, with an ontological rather than a legal fiction, something which leaves us essentially unchanged?

Torrance insists that this is not so, since all that Christ is and does, he is and does "for us" and not for himself. In the incarnation, he writes, "God has drawn so near to man and drawn man so near to himself in Jesus that they are perfectly at one."[25] What this means, for Torrance, is that all humans have drawn near to God in and with the one man Jesus. How is this possible? To make sense of it Torrance appeals to the category of Christ's "vicarious humanity."[26] In assuming the "flesh" which belonged to us, he urges, the Son of God identified himself with our condition and thus united us to himself, establishing an ontological bond by virtue of which his particular humanity was rendered inclusive in its relationship to ours, and we thereby included "in" him prior to and apart from any knowledge of or response to God's redeeming action in him for our sakes. What takes place in him on our behalf, therefore, is no "fiction" but already has an impact at the roots of our own being, since we have no existence apart from the ontological solidarity which, by taking flesh, God has established between us and his incarnate Son. The context for making sense of this solidarity is not, as in some accounts of the idea, an anthropology drawing on extrabiblical categories (such as the classical philosophical notion of "concrete universals," or primitive notions of "corporate personality"),[27] but rather the specifically Christian theological claim that in Jesus it is the Creator Logos, in whom we already live and move and have our being, who now takes to himself our humanity and thereby bonds us to himself humanly as well as by virtue of his existence "as God."

All humans, therefore, are united to the regenerated and sanctified "flesh" of the Son, and through it granted access to the life of sonship which he enjoys both eternally and now humanly. But inasmuch as this is something done by God *for us*, objectively and once for all in his atoning incarnation, death, and resurrection, it is not the whole story. Substitution must subsequently be complemented by and come to fruition in active participation as individual men and women are drawn by the Spirit which was in Christ to live out and "become" what, by virtue of their union with him, in a deeper sense they already are. "This union of Jesus Christ with us in body and blood by virtue of which he became our Priest and Mediator before God demands as its complement our union with him in his body and blood, drawing near to God and offering him our worship with, in and through Christ."[28] This latter, secondary union comes to sacramental expression in baptism and the Lord's Supper, both of which testify in a visible way to the fact that Christian existence is neither more nor less than faith's appropriation, through the Spirit's enabling, of what is already ours (established for us in his self-substitution for us before the Father) in Christ. For Torrance, therefore, in granting faith the Spirit does not *establish* our union with Christ but rather reestablishes and confirms it, creating in us a new level of that same union which, in the virgin's womb, he established once and for all. Thus, while the activity of the Son and the Spirit are distinct, they are nonetheless thoroughly correlated and interpenetrate.[29] It was in the Spirit's power that the Son, as the *Mashiach* or anointed one, regenerated and reconciled our broken and alienated nature from within; and now that same regenerative and reconciling activity is continued in others, as the same Spirit is poured out on all flesh, enabling their active participation in Christ's redeemed humanity as sons and daughters of the Father.

§4. Deification, Mediation, and the Humanity of God

On what basis, then, could this view of salvation as a participation or sharing in the regenerated humanity of the Son be made sense of in terms of the language of "deification," as I have suggested it might? The answer lies in the way in which Torrance situates his soteriology ultimately within the womb of his Trinitarianism. What we see in the history of the man Jesus, he argues, is nothing less than that place in human space and time where eternal relations between the three divine persons are historically *earthed*. *Sub specie aeternitatis* the Son relates to the Father and the Father to the Son in the power of the Holy Spirit. Historically speaking, when the Son takes flesh he relates (humanly) to his heavenly Father and the Father to his only beloved (now incarnate) Son in the power of this same Spirit, moving mysteriously in the virgin's womb, poured out at Jesus' baptism, and erupting from the darkness of the closed tomb, to mention just three key moments in what must nonetheless be supposed to have been a continuous if not uniform presence and activity. The life of intimate love between Father, Son, and Spirit, now interwoven with human history in a wholly new way, is thus both the immediate context for and the substance of the outworking of human redemption; atonement and regeneration take place within the depths of God's threefold being, and in the Son's "flesh" humanity is drawn into the dynamics of that same being, while yet remaining fully human throughout (the two "natures" of the Chalcedonian Confession remain properly distinct in the union).

By way of brief elaboration, three points stand out as worthy of particular mention. First, the one who becomes incarnate and unites us to himself is none other than very God himself, and thus our participation in his humanity is precisely a participation in the humanity of God, a "fleshly" fraternity with the Creator who empties himself for our sake, but in doing so remains the One who he always was and is and shall be.[30] Second, the Spirit who, in due course, draws us severally to Christ and enables our personal sharing in his communion with the Father, is himself none other than the Spirit of Christ, the one who is eternally *homoousios* with both the Father and the Son and who condescends to indwell us just as he indwelt (and still indwells) Jesus, lifting us up and enabling our personal response of faith and obedience and worship.[31] Thus the "Godness of God" itself is present in the temples of our bodies in the person and the power of the Holy Spirit, a point Torrance learned well from Athanasius' *Letters to Serapion*.[32] In redemption, therefore, we are united to God's own humanity, and we are filled with God himself in the person of the Spirit. And, third, we are defined now by our access (by grace) to the Father-Son relation which lies at the heart of God's eternal being, "the inner life of the Holy Trinity which is private to God alone" but "is extended to include human nature in and through Jesus," and with him all those to whom he has bound himself in love.[33] While one might argue, therefore, that the central motif in Torrance's soteriology is that of participative sonship, it is clear that this particular notion of "sonship" has nothing whatever to do with its Liberal Protestant counterpart in which God's universal "Fatherhood" is traced from the doctrine of creation, turning it into a "natural" and ethical relation rather than one of pure grace;[34] for Torrance, God's

Fatherhood has nothing to do with his role as Creator, but is to be understood purely in terms of the eternal triune being in which God is the Father of the Son and the Son of the Father in the power of the Spirit who binds them in love. It is this relationship of *koinonia* and self-giving lying at the heart of what God eternally is that, in grace, is opened up to human sharing by the economy of the incarnation.

We should note that Torrance's insistence on wedding *theopoiesis* firmly to the incarnation (it is, Torrance insists, the obverse of Christ's "inhomination" and utterly contingent on it)[35] obviates the need for mediating categories such as "created grace" and the "divine energies" appealed to in Western and Eastern versions of the idea respectively as that by virtue of their participation in which humans are duly "deified." Since *theopoiesis* is not a direct communion of the believer with the Father or the Spirit but a reality mediated via our union with the incarnate Son, it is precisely the flesh of Christ in which we participate, and which provides the mediating term between our own humanity and the divine life in which we are given to share. The problem of the interface between God and humanity does not arise, in other words, in any form lying beyond the scope of that addressed in the careful terms of the Chalcedonian Confession to which Torrance is so committed, for the relevant point of contact between God and our nature is precisely the one which God himself established when he entered the womb of the virgin. No closer or alternative union between divinity and humanity can be imagined or entertained than this, for this is where God himself enters into our nature and makes it (and us) his own by uniting it with his own nature in the person of the Son.

Hence, while we may well think of salvation as a matter of *huiopoiesis* (the making of sons and daughters), it is nonetheless both appropriate and important to understand this also as a matter of *theopoiesis*—not the "divinization" of our humanity, to be sure, but its being granted to share nevertheless in who and what God eternally is, by virtue of an act of grace in which he has first become what we are. "Deification," while an unfamiliar term in Protestant soteriology, is thus the one which best captures and expresses the larger pattern of Torrance's understanding of salvation in which atonement, incarnation, and Trinity are not discrete but interpenetrating doctrinal loci, because the complex reality of divine being and action to which each in its turn refers resists easy dissection other than at the cost of the death of the patient.

III

Christology in Contemporary Context

11

Impeccability

§1. Incarnation, Temptation, and Human Freedom

A Dilemma

Our concern in this chapter is with the traditional Christian claim that Jesus of Nazareth was "tempted in all respects as we are, yet without sin" (Heb 4:15). In its dogmatic, as opposed to its biblical, version, this claim can be identified in two distinct forms. First, there is what we may denote the weaker form, in which it is claimed simply that in actual fact Jesus committed no sin, and second, there is the stronger form according to which he was actually and in principle quite incapable of committing sin. Put differently, in terms of the distinctions of scholastic theology, we may either confess of the incarnate *posse non peccare* or *non posse peccare*.

Traditional dogmatics has for the most part insisted on the stronger form as a necessary inference of the doctrine of incarnation. Only the recognition that Jesus could never actually have sinned, it has been contended, safeguards both the integrity of the incarnation as a manifestation of the life of God, and its redemptive efficacy. For Christ to have faced the genuine possibility of the commission of sin puts all this at risk, a risk which, it is implied, is just as incompatible with the character of God as sin itself. In a discussion of the subject, H. P. Owen[1] goes further, arguing that a genuine capacity for sin logically already entails that condition of the human flesh which is inherently sinful, and therefore utterly incompatible with a de facto sinlessness. In the language and categories of tradition, the capacity for actual sin is inseparable from original sin, and to be possessed of the latter is by default to be sinful and in need of redemption rather than the agent of it. So, if we are to be true to the central tenets of incarnational Christology and soteriology, we must affirm that the man Jesus was utterly incapable of embarking on a sinful course of action, no matter how frequently or intensely he might have been subjected to temptation.

But it is precisely here, of course, that a major problem seems to arise for Christology. Namely, if Jesus was at no time in his life faced with the real possibility of sinning (if, as we might say, he was never really "free" to sin) then in what precise sense are we able to affirm the integrity of his human experience, and in particular the claim that he "was tempted in all things as we are"? It may be argued that sin as such has no legitimate place in true human existence, and that Jesus' being truly human is thus perfectly compatible with his sinlessness. Some such claim would indeed seem to be a necessary inference of orthodox Christology. But it does not of itself resolve the thorny problem of knowing precisely where the line which differentiates his "truly" human experience of life from our experience of it should be drawn. If we draw that line in such a way that it removes from Jesus all possibility of sinning, are we not thereby precisely robbing him of the experience of being "tempted in all things as we are"? Is the genuine potential for sin not analytic in some way in the very notion of temptation? Certainly it would seem to be basic to human temptation as we know and experience it. What exactly *is* temptation, it may be asked, if the freedom to sin is removed, if the choice of the evil over the good, of sin over obedience, is rendered null and void from the outset?

To question thus is not simply to insist on a Christology which takes as its point of departure the allegation that "whatever else he was, Jesus was certainly a man," and moves rapidly on from there to sweeping statements about the probable nature of his experience based on the assumption that, being human ourselves, we know what his human experience must have been like in certain fundamental respects at least. Such an approach may have something important to offer, but, starting as it does with general and empirical categories, it certainly does not furnish us with a sufficient basis for constructing a Christology rooted in the particularities of the story of Jesus, where, as Stephen Sykes has noted, we cannot in the end avoid the question of that in Jesus' human story which marks him off decisively from all others.[2] Nor is it simply to insist on due weight being accorded to the specific statement of Hebrews 4 or the Gospel portrayals of Jesus as one caught up in an ultimately victorious conflict with the attempts of the powers of evil to deflect him from his messianic mission under God. Important as these are, they are capable of interpretations which relieve us of the dilemma rather than addressing it.

In addition to these and other possible motives for questioning the ascription of impeccability to Jesus, we may note that there are motives for doing so which seem to emerge naturally and equally urgently out of the very same mesh of incarnational and soteriological understanding which have led to that same ascription. There are those, of course, who have insisted that the humanity of Christ must actually be "fallen" in order for his incarnate economy to be possessed of real redemptive significance for us who exist in fallen flesh. But it is not necessary to endorse this claim in order to acknowledge the existence of genuine soteriological difficulties with the doctrine of impeccability. There are few soteriologies, for instance, which do not in practice make considerable capital out of the perfect human obedience of Jesus: whether as an example to be followed, an ideal personality affecting our inner life, a necessary prerequisite to the supererogatory *satisfactio* constituted by his death, or whatever. But remove from Jesus all possibility of doing anything other than he in fact did from moment to sinless moment in his life, and arguably one has undermined all soteriological talk of obedience and of victory. For what is obedience if there can never be any serious question of disobedience? And what is victory if the enemy never stood any serious chance? Formally the terms may remain, but morally they are emasculated. So, at least, it may seem to some.

"It is here," writes L. W. Grensted, "that a protest becomes intelligible. Man urgently desires a Leader who has fought His way through to victory. Even though the victory were incomplete, that is better than a victory that is no victory at all, but an irruption upon us of another world-order, robbing us of our very birthright as well."[3] Soteriologically speaking, therefore, what would seem to be desired is a way of making sense of the dual claim that in the case of Jesus temptation was fully real while yet the victory over sin was equally complete at each moment. The traditional christological insistence on the *non posse peccare* appears in effect to rob Jesus of that moral freedom which allows his temptation to be viewed as genuine. The dilemma we face, therefore, is that the more we seek to bolster and secure the sinlessness, the more we seem to put at risk those very moral conditions which render it soteriologically significant. To cite Sykes again, "The more a theologian insists on the particular humanity of Christ, the more need he has of a concept of its representative status," since "the theme of identification is theologically effective only if what Jesus was and did can in some sense be shown to be typical or representative of the human condition and human experience."[4]

§2. Forsyth's Proposed Solution within the Context of a Kenotic Christology

Forsyth addresses this very dilemma in the context of his development of a kenotic Christology in chapter 11 of *The Person and Place of Jesus Christ*.[5] The basic theme of kenotic Christologies, of course, is that in becoming human the preexistent Son set aside for a season his divine fullness in order to enter fully into human experience. But, however this process of self-divestment be thought of (and Forsyth, it will be recalled, favors the model of a "retraction" rather than an abandonment of attributes), there must in certain instances remain some clear and positive relation between these two stages or modes of the Son's existence, otherwise we drive a wedge between them which renders the humanity of Jesus empty of both revelatory and redemptive significance. Specifically, we cannot think of God divesting himself of holiness in order to enter into experience of human sinfulness. We may need to think through just what perfect holiness might mean when adapted to a human mode of existence, but it is vital that we hold on to it, since holiness (sinlessness if we prefer the same thing viewed from a negative relation) is so integral to the character of God that to set it aside or to compromise it would be tantamount to God ceasing to be God. Whatever kenosis means, it cannot mean or entail this. Thus, Forsyth argues, we reach a limit when we come to the human experience of sin, and we must confess with the church through the ages *non potuit peccare*.

So then we are back with our dilemma, apparently denying to Jesus the conditions proper to human morality, and thereby just as surely creating a serious problem for Christology and soteriology. "But," Forsyth asks, "what if it were thus?" (and here we quote at some length). "What if his kenosis went so far that though the impossibility was there he did not know of it? The limitation of his knowledge is indubitable—even about himself. . . . Did that nescience not extend to the area of his own moral nature, and so provide for him the temptable conditions which put him in line with our dark conflict, and which truly moralise and humanise his victory when *potuit non peccare*? He knew he came sinless out of each crisis; did he know he never could be anything else? How could he? Would it have been moral conflict if he had known this?"[6]

Here, then, we have the suggestion that the doctrine of kenosis enables us to make sense of the apparently self-contradictory claim that Christ could never have sinned and yet experienced precisely the same sort of moral conflict which all other humans endure daily, thereby investing his obedient and sinless behavior once again with genuine moral value. The key lies in a distinction which may be drawn between the ontological and the noetic. In reality Christ was not able to do any other than the good. He was not free to sin in that sense. But from his human perspective he could not know this; it appeared to him as if he were genuinely free either to sin or not to sin. In this qualified sense, therefore, we may speak of his moral freedom. To introduce a familiar distinction in Christology we may put the matter thus: viewed "from above," Christ was not free to sin; viewed "from below," he seemed to be, and had to engage in moral struggle just as if he had been. In practical terms his immunity made no apparent difference to his circumstances.

This suggestion certainly shortcircuits the sort of tacit Apollinarianism which some attempts to secure the *non posse peccare* appear inevitably to slide into. Further consideration suggests a direct parallel in a facet of our common human existence, namely the way in which our conscious self represents only the tip of the iceberg of our psyche, and at any moment it is true of us that we both know and yet paradoxically do not know (i.e., are not consciously aware of) many things. Indeed, depth psychology suggests that any and every decision which we "freely" make in life is inevitably going to be shaped by that which lurks unobserved in our subconscious—repressed memories, psychological scar tissue, the emotional inheritance of a childhood spent in a secure and loving home environment, and so on. We may not (perhaps almost certainly will not) be aware of the influence of these things, but they will be there nonetheless. It is interesting that William Sanday, in a book published just one year after *The Person and Place of Jesus Christ*, was to seek to develop a model of the hypostatic union employing these very same categories.[7] But while this suggests how, from a psychological angle, we might make sense of the idea that Christ was absolutely impeccable without being aware of it, it does not, of course, address the metaphysical question of whether the presence of a foregone immunity to sin, known or unknown, is compatible with genuine moral struggle. To put the matter differently, it does not tell us whether necessity is compatible with human freedom.

§3. Parallels between Forsyth's View and "Compatibilism" Observed

With this further question we reach a point where we may identify certain formal parallels between Forsyth's proffered account of Jesus' experience of temptation and the philosophical position usually referred to as compatibilism, and may ask whether the latter might not furnish a philosophical basis for the development of the former. Compatibilism, according to one of its exponents, J. L. Mackie, is the view that determinism and human freedom are compatible with one another; that if, that is to say, all human actions can be accounted for sufficiently in terms of identifiable antecedent causes so that, given the particular combination of factors and circumstances leading up to an action or choice, the particular outcome may be said to have been inevitable and in principle predictable, nonetheless, we can still speak in perfectly meaningful terms about morality, responsibility, desert, and so on.[8] One key factor in the case for compatibilism is the claim that moral responsibility is tied directly to intentionality: in other words, I am responsible as a moral agent for all those acts which I engage in intentionally, and not for any others. There is, of course, considerable scope for clarification over what precisely constitutes an intentional act in this sense, and room for multifarious exceptions to be identified (when, for example, I am coerced by some external physical force or forces to commit a conscious act for which I may yet be deemed not responsible); but basically the "straight rule of responsibility," as Mackie calls it, finds me responsible for all those acts which I choose to do, for whatever reason. Insofar as this same choice or decision may theoretically be the result of unseen antecedent causes, moral responsibility thus defined can indeed be seen to be perfectly consistent with the determinist hypothesis.

Two particular points of comparison with Forsyth's kenotic treatment of the *non posse peccare* may now be identified. First we should note that the truth or falsity of the determinist hypothesis is neither knowable nor demonstrable. In order to prove it we should have to be able to produce evidence for the existence of sufficient antecedent causes to account for all particular actions, and no reasonable determinist would claim that such an analysis is or is ever likely to be possible. Indeed, since such demonstration would in any case have in principle to apply to the process of analysis itself, the results generated could never be conclusive. To this extent, as David Wiggins puts it, "getting evidence for determinism would certainly be like filling a broken pitcher."[9] It constitutes an epistemological impossibility to step outside the circle of alleged causality in order to achieve an objective viewpoint; thus there is a self-referential problem involved in any attempt to verify (or indeed to falsify) determinism. Such a "God's eye view" of things is not available to us as moral agents. On the other hand, the appeal of libertarians to what might be termed the common-sense factor, namely the appeal to "a feeling or direct experience of freedom" on the part of human beings as they go about their moral business, must be deemed equally inconclusive. As Mackie argues, "What we would most naturally take as a feeling of freedom is the consciousness of the effective operation of our thoughts and decisions," and while this may furnish evidence for "voluntariness," it does not demonstrate the presence of "contracausal freedom."[10] Again, the circle of our experience cannot be stepped beyond. We can never know for sure that our experience of freedom is not itself sufficiently accounted for by antecedent causes, even though there may be good reasons for suspecting this to be the case.

Where all this leaves us, then, is with the observation that whether the determinist hypothesis is true or false, human experience of moral decision making on the ground may look and feel just the same. It makes no practical or experiential difference to our wrangling with a moral problem whether or not the various stages in that wrangling can be accounted for causally. That we could never do otherwise than in a particular set of circumstances we actually do is altogether beyond our ken if it is true, and therefore makes no difference whatever to our moral consciousness. Here, then, there is an obvious point of contact with Forsyth's contention that Jesus' sinless actions were necessary (i.e., in some sense at least predictable and determined) and yet such necessity remained altogether unknown to him and made no practical or experiential difference to his human moral pilgrimage. If determinism is a correct hypothesis, in other words, then this is true not only of Christ but of all humans at all times.

The second point of comparison between Forsyth and compatibilism lies in the explicit suggestion of the latter that judgments of moral integrity and worth survive even if our every action is inevitable and the possibility of acting otherwise was never open to us in any real sense. For the compatibilist it is the intention of the agent considered from the standpoint of the agent which matters rather than the hypothetical presence or absence of causes sufficient to account for that intention. If we distinguish between the standpoint of the moral agent and that of the "scientific spectator," then what compatibilism claims is that while the latter may (in principle) have inductive and predictive knowledge of the actions and decisions of the agent, the agent him- or herself cannot be party to this same knowledge, and therefore our ordinary everyday assumptions concerning moral agency and responsibility remain intact.[11] Thus in the case of Jesus we might say that while his sinless perfection was in principle predictable, attributable to some unseen but nonetheless real determining factor or factors (presumably, e.g., his personal identity as the eternal Son), nonetheless, inasmuch as his actions were the result of the normal processes of human moral psychology, moral value is ascribable to them. If this is so, then we can see how their significance for soteriology and for a truly inhominational christology might be preserved alongside the confession of the *non posse peccare*. Again, of course, this moral paradox pertains not only to Christ but to all humans considered as moral agents in all their actions.

§4. Critiques of Compatibilism and Questions concerning Human Freedom

The chief problem with compatibilism, according to its critics, is that it posits compatibility where there is in reality none to be had, and that it does so by engineering a subtle but all-significant shift in the sense of traditional terms. Thus Richard Swinburne observes that, while compatibilists claim to show that determinism is consonant with human freedom, what they really mean is that it is consonant with human moral responsibility, a closely related but (he maintains) nonetheless logically distinct thing.[12] Focusing on the "straight rule of responsibility," compatibilists proceed to identify the human ability to choose (an activity of the will which in theory at least may be either caused or uncaused) with freedom of the will. Thus "insofar as he acts intentionally, [an agent] has free will in the compatibilist's sense."[13] But, Swinburne insists, such freedom is certainly not freedom in the obvious and generally accepted sense of that term, which entails the insistence that in human choice the will is "free from necessitating causes."[14] Clearly, freedom of this sort could never be compatible with determinism since it constitutes its logical opposite, as surely as not-P stands over against P. And for Swinburne, true moral responsibility is definable not in terms of intentionality alone, but intentionality within the context of this libertarian understanding of the freedom of the will. "Men," he concludes, "having moral beliefs, are morally responsible for their actions if and only if they have free will in the traditional sense that their intentional actions are not causally necessitated in all their detail by prior causes."[15]

Some such appeal to what has been termed elsewhere the "categorical substitutability" of choices and actions[16] (i.e., the claim that a particular choice or action might genuinely have been different even given the same precise set of circumstances), in which moral responsibility is closely tied to purposive explanation which is neither reducible to or entirely compatible with causal explanation of a physical kind, would seem likely to find a sympathetic ear among Christian theologians. A number of factors inherent in what most at least would hold to be a Christian view of human existence seem to be endangered by its erosion or denial. It is not clear, for example, precisely how such doctrines as those of sin and redemption, or Christian ethics, can ultimately survive the ascription of everything that happens, both good and bad, to the direct will of God as a doctrine of creation informed by determinism would seem to require. Again, the fundamental appeal of the gospel to love, both as the nature of God and as that mode of existence to which humans are uniformly called, would seem to conflict with determinism. Love that is in principle predictable, the theologian might well protest, is simply not love, either in God or in human beings. Finally, we may note that the logic of determinism also calls into question the integrity of human personhood. "The doer," writes Nietzsche, "is merely a fiction added to the deed—the deed is everything."[17] In similar vein the determinist finds him or herself with no need to posit the existence of a so-called metaphysical or nonempirical self in order to account for human moral behavior. All that a particular human being "is" at a given moment in time is satisfactorily accounted for in empirical and causal terms as a combination of feelings, desires, character, and so on. And since these factors will vary from one moment to the next, there is no need to posit any absolute and enduring identity of persons through time. As Swinburne notes, the net result of this is the denial of continuity of personal responsibility and Nietzsche's insistence that "bad consciences . . . should be abolished."[18]

But if, for these and a host of other reasons, the Christian theologian is likely to be ill disposed to a consistent philosophical determinism, nonetheless the alternative can hardly be a headlong rush to embrace the sort of optimistic libertarianism popular in many quarters since it was espoused by Kant at the end of the eighteenth century. As Donald Baillie pointed out long ago, Kant's maxim that it must be possible on the basis of a moral ought to posit a universal human capacity to choose to do what that ought prescribes amounts to little more theologically than Pelagianism.[19] Even if the more pessimistic excesses of certain Protestant anthropologies might reasonably be avoided, it would, nonetheless, seem to be basic to Christian understanding to insist that humans are in some sense enslaved by sin, and require to be set free from its bonds in order to live life in accordance with God's creative purpose.

Quite apart from this specifically theological consideration, it would seem in any case to be clear that whatever human freedom consists in it is not a condition characterized by complete and utter lack of determination. If reactions against determinism suggest that it is thus, then they can only mislead. As Baillie observes, such "capricious freedom," far from enhancing moral responsibility, would actually undermine it altogether. "Surely," he writes, "we are responsible for our actions precisely because they do not spring 'out of the blue,' utterly undetermined and accidental, but spring from what we are, by a kind of determination quite different from the chains of mechanical causation which determine the behaviour of material things; it is the determination of personal choice."[20] Our choices are affected by a great many things: things concerning the world in which we live; and those in relation to whom we exist, and things "internal" to us as particular persons, our specific genetic coding, our temper, our "nature," and so on. We cannot begin to understand the choices which people make without according due consideration to such things, which may perfectly legitimately be referred to as "causes" of their behavior if that term be preferred.

Thus we may allow Mackie his complaint that libertarians cannot in the end avoid the category of causality if they are to ascribe motive (and thereby morality) to human actions.[21] But to concede this is certainly not to capitulate to determinism. Freedom within causal constraints, be those constraints ever so great, is still recognizably freedom: not freedom defined as freedom *from* all constraints certainly, but rather the freedom which exists in the space which remains for contingency after every antecedent cause has been taken fully into account. Thus, as Downie and Telfer put the matter, while the agent "may be circumscribed by features which he cannot influence, including his own desires, . . . some room is left for his own decision to contribute to events."[22] Freedom is, in the words of Sartre, "the small movement which makes of a totally conditioned social being someone who does not render back completely what his conditioning has given him."[23] Such freedom may in the end be simply the freedom to choose which set of determining or causal factors shall prevail. The space left for it may not necessarily be very great: it may be more or less, so that sometimes, when the antecedent determining factors are weighed, we may certainly speak of the extreme likelihood or probability that a person will behave in one way rather than another. That is, presumably, what we mean when we say, for example, that we cannot imagine Mother Teresa committing a violent crime, or that she "could not" do so, language which we employ readily in this context. But for the libertarian there must always be the chink of daylight left when all the causal bricks have been slotted into place. By the phrase "chink of daylight" it is not intended to suggest that a person might in some way step momentarily outside of their personal and natural specificity, "freed" from the constraints of who and what they are, but simply to insist that who and what they are does not render their choices inevitable but has an element of behavioral contingency built into it. To cite Wiggins again: "It may not matter if the world *approximates* to a world which satisfies the principles of a neurophysiological determinism provided only that this fails in the last resort to characterise the world completely."[24] Causality, however great it may prove to be, must not be absolutely irresistible if moral responsibility is to prevail; it may be necessary but can never be sufficient.

It would seem, then, that determinism, even in its compatibilist versions, fails to provide a philosophical base sufficient to undergird a comprehensive Christian theology. A perusal of Forsyth's writings rapidly betrays the fact that he for one could not have embraced it. Yet if some form of libertarianism is the only alternative, then it would seem necessary to insist that in order to take account of the Christian doctrine of sanctification and Christian ethics, it will have to be a form which comes far closer to determinism than has often been supposed. With this in mind we turn finally and briefly back to the problem of Christ's human freedom and the *non posse peccare*.

§5. Baillie's "Paradox of Grace"

An Alternative Model?

In an essay on the theology of Donald Baillie, George Hall suggests that Baillie ought logically to have embraced compatibilism in order to bolster his own exposition of the so-called paradox of grace.[25] Significantly, Hall does not refer to the essay "Philosophers and Theologians on Freedom of the Will." If he had done so he might have modified this suggestion, as it becomes clear in this essay that what Baillie envisages as human freedom, while allowing for free choice to be determined to a considerable degree, is nonetheless quite incompatible with determinism in the strict and proper sense. But Hall's comment directs us helpfully to the fact that Baillie's paradox of grace comes close in appearance at least to compatibilism, and thus prompts the question whether or not we might usefully turn here for an alternative way of making sense of Forsyth's christological proposal. This possibility is lent weight by two considerations: first, the fact that for Baillie himself the paradox of grace is precisely a means of understanding, by means of an analogy in our own experience of God's grace, just how the divine and the human might be related in the incarnate Son; and second, Forsyth, in seeking to illuminate how it might be that Christ's obedience could be both determined and yet free, makes brief appeal to the very same facet of Christian experience.[26]

What both theologians direct us to is the conviction of the Christian that somehow every good thing in her and everything which she does in the service of the kingdom of God is wrought not by her but by God through her. And yet there is no suggestion that the Christian is not every bit as free and responsible in doing it as she ever is. It is and remains fully her own act; and yet she can claim none of the credit for it, as if it were an independent achievement. It is both fully her own act and yet mysteriously fully God's act. There is no other way to express the matter. And in submitting to the divine determination (if we may call it such) of her actions, the Christian feels not less but mysteriously more free, liberated from other negative determining factors which lay constant claim to her allegiance. This experience of "determined freedom" accords well with the view of freedom outlined in the previous section of this chapter, and, Baillie suggests, may help us to resolve the matter of Jesus' relationship to sin.

On one hand we can say that Jesus' moral life was fully human, yet on the other that his goodness was the very work of God himself, as, indeed, it is in all Christians when it occurs. There remains, of course, a very basic difference between Christ and us. His life, being sinless, must be supposed to have been determined from start to finish by this work of God, whereas ours, in the process of gradual sanctification, wavers from determination by grace to determination by other, less savory influences. This is where our genuine ability to choose manifests itself negatively; we remain able to surrender true freedom by submitting to causal factors other than that of our relationship to God, by "submitting again to a spirit of slavery" as Paul puts it, by spitting in the face of the Spirit who through the determination of love seeks to draw us to himself. While this difference itself raises a number of important theological questions and must be accounted for, it does not, however, undermine the analogue as one way of thinking about how the basic conditions of Jesus' moral life might be essentially the same as ours, while yet he remained in some real sense unable to sin.

How, then, might we account for the difference? We might, I suppose, choose to think of the operation of the Holy Spirit poured out at Jordan as such a major factor in the determining conditions proper to Jesus' moral life that it really was impossible for him to sin, in precisely the sense that we might say it would be impossible for Mother Teresa to commit some violent crime against humanity. But at this level, of course, it is in principle possible for *our* freedom to be determined by the very same factor, which, presumably, is what sanctification and Christian discipleship consist in. That has been the challenge of Christian perfectionism through the centuries. Adopting a different perspective on the same basic fact, we might say instead that his freedom is determined by the personal relationship which, as the incarnate Son, he enjoys with the Father and the Spirit, precisely as all our free acts are determined by who we are in our relationships to and with others. Here, then, we appeal to a factor of Jesus' personal makeup, a causal element in his determined freedom, which sets him apart decisively from all others in the human series and which might, therefore, reasonably be thought to go some way to dissuade proponents of the view that "if it was possible for Jesus it must be possible for me" of the verity of their cause.

It may, perhaps, be objected that the account of freedom employed in our discussion is an inadequate or inappropriate one within the theological context, that we have, for the most part, assumed in an uncritical manner a definition offered by the Western philosophical tradition. Freedom, it might properly be objected, ought not to be thought of simply in terms of a capacity to choose to act either in one way or another. Rather, freedom may be defined as the ability (granted by grace) to act in accordance with our nature. Thus it might be suggested that freedom from sin (as that which distorts and twists our human existence) is genuine freedom, and that to think of Jesus as utterly incapable of sin is not, therefore, to rob him of his freedom but rather to affirm it. Some such redefinition of the term may well be in order. Nonetheless, it remains true that this definition of freedom is not the one which has predominated in the philosophical dialogue concerning free will and determinism, and for us to have adopted it at the outset would inevitably have been to complicate the subsequent exposition at every turn. Nor, whatever definition we decide to attach to the word freedom in the theological context, can a simple shifting of terminological goalposts relieve us of the responsibility of accounting for the continuing involvement of humans in sin, notwithstanding the gracious initiative of God toward us in his Son. It is a fact of our experience that we may either submit to the prompting of the Spirit, or else turn our back on that prompting and persist in sinful rebellion. If we choose not to express this by saying that this is because we are still "free to sin," if this phrase be deemed somehow oxymoronic, then we must find some other way of saying the same thing, for it is this very "thing," the genuine choice which faces us as moral agents between good and evil courses of action, the "categorical substitutability" of our moral choices, which lies at the heart of the discussion concerning moral responsibility and therefore that concerning the reality of Jesus' participation in our human condition.

If some such account of Jesus' moral life as that offered above is in any way an appropriate one to develop, then it is clearly still possible to incorporate Forsyth's suggestion that he would not have known that he "could not" sin. After all, which of us is aware of all the things or even the most significant things which determine our personal exercise of freedom? At the end of the day, however, it will be noticed that the paradox of grace, determined freedom, or whatever, if it be applied to the *non posse peccare*, entails a substantial weakening of it. It is still possible to say "Jesus could not have sinned," but the meaning attaching to these words must immediately be qualified to the point where they can only mean "given the determining factors operative in his moral life, it was supremely unlikely that he ever would sin." If we insist on the stronger sense of *non posse* we shall very likely be driven to embrace a deterministic framework with all the theological ills that accompany it.[27] But do we really need to go further than making the weaker, probabilistic affirmation? We certainly should not underestimate its force. If the response be given that anything less than a clear-cut, predictive *non posse* can secure the incarnation and all that rests on it form the risk of frustration and failure, is it not at least worth posing the question whether some such almighty risk is not intrinsic in the scandal of the message of a God who empties himself and embraces the life of the flesh in order to redeem it?

12

Universality

§1. Between Orthodoxy and Heresy

John A. T. Robinson is best remembered nowadays as an *agent provocateur* in ecclesial and theological terms. The self-confessed "radical"[1] became a household name more or less overnight in the early 1960s as a result of two particular acts of self-conscious provocation. First, he appeared at the Old Bailey to defend Penguin Books against charges of obscenity in connection with their publication of an unexpurgated text of *Lady Chatterley's Lover*.[2] Then, just as the dust was settling and the press pack losing interest, Robinson published his own "sensational" paperback, *Honest to God*, a popular work designed to introduce the "man on the Clapham omnibus" to the putative intellectual and religious gains of a nonrealist theology. The consequent notoriety was generated, of course, not by the man and his ideas alone, but by the office that he held.[3] Robinson was the British media's original "Bishop behaving badly," and the same ideas promulgated from the corridors of academe would have attracted far fewer column inches (and sold fewer copies of the book) than they eventually did. In reality, the arguments of *Honest to God* were not in any case especially radical when weighed in the balance by the theologically trained reader; but, served up in popular form to a theologically uneducated public by one whose ministry was supposed to be a sign and guarantee of Apostolic truth, they seemed quite radical enough, and the words "controversial," "notorious," and "unorthodox" were quickly drafted into service by the writers of banner headlines and chat show hosts.[4]

Given all this, the fact that in his writings on eschatology Robinson should break with the mainstream of Christian orthodoxy across the centuries, declaring himself to be a convinced believer in the final restoration of all things, might be thought likely to provoke little surprise. What *may* surprise us, though, are the grounds on which he had arrived at this conviction and the sorts of arguments he deployed in articulating and defending it. Far from sitting loosely to or uncomfortably with the core tenets and claims of biblical and creedal faith, Robinson situates himself and his argument in the thick of them, building his case by constant and careful reference to the character and purposes of God as revealed in Scripture, and to the human condition as laid bare by God's response to it in the person and work of Christ. *Apokatastasis*, he argues, is a doctrine to be believed passionately precisely on the basis of all this and not in spite of it, being the most fitting and appropriate vision of the world's end in God's hands given the larger shape and substance of divine revelation to humankind. Thus, in his earliest published treatment of the question, Robinson took as his starting point Emil Brunner's description of the doctrine of universal restoration as a "menacing heresy, endangering the Biblical faith," and argued directly the contrary: universalism was, he insisted, both profoundly biblical and, in that sense at least, profoundly orthodox.[5]

The essay in question, though, was not written by the author of *Honest to God* but more than a decade earlier when Robinson was tutor in New Testament and Ethics at Wells Theological College, and it contained materials dating back even further than this.[6] The piece appeared in the pages of the recently established *Scottish Journal of Theology*, earning an immediate published rejoinder from one of the journal's founding editors, the Rev. T. F. Torrance.[7] The editors afforded Robinson the courtesy of a brief reply, in which he graciously but firmly held his ground, insisting that Torrance had misunderstood both the grounds for and the nature of his major lines of argument.[8] Evidently, what was needed in order to forestall further misreading was a fuller treatment, laying bare some of the methodological and substantial commitments that undergirded and surrounded his articulation of the doctrine of *apokatastasis* itself. The opportunity for this came with an invitation to contribute a volume on eschatology to a series on "Theology for Modern Men." *In the End, God . . .* , Robinson's first book-length publication, duly appeared in 1950, including in its introduction a note of thanks to "Dr T. F. Torrance for kindly reading the whole MS. and suggesting invaluable criticisms."[9] Consideration of the last things had definitely come first, then, in the chronology of Robinson's career as a scholar and writer, and while he was still some years away yet from his personal concern with "the end of God" in the other sense.[10] And while the Robinson of 1949–1950 was certainly no theological conservative, this accounts in large measure for the unashamedly confessional tone of his eschatology and his preoccupation with establishing *apokatastasis* as an orthodox Christian hope (a consideration not naturally associated with the doyenne of "South Bank Religion").[11]

In his response to Robinson's 1949 article, Torrance had laid at least five key charges at his door: first, that his case was one based at critical points on abstract human logic rather than the alternative "logic" of God's self-revealing in Christ; second, that it failed, as a result, to do justice to the atonement, deploying a model of love drawn from general human experience (and then "raised to the nth degree")[12] rather than the concrete circumstances of the encounter between God's love and human sin; third, that it failed to reckon adequately with the fundamental irrationality of sin whereby some are hardened in their opposition rather than persuaded by the approach of divine grace; fourth, that it could not account for the preponderance of biblical teaching concerning a final division of humankind between the children of light and the children of darkness; and fifth, that it cut the nerve of eschatological urgency underlying Christian proclamation, and thus finally relativized the significance of the response of faith. Robinson's was not, in other words, to be considered in any proper sense a Christian argument, being based in considerations lying outside the framework of revelation and corrosive with respect to core doctrines of the faith. Far from bringing universalism within the fold of orthodoxy, Robinson had simply demonstrated how and why the doctrine in all its forms was (and could only ever be) an "abiding menace to the Gospel."[13] This is a fairly comprehensive and emphatic rejection! In what follows I suggest that in significant part at least it is mistaken and unsustainable, unfair to Robinson's intentions and perhaps to his achievements too, certainly as these were further clarified in his immediate response to Torrance and in the pages of the 1950 book.[14] Whether or not we are finally persuaded by his argument for *apokatastasis*, we must do justice to it, and recognize the extent to which it was deeply rooted in the soil of Scripture and tradition, driven from first to last by a distinctly Christian apprehension of the character and purposes of God, and thus deserving of recognition at least as a legitimate variant of Christian hope rather than something fundamentally alien to or incompatible with it.

Robinson's argument may be treated for convenience as falling into four closely related parts, having to do respectively with the witness of Scripture, the nature of divine love (as omnipotent and holy), the relation between divine purpose and human freedom, and the abiding reality of hell. Before turning to these, though, it behooves us first to consider his wider understanding of the nature and task of theology as a practice, and the particular status of eschatological utterance, since this has a direct impact on everything else that he has to say, and is vital to a proper understanding of it. For some readers, indeed, it will be a refusal to follow Robinson here, in certain methodological moves he makes (and, as always, makes quite openly and unashamedly), which determines most fully their inability to concur with his conclusions; others, while sharing to the full his theological commitment to those same conclusions, may nonetheless find themselves compelled to reach them by a rather different route.

§2. An Empirical and Existential Theology

One of the constants in Robinson's writing over the decades was a deep apologetic impulse, determined that no one should reject the Christian gospel merely because it had been presented in ways which were intellectually lazy or irresponsible. Faith in Christ, he insists, must be able to hold up its head with dignity and confidence in the midst of the very best and most up-to-date of human learning rather than skulking in the shadows, nervous that what it has to offer may lack the credentials to be taken seriously. Such legitimate concern to commend itself to "the modern mind" must not, of course, entail any simple kowtowing to the dominant intellectual dogmas or methodological prescriptions of the age. On the contrary, the church must remain utterly faithful to its charge to bear witness to something revealed to it, a reality not discoverable or demonstrable through the exercise of human intellect alone and which demands its own unique categories of interpretation and understanding.

In walking this fine line between the demands of nonnegotiable fiduciary commitments and intellectual respectability, the Robinson of 1950 drew enthusiastically and fully on the model of theology as an "empirical science" articulated three years previously by Alan Richardson in his *Christian Apologetics*.[15] The proper task of the theologian, Richardson had argued, was not (as for long ages it had been reckoned to be) the deduction of truths from explicit and infallible statements contained in the Bible[16] but, as in all modern science, an inductive task in which relevant data are first carefully collected and then systematized in accordance with appropriate intellectual categories. These categories necessarily trespass beyond the data (and may or may not themselves prove finally to be susceptible to empirical verification), their role being precisely to situate the "facts" within a larger meaningful pattern which enables them to be interpreted and understood. In this sense, Richardson maintains, science is not finally concerned with the demonstration of the truth of its conclusions (since other ways of configuring the data are always possible), but with offering an account that seems to make the *best available sense* of the data set presented to it. The "data" for theology, he argues, are the many and varied phenomena of church life, past and present, and the theologian's responsibility, by direct analogy with practitioners in other sciences, is to offer an account of this data which makes the best overall sense of it, conducted in "the full light of our modern knowledge,"[17] and formulating and deploying whatever categories and hypotheses appear to be warranted or demanded. Again, the job in hand is not to test or to demonstrate the *truth* of faith's claims, but to situate these together with the rest of the phenomena of Christian existence within a bigger picture of things which permits the best possible sense to be made of them.

Robinson echoes this account point for point in his own description of the theological task, and duly applies it to the field of eschatology. The formulation of eschatological doctrine, he insists, is not about coordinating a set of divinely revealed propositions pertaining to the future but developing and constantly recalibrating a set of categories sufficient to explain (i.e., give a meaningful and coherent account of) the data of Christian existence.[18] For Robinson, the most relevant data in this regard are "given in the present encounter with Christ in His flesh and in the Spirit,"[19] known and borne witness to from the vantage point of faith. Revelation, in other words, is basic to the data with which theology must grapple. "Revelation," though, is understood here to refer not to a body of information divinely divulged and underwritten but to a dynamic personal encounter with, apprehension of, and response to the presence and character of the living God himself. All revelation, Robinson insists, is "of a Now and for a Now," a matter of personal and present summons and response, and not as such the source of information about either the past or the future.[20] Of course what is known of God in this way ("given and verified in present experience")[21] has far-reaching implications for our understanding of both the past and the future (not least the primordial past and ultimate future), and these must duly be thought through and articulated in a responsible manner.

This, according to Robinson, is precisely where eschatology fits into the theological scheme of things; beginning with the content of what is known with conviction about God by faith in the present moment, eschatological doctrine constitutes a projection or extrapolation of that same reality into the farthest reaches of both individual and historical futures and their respective "ends" in God's hands.[22] "It is the explication of what must be true of the end . . . if God is to be the God of Biblical faith."[23] Thus the content of Christian eschatology *must* cohere with the reality of faith's present awareness of the living God, for it is derived directly from it, an imaginative "transposition into the key of the hereafter" of what faith already knows to be true in the here and now. Just as the people of Israel pictured the primordial events of creation in terms of the God they already knew as the LORD of Sinai, so, for its part, the church configures its account of what will hold good at the end of time in accordance with the character of the Lord of the new covenant. "All eschatological statements can finally be reduced to, and their validity tested by, sentences beginning: 'In the end, God . . . ,'"[24] the word "God" being defined rigorously and solely by the content of faith's encounter with Jesus Christ.

In substance, what all this boils down to is a particular version of the claim lying at the heart of many Christian universalisms, namely that in eschatology it is finally our doctrine of God itself that is at stake, since God's character is irrevocably bound up not just with the provenance and shape of creaturely existence in the world but most fully with its destiny and telos, and hence with its very raison d'être. In Robinson's terms, for Christian faith every truth about eschatology is ipso facto a truth about God, and every truth about God is ipso facto an assertion about the end, since God is what in the end he asserts himself to be, and the ultimate truth about God is necessarily the final event in history.[25]

§3. Revelation and Scripture

Despite Robinson's insistence on revelation as dynamic personal encounter and thus, in one sense, always concentrated on the particular temporal present, it is clear that he does not envisage an essentially noncognitive event wholly unrelated to propositional content. On the contrary, revelation is vitally related both to Scripture's narration of events in history and to its imaginative vision of the world's future in God's hands. Robinson's point appears to be the Kierkegaardian one that, apart from a personal and present encounter with the living God of whom these texts speak, the texts themselves remain inert and have nothing of any significance to say to us.[26] It is notable, therefore, that Robinson begins his own treatment of the doctrine of universalism precisely with exegetical and hermeneutical considerations.[27] What, he asks, according to the Bible, is God's purpose for the world he has created? More precisely, what do the central facts of God's redemptive action in Christ as narrated in Scripture tell us about who God is, and thus about the answer to Kant's third great question, What may we legitimately hope for? The apostolic message, Robinson insists, bears witness to "one decisive act of God, once and for all, embracing every creature,"[28] and our eschatological doctrine must be worked out from first to last in the light of that established reality and take it fully into account. Thus a "biblical" approach to the doctrine can never mean one that simply stacks up texts alongside one another but that will seek points of logical and hermeneutical priority within the pattern of the biblical witness, allowing texts to interpret one another in an appropriate fashion.

Nonetheless, Robinson is vociferous in his insistence that in this field of theological concern as in every other, a biblical approach will be one that gives full and careful consideration to the *whole* body of relevant textual evidence rather than securing the conviction of its case only by failing to do adequate justice to a significant part of that evidence. The question is, of course, What will "doing justice to" mean in particular circumstances? The main challenge facing us in our formulation of doctrine concerning the ultimate destiny of God's creatures in his hands, Robinson notes, is the existence in the New Testament of two quite different and seemingly contradictory "mythic"[29] representations of the relevant state of affairs. First, there are projections of a universal restoration of all things to God their maker, directly related to and based securely on the universal scope and "finished" nature of the accomplished fact of divine redemption in Christ.[30] Over against these, though, we must set texts (and Robinson acknowledges that they are plentiful and many of them occur in accounts of dominical teaching)[31] that seem "to point to a very different issue,"[32] namely the final separation of some who are "saved" from others who are "lost."

We should recall that for Robinson neither set of texts can be treated as literal predictions of some "factual" future state of play; each consists in an imaginative projection envisaging how things must end, given the nature of reality (and specifically the reality of God) as presently experienced. Were they literal forecasts, Robinson observes, one set would have to be concluded true and the other false, but understood properly as myth, the contradiction between them is not fatal but theologically and spiritually rich; we can, and we must, he insists, hold them together and avoid

premature resolution of the tension generated by their juxtaposition,
since both pertain to a truth in our present human circumstance before
God (viewed in relation to its future outcome). Both myths must be taken
with absolute seriousness and thereby granted their existential force, even
though, in our doctrine of the end, their respective significances may have
to be weighed rather differently.

Robinson begins his consideration of the doctrine of universalism,
then, from a standpoint deliberately and (he argues) necessarily situated
within the logic of Christian claims about revelation. It is the character of
the God known by faith on the basis of the once for all and finished work
of Christ as witnessed to in Scripture that dominates his concern, and he
determines that serious wrestling with the whole range of relevant biblical
materials must form part of an adequate theological defense of the doctrine. In his response to Robinson's original 1949 article, Torrance argues
that, while Robinson allows Scripture to raise the relevant questions for
him, "his real answers are not given on Biblical lines."[33] This claim may be
a helpful one to bear in mind as we consider the case Robinson builds both
in that article and in the book that followed it.

§4. Spoiling the Egyptians

Omnipotent and Holy Love

How, then, can we do justice both to the universalistic and the dualistic
myths of the end contained in Scripture? In what is effectively a ground-
clearing exercise, in chapter 8 of In the End, God . . . Robinson considers and
dismisses some traditional ways of answering this question which he deems
to be theologically inadequate in one way or another. His dismissal of two
of them is swift: We cannot, he insists, suppose (as the Reformed doctrine
of a double decree supposes) that the myths refer respectively to two groups
of God's creatures, the elect (all of whom will be saved) and the reprobate;
quite apart from the horrendous doctrine of God lurking behind this idea, it
rests, he contends, on a mistaken exegesis of Romans 9:22–23. Nor can we
understand the two imaginative projections to refer to possible but alternative eschatological outcomes, only one of which will be fulfilled, contingent
on the exercise of freedom (by creatures, and by God himself). Superfi-
cially attractive in its humility, this is actually, he insists, the most unbiblical of views, basing eschatology not on what Scripture declares as "Divine
fact, which has foreclosed all possibilities, but on human speculation which
ignores the decisiveness of what Christ has done."[34]

According to the third view (to which Robinson grants more space), both the universalistic myth and its dualistic counterpart can be held to treat realities rather than mere possibilities, because "God *will* finally be all in all *despite* the damnation and destruction of many of His creatures."[35] Neither God's omnipotence nor his love is compromised by dualism (wherein the purposes of his love are necessarily modified) because the divine nature is characterized equally by justice, and it is this which duly prevails and through which God finds fulfillment precisely in the punishment of the impenitent. This view, too, Robinson insists, is one that may only be entertained at the cost of a genuinely Christian doctrine of God. The very idea of God being "fulfilled" rather than grieved at the loss of any of those he has created in and for loving communion with himself is, he argues, intolerable if the word "God" means what according to the revelation in Jesus Christ it does mean. The fundamental failing of the view, he suggests, is its failure to recognize that the words "love" and "justice" as applied to the God of the Bible are not parallel attributes with competing demands but two aspects of one single reality. God's love "is a love of cauterizing holiness and of a righteousness whose only response to evil is the purity of a perfect hate."[36] If we lose sight of this vital distinctive of the use of the word "love" in theology, our understanding of love becomes sentimental, forgiveness immoral, and justice sub-Christian. By the same token, though, the God known in Jesus Christ (and him crucified) has no power and no purpose other than the power and purpose of holy love. This being so, Robinson argues, the final loss of any must arise within the jurisdiction of this same purpose, and in some clear sense constitute its frustration. In other words (borrowing again from the classical philosophical terminology of Aquinas whose theology he takes to represent this view), what cannot be maintained is the eschatological demonstration of "omnipotence" ("the complete fulfillment of the Divine will") in tandem with an adequate notion of God's "love" as understood biblically. The recalcitrance of the impenitent sinner limits God's power and purpose to forgive.

According to Torrance, Robinson's argument for universalism rests at this point on human logic rather than on solidly theological grounds, taking "omnipotence and love as logical counters," and deploying Aristotle's law of noncontradiction to sweep aside the various nonuniversalistic options.[37] Perhaps there is some credence for such a reading in Robinson's 1949 article, where syllogistic logic is indeed introduced early into his discussion and shapes much more fully the form of his approach to the subject.[38] We should note, though, that both here and in the reworked version of his argument in the 1950 book Robinson is concerned chiefly with engaging Aquinas' argument (in *Summa theologiae* 1a, q. 19, a. 6) for the logical compatibility of divine love, divine omnipotence, and eschatological dualism. In a bid to show why this same argument fails even on its own terms, of course, Robinson must indwell its logic, whatever his own preferred eschatological starting point. The syllogistic treatment of "omnipotent love" may, in other words, be intended primarily as an exercise in "spoiling the Egyptians" rather than the logical ground or driver of Robinson's own view. Robinson himself (in his permitted "last word" in the exchange) insisted that this was the case,[39] and appears subsequently to have adjusted the articulation of his case in order to make this clearer. Thus, in *In the End God* . . . things are set up rather differently, all talk of syllogistic logic being reduced by comparison to a minimum, and here (as indicated above) it is quite clear that what drives Robinson's response to Aquinas is a deep theological conviction about the character of the God revealed in Jesus Christ (not least the peculiar sense which the word "love" bears in its application to him) and the "Divine fact" of his finished work. Any remaining appeal to logic is subordinated entirely to these properly theological considerations. And if Robinson remains concerned (as he does) with questions concerning the relationship between divine sovereignty and human freedom ("the omnicompetence of God to fulfil his great purpose of love"[40]) in the remainder of his argument, this concern too seems to arise chiefly from the substance of revelation (along "Biblical lines"), and not from the substitution of abstract logical or general experiential considerations for that.

§5. Love's Omnicompetence and the Paradox of Grace

The doctrine of universalism, Robinson notes, has often been defended in ways and under forms which do it little credit, whether grounded on some essentially optimistic anthropology, or sustained by appeal to the supposed demands of reason or even of human longing. But, he insists forthrightly, "There is no ground whatever in the Bible for supposing that all men, simply because they are men, are 'going the same way'—except to hell," and the sole basis for the doctrine, therefore, is the work of God in Christ, "the Divine 'nevertheless,' intervening beyond any expectation and merit"[41] and providing the only grounds for the assurance of faith rather than mere wishful thinking. We should note in passing, therefore, the central place which the atonement plays in Robinson's view. Far from being displaced or short-circuited by a universalistic vision,[42] it becomes a central plank in the argument: for if God has indeed done this thing "once for all," and if "it is finished," then the sole remaining relevant consideration is not whether anyone may yet be "saved" apart from the cross (since none actually exist apart from it any more than they exist apart from Christ), but what their personal response to it will be, and how the response of any could yet be supposed capable of frustrating the sovereign purposes of God's holy love. Thus the next step in Robinson's argument is directed precisely toward this question of the sinner's response, and how it might be possible to think together the "necessity" of grace's ultimate triumph and the inviolability of human freedom, something he insists we must seek at all costs to do.

Here again it is revelation (and Scripture as the normative textual mediator of revelation)[43] that drives his argument. The voice of the text demands that we take seriously both of these seemingly contradictory facts. For, in the very moment that it points to a universal restoration predicated on the finished work of Christ for all, Scripture immediately complicates the circumstance with repeated and strident insistences that each must yet respond to this objective achievement personally, and frightening evocations of the hellish consequences of choosing death rather than life. Robinson echoes the suggestion of Schleiermacher, insisting that what we must reckon with here is a single divine decree whereby the positive response of each is secure in God's hands and in God's good time.[44] He is emphatic, though, that we cannot think merely in terms of a numbers game; it is the quality and not simply the direction of the response each person will make that matters. "Being saved" is precisely a matter of coming to love God, a love born of gratitude and duly finding its fulfillment in a disposition of trust and obedience. The response of "faith" that God longs and waits to receive from each sinner is therefore not so much a condition of salvation as the point at which a salvation already objectively established bites into the subjectivity of individual lives with redemptive effect. By definition, we cannot ever be saved "against our will" by force (physical or emotional) because the free exercise of our will in love is itself the subjective pole of that relationship in which salvation (being saved) consists. Robinson cites Kierkegaard's Concluding Unscientific Postscript to reinforce what he takes to be a fundamentally biblical insight: "It would help very little if one persuaded millions of men to accept the truth, if precisely by the method of their acceptance they were transferred into error."[45] Salvation, like Kierkegaard's truth, must be acknowledged at this point to be a matter of genuine "subjectivity,"[46] and the infringement of freedom would thus amount to a contradiction of its essential reality.

So we return to the apparent standoff: can we think the inviolable freedom of human choice and the reality of hell consistently together with the claim that God's holy love must finally triumph (because in a real sense it has already triumphed in Christ)? If we cannot think these together in a consistent manner then we must certainly hold them together and permit the contradiction to stand, because to do otherwise, Robinson insists, would be untrue to the explicit teaching of the biblical writers.[47] But surely, he suggests, it is the task of the theologian not to capitulate too quickly at this point, seeking instead responsibly to discover and explore different ways of modeling things which might help us to imagine the circumstance afresh, and perhaps to grasp it under an aspect where it appears altogether less contradictory and baffling.[48] Perhaps, in this matter of the relationship between divine sovereignty and human freedom, we have been held captive by a particular picture of how things stand, and by reconfiguring things into a different pattern we may yet find a way of making sense of the suggestion that both claims—the necessary triumph of divine love and the inviolable freedom of human response—could be true at the same time.

The analogy which Robinson offers us is drawn from the world of persons, and from those particular experiences of human love where its manifestation by another *constrains* us to reciprocate. In such circumstances, he writes, "We cannot help ourselves, everything within us tells us that we must [respond]. Our defences are down, the power of love captures the very citadel of our will, and we answer with the spontaneous surrender of our whole being. Yet, at the same time, we know perfectly well that at such moments we can, if we choose, remain unmoved; there is no physical compulsion to commit ourselves."[49] Under this "strange compulsion," Robinson notes, far from feeling that our freedom has been infringed or our personhood violated, we tend to feel more fulfilled and free than ever before, more fully ourselves, indeed, than were we to assert ourselves and our self-will in the face of such love, deliberately resisting its draw. From within the dynamics of a personal encounter of this sort, in fact, it is the alleged logical contradiction between freedom and compulsion that seems to make little sense, rather than their compatibility. Clearly, a different sort of logic is being appealed to.

If, though, something like this pertains at the level of the finite, in our dealings with other human persons, then, Robinson asks, might something similar not be imaginable in the logic of our dealings with a personal but infinite and all-powerful God? If human love can sometimes be too strong for us to resist, what then should we think of divine love? May we not suppose that a similar alternative "logic" could apply here too, and imagine a divine *Thou* whose love pursues and woos us relentlessly and perfectly until, at last, we can hold out no longer but must yield, our freedom remaining fully intact and actually *fulfilled* in the process? If the word "love" functions analogously to bridge the gap between God's existence and ours, then there is surely warrant for conducting such a thought experiment. And, whether or not this is *in reality* how things stand in the mystery of the relationship between God's love and our eschatological freedom, this model at least enables us to picture how it *might* be, and thus to *make sense* of what otherwise remains an apparent contradiction. More than this the model must not be forced to do, but more than this it is not intended to do.[50]

It is particularly important to stress this last point. Torrance criticizes Robinson for missing the point made helpfully by Aquinas in his doctrine of analogy, and therefore clumsily projecting the conditions of a shared human experience onto God in an inappropriate act of univocal predication.[51] Again, though, this misses the point of what Robinson intends. His concern is not with establishing *what is in fact true* of the relationship between God and human persons through an analysis of personal existence as such. It is true that the theologies which particularly influenced him were inclined to trace stronger connections between the world of human persons and talk of God as "personal" than Torrance would ever be comfortable with,[52] but in this context Robinson's stated ambitions are much more modest. He is, we should recall, engaged in a strictly "scientific" exercise, so mapping the territory of metaphysics lies in any case beyond his theological remit. His avowed aim here is to insist that the "paradox" of human freedom and divine sovereignty may be less baffling than first appearances suggest if we model it along the lines of this circumstance familiar to us from the texture of finite I-Thou relations. It is an exercise of a hypothetical sort and one entertained in the theologian's pursuit of coherence, suggesting how various facts might be imagined to hold together in the wider scheme of things,[53] rather than insisting that "this is in fact how it works, because God is personal, and we all know how our relationships with persons work."

Nor is Torrance's suggestion that Robinson would "have been better to learn from Biblical analogies" rather than seeking them in the structure of personal existence as such entirely fair.[54] In fact, in order to achieve his purposes as we have just outlined them there is no good reason why Robinson should appeal to biblical examples at all, though it is perfectly reasonable to suggest that he should subsequently reckon with a spread of them in order duly to "test" his hypothesis, applying it to the relevant body of empirical "data." Even here, though, we may find reason to defend him, since his discussion moves on identifiably from appeal to the wider phenomena of a shared human existence and is transplanted to the soil of the particular Christian experience of God (as witnessed to in Scripture). There is, Robinson insists, in every Christian's experience something which resonates profoundly with the model of an irresistible love which leaves our freedom unscathed, thus eluding the "objective" schema of cause and effect; namely, the believer's awareness of feeling no contradiction whatever between "what he does and what God does in him,"[55] the phenomenon testified to clearly by the apostle Paul (1 Cor 15:10) and referred to by Donald Baillie (just a year before the appearance of Robinson's 1949 article) as "the central paradox" of Christian life.[56] Of course, Robinson observes, this paradoxical aspect of God's grace can finally be made sense of only by those who have experienced and continue to experience it,[57] and it escapes us if we try to net it (to explain or describe it) within the categories of objective logic. As a central "fact" of Christian existence, though, it seems to lend further warrant to the imaginative modeling he has already undertaken and, further, without in any way collapsing the distinction between the two distinct personal circumstances (that of the sinner's encounter with God and the wider nature of I-Thou encounters in the human sphere) to point to the possible fruitfulness of applying the same model to the eschatological context where parallel issues (i.e., to do with sovereignty and freedom) offer themselves for consideration.

Torrance mentions one specific biblical instance which, he argues, threatens to confound Robinson's appeal to the compulsion of love, namely, the I-Thou relation between Jesus and Judas. "If all that Dr Robinson has said were true," Torrance writes, "one would be utterly at a loss to understand why Judas who for several years had the priceless privilege of enjoying to the full the love of the Son of God should not have found that love irresistible."[58] Here, in other words, we find "omnipotent love" incarnate in our very midst, and Judas' "dastardly kiss" in Gethsemane suggests precisely that the surd quality of evil may yet not be won by it but reject it "to the very last." Whether Judas did indeed resist and reject the approach of grace "to the very last" may be a moot point even in exegetical terms, but the wider point is clearly an important one: Robinson's model needs to reckon squarely with evil as a surd rather than relying on any more optimistic account of its (and thus our) "capacity for redemption." In response, Robinson echoes Augustine's insistence on a capacity within God's grace to lay hold of and redeem even that which is most fully immured in evil's clutches, and therefore most fully antagonistic to the approach of holy love.[59]

It is this alone, he argues, and not any form of humanist optimism that provides the Christian with reasonable grounds for hope. What is at stake is precisely the question of whether the God who is undoubtedly *capable* of rescuing even surd-like sin from a hell of its own making and choosing, and objectively in Christ has already established the conditions for and completed the larger and decisive part of the rescue, will now continue his redemptive engagement and bring it to completion in the existence of each of his creatures, no matter how far they may have fallen. And if not, why not? For Robinson, the character, purpose, and objective achievements of the God revealed in Christ lead (indeed require) faith to answer this question in the affirmative, but equally to suppose that the relevant redemptive encounter will and must be one which occurs in and through, and not despite, the exercise of freedom, even in the most depraved of creaturely cases.

§6. Hell

The Reality That Must Be Not Chosen

The final condition which "any sound doctrine of universalism must satisfy," Robinson insists, is that of demonstrating that it can take seriously the integrity of the Bible's extensive teaching about hell, and thus do justice to the genuine *reality* of hell as such, rather than reducing it either to a mere eschatological possibility or a rhetorical fiction (an "indispensable bluff" designed, as it were, to scare the hell out of us and thereby keep us moral).[60] We can do so, Robinson argues, by recalling that the two scenarios which Scripture holds awkwardly together (*apokatastasis* and dualism) are cast in the form of existential myths rather than constituting alternative and contradictory predictions of actual futures. They are imaginative extrapolations of what the end times must surely hold, given the revealed realities confronting human beings in the existential present, but they represent two quite different existential standpoints within that present.

From the standpoint of those who have chosen Christ, there is now only one reality to be reckoned with seriously, namely the fact of what God has purposed and done for all, so that even now no one can be reckoned outside of Christ and the salvation which is in him. It is from this standpoint alone that the truth represented in the myth of universal restoration can be known or taken into account. The other myth, in which heaven and hell appear as alternative destinations, represents a different truth about Christ as he confronts us in the here and now, namely that he must indeed be chosen freely or, put differently, that hell must be consciously not chosen.[61] Such deliberate decision for Christ and against hell Robinson holds to be part and parcel of that reconciliation of each person to God in which "salvation" actually consists. Thus, from the standpoint of not yet having made this choice, two realities do and indeed must exist and be reckoned with: the reality of a continued hellish existence in alienation from God, and the reality of the gracious divine "nevertheless" embodied in Christ. Only if and because there are two realities confronting us can there be a meaningful choice to make at all.

There are many, Robinson affirms, who, when the divinely engineered moment of crisis and decision arises, choose death, and choose it repeatedly, because they do not not choose hell. "The believer, . . . seeing the matter, as it were, from the other side of the Divine act in Christ, knows that God cannot let it rest there; He must and will win all men."[62] But this is not true "objectively" (i.e., in a manner demonstrable to all) and cannot and must not be believed by those in the condition of not having yet chosen. It *must* not be believed by them (or preached to them as "true," which, for them and as yet, it is not) precisely because salvation itself is a matter of *having chosen*, of freely and deliberately setting hell aside as an option and embracing God in gratitude and love. Thus any attempt to lessen the genuine urgency and seriousness of such a choice or render it needless is bound in effect to keep people at arm's length from their salvation, leaving them bound in the grip of a hellish existential present. For "as long as a man refuses to become a 'subject,' as long as he presumes that the truth of universalism relieves him of reckoning with hell or making a decision, then he is not even on the road to the valley—or, rather, he has implicitly chosen hell."[63] As long as I do not choose Christ over hell, hell has me securely in its grasp; it is what dominates the horizon of my tomorrow as well as poisoning my today and polluting my recollected past. Hell is thus, according to Robinson, an all-too-present reality and, unless and until each person arrives at the point of not choosing it, turning away from it by turning to Christ, it can only remain such. Thus, he concludes, "there could be no greater calumny than to suggest that the universalist either does not preach hell or does so with his tongue in his cheek."[64] Hell is that reality which each of us must reach the point of deliberately renouncing for the sake of Christ, and its reality is essential to the genuineness and meaning of the choice itself.

In theory, of course, at this point Robinson's account accepts that, were any not eventually (in God's time) to make this choice, were they to continue (implicitly or explicitly) to choose hell rather than not choosing it, then hell would indeed remain existentially real for them "in the end." His parable of the compulsion of love is intended to undergird faith's intuition/conviction that, within the purposes and sovereignty of God, all *will* finally and freely choose Christ, rendering hell at best an empty reality that can be allowed to fade and crumble until it is no longer a reality at all, there being none for whom it has any further relevance as a live option. Were it to be otherwise, were there finally to be "a concentration camp set in the midst of a blissful countryside," then all that God is and all that in Christ He has done is effectively denied.[65] Again we see the extent to which Robinson's view is driven ultimately by convictions arising out of the substance of revelation itself. Perhaps in the end, he acknowledges, we shall not actually be able to make any sense of this claim which faith finds itself compelled nonetheless to make. Theology must certainly seek understanding of what faith holds to be true, but faith is not constrained by what the theologian cannot render thinkable (any more than the scientist abandons data for which he cannot yet account adequately in terms of any hypothesis). The good news revealed to faith, he insists, is precisely that "the incredible must happen, because in Christ the incredible has happened.... The world *has been* redeemed."[66] That this divinely purposed and accomplished redemption, in which God's character as holy love is laid bare, should finally be frustrated by sin's recalcitrance would be either "the most terrible defeat" of such love or (worse and unthinkable) the revelation of a very different, occult character of God lurking (to borrow a convenient phrase from another theologian) "behind the back" of Jesus.[67]

§7. Conclusion

My chief concern in this chapter has been to reckon with Robinson's argument for universalism on its own terms and thus to help the reader to understand its logic more clearly. I am conscious that in doing so I have ended up defending him from what I take to be some basic misunderstandings or unfair criticisms, insisting, contra the thrust of Torrance's argument, on his right to be counted as a "Christian universalist" in the strong sense—that is, one whose universalism is solidly grounded in the wider substance of the faith, identifiably nourished by Scripture and tradition, rather than an anomalous "bolt-on" driven by extraneous considerations. This does not mean, of course, that there are no flaws to be identified in his argument or points at which it remains vulnerable to criticism, perhaps even of a fairly fundamental sort.

The most significant weakness by far surely lies in Robinson's treatment of biblical texts, which has all the appearance of inconsistency embraced in the interest of convenience. Some readers, of course, will be unhappy in principle with his way of reading eschatological texts as "existential myths." Even if we grant Robinson's own conviction that such a reading leaves the texts' authority and normative status unscathed, though,[68] we may reasonably demand much more justification than he supplies for treating them in this way, and for his denial that such texts could be "revelatory" of any future circumstance at all (a claim which is simply tacked on to—but does not follow necessarily from—his recognition of their highly imaginative form and concomitant eschewal of inappropriate "literal" readings).[69] His straightforward appeal at other points to the "facts" of God's once-for-all redemptive action in Christ simply heightens the reader's sense of frustration,[70] and reinforces the suspicion that the epistemic force granted to particular texts (or sorts of texts) is informed as much by the particular demands of Robinson's own argument as by any objective considerations. And, as Reginald Fuller notes in an early review of the book,[71] there is in any case a final inconsistency in the epistemic significance afforded to the two types of eschatological "myth" which Robinson identifies, one of which turns out eventually to be a fitting imaginative vision of how things will indeed end in God's hands (and thus in some sense, we must suppose, "revelatory" after all). Everything rests on Robinson's assertion that the dualistic texts are indeed best read as existential myths, and the reader has a right, therefore, to expect more by way of warrant for this claim than he ever actually provides.

Other charges may easily and reasonably be leveled, and mention of just a few must suffice here. Torrance's third charge still has some mileage in it. Notwithstanding his formal acknowledgment of the surd-like nature of human sin and God's "omnicompetent" capacity to redeem it, it seems nonetheless that Robinson's vision of the soul's redemption is mostly a more pastoral one in which the sinner is at the last "gently led" back to God.[72] Yet "wooing" is neither the only nor often the first weapon in the armory even of human love, and if we take the crucifixion as our starting point and permit the wider teaching of the Bible and the testimony of Christian experience to guide us, it seems that hell may more often than not be renounced (albeit freely and gladly) only after a considerable struggle and some hard blows have occurred first. These are "data" which feature less than prominently in Robinson's model, despite its technical capacity to accommodate and make sense of them, and a fuller reckoning with them would have strengthened his case. Furthermore, having collapsed the temporal horizons of eschatological myth into the present moment, Robinson has little to say about the realities of divine judgment outside the fact of their having been dealt with once and for all in Christ. Second advent and resurrection to judgment are understood wholly as ways in which the biblical writers make sense of "the finality of the events of the Incarnation,"[73] and neither God's judgment as an experienced present reality (for the Christian) nor as an occasion yet to be faced has any serious place in his scheme of things. Nor does Robinson's argument reckon adequately with the claims of annihilationist eschatologies, sweeping all such notions aside as reflecting an unbiblical anthropology,[74] and thus presenting eternal conscious torment ("a concentration camp set in the midst of a blissful countryside") as the only biblical alternative to a doctrine of universal restoration. While it is true that interest in the exegetical basis for a doctrine of conditional immortality has burgeoned in the decades since 1950, the idea itself was already a familiar one, and Robinson's failure to engage its distinctive version of eschatological dualism must be considered a lack. These are hardly trivial criticisms, and plenty of others like them could no doubt be marshaled. In each case, though, it is clear that we are dealing with considerations arising identifiably within the camp of Christian theology, and not defending the camp from hostile forces originating outside it. Robinson's argument undoubtedly has its problems, but we are unlikely to encounter an argument that does not have problems, and in this field in particular it is a matter of which theological problems one feels able to live with.

Finally, there is the charge that his dogged pursuit of consistency leads Robinson to trespass into arrogance, boldly asserting what God "must" finally do rather than resting content with the sort of "holy silence" or "reverent agnosticism" which gladly hopes and prays for the salvation of all but never permits this hope to be handled dogmatically.[75] In part, of course, this is a function of his understanding of the theological task as a "scientific" one, and a different modeling of the task would almost certainly have yielded a quite different statement of things. For Robinson, the universalistic vision or "hypothesis" is the only one that properly "fits the facts," being grounded "in the very necessity of God's nature"[76] apprehended (as alone it can and must be) by those who have made the leap of faith and stand now in the truth of Christ. But his commitment to the doctrine is, of course, more than a matter of intellectual gratification. It has a deep moral and religious root, shaped by what he takes to be the mind of Scripture and of Christ, and contingent on faith's intuition that, *mutatis mutandis*, there is no God who is not like Jesus. This being true, he finds himself driven out of silence to take the risk of "holy speech." "In a universe of love," he writes, "there can be no heaven which tolerates a chamber of horrors, no hell for any which does not at the same time make it hell for God. He cannot endure that, for that would be the final mockery of His nature—and He will not."[77] And if it is *not* true, then, for Robinson (as for many of those who have been driven to embrace a universalistic eschatology), much more is at stake than the truth or falsity of this particular doctrine alone.

13

Particularity

In this chapter I hope to accomplish at least two things: first, to bring together some of the theological concerns identifiable in my colleague Richard Bauckham's work over the years,[1] and, in doing so, to draw renewed attention to a short article, "Christology Today," published in the South African journal *Scriptura* in 1988.[2] Although the article is relatively little known, I have always found it particularly helpful and suggestive, and have both recommended it to students and returned to it myself on numerous occasions over the years. Some of the themes and ideas explored in it, such as the centrality to its argument of the categories of identity, identification with and identification as, have duly been taken up and taken further in later publications such as *God Crucified* and *Jesus and the God of Israel*.[3] Others remain as yet to be worked out at comparable length, hopefully in the years of productivity still to be looked forward to. At the heart of the piece lies a characteristic upending of the assumptions in terms of which a familiar philosophical and theological problem is typically cast, namely the relationship (typically construed as a dialectic) between the universal and the particular, especially as that plays out in Christology and soteriology in one form or another of the so-called "scandal" of particularity. It is with this cluster of issues, albeit approached for the moment from a slightly different angle, that I begin.

§1. Between Parmenides and Plurality

Pursuing a Community of the Different

In his 1992 Bampton Lectures, Colin Gunton observes that the question of the one and the many, the universal and the particular "takes us to the very beginnings of philosophy and theology" and unites the concerns of ancient human wisdom with those of the modern and postmodern condition.[4] These concerns themselves, Gunton suggests (with his tongue only lightly lodged in his cheek), are thus at least recurrent if not universal in the history of human thought, though, irritatingly, of course they arise in a host of different particular forms. Among the recurrent features seemingly essential to the debate is a tendency to view universality on one hand and particularity on the other as opposing principles in an unstable dialectic constantly threatening to resolve itself unhelpfully so as to privilege one term (by bestowing on it logical and ontological priority) to the inevitable detriment of the other. Gunton adopts the pre-Socratic monism of Parmenides (for whom "what is" is timeless, uniform, necessary, and unchanging) as a convenient figure representing philosophies tending finally toward a "homogenizing abolition of particularity" (a tendency Gunton finds prevalent in much post-Enlightenment modern thought),[5] while Parmenides' contemporary, Heraclitus, taking his stand resolutely in the flowing waters and slippery banks of plurality and flux, serves as the champion (if not the essence, since that would be self-referentially incoherent) of the radically plural and the particular, and thus the patron saint of postmodernity. The seemingly ethereal questions of ontology and theology from which discussions about such things take their bearings and to which they finally return are, nonetheless, Gunton notes, bound up with very down-to-earth and practical considerations, such as the quest for rationality and meaning, and the desire to negotiate the peaceful ordering of human relationships.[6]

If we turn to Christian theology in particular, then here too we find that questions about universality and particularity, sameness and difference, what is shared and what sets things and people apart from one another arise and solicit answers from us at almost every turn. They are to be found, for instance, at the heart of the doctrine of creation, which both posits a vital relationship between God and the world while yet, through the asymmetry of that relationship, setting God equally clearly apart from the world as its uncreated source, and thus radically and uniquely "other." Such questions are fundamental, too, of course, to the grammar of Christology and its attempts to parse the claim that in Jesus of Nazareth the eternal Word or Son has taken flesh and become a man. In the Christologies of the Nicene and Chalcedonian formularies just as surely as in the prima facie blasphemous biblical conjunction of a particular human life with the identity, presence, authority, and action of the Holy One of Israel, it is precisely questions about sameness and difference, unity and distinction, universality and particularity, the one and the many that are at stake. And here, too, questions of such enormous metaphysical import are finally inseparable from questions of praxis, and thus of a distinctly Christian way of modeling human community (i.e., one earthed in, growing naturally out of, and reflecting the answers we give to such questions about reality's ultimate provenance, nature, and destiny in the hands of the God we know as the Father of Jesus Christ).

For the sake of argument, one might summarize the character of authentic Christian community—modeled in the church not just *ad intra* but *ad extra* too in its ways of *being* the church in the midst of the world for the sake of which it exists—as one marked by an unconditional respect and love for the other as other, by becoming what Jürgen Moltmann calls a "community of the different."[7] Of course, difference obtains at various levels of personal existence—between individuals, between social and economic groups, between nations, between ethnic groups, between religions, between civilizations, and so on. It all depends where we choose to draw the relevant boundaries.[8] And we must avoid reifying or absolutizing difference in unhealthy or dangerous ways. The idea of that which is "other" is susceptible to all manner of abuse socially and politically. As a social construct, "otherness" has much to answer for in the long history of man's inhumanity to man, being grist to the mill of every form of tribalism.[9] So, for a Christian, acknowledgment of the genuine and significant differences that do exist must always take place within the context of a countervailing recognition of what is held in common (even when this cannot always easily be specified), and the recognition of the "other" first and foremost as a fellow human being made in the image and likeness of God and heir to the covenant promises of God. Yet the danger exists, too, of failing to respect the particularity of others, of a "homogenizing abolition of particularity" which either seeks to marginalize the things which others hold dear in the interests of a peaceful coexistence, or else demands that they abandon them and become like us as the condition of their acceptance. This, too, Moltmann argues, is an error Christians must avoid.

In his essay "The Knowing of the Other and the Community of the Different," Moltmann identifies both of these errors as products of the ancient epistemic principle that "like is only truly known by like," which he traces back to Aristotle's *Metaphysics* (2.4.1000b) and dubs the "principle of analogy." In this case, he observes, what is genuinely other cannot be known at all, and our acquisition of knowledge about the world, the other person, or God himself amounts only to "the continually reiterated self-endorsement of what is already known."[10] As regards knowledge of God, Moltmann observes, this principle necessarily supposes that the human self is in some sense already "divine," otherwise it could not recognize that divine reality which transcends it.[11] It is thus constantly prone either to the deification of the human knower or the reduction of God to a projection of the creaturely imagination. In personal, social, and political terms, the conviction that "like is only known by like" tends to be either indifferent toward or anxious about that which is different (and thus forever alien) in the other, rather than curious about or fascinated by it. It typically seeks to neutralize and domesticate otherness, either by force (some version of exclusion, colonialism, or globalization), or by the more humane but equally disrespectful mechanisms of a "dialogue" intended to establish a shared denominator of human experience and outlook as "what really matters," and to secure homogeneous cultural expressions of the same, thus marginalizing and belittling the very things that grant particular identities their value and color.[12]

The second principle Moltmann identifies is that according to which "other is only truly known by other" (the "principle of dialectic"), a model that he also credits to Greek philosophy (Euripides, Anaxagoras) but for which he finds significant theological grounds in the dialectical relationship that occurs in communion between ourselves and the God who is Wholly Other. We might add—though Moltmann does not in this context—the distinctly Christian conviction that in God himself there is eternal communion between three persons constituted as much by their differences from one another as by their sharing of a single nature. Triunity, in other words, is at one level an exemplification of communion evinced and constituted in genuine diversity, albeit one only analogously related to the creaturely circumstance. Where creatures (and fallen creatures at that) are concerned, Moltmann notes, our initial experience of that which is different, strange, or new is one of resistance to the self and attendant pain or suffering caused. Genuine otherness is discerned by way of contradiction and contrast rather than correspondence, and we quickly

sense "the claim of the new" and our need to accommodate it or adjust ourselves accordingly.[13] The point here, of course, is precisely that knowledge
of difference and knowledge of self/same arise together and dialectically.
Knowing ourselves, we are able readily to identify that which differs from
and resists ourselves, and become curious and wonder about the contours
of its otherness. "I can only understand [what is other]," Moltmann writes,
"by changing myself, and adjusting myself to it. In my perception of others
I subject myself to the pains and joys of my own alteration, not in order
to adapt myself to the other, but in order to enter into it."[14] It is by way of
such willing subjection and the imaginative transcendence of the established boundaries of "self" alone that genuine community rather than
artificial homogeneity can be established and sustained. Thus, universal
and particular, sameness and difference arise here not in a self-destructive
tension but in a mutually defining and mutually enriching, albeit costly,
interplay.[15]

§2. Scandalous Particularity

Jesus and the Self-Identification of God

In "Christology Today" Bauckham traces parallels and resonances with
all this not in the doctrine of God as such but in Christology and its wrestling with the question of how the historical Jesus can be identifiable as the
One who made and sustains all things in heaven and earth, and how the
accidents of his particular life and death and resurrection can be of universal redemptive significance. On one hand, in "taking flesh" and sharing
creatureliness with us, the Son of God held in common with us all that
is shared in our human "nature" and existence, thus identifying himself
with us. Yet, since humanity does not exist as an abstraction but only in
the form of particular human lives lived, this same Son of God embraced
to the full the contingency of historical existence, becoming the particular man Jesus of whose actions, words, and suffering the Gospels are concerned to tell us.

It is precisely in this latter acknowledgment or insistence, though,
that various strands of modern Christology have identified a problem
for soteriology, generating different versions of a scandal of particularity. One prominent strand of this presupposes something very like what
Moltmann identifies as the Aristotelian "principle of analogy," insisting
now that "like can only be *saved* by like." A forthright and persuasive statement of the case that particularity (or "difference") is corrosive of Jesus'

universal redemptive significance in this way is found, for instance, in its (post-Christian) feminist version in the writings of Daphne Hampson.[16] For Hampson, unsurprisingly, it is Jesus' maleness—the fact that the incarnation necessarily entails gender specificity—that is the problem. The claim that God has entered the stream of human history as a man, she argues, is by definition at odds with the other claim Christians typically make, namely, that in his redemptive significance Christ is inclusive of all humans.[17] On the contrary, Hampson insists, a God who, in becoming flesh uniquely, actually becomes *male* flesh entails the unique symbolizing of God in a manner which suggests that maleness is identifiable with God in a way that femaleness is not, thereby preventing women from ever finding themselves in God in the way that men now can and might be encouraged to. Hampson traces to this singular fact the whole history of Western religious thought (and much of Western culture in its wake) as "ideologically loaded against women."[18] Considered on its own terms, Hampson's case is robust and well made—though, as Bauckham points out, maleness is only one significant marker of difference among humans, and there is no reason why, in our plural and postmodern context, parallel cases might not be made by others on the grounds of race/culture, marital status, age and breadth of life experience, economic status, the fact that (so far as we know) Jesus had to endure no physical or mental disability, and so on.[19] In each case it might be argued by some that, precisely because Jesus was "different" from them in one way or another, he could have no ultimate religious significance for them.[20] Indeed, since no human life is ever wholly like another, the logical *reductio ad absurdum* of the case would be the denial that a genuine human life (i.e., one lived in all the unique particularity that in reality marks *every* human life out as different from any other) could never be redemptively significant for any other, let alone for all.

What makes Hampson's case persuasive (though not immune from susceptibility to the *reductio* alluded to above) is the extent to which she engages directly with Christian attempts to address this perceived problem. In particular, she attends closely and carefully to the development of patristic Christologies that attempt to do precisely this, and finally finds them wanting for reasons which Bauckham himself in part shares.[21] The patristic theologians, Hampson notes, recognized that human difference in the context of an incarnational Christology was intrinsically problematic for soteriology, and sought to address it. Precisely because (in the familiar terms coined by the Cappadocians) "what is not assumed is not healed," theologians from Irenaeus onward sought to maximize and draw attention to the levels of *likeness* between the incarnate Son and those he came to save. This led most notably to their insistence that what mattered soteriologically (and, by association, christologically) was the fact that in Christ God took upon himself our common human "flesh" (the "human nature" in which, regardless of our gender, we all share) and redeemed it. Thus, considerations of a more particular sort can be set aside (deliberately or tacitly) as christologically and soteriologically *adiaphora*. Jesus' Jewishness, his masculinity, his having lived for only thirty or so and not eighty years, his lack of experience of married life or of being a parent, or of being demon-possessed, and so on—all of this can be safely acknowledged, leaving his salvific significance "for all" essentially unscathed.[22] Because what he did "for all" was done precisely at the level what the "all" in question have in common, namely our shared "human nature" in which he suffered and died and rose again.[23]

Having reckoned fully with this attempt to redress the scandal of particularity, Hampson finally rejects it. Her reasons for doing so are, chiefly, its alleged reliance on a Platonic philosophical notion of "universals" which modern (and postmodern) humans can no longer take seriously.[24] In doing so it plays down the importance of particularity and specificity in a manner that is no longer tolerable. Bauckham too demurs from the emphasis of much patristic Christology on relatively abstract notions of humanity, but his reasons for doing so are more solidly theological. Whatever their merits, he insists, there can be little warrant in theological terms for stripping Christology of so much of what the New Testament is concerned to tell us about Jesus, in effect overlooking the particularity of the Jesus whose ministry is related in the Gospels, and moving quickly to a much more abstract theological principle concerned with "natures" and the mode of their hypostatic union.

The reason that Hampson can spend so long sympathetically entertaining the christological views of the church fathers, it seems, is that she shares with them the same basic soteriological premise, namely that in the final instance "like can only be saved by like," and that human particularity is therefore a significant stumbling block rather than a positive consideration in the attempt to develop an account of the universal relevance of the incarnation. Yet it is precisely this premise that Bauckham is concerned to reject. If we abandon the tenuous supposition that the redemptive significance of Jesus for each of us consists only (or even primarily) in whatever we happen to hold in common with him and he with us, he argues, then a wholly new christological and soteriological vista opens up for our consideration and exploration.

Instead, Bauckham maintains, it is by virtue of a complex *interplay* of sameness and otherness that Jesus' redemptive being and action is realized, his "universal" saving significance being bound up just as thoroughly with the particular and peculiar things he is reported to have said and done and suffered as it is with his assumption of "humanity" and sharing of "the human condition." Thus it is precisely the shape of Jesus' character and personhood (whether encountered in first-century Palestine in the flesh or through the narration of his story in the church today) which, as it interacts with others, transforms them redemptively; and the form of his identification with some (the poor and the downtrodden) will differ significantly from his identification with others (the Pharisees and teachers of the law), because their particularity is respected rather than marginalized, and demands a wholly different response and relationship from the particular person Jesus himself is. In Jesus, Bauckham insists, the universal Lord identifies himself with humankind not in some homogenous or abstract manner which robs both him and us of the very particulars which make us each who we are, but in the particular form of Jesus of Nazareth whose story intersects and interferes with our particular stories in a plethora of possible ways and combinations, each redemptive but each equally distinctive. Thus God's solidarity with us is not that of a symbolic Everyperson but precisely a "differential solidarity," global in its reach but infinitely variegated in its precise configurations, a solidarity "with people not only in the common human condition," as Christology is sometimes prone to suggest, "but with people in all the varieties of the human condition." Again, sameness and difference, universality and particularity are here not locked in mortal combat with one another, their respective concerns to be secured only despite one another, but instead belong together in a fruitful if at times complex and costly give and take.

Notice that, here, the concerns of two distinct strands of contemporary christological reflection are held together and seen properly to belong together rather than pulling in different directions. On one hand, a concern to reclaim and make sense of the heritage of creedal profession of the incarnation of God's eternal Son, and on the other an insistence that we do justice to the specifics of Jesus' particular history as narrated in the Gospel traditions. So, christologies "from above" and "from below," as they have often been dubbed, prove to be not at all feasible as opposites but only as emphases which require and complete one another within a more unified scheme of things. The one who comes to us from above is never known or knowable to us as a *logos asarkos* but only as one clothed in the contingencies of a particular historical existence, while the story of the man Jesus has universal redemptive significance (or for that matter *any* significance for us other than as a historical curio) precisely and only because it is held to be the concrete form of God's own self-identification in the world. Matters of epistemology and soteriology stand and fall together here, since it is precisely the particular form of God's self-identifying which cuts across our existence with redemptive effect, banishing the idols which religious imagination so readily sets up, and, by showing us the Father's heart of holy love, drawing us back from our alienated state to receive our adoption as forgiven sons and daughters.

Of course, the incarnation does not reduce God to this particular form: God remains mysterious and beyond the grasp of our thought and speech even in the midst of his self-identifying; but here, God also "comes out of his mystery and gives himself a particular this-worldly identity by which we may identify him,"[25] thus meeting the fundamental religious need to specify who God is, and to form a concrete image of him. This insistence provides a helpful corrective to crypto-Hegelian suspicion of the economy of the image as such in Christology, such as T. F. Torrance's insistence that all images must properly give way in theology to an "image-less" relation secured by the superior mediation of our knowing by "pure concepts."[26] Visibility of sorts is, whether we like it or not, one of the characteristics of the flesh and of our embeddedness as creatures in the world of the senses, and we cannot strip it away to the point where it ceases to be noticed (becoming, as it were, not just transparent and translucent as a mediator of the divine reality but in effect *invisible*) without removing it altogether, thereby effectively reversing the direction and the accomplishment of the incarnation and God's accommodation to our epistemic condition. Again, God is not reduced to the form of Jesus' humanity; but if our knowing of God is always about more than the human Jesus alone, it is never about anything less, and the extent to which it drifts free of its moorings there is the extent to which it is in danger either of agnosticism or of the sort of sheer imaginative construction which was Feuerbach's diagnosis of the whole religious and theological enterprise.[27] The doctrines of the resurrection and the ascension are our theological warrant for insisting that the humanity of Jesus remains theologically basic rather than a fleeting flirtation with the flesh to be transcended both by Christ and by us as we ascend instead to some fleshless and timeless sphere of forms. That, surely, is one of the most basic differences between a Christian account of reality and any one of those derived variously from the philosophy of Plato. And, to reiterate the point, the humanity of Jesus we are talking about is no bloodless abstraction, but the historically particular flesh-and-blood individual who lived and died and rose from the tomb somewhere around 33 CE in Palestine. Whatever sense we make of this, it is precisely *this* that we must make sense of, and not something else.

It should not be supposed, though, that Bauckham dismisses the importance of christological and soteriological claims directed toward what is shared among human beings, and thus between Christ and those for whom he is held to be salvifically significant. Indeed, Bauckham takes the apostle Paul's concentration on Jesus' death on the cross as "the ancestor of all those atonement doctrines which find Jesus' universality in his relevance to the human condition as such" (i.e., our shared subjection to sin and condemnation, and our need of forgiveness and reconciliation to God).[28] But while this may be important it is not the whole truth with which soteriology must grapple. Put bluntly, "We are all sinners in different ways,"[29] and an adequate soteriology must get to grips too with the particularities of *our* lives, and the ways in which Christ is religiously significant for those. And it is precisely here, Bauckham argues, that the particularities of Jesus' humanity as transmitted to us in the gospel accounts can and must be brought fully into play. Appealing again to the categories of narrative as a way of speaking both about Jesus' particular identity (and of God's self-identification in him) and of our identities, he thus insists that there are both points at which "Jesus' story intersects every other human story in the same way" and others (an infinitely varied number) where his story and ours intersect uniquely, being the interplay of one unsubstitutable human identity with another.[30] Jesus' "identification with" us, in other words, involves both an engagement of like with like *and* an equally vital play of difference with difference. And within this salvific play of difference, Bauckham observes suggestively, it is both the radical particularity of the Jesus of the Gospels which cuts across ours redemptively (uttering words of judgment, or encouragement, or healing, or forgiveness, or whatever the particular manifestation of sin in our lives might demand) and his identification and solidarity with those who are very different from ourselves. Thus, "When American black theologians began to claim that 'Jesus is black'—which I have suggested can be understood as 'black by identification'—they did not, if I have understood them, mean only that Jesus is black for blacks. Jesus is also black for whites—just as, for the Pharisees, Jesus was identified with tax collectors and sinners. They could, as it were, only know his solidarity with themselves via his solidarity with the people they excluded."[31]

§3. Ascension, Parousia, and Eschatological Imagination

Insofar as our salvation is contingent on an encounter with the particularity of Jesus, of course, it quickly presents yet another version of the scandal of particularity. Bauckham insists that "Jesus is God's loving identification with all humanity," which is, as such, "in principle unlimited and potentially universalizable."[32] If, though, this loving identification is mediated uniquely through the particular history of Jesus, if Jesus is, as Bauckham puts it, "God's own particular, this worldly identity, and so . . . the form in which God can be encountered and known,"[33] then a question quickly arises about the de facto rather than the de jure scope of such redemptive encounter. Prima facie, as Bauckham himself notes, such encounter is in one sense limited to the circle of Jesus' empirical human acquaintance, that is, "the actual men and women Jesus encountered in his earthly life."[34] Bauckham's appeal at this point to a version of narrative theology (Jesus' particular identity, which is the form of God's self-identification with us and for us, is subsequently narrated in Scripture and thence in the teaching, preaching, and other proclamation of the church)[35] certainly widens the scope of the circle considerably but does not yet universalize it. It continues to exclude all those (doubtless fewer and fewer today, but across the history of humankind as a whole surely the vast majority?) who have never heard the story. It was this problem of "epistemic particularism" and its apparent soteriological implications which motivated John Hick and others in the 1970s gradually to abandon the doctrine of the incarnation, conveniently discovering its origins as a "myth" separable from the redemptive significance of Jesus, and identifying the latter in generic and universalizable religious considerations which could be abstracted from the body of Jesus' recorded teachings and example just as surely as the notion of "human nature" had earlier been abstracted from the more complex contours of biblical Christology as a whole.[36] More theologically orthodox responses to the circumstance have also tended to move quickly from the complexities and contingencies of Jesus' life and ours to embrace a drama seemingly conducted at a higher level and, in practice, over our heads. So, for instance, Vernon White argues boldly for an atonement conducted by the incarnate Son objectively "for us," our inclusion in which does not demand any knowledge on our part of the drama's having occurred, let alone of the details of Jesus' life and ministry.[37] No matter how helpful and rich many of the things White's argument affirms may be as versions of a Christian understanding of the person and work of Christ, Bauckham's steadfast resistance to the abolition of particularity in Christology and soteriology seem bound to preclude his accepting it as an adequate response to religious pluralism of the sort Hick espouses. Again, both positions (i.e., White's and Hick's) are premised on the flawed notion that Jesus' universal significance can only be had (and may in fact be had) at the expense of a full-blooded reckoning with and insistence on the historically particular shape and substance of his humanity.

We return, though, to the historically ungainsayable point that many, and probably the greater bulk of particular human souls who have ever lived, have never enjoyed the opportunity for the sort of meaningful encounter with the particular identity of God manifest in Jesus to which Bauckham refers us. If, as he maintains, this sort of encounter is important for a full understanding of Jesus' religious and redemptive significance, rather than readily elided or substitutable with encounters of other sorts, then to make sense of the claim that what is in principle *universalizable* here may finally become *universal* in its actual salvific reach we must begin to reckon with questions lying solidly in the domain of another of Bauckham's major theological concerns, namely eschatology. More broadly, indeed, since few believers will suppose that their redemptive encounter with the Jesus revealed in the Gospels is likely to be wrapped up satisfactorily by the point of their death, some continuation of that same encounter beyond death must meaningfully be imagined. Readers who balk at the use of the term "redemptive" in the context of anything occurring postmortem should feel free to coin some alternative vocabulary. The point remains one to be grappled with. Thus P. T. Forsyth once averred that the Protestant church, in its abandonment of the medieval doctrine of a purgatorial state, had thrown the baby out with the bath water, and that—shorn of its association with spiritually toxic notions of postmortem atonement for personal debts laid up in this life—the idea of a continuing relationship with Jesus in which we are changed ever more fully into his likeness (albeit by an encounter precisely with his *difference* from us) was a perfectly cogent and warranted one. More recently, Jürgen Moltmann has suggested something similar in his sustained wrestling with eschatological questions.[38] Whether or not we choose to entertain and explore such eschatological scenarios, though, Bauckham's insistence that it is in, and not apart from, the particular identity of Jesus that God identifies himself as "God for us" has profound eschatological implications, for it entails the further claim that it will only be through a continuing encounter with Jesus (and not some "fleshless" eternal Son) that our knowing of God in eternity will be enjoyed. In other words, the knowledge of God "face to face" may well transcend the knowledge we have now "through a glass, darkly," but it will still in some identifiable sense be an encounter with the face of Jesus. Again, the theological force of the christological doctrines of resurrection and ascension provide vital ballast for such a claim. The incarnation is no mere temporary theophany but a permanent tabernacling of God in the enhistoricized "flesh" of our humanity, through encounter with which alone—now and "for ever"—we may properly apprehend and commune with God's glory.

Bauckham's insistence on the self-identification of God in history in the story of Jesus provides, in fact, a vital clue to help us grapple with the wider problem of eschatological imagining—the problem, in other words, of thinking beyond the thresholds not just of human history but of the present space-time reality itself, and thus beyond the warranted range of human language and conceptuality as such.[39] Just as Israel's protological saga is identifiably bathed in the light of her historical relation with *Adonai*, creation itself being presented as an act of grace consonant with the character of the One who delivered her from slavery and called her into covenant fellowship, so, too, for Christians the constant which straddles the logical gap between historical present and posthistorical future is precisely the *character* of the God of the promise, who himself transcends all creaturely reality but who has identified himself concretely and definitively in the contingencies of the historical Jesus. To repeat: God cannot be reduced or limited to the form of Jesus' humanity, but if this is the form in which God particularizes himself for us, then we can never set it aside or skirt around it in our knowing of God, even in eternity.

If so, then in the meanwhile this same concrete form must shape our own imaginative trespass beyond what can meaningfully be known or understood about the eschatological future, providing the vital template and compass for our thinking about the substance of the divine promise. In particular, in closing, it would seem that one vital theological function of the doctrine of the *parousia* or second coming of Christ is precisely to insist that the eschatological judgment of the quick and the dead (a scenario more prone than most, perhaps, to flights of imaginative fancy and projection as the history of Western visual art bears eloquent witness) lies securely in the hands of the one who characterizes himself most fully in having borne the place of judgment for us, making it his own, and thus robbing us of any right to the leasehold. The one who comes to judge us is not just some abstract "Risen Lord," but the selfsame Jesus whose character we know from the Gospel accounts, and who bore our sins to the cross in his body. Whatever account of final judgment we have to offer, therefore, it cannot and must not be one developed without constant reference to the judgment already borne for us on Calvary, or the character of the judge who allowed himself to be judged in our place and "descended to the dead." Unable to hold him—the one who is like us in all things, and yet (thank God) so very different—the gates of that death have been broken wide open by his rude departure from it, once and for all. No more theologically basic or ultimate characterization of God must be permitted to haunt our eschatological imagination, for anything that seeks to go behind the back of Jesus in this way resorts, in effect, to the fashioning of idols again, albeit ones crafted with the flotsam and jetsam of scattered biblical texts and fired by exegetical enthusiasm.

14

Availability

§1. Elusive Presence

It is by now a commonplace, perhaps a truism, to suggest that the prevailing climate of thought and of feeling in contemporary (modern or postmodern) European culture is that of "a vivid sense of the absence of God."[1] God survives, according to his self-satisfied executioners, only by clinging to culture as "a phantom of grammar, a fossil embedded in the childhood of rational speech."[2] But in at least one sense, therefore, the suggestion can be seen to be misleading. The postulate or dogma of God's *nonexistence*, it seems, is not at all the same thing as the experience of God's *absence*, a sense bound up closely with the postulate of his presence, or at least the possibility of his presence.[3] Insofar as the claim is true, furthermore, I want to suggest that far from being a consequence of the successful overthrow of our biblical heritage, the problem of God's absence (or, as we might say somewhat inelegantly, God's "absence/presence") is bequeathed to us precisely by that same heritage, and in particular by its roots sunk deep in the soils of Hebraic and Judaic sensibility. For here what we find is a theology of divine presence which is at once profound and problematic, which gives with one hand what it appears only to take away again with the other, compelling an epistemic and moral disposition which human beings who have "come of age" have always found uncomfortable—namely one of trust:

trust in the God who makes himself present yet refuses to give himself over into human hands to be held on to or commandeered into our various programs and agendas, who gives what is for us in his judgment sufficient but never as much as we think we should actually like of his presence (even though in reality it may often also be as much as, for the time being at least, we can bear).[4]

According to Samuel Terrien's eponymous essay in the field of biblical theology[5] it is a distinctive theology of divine presence (rather than one centered around the theme of covenant) which sets Israel apart most clearly from the religious cultures of her immediate neighbors and provides the golden thread holding both the various stages of her historical development and the texts in her canon of Scripture identifiably together.[6] The peculiarity of this sense of presence is, Terrien suggests, precisely its persistent complication by and compounding with an attendant awareness of absence, a sense of isolation from the proximity of God.[7] It is a presence both undeniably real, and yet more often than not either remembered or (on the basis of divine promise) looked forward to, rather than experienced directly or "purely." It is, in this sense, we might say, both dialectical and eschatological. Ingolf Dalferth characterizes the whole history of Israel as one of "suffering from the experience of God's absence, and . . . longing for his definitive and real presence"; Jesus' announcement of the kingdom of God, Dalferth suggests, must be understood in this light as the announcement that "the time of God's absence had come to an end and that the longed for presence of God was about to begin here and now."[8] But, while in some sense Christians must hold this to be true, the dialectic is not resolved here into any Hegelian higher synthesis: the pulse of Hebraic iconoclasm beats powerfully in the breast of the New Testament too, and maintains a tension, as Terrien puts it, "between divine self-disclosure and divine self-concealment." In many ways, indeed, the presence of Christ in the world sharpens and heightens the tension, the presence of the Risen Lord remaining "elusive" rather than available on tap, communicated by the Spirit who blows where he wills, and arising not as "sheer presence," but shaped from first to last by elements of narrated past and future, that is to say of remembrance and hope (including the abiding hope for an unambiguous presence, when God will be known to be "all in all").[9] If, as Dalferth properly insists, for Christian believers questions about divine presence and absence must be informed above all by considerations of Christology, therefore, we certainly should not expect the answers to those questions to be easily had, for at the heart of

Christology we find events that serve precisely "to intensify the sense of the absence of God rather than disclose God's presence."[10]

Questions of presence and absence have spilled over identifiably from the explicit concerns of biblical religion and theology to generate some deep-seated anxieties in the patterns of our wider culture, and it is worth pausing at least to notice the resonances arising from their common (albeit often disputed or unacknowledged) paternity. Thus, according to George Steiner,[11] the postmodern "broken contract" between word and world, sign and thing signified, deeply questioning whether any "presence" (authorial, readerly, or other sort) may in fact reliably be discerned through our engagements with "language" in the widest sense of the word, may confidently trace its roots and antecedents (if not its warrant) in the same biblical matrix of "elusive presence." Judaism, Steiner notes, is marked equally by its profound respect for the holiness of the divine presence and its attention to the sacred text as, in effect, an extension of the tent of meeting. One consequence of this, he argues, is the prominent phenomenon in Jewish culture of the textually secondary, keeping, as it were, a respectful distance from the *qodesh qodashim*, always preferring commentary—and commentary on commentary—to those primary performances of the text which inevitably risk the idolatrous suggestion of semantic closure. Hermeneutic unendingness, "reading without end," the midrashic gloss and marginalia not just on the sacred text but on all previous readings of it, deferring definitive resolution of questions of the text's meaning, all sustain a dialectic precisely similar (because in reality wedded) to the interplay of divine presence and absence, self-disclosure and self-veiling. "The lamps of explication must burn unquenched before the tabernacle,"[12] precisely because the presence discerned there is one not to be pinned down through the semantic, lexical, and grammatical tools at our disposal but always elusive and thus in a manner "absent" (refusing more than a partial and fleeting, let alone a final, determination) even in the midst of its own elected presence. Paradoxically, Steiner notes, the same religiously driven impulse toward the underdetermination or destabilizing of textual meaning also liberates the sacred text both from "historical-geographical contingency" and from "the threat of the past tense," acknowledging its capacity to speak in ever new times and places. "In dispersion," he notes, "the text is homeland."[13] But all this, Steiner admits, has in due course borne some strange fruit, and it should come as no surprise to anyone that some of the high priests of textual deconstruction are to be identified among the tribe of Israel. Thus, poststructuralist versions of "reading without end" and la *différance*, endlessly adjourning the sterile fixity of definition,[14] are in their own way rooted in the selfsame theological concerns about potentially "idolatrous" misappropriations of presence ("logocentrism"), but, far from preserving the dialectic of "elusiveness," deconstruction posits an *aporia*, a semantic "transcendence" so radical as in effect to explode the dialectic, leaving available only the dubious consolation of the assurances of absence. So, Steiner writes, "Deconstruction dances in front of the ancient Ark. This dance is at once playful . . . and, in its subtler practitioners . . . instinct with sadness. For the dancers know that the Ark is empty."[15] Although he rejects the postulates of deconstructionism, Steiner insists that, on its own terms and planes of argument, like all forms of philosophical skepticism, its challenge is a difficult one to refute. In the final analysis, he suggests, the reality of any "presence," that is, of something other than ourselves and meaning-full "out there" to be reckoned with, responded to, and "made sense of," is one which remains elusive, and thus, while we may have a grasp or sense of it sufficient for our practical needs (indeed it is difficult to see how these can be sustained in the teeth of its denial), resists our desire and attempts to master and possess it completely. It can only be known at all, he suggests, on the basis of a "wager," a willingness to trust which is wedded both structurally and ontologically to the prior wager on the reality of God's own elusive presence.[16]

§2. Orientating Presence

Despite the necessity for and importance of such disclaimers, "presence" remains fundamentally a term of orientation rather than disorientation. Specifically, it indicates our attempt in language to locate and situate ourselves—in relation to everything that is (things, persons, thoughts, events, actions, facts, and so on[17])—in space and in time. Thus that which is "present" to me[18] is that which is here and now, not there or then. That which is "real" we typically take to be characterized by its "thereness"[19] (it is that which "presents itself" to me from time to time and place to place, which I apprehend with a certain "psychical immediacy"[20] and in the face of which I am compelled to respond),[21] and by its being neither past (that which "is" no longer) nor future (that which will or may in due course "come to be" but "is" not as yet).[22] Such coordinates are, to be sure, often difficult to plot precisely in the manifold of experience—we draw the line between "here" and "there" variously as practical circumstance demands, and the "present moment" is notoriously subject to slippage (like our shadow it shifts whenever we seek to step back and grasp it) and never pure (always interrupted and conditioned by the flashbacks of a remembered past and the particular hopes and aspirations regarding what may yet come to be).[23] Nonetheless, what we refer to as "presence" is, we might venture, a function of the way in which God himself situates us within his world, giving us (despite the vertigo-inducing infinity of cosmic time and space posited by modern physics, and notwithstanding the universalizing aspirations of various philosophical idealisms to transcend the constraints of any and every particular time and place) both the "space" and the time sufficient to live the lives he calls us each to live,[24] lives which must be lived, furthermore, *coram Deo*—before the face of God himself, and thus in his presence.[25]

As theologians across the ages have reminded us, time and space are themselves functions of God's creation rather than conditions of it,[26] and God's own relation to us as such is, strictly speaking, neither spatial nor temporal despite the inevitable "mythologizing" of our religious language ("he came down from heaven," etc.). God relates to creatures existing in time and space but is not himself spatially or temporally located in or related to his creation.[27] Traditional claims concerning the ubiquity (or "omnipresence") of God must therefore be interpreted with care lest they mislead. If God is in some important sense "everywhere," it is not as a spatially extended backdrop which, as it were (being "bigger, wider, and deeper" than the cosmos itself), runs over the edges of creaturely space and time so as to cover them completely with and swallow them within itself ("God . . . the final frontier . . ."), but as a personally willed presence *to* every creaturely present as it arises, more helpfully pictured, perhaps, as the intersection between two otherwise quite incommensurate planes or dimensions.[28] Thus Aquinas notes that, strictly speaking, it is no more correct to say that God "contains" the cosmos than to suggest that the cosmos may contain God (i.e., that God may crop up as an object located "within" it), except in that peculiar sense of the word "contain" which means "to hold together" ("I could hardly contain myself," etc.).[29] In the latter sense, God does indeed "contain" all things by his continual presence to them, such presence being the very condition for their existence, power, and activity, but again, Aquinas stresses, this is a matter not of mere ontology but of moral agency—God acts (and thus chooses) to be present (in Dalferth's phrase, he *becomes* present to every present[30]) and thereby to hold the world in being from moment to waking moment of its creaturely existence. So, talk in the abstract of divine "presence" may also mislead if it is taken to connote some essentially static state of affairs: For God to *be*, Dalferth reminds us, is, according to Christian theology at least, for God to be *active*, and therefore divine presence is always a matter of God's *becoming present* as the one who acts,[31] whatever the precise mode of that presence and action may be. This in turn draws our attention to a further potentially misleading abstraction: God's "presence" is not only of a single sort but can be identified in various modes, and sometimes in more than one at the same time. Dalferth himself identifies for us three key modes of this divine presence-in-action, and he maps these conveniently onto the Christian naming of God as Father, Son, and Holy Spirit. Thus God, he suggests, is present as Father/Creator as the one who is "time free present"[32] in the same way to every presence (as the necessary condition for every occurring event and every person in whose presence it occurs); he is present, secondly, in a wholly distinct mode as the incarnate Son/Savior (in whom he has "made himself *temporarily present* to us *in a specific way in human history*"[33]); and he is, in a different way again, "multi-present" as Spirit/Perfecter, making his presence felt in a manner which will be unique to each individual circumstance, and drawing particular persons to faith as the pattern of life lived consciously in God's presence. Without following Dalferth's precise way of mapping these modes onto the *Seinsweisen* in the triune life, in the remainder of this chapter I follow at least in broad terms his example of differentiating modes of God's presence along identifiably Trinitarian lines.

§3. Creative Absence

God Makes Room for the World

According to a familiar graffito, "Time is God's way of stopping everything from happening all at once," in which case we might surmise that space is his way of avoiding the need for everything to be in the same place at the same time, a level of cohabitation the very suggestion of which is likely to send even the agoraphobic and the extrovert into a panic attack, and puts a whole new (and paradoxical) complexion on the phrase, "You're trespassing on my space." God the Creator makes room for his creatures to exist and to coexist fruitfully alongside one another, however they may subsequently choose to distribute that space. Unlike embodied creatures such as ourselves, though, Aquinas suggests, "God's presence in a place does not exclude the presence of other things."[34] God, it seems, is the perfect cohabitee. This, we have already suggested, is precisely because

God does not occupy any space ("take up any room") in the world, being related to it (except, we must now say, when he takes flesh in the economy of the Son) in an essentially nonspatial manner.

Notwithstanding this, Jürgen Moltmann insists that it is important to reckon with the claim that in a more profound sense God as Creator must and has "made room for" the world itself to exist alongside himself, though what he has in mind, of course, is not a literal but precisely a metaphorical *Lebensraum*.[35] Although we speak and think (and cannot do otherwise) of God's various *operationes ad extra*, Moltmann notes, strictly speaking there is no *extra Deum* either before creation or after it. Yet, he suggests, it may nonetheless be theologically fruitful to stretch our language and our imagining of the primordial circumstance in this direction. "Prior to" creation (again, we cannot help borrowing from the temporal conditions to which human speech is naturally fitted), God took up, as it were, all the available space, since God was all there was. God's self-determination as Creator thus, we may suppose, necessarily involved a withdrawal or contraction of himself into himself, a divine "shoving up" in order to make room for something genuinely other than himself to exist at all. In the first instance, this appropriation of the Jewish kabbalistic image of a divine *zimsum* (contraction) is offered as a way of imagining very concretely (albeit "mythologically") what is entailed by the Christian doctrine of *creatio ex nihilo*, and avoiding the twin theological errors of monism and dualism. Moltmann presses further, though, playing on the image in a manner which foregrounds questions of divine presence (and divine absence) in a much more far-reaching manner.

Zimsum entails divine self-withdrawal, and thus divine absence from the "space" freed up by it. What arises as a result of this deliberate action of God *ad intra* is precisely "Nothingness." While Moltmann alludes to this new existent as something "created,"[36] strictly speaking for him the space concerned exists precisely as a *condition* of the creation of something other than God. (In this sense it is, we should recall, a metaphorical and "logical" rather than a literal space.) It is, Moltmann suggests, quite literally "God-forsaken" space, space from which God is now absent in his presence and power. It is a "Nihil," albeit one paradoxically and necessarily enfolded within God's own otherwise omnipresent being. And it is into this same space or void that God subsequently creates, filling it not just with a cosmos but thereby once again with his own presence, being present to it now, though not as he is to his own being but as the one who by an act of gracious will holds something other in being alongside himself. Yet the void remains, if only as the logical (and possible) alternative to our originated and continuing existence as contingent creatures in God's presence. It is that which, should God ever withdraw his presence again, is all we may look forward to—disintegration and the abyss of nonbeing. As such, for now it exists or is present (it is precisely that which "waits over against" us—*die Gegenwart*) only as a threat, the threat of absolute death and hell which has no purchase apart from the further fact of human sin and god-lessness (which is not as such yet *God-forsakenness*), but for that very reason has purchase. The possibility of "annihilating Nothingness" is precisely the threat of divine absence in which the self-isolation of the creature in sin is met by God's final turning of his face away from it, permitting the primordial chaos out of which it was created to rush in again and take its place.

What, then, are we to make of all this? Is it anything more than a colorful (and speculative) remythologizing of a circumstance lying beyond the range of legitimate human (even theological) concern? Well, we cannot help, perhaps, imagining some state of affairs pertaining prior to, and in and through, God's primordial creative act, even if we subsequently submit our imaginings to rigorous apophatic qualification and cleansing. Even discussions about God's "freedom" to create (or lack of it) entail some element of that. No doubt Moltmann's "myth" has its particular theological limitations and dangers. (Spatializing the relation between God and a "mystical primordial space" of Nothingness, for instance, tends inevitably toward an imaginative reifying of the latter (as an ontological rather than merely logical space), and, duly incorporated into an account of evil, in the direction of at least a "soft" dualism.[37]) What, then, are its gains, if any? We might list four: (1) It encourages a consistent portrayal of God's character across the whole narrative of creation and redemption, as one who from first to last willingly undertakes a form of "self-limitation" (*kenosis*) for the sake of the creature;[38] (2) it furnishes a theological context in which human experiences of divine "absence" may be taken radically seriously (as authentic felt approximations to or foreshadowings of a real creaturely possibility) within an overarching theology of Creatorly ubiquity (i.e., universal presence); (3) it holds the doctrine of creation together with Moltmann's own distinctive account of the cross as a paradoxical divine sharing in the experience of "godforsakenness"; (4) it situates creation within a Trinitarian narrative of expectation in which absence (the Nihil) will itself finally be annihilated as a meaningful threat to anyone, and God will at last become truly "all in all."[39] To see how, we turn next to reckon with yet another mode of God's presence in the world.

§4. Incarnate Presence

God Makes Room for Himself in the World

We have seen how Moltmann puts his finger on a seeming paradox whereby both divine absence and divine presence are in some sense necessary conditions of the world's existence. It is not a genuine paradox, of course, because we can recognize both presence and absence as existing in different modes (or, we might say, at different levels); and, whereas God must withdraw (be absent) in the mode in which he is otherwise present to his own being as God precisely in order to make room for the world's existence alongside himself as a genuine "other" (i.e., rather than a further form or "emanation" of God's own existence), in an equally fundamental sense (but at a different level of consideration), as the world's Creator, God can never be absent from it, since this would involve its inevitable and immediate disintegration and death. Christian theology, though, knows of yet further comings and goings on God's part, the most radical of which, of course, lies at the heart of its own testimony to Jesus Christ as "Immanuel," God with us—God with us now, that is to say (since in another sense God is always "with us"), in a wholly unprecedented manner, *as one of us*. As Torrance expresses it, the "flesh" or humanity of Christ is "a place within our created and historical existence where God has made room for Himself,"[40] becoming the τόπος or *locus* in space-time where God is to be found present (and known to be so) most fully,[41] accommodating himself fully to the conditions of creatureliness while yet remaining "wholly present everywhere, for He became man without ceasing to be God."[42] Fortunately, we need not trouble ourselves here with all the complexities of incarnational Christology, as it suffices to note that this quite distinct and "new" mode of God's presence logically entails an act of self-distinction not just between two modes of presence but between two discrete "modes of being" (*hypostases* or "persons") within God's own life. For, as Calvin notes, "The Son of God became man in such a manner that he had God in common with us."[43] Moltmann glosses this (following much of the tradition including Calvin himself but offering his own distinctive account) to observe that the incarnate Son has not just God but *God-forsakenness* (the experience of divine absence) in common with us too.

If God's incarnate presence in the world (the preposition being used for the first time with impunity and without qualification) is something unprecedented, it is not, Moltmann notes, wholly unanticipated. Already, he insists, in the older Jewish accounts of God's Shekinah (and the attendant theologies of tabernacle and temple) we find a foreshadowing of and natural prelude to the logic of incarnationalism—a presence of God which is special, willed, and promised, God present at a particular place and at a particular time among particular people, and in a manner distinct from God's essential omnipresence.[44] The Shekinah, Moltmann insists, is no divine attribute but God himself as present, yet present now in an earthly, temporal, and spatial mode "at once identical with God and distinct from him."[45] Thus already, he argues, we have to do with a "difference in God" between two modes of presence that logically entail two modes of being, a "self-distinction," a "difference in God between what distinguishes and what is distinguished, between the self-surrendering and the self-surrendered God." For in sending his Shekinah into the world, God surrenders himself to and identifies with the conditions and the fate of his people, sharing in their exile, rejoicing in their homecoming. The Shekinah too, then, Moltmann suggests, even as a mode of divine presence, in some sense suffers from the absence of God by virtue of its solidarity with Israel: "It is now alienated from God himself. It is grieved and hurt. . . . It suffers in the victims and is tormented in the perpetrators. It goes with sinners on the wanderings of their estrangement" and "with every bit of self-seeking and self-contradiction which we surrender to the will of the Creator who loves us, the Shekinah comes close to God . . . is united with God himself."[46] Of course all this trespasses significantly beyond the limits of the biblical theology of God's Shekinah, but Moltmann urges that it does so in a way which is a natural extrapolation of it. Whether we judge it to be helpful or fanciful, it at least serves as a further clarification of what it might mean for God to exist not just in two modes of presence but in two modes of being which are, as it were, "present to one another" at the same time. Whether or not any such notion is present (or even latent) in the theology of the Shekinah I leave for others better qualified to judge, but it is certainly an important component of the incarnational Christology which Moltmann sees as the natural heir to the Shekinah and temple traditions. Indeed, as Dalferth notes, where God is present and active in more than one way at once, both *in Christo* and *extra Christum*, the two activities may sometimes run not in parallel but contrary to each other,[47] a difference between God and God exemplified supremely and decisively, at the point of Jesus' suffering and death on Golgotha, to consideration of which we now turn.

According to Dalferth, "*What it means* for God to be present is definitively shown in the life and death of Jesus Christ."[48] So, too, we might insist, what it means for God to be *absent*. The two belong naturally together, for, as we have already seen, the experience of divine absence is precisely a reflex or at least a reminder of the sense or apprehension of God's presence rather than its contradiction or opposite. So: "the sense of the absence of God is tied to—at least the possibility of—God's presence just as the sense of God's presence is always contrasted to—at least the possibility of—God's absence."[49] What we experience as God's absence cannot be absence or at least not absolute absence (since there can be nothing to experience and no one to experience anything apart from God's presence to us), but "hidden presence,"[50] a loss of the *apprehension* of God as the one who is present to us and in whose presence we live our lives. Thus the dialectic between divine presence and divine absence is best understood through consideration of the life of the community of believers, for it is only those who confess God's presence who can suffer his absence in the proper sense of the term, in the conflict between what faith believes and what experience of living so often suggests to be the case. The deeper the sense of God as a living presence, the more constitutive it is of the very pattern and fabric of our way of being, the more acute the pain of his seeming absence is bound to be. For this very reason, we may suppose, the suffering of God's absence in the death of Jesus on the cross is paradigmatic, and must inform and shape Christian faith's experiences of absence in whatever context they may arise.

In his discussion of providence and suffering, H. H. Farmer suggests that, given the nature of our experiences in life, there is only one way in which faith in the overshadowing wisdom and love of God can truly be succored, and that is "for it to be able to grasp its object, or be grasped by it, out of the heart of those historical happenings which otherwise give it the lie"[51]—all the "confusion and heartbreak and frustration of life, the sins, follies, accidents, disasters, diseases, so undiscriminating in their incidence, so ruthless in their working out,"[52] all that is least patient of interpretation as a manifestation of divine meaningfulness or compatible with God's presence and activity as one who loves us. But in the cross, Farmer suggests, this is precisely what faith grasps, not directly but precisely *sub contrario*, through an occurrence "including in itself something of almost every darkness to which human life is liable—sin, hatred, physical agony, premature death, the innocent suffering for the guilty, the bitter disappointment of high ideals."[53] Even here—no, *precisely* here—faith discerns and grasps unexpectedly the holy love of God present and working its purpose out, and doing so in more than one way at once.

Thus, at the cross the eternal Son whose personal being is bound up inextricably with both the love of and love for his Father, experiences the darkness of absence, unable any longer to apprehend his Father's face in the horror and awfulness of the circumstance he himself now faces. A postresurrection, Trinitarian reading of the cross suggests, though, that far from being absent God was never and nowhere more fully present than in his "hiddenness" in this same dark event: present as the Father whose judgment on the Son remains even here the same as that promulgated at Jesus' baptism—"This is my beloved Son in whom I am well pleased!"; present as the Holy Spirit who both drives Jesus to the cross and is in turn duly offered up by him to the Father as the climax of a supreme act of liturgical self-offering;[54] and present as the incarnate Son himself, standing alongside us and in our place, making our "darkest hour" (death without God) his own, and thereby robbing it (and us) of its perverse promise of sanctuary from the divine presence. Here, the psalmist's words acquire a radical new surplus of meaning: "Even if I go down to the pit, Thou art there also." Thus, Moltmann insists, the crucifixion is no mere paradigm but the decisive point at which absence meets its nemesis, the threat of death being emptied of its power, and the gates of hell finally broken open. "By yielding up the Son to death in Godforsakenness on the cross, and by surrendering him to hell," Moltmann writes, "the eternal God enters the Nothingness out of which he created the world . . . [and] pervades the space of Godforsakenness with his presence."[55] Here, and only here, in the divine "occupation" of the Nihil as a human, he suggests, does God truly become "omnipresent," present humanly and fathoming even his own absence, and thus exhausting it of its power to isolate us from him. Indeed, there is a sense in which, for Moltmann, we are never closer to God than in such profound experiences of seemingly "godless" suffering, for God has made his own bed (pitched his own tent) there with us. Of course this is not the end of the story (that would be not good news but the very worst news of all—that God loved us so much that he sent his only Son to be with us in the hellishness of life and death, and left him there). For Moltmann, as for Dalferth, therefore, it is precisely the *resurrection* that grants the experience of God-forsakenness on Golgotha and Holy Saturday its redemptive force. But in a vital sense Easter Day does not (and must not) undo or erase but rather affirms, reveals, and lays bare the reality and significance of what precedes it, enabling us now to look the very worst experiences of God's hiddenness when they occur (whether to us or to others) fully in the face and yet remain creatures of hope rather than despair.[56]

For we know that even out of this—no, *precisely* out of this—God can and has and has promised again to bring forth something new, something of supreme value and benefit for which we hardly dare hope—life, and life in all its fullness, because life lived eternally in his presence. "Nothing comes of Nothing" is the testimony of common sense, and based on all but global experience, yet faith's testimony is precisely that at this point it knows better: Neither the world itself nor its future in God's hands can or will be made sense of in those terms, because in the peculiar interplay of divine absence and presence in the cross, *creatio ex nihilo* is matched precisely by a *redemptio ex nihilo*, anticipating and earthing the miracle of God's new creation, the miracle in which God himself will at the last be all in all.

§5. Acknowledged Presence

Generosity, Response, and Particularity

"The truth of God's presence," Dalferth observes, "does not depend on whether it is believed, denied or ignored."[57] This is true whether what we have in mind is God's presence to the world as its Creator, his incarnate presence in Christ, or some other instance and mode of God's being together "with us." From what we have seen thus far, though, it should be apparent that the "fact" of God's presence (in whatever mode) is far from self-evident.[58] It is perfectly possible, and common enough for the reality of that fact to be obscured from us or to go unrecognized. This is true not just of faith's lament (the felt "absence" of one for whose presence we long) but equally of various shades and forms of "unbelief." So, we are compelled to distinguish between presence itself and the *acknowledgment* of presence, and to ask who may legitimately be supposed to apprehend or respond to God's presence (or as the matter is sometimes more broadly cast, to have a "sense" of it) and how such apprehension/response arises. Where it occurs in its most developed form (so that we sense the difference it makes to live in God's presence and articulate that difference to ourselves and to others in terms of some particular religious symbolics), it is, Dalferth argues, always a matter of God himself becoming present to us in a further, new way, opening our eyes to something which is already true. This distinctive mode of divine presence and action, he suggests, is most naturally ascribed to the third Trinitarian person, the Holy Spirit.[59] There are, though, Dalferth suggests, other "lower" levels of apprehension or "sensing" of God's presence and our existence in God's presence. Indeed, since God is ubiquitous, God's presence is "somehow apprehended" in (or as an aspect/dimension of) *all* experience (i.e., by everyone who has experience of any sort), though this is to be distinguished sharply from awareness or consciousness (and religious or theological "naming") of what it is that we apprehend.[60]

Similar suggestions are theologically widespread, and often less determined in their insistence on disentangling "apprehension" from "awareness," softening the distinction in the interests of globalizing the "sense of the presence of God," and seeking thereby to address the awkward "scandal of particularity" that otherwise haunts the proclamation of God's essential goodness and redemptive purposes for all his creatures. A good example of this is the work of David Brown in which he seeks a "reinvigorated sense of the sacramental" (yet another mode of presence we might have explored).[61] Brown's basic thesis is that "if God is truly generous, . . . we [might] expect to find him at work everywhere and in such a way that all human beings could . . . respond to him."[62] This duly becomes the basis of a new version of "natural religion" in which aspects of the human experience both of nature and of culture are pursued as extra-ecclesial loci "where God can be encountered, and encountered often."[63] Such diverse phenomena as architecture, sport, horticulture, humor, the natural world, and the arts are all explored as containing within them "a reflection of the divine, there to be experienced as such,"[64] and thus interpretable as the initiatives of the God of grace, operating now beyond the limits of the gospel, in seeking and saving the lost.

Comparable initiatives can be identified in the work of earlier British theologians. Thus, for instance, in his Gifford Lectures (1961–1962) John Baillie argues for a universally available "sense" of God's presence directly analogous to our apprehension of other nonmaterial realities (e.g., personal, moral, aesthetic), and given in, with, and through the complex manifold and gamut of day-to-day experience which "presents itself" to us. In particular, Baillie emphasizes personal and moral entities as among those of the reality of which (whatever empiricists and naturalistic positivists may insist) we are most fully assured in the living of life, and with which our sense of God as personal other is, he argues, most directly bound up. Whatever the place of a distinct "sense of the numinous," such as that posited by Rudolf Otto,[65] our apprehension of and dealings with God are, Baillie suggests, most solidly grounded on and mediated by (and, when manifest in the form of faith, in their turn transfigure completely) our wider consciousness of dwelling in an objective personal and moral environment, and the particular demands made on us by that. Since these are, so far as we know, universal human apprehensions, the Christian apologist, Baillie insists, rarely if ever faces the complete absence of any trace of a sense of God's presence, whether this is acknowledged and named in terms proper to any religious or theological frame of reference or not. In almost all cases there will be at least the glimmer of something which the theologian or religious believer will identify as God's presence and action, something apprehended as real by unbelief too, albeit unrecognized and sometimes even denied.[66] Farmer also speaks of the conditions for a living apprehension of God as personal being given in and through our experience of the world as a morally significant environment.[67] He identifies two strands in this: (1) our experience of natural phenomena, processes, and events as either frustrating or cooperating with our personal projects and purposes (e.g., apprehended as blessing or injury) or—at a more basic (largely unconscious) level of creaturely perception—as conflicting with or furthering the interests of our "immanent teleology" as organisms; (2) our awareness of other persons as centers of will and activity who are present to us and whose presence impinges on us, variously resisting and facilitating our own projects and (more importantly) placing us under certain moral obligations. In, with, and under all this (our common human experience of natural and social environments), Farmer argues, God approaches us, "resistantly and savingly,"[68] unveiling himself, giving himself to be known as a genuinely personal reality must if it is to be known at all,[69] and giving himself to be known both as "absolute demand" and "ultimate succor." Significantly (in light of our earlier discussion of Steiner), Farmer suggests that the world becomes in effect God's "language,"[70] thus necessitating precisely both a certain absence from and presence to it: language is precisely a medium, a means by which we communicate indirectly (and thus with attendant risk of misunderstanding or loss of meaning) rather than "forcing our meaning into" our hearer or reader directly and thereby subverting the need and opportunity for responsible personal response.[71]

In Farmer, then, more completely than either Baillie or Brown, we find an emphasis on "revelation" as the necessary condition for a meaningful sense of the presence of God as *personal other.* Nor will he take easy refuge in the time-honored category of "general revelation." Revelation, Farmer insists, always arises as a "point of crisis" in a particular life lived, an encounter (whether recognized and named as such or not) with the living God apprehended as "holy will," namely as "present within the immediate situation, asking obedience at all costs and guaranteeing in and through such asking the soul's ultimate succor."[72] Each and every such encounter is one in which "the soul must take either a step forward or a step backward in understanding of God and in stature as a child of God."[73] While Farmer's account certainly sees a fundamental continuity between such putative revelatory encounters and the lower-level, universally available apprehensions of the world alluded to a moment ago, his account has the distinct advantage (certainly over that of Brown and, to some extent, that of Baillie too) of identifying specific criteria in terms of which such encounters might be identified as such. He is quite explicit: wherever and whenever God is apprehended as present within the immediate situation as both absolute demand and ultimate succor (whether or not he is identified and named as such), "there is revelation."[74] Clearly, though, while disentangling revelatory encounters from the infinite sum of human experiences (as though God were not just present but "available" for encounter anywhere and everywhere in some undifferentiated manner), this account nonetheless identifies "revelation" as both possible and actual well outside the boundaries of the Christian proclamation of Christ and its impact. Dalferth's account is equally emphatic in its insistence on revelation. Believers, he insists, are those who feel that their lives have in some sense been "broken into," God having "made his presence felt" in an unmistakable manner.[75] Furthermore, for this sense of the presence of God to arise, there must be both divine self-presentation and acts of human re-presentation, responses to that presence in terms of some more or less appropriate and adequate symbolics.[76] Whereas Dalferth himself, of course, presents all this in terms of the particular symbolics of Christian faith (it is the Holy Spirit who interrupts us, "opening our eyes" to God's present reality in our lives and enabling our response of faith and obedience), his account too seems to permit the possibility of revelation and belief arising in other religious (and perhaps even nonreligious) contexts, as what exists universally as the apprehension of life's essentially precarious, contingent, and "gifted" nature[77] breaks in now with new, interruptive, and life-transforming force on those who nonetheless, because of their particular cultural-linguistic *Sitz im Leben*, symbolize it in terms of a set of "doxastic practices" quite distinct from those proper to Christian faith as such.

I end with a quotation and a question. The quotation is from Hendrik Kraemer, who, having wrestled long and hard with the issues raised by Karl Barth at the Tambaram World Missionary Conference in 1938, expressed his considered view that "God is continuously occupying Himself and wrestling with man, in all ages and with all peoples," and that, "while the religious and moral life is man's achievement," it is "also God's wrestling with him."[78] God, we have suggested, following Dalferth's lead, is always present to every present and to every personal presence at that present. Furthermore, it is both God's desire and his promise that he will finally be present as "all in all." It is likely, therefore, that whether or not we single out the spheres of morality and religion for special consideration,[79] most readers will nonetheless warm to Kraemer's basic intuition of God as present to all not just as their Creator but equally as their Redeemer, doing whatever he can to draw them closer to that knowledge of himself and his presence in which salvation properly consists. And yet for Christians, God, we have also seen, is present in the world as Savior in a manner that deliberately excludes ubiquity, concentrating his presence, his purposes, and his actions in a very particular place and time in a manner which may seem, prima facie, to an age of globalization an uneconomic and highly inefficient way of securing a supposedly "universal" purpose. But, as Lesslie Newbigin observes, in the pattern of Scripture these two themes are typically woven together without any apparent sense of incompatibility or embarrassment, salvation being communicated in the final analysis (because by nature of the case it *must* be) not through a universal series of individual communications vertically "from above" and regardless of time and place (or cultural-linguistic matrix) but through the undoubtedly messy, contingent, and fragile dealings of human beings with one another reciprocally as bearers and receivers of a gift.[80] My question, therefore, is whether theological reckonings with this question of "acknowledged presence" of the sort we have considered may, without compromising the fundamental perception of God's universal redemptive purposes and his wisdom to achieve those purposes, need nonetheless to face rather more squarely the implications of yet another mode of God's flickering "presence" and "absence" in history—namely, that which is concluded under the rubric of the biblical doctrine of "election." That God chooses some rather than others means that we must be willing to grasp the nettle of "absence" and the scandal attendant on it; that he chooses some *for the sake of* others means equally that such absence is only ever permitted to be temporary, and we may properly expect that in God's good time it will indeed give way to an acknowledged presence corresponding precisely to that universal "truth of God's presence" which "does not depend on whether it is believed, denied or ignored."[81] In the meanwhile, the call to believers, it might reasonably be suggested, is not to draw our neighbors' attention to something which they already apprehend (however accurate the putative reidentification of it may in fact be), but to bear into their presence the gift of that name by which alone access into the presence of the Father is finally granted.

15

Imagination

Christology and human imagination are, I believe, topics of consideration naturally rather than unnaturally yoked, despite the fact that they have rarely been explored together. This may seem an odd, perhaps even a pre-posterous claim at first blush, so let me unpack it a little. Christian theology itself, I am suggesting, by virtue of the nature of its proper and primary object (the God made known in Jesus Christ) and its own nature as an activity shaped and determined by that same object, is closely and necessarily wedded to acts of imaginative human *poiesis*. And commitment to a properly incarnational Christology in particular, I will argue, compels our acknowledgment that any and every statement we make about God comes charged already with a high IQ—a high imagination quotient.

§1. Imagination, Meaning, and Reality

Let us be quite clear about this: we are not speaking now only of those moments where faith, in its attempt to articulate and express itself most fully and clearly, finds itself compelled to burst explicitly and unasham-edly into full-blown poetry, to harness the resources of storytelling, or to trespass imaginatively into other worlds the forms of which bear little direct or obvious resemblance to our own. This sort of thing is rife, of course, both in Scripture and in the tradition of the church across the cen-turies, and if it is to be faithful to the witness to either of these, theology itself cannot wholly eschew self-consciously imaginative forms. But my point here embraces the whole spectrum of what theology does, rather than what might be deemed by some to be occasional and necessary lapses into more poetic and less precise and scientific modes of engagement. No doubt there are more and less poetic forms of theology, some better suited to particular subjects and contexts than others. But my claim here is that *all* theology, no matter how "scientific" and precise its aspiration or achievement, is nonetheless also "poetic" and contingent on acts of deep human imagining from the outset.

The etymology of the verb *theologein* must not be permitted to mislead us at this point. Even the most rigorous and tightly defined uses of words and ideas (the usual connotations of *logos* in theology and elsewhere) that we are capable of as human beings are inseparable from and dependent on prior and continuing acts of imaginative *poiesis*.[1] Among Christian writers on the subject, none has seen this point more clearly than C. S. Lewis, writing now in his professional capacity as a philosophically trained literary critic rather than as Christian apologist, though his theoretical insights in the one field shaped his practice in the other from first to last.[2] Reason, Lewis observes, can function only if it has something to reason about, otherwise it is empty, and he follows Kantian precedent in ascribing to the logically prior and occult activities of imagination the responsibility for furnishing the relevant materials.[3] What imagination supplies, Lewis suggests, is not just a cornucopia of material objects to be experienced but the webs of relationship within which these objects are situated and in terms of which we are able to "make sense" of them. Imagination, he insists, is thus not the organ of truth but of *meaning*. And, since "meaning is the antecedent condition both of truth and falsehood, whose antithesis is not error but nonsense,"[4] imagination is evidently a necessary if not a sufficient condition of all our most carefully reasoned and rational engagements with the world. Having made this most fundamental and vital point, Lewis then proceeds to concede that imagination functions at a "lower" level than reason, which he supposes must be appealed to finally as the arbiter of truth. This, though, hardly seems to go far enough in its efforts to rehabilitate the profile of imagination. After all, when one turns to consider some of the activities typically associated with "reasoning" of the sort Lewis clearly has in mind, a moment's reflection reveals them to be in reality themselves activities of a highly "imaginative" sort, trespassing far beyond the immediacy of the empirically given. Devising experiments, testing, theorizing, calculating, and so on are clearly very different sorts of activities from daydreaming, fantasizing, or constructing artistic alterities (let alone the deliberate construction and perpetration of lies), but they are activities, nonetheless, which are not only contingent on *prior* acts of an imaginative sort but continue to rely on our capacity for imagination at every point. Unless we choose arbitrarily to define our terms in ways that posit an artificial antithesis, it seems that we must reckon with a much more perichoretic relationship than even Lewis permits between the imaginative and what we hold to be our most reliable and "hard-edged" encounters with reality.

This is true, we might observe, of our intellectual engagements with objects of all sorts, but—in one of the great ironies to be grappled with in these matters—it is especially true at the cutting edge of such engagements, those frontiers of knowledge where established patterns of language and conceptuality let us down (precisely because we are confronted with something genuinely new for which we possess as yet no intellectual or linguistic currency). In situations like these we are driven to acts of catachresis, bending and extending the natural range of our language through the undeniably poetic devices of analogy and metaphor, teaching our old words new tricks in order to fill the gaps in the lexicon,[5] and, by effectively adjusting or accommodating our language to the structures of the world in this way, granting ourselves enhanced epistemic access to it.[6] Thus, there are poetic fingerprints to be found all over the precise and technical vocabularies of the sciences, in talk about electromagnetic fields, sound waves, particles of light, genetic codes, and preprogrammed motor responses, for instance. The glow associated with poetic origination may long since have dulled with use, of course, but in each case we can see how an eye for metaphor and acts of imaginative creativity are as vital to the advancement of scientific understanding as any intellectual or practical skill. Here the poetic and the heuristic impulses appear naturally to stand and fall together rather than necessarily tugging in opposite directions.[7]

In the particular case of Christian theology, the shortfall of our day-to-day utterance with respect to its putative object is even more daunting than that confronting us at the limits of empirical exploration and (much more frequently) the stubborn resilience of so many day-to-day realities that will not be measured, weighed, or reduced to the terms of any convenient calculus (the gnawing anxiety caused by a delayed medical diagnosis; the sacramental charge of an unexpected smile; the veil of mystery that remains intact even amid a lover's passionate embrace). Here too, therefore, we must insist on a vital symbiosis rather than a putative opposition between the logical and the poetic, the word/idea and the image.

The poetry of R. S. Thomas is perpetually haunted by questions of God's presence and absence, and of the capacities and incapacities of human language in the face of one who is, in Kierkegaard's phrase, "wholly other," yet closer to us than we are to ourselves. In "The Gap," the poet imagines God himself contemplating the dictionary of human speech, the glaring blank alongside his name a convenient index of the gulf remaining between them. Rather than tolerate any attempt to scale the heights of divine mystery and place him under the arrest of lexical definition, this God chooses instead to define his own name, making "the sign in the space / on the page, that is in all languages / and none; that is the grammarian's / torment . . . / . . . and the equation / that will not come out."[8] When God places himself within the order of signs, the poem suggests, matters are far from straightforward, the accommodation being as much a matter of judgment as of grace, and leaving God's mystery and freedom unscathed, veiling his elusive reality even as it shows it.

When it comes to the *logos* concerning *Theos*, in fact, for reasons bound up directly with what is widely held to be true of this God, we are necessarily reliant on language of a poetic sort. This is widely acknowledged in discussions of religious language, but its implications are not always taken fully on board or kept sufficiently in view in the wider task of doing theology.

§2. Analogy, Meaning, and the Incomprehensible

One classic discussion of the status and force of human language used to speak of God is that provided by Thomas Aquinas in the opening chapters of the *Summa theologiae*.[9] Aquinas is, on the whole, more positive about the wider circumstance than R. S. Thomas' poet, yet his account remains a very measured and carefully qualified one, and certainly provides little encouragement for those who would wish to pin God down on the basis of any sort of lexical logic-chopping attempted "from below." According to the claims of Christian faith itself, Aquinas reminds us, the uncreated and infinite reality we know as "God" by definition transcends the created and finite world inhabited by his own creatures, and as such can, in the strictest sense, neither be comprehended by creaturely minds as such nor spoken about in terms of the meanings attaching ordinarily to our discourse. Here it becomes necessary at once to lodge a significant disclaimer, and to notice something that is perhaps not often enough noticed about Aquinas' account. God being God, he insists, it is quite impossible that any created mind should see the essence of God by its own natural powers.[10] The key phrase here, though, is "by its own natural powers," and Aquinas proceeds to affirm at once that, when the soul is finally freed from its present entanglement with material things by death, and by virtue of an act of divine grace uniting the soul directly to God, knowledge (or "seeing") of God's essence will indeed be possible even for creaturely intellects. This, indeed—the enjoyment of the so-called "beatific vision"—is Aquinas' firm eschatological hope, and all that he says subsequently about what our minds and our language are capable of *in the meanwhile* is set consciously in apposition to this hope, as something by comparison "so exiguous as to be hardly worth discussing."[11] While ever we labor in a human "nature" in which soul and body are inexorably intertwined, Aquinas insists, our forms of creaturely knowing and our language alike are constrained by the limits of that which also exists in close conjunction with corporeal objects and whatever can be known through a process of logical abstraction from the same. God, being infinite, clearly *cannot* be known in this way, and thus while God may from time to time grant individuals a miraculous glimpse of his "essence" in this life, our *natural* epistemic and linguistic capacities, being hopelessly wedded to the senses, are bound to fail in any attempt to encompass it.[12]

The categories used by Aquinas in question 12, of "knowing" or "seeing" God's "essence," are ones unfamiliar to us today, and Herbert McCabe suggests helpfully that the force of his point would come across rather more clearly if he had said instead that in this life we do not actually know what "God" (or any creaturely term applied to God) really means, and are thus compelled to use words to mean more and other than we can ever understand. We cannot get either our heads or our words around the reality of this God, because his reality is literally mind-blowing and lies well beyond the natural range of any language suited to the dealings we have as human beings with the world around us. But, Aquinas observes, that is actually the only sort of language available to us as human beings.[13] The fact that, paradoxically, notwithstanding all this we are able to speak *meaningfully* about God and thereby obtain some appropriate grasp on his reality lies at least in part, Aquinas suggests, in the plasticity of language and its capacity to be redeployed in imaginative ways.

Words coined originally to speak of one thing can be taken up and made new, their semantic patterning modified and stretched creatively so that they come to refer fittingly to other, quite different things, enabling us

to talk and therefore to think about them. If, as Aquinas readily acknowledges, this sort of thing is basic to the ways in which we expand and order
our knowledge of the world itself, straddling the interstices and simultaneously plotting the (sometimes far from apparent) connections between
different creaturely realities, in the case of our knowing and speaking of
God who is, Aquinas reiterates, "more distant from any creature than any
two creatures are from each other," it is clearly essential to the circumstance.[14] In this case above all others, univocal predication (a particular
word or phrase used more than once and bearing exactly the same sense
on each occasion) is not an available option, and if we are to avoid the
hermeneutic emptiness of utter equivocation, therefore, we are bound to
rely instead on the imaginative stretching of our terms to bridge the gap.

§3. God, Analogy, and Metaphor

Aquinas identifies different forms of this stretching in our talk about God.
In doing so he puts his finger on and seeks to account for something that
most Christian readers would almost certainly concur with; some human
terms, we tend naturally to suppose, apply to God more fully and properly than others, so that there is apparently less of an imaginative stretch
involved in referring to God as good or wise than there is in calling him
a shepherd, let alone a rock or a lion. This, Aquinas tells us, is because the
former terms apply to God by way of analogy, whereas the latter are merely
instances of metaphor.[15] How, then, does he account for the difference
between the two?

Words that refer *analogically* to God, Aquinas argues, refer to nonmaterial qualities ("perfections") that God actually possesses in common with his creatures (though he possesses them, Aquinas reminds us
at once, in a manner befitting his own eternal and infinite nature, which
thus far outstrips our intellectual and imaginative grasp). We know that
these perfections are possessed by God (though not how he possesses
them), Aquinas contends, because we find them present in his creatures
and, he maintains, the transcendent "first cause of all things" must itself
first possess whatever perfections it duly imparts to its creaturely effects.[16]
Presuming this to be so, of course, such qualities (being, goodness, and
wisdom are some of Aquinas' chosen examples) belong primarily and
properly to God and only secondarily and in a derived way to creatures.
Furthermore, the meaning of the relevant terms (what Janet Soskice calls
their natural or proper "domain of application"[17]) is for Aquinas centered
precisely on their applicability to God rather than on our more familiar

uses of them.[18] In calling God "good," therefore, he insists, we are actually involved in literal rather than figurative speech. The way in which the term applies to God (its *modus significandi*) is going to be vastly different from the sense it bears in the statement "Thomas is good," and in this life we cannot know what it means to speak of God as good. But, for reasons just indicated, it will involve no trespass beyond the term's primary and proper domain of application. So, by definition, analogy is quite different from univocal predication but it is, Aquinas insists, a form of the *literal* rather than a *figurative* use of words.[19]

How, then, does all this differ from a metaphorical use? According to Aquinas, in several basic respects. Both involve the semantic stretching of terms across difference, but otherwise they are themselves quite different from one another. To begin with, Aquinas argues, the primary and proper domain of application of the words we use metaphorically is limited to creaturely realities,[20] so that the trajectory of meaning travels, as it were, identifiably from below to above, and words are compelled to operate well beyond their natural comfort zone and to do work quite other than that for which they were designed. Here, we might say, the domain of application of the relevant terms is not only stretched, it is in effect ruptured, and words are left isolated, functioning in places where they did not expect to find themselves and do not properly belong. Secondly, therefore, Aquinas holds, human terms used to speak of God in this way do not name perfections God *actually possesses* in common with us, but, being semantically inextricable from their flesh-laden context of use,[21] only point obliquely to a "certain likeness" or "parallelism" (*similitudo*) suggesting itself between God and mundane realities.[22] Presumably, if such metaphor works rather than falling flat, the similitude may be taken to be appropriate rather than arbitrary, but the sense of "fit" will nonetheless be of a wholly different order than that involved in analogical speech. We inherit lots of images of this sort from Christian Scripture itself, of course, which pictures God variously as a rock, a refreshing drink, a lion, a vintner, an artist, a husband, a woman in labor, a shepherd, and many other things besides. And we might suppose (though Aquinas himself does not deal directly with the question), we reach intuitively for others on occasion in order to grasp or articulate some distinctive feature of faith's living encounter with God.

§4. Analogy and the Apophatic Contra-indication

Despite such alleged differences, these two ways of stretching our language in order to speak of God seem to me to fall rather closer together in

Aquinas' account of the matter than first appearances might suggest. To begin with, the broad structure and direction of linguistic use is the same in both cases, for, as Aquinas readily admits, even in analogy it is true that, whatever its meaning may be *sub specie aeternitatis* or from a God's-eye point of view, "from the point of view of *our use* of the word *we apply it first* to creatures because we *know* them first,"[23] and thus only secondarily to God. Aquinas' insistence that such reference is in reality "literal" rather than figurative makes no practical or structural difference at this point. God is no more "good" or "wise" *in the way that we are* (and thus in any of the senses that we attach to our use of those terms in familiar human discourse) than God is a rock or a shepherd, and there thus remains a clear and considerable stretching of language and imagination moving from below to above in applying them meaningfully to him. In neither case are we able to define precisely what we mean or cash things out fully in "literal" terms; indeed, were we able to do so, the theological resort to the poetic image with its capacity to *suggest* what cannot be grasped or stated in a categorical manner would be wholly unnecessary and, we might add, our engagement with things considerably less rich. Aquinas' own indications that some such clarity of vision is what awaits us in eternity need not detain us here, other than to observe that it need not be interpreted as the eschatological endorsement of the sort of rationalism which wants no more and no less than it says and can define exactly—as though God were a giant, hitherto unclassified species of moth to be pinned conveniently under glass and labeled at last by a nineteenth-century amateur collector,[24] rather than the ultimately unfathomable mystery, to be united with whom is to be ravaged and undone by love, and so to lose all interest in considerations of a merely intellectual sort. Indeed, as analogues for the beatific vision go, while certain acts of intellection may well fit the bill, it is more likely to be those most evidently woven together in our experience with imaginative, aesthetic, affective, and moral realities (the sense of wonder and awe attendant on some new scientific discovery; the compelling "beauty" of a newly apprehended mathematical or logical pattern; the goodness and "rightness" of responding in a particular way to an unexpected initiative of personal self-revealing) and not the rarefied abstractions inscribed for convenient reference and computation on the pages of the dictionary or the manual.

The other aspect of difference Aquinas identifies between analogy and metaphor as we have seen has to do with the respective levels of similarity and dissimilarity understood to pertain between predicate and object, and the relative felt sense of propriety and impropriety therefore involved in conjoining them. Appeal to something like this is also commonplace in more recent attempts to distinguish the two linguistic forms. Whereas in the one circumstance, Sallie McFague suggests, what is indicated is "profound *similarity* beneath the surface dissimilarities," in the other we point only to the slightest "thread of similarity between two dissimilar objects,"[25] a formulation which echoes Aquinas' talk of shared qualities versus mere fleeting similitudes. Consequently, Soskice suggests, from its inception analogical use "seems appropriate" and "fits into standard speech without imaginative strain,"[26] while the relatively wayward and risqué nature of the metaphorical is captured nicely in Nelson Goodman's colorful (and highly metaphorical) description of it as "an affair between a predicate with a past and an object that yields while protesting."[27] Where there is metaphor, it seems, there is some evident felt sense of conflict or tension, the conjunction between two things being "to some extent contra-indicated."[28]

Again though, the two allegedly distinct forms evidently hold something basic in common. In each, the relevant use of words is designed to indicate some level of similitude apprehended in a relation characterized otherwise by nonidentity and dissimilarity between two things or circumstances, and thus, even though the *ratios* of similarity to dissimilarity indicated may differ significantly, we have to do in both cases with a use of words designed to hold like together with unlike, and one which therefore, in McFague's paraphrase of Paul Ricoeur, contains the whisper "it is, *and it is not!*"[29] The audibility of the whisper will indeed vary with the degree of difference we suppose to exist and, as we have seen, in this regard metaphor is generally located at one end of a putative scale and analogy at the other. But this, surely, is a convenient place to remind ourselves of the theological conviction that accompanies and undergirds Aquinas' ruminations about theological language in the first place, namely his insistence that the difference between God and finite creatures is so great as to be unimaginable, and that even in the case of analogical speech about him, therefore, in the very instant that likeness of any sort is dangled tantalizingly before us, it is at once snatched away again to be offset and qualified by the equal and opposite suggestion of a profound difference remaining unscathed and unfathomed. Even here, surely, "from the perspective of human use" there is something remarkable and striking about being willing to use the same word in both cases? God is good, we say; but being God, God is good in a way lying far beyond our intellectual and imaginative reach, so that we cannot understand our own words even in uttering them. We may trust that they bear some positive relation to their several mundane uses, but precisely what that relation is, we can neither know nor say.

§5. Semantic Slippage and the Problem of Petrification

Some theologies would be inclined to widen the ontological and epistemic gap between divine and creaturely reality even further than Aquinas himself does, perhaps challenging in doing so the idea that any "qualities" could meaningfully be supposed to be held in common between them, or at least that we could *know* them to be so by a process of logical inference. Indeed, those unwilling to follow Aquinas' metaphysic in tracing the perfections evident in creaturely effects to their preexistent type in a divine exemplar (God), will have no abiding reason to distinguish between the analogical and the metaphorical in the precise way that he does, and will seek different grounds for choosing to deploy some terms to speak of God and resisting the use of others, or for granting some terms more priority and weight than others within the patterns of religious and theological discourse. While unlikely to collapse all our anthropomorphic images for God down to the same level (as though to call God Father, for instance, were no more and no less fitting or significant than to refer to him as a farmer, let alone a rock or maggots)[30] such theologies will nonetheless tend to insist that any and every human term *when applied to God* is, by nature of the ontological and epistemic circumstance, striking and surprising in its first use at least, and thus charged with that tension and sense of resistance generally ascribed to metaphorical utterance.[31]

Furthermore, in the case of our speech about God all this is bound to remain, properly speaking at least, a permanent rather than a temporary state of affairs. In our human dealings with creaturely things, the poetic image often petrifies, passing eventually into more prosaic and "literal" modes, its work as a tool of exploration now successfully completed and the relevant territory, if not exhausted, at least now mapped to our satisfaction. Metaphors, as it is commonly put in the literature, eventually "die," their capacity to shock or surprise (and in doing so to draw our attention to something hitherto unnoticed) having been dulled through the familiarity of sustained use. Such death, of course, far from being an indication of failure, is precisely a function of the success of the image and its ready assimilation by the wider language. So, for instance, in his discussion of this semantic slippage across time, Colin Gunton reminds us of the once metaphorical status of the word *muscle*, which, "when first used presumably drew upon some of the associations of the Latin *musculus*, 'little mouse.' No one now thinks of those associations, but that is because it has been so successful."[32] Gunton describes this as the passage of the relevant term from metaphorical to "literal" status within the language, a shift which means simply that what was once a striking and unfamiliar use has now "come to be accepted as the primary use of the term"[33] or, we might say, been adopted as a use located securely within the range of the term's primary domain of application.

Soskice, acknowledging the importance of such diachronic developments in the patterns of language use, yet preferring to follow Aquinas in differentiating literal (including analogical) from metaphorical predication on the basis of something more than usage alone, distinguishes instead between literal use and what she identifies as "dead" and "short-lived" metaphors, respectively. The latter, she suggests, function within language in ways closely related to analogy, but native speakers of the relevant language can, on reflection, readily identify that the usage is inconsistent with the word's "original domain of application."[34] An analogy, Soskice suggests, has never possessed any "modeling" or heuristic capacity, having stayed at home and led rather a dull linguistic life, whereas a "dead metaphor" has had a colorful past, even if we find it now settled down to a quieter form of existence. It is tempting at this point to raise all manner of questions about the notion of a consistent and unchanging "original domain of application" and its alleged nonsusceptibility to the contingent fluctuations of time and place. Depending on exactly where and when one enters the relevant conversation, it might be argued, one's sense of what counts as the primary domain may be calibrated quite differently, and talk about muscles, and magnetic fields, or, for that matter, God as Father, Lord, and perhaps also "good" and "wise,"[35] might then, even on reflection, strike one as having something odd and out of place about them or as entirely unsurprising and proper.

We cannot (and fortunately need not) resolve these interesting and contested differences of understanding here. Allusion to them, though, leads us conveniently back to my main point: Where our discourse about the phenomena of creaturely existence in the world is concerned, words can and do shift in their range of applications with impunity, however we may choose to describe or theorize that shift. What was once a striking and surprising use of words becomes less so, eventually being taken for granted as part of a perfectly natural and ordinary way of speaking about things. But in the case of our talk about God, I would suggest, there is a vital sense in which this process of assimilation ought never to be allowed to happen, not entirely anyway. I say "ought" because, of course, it does happen, and in the case of lots of human terms (Father, Lord, King, and others) many Christians have long since forgotten the oddity of just what we are doing when we use them to speak of God. But we ought not to forget it. We should deliberately keep the relevant images alive, no matter how accustomed we have become to their use, because, in a unique manner and to a unique extent, God remains forever elusive and resistant to convenient classification, escaping our grasp whenever we try to tighten up our definitions or pin him down more precisely. To forget this, or to overlook it in practice, is both to run the risk of religious idolatry and to miss the power of the poetic image to transform and renew the vulgate, the breaking open of our terms on the rock of divine otherness compelling constant reconsideration and reevaluation of their familiar meanings. To call God "King," for instance, cannot leave human models of kingship unscathed but must be permitted to come back eventually to bite not just our political theologies but our politics, God's "kingship" calling its creaturely equivalents severely into question.[36] It is typical of poetic images that their juxtapositions of like and unlike transform our understanding of all relevant terms in the relationship. In the case of God and God alone, though, we might properly insist, such mercurial otherness is not just de facto but de jure, a feature of who and what God himself is in his proper relationship to the world. Here, the "split-reference," the mysterious and fluid interplay of "it is" and "it is not," which Ricoeur identifies as the very hallmark of the truthful poetic image,[37] remains and must remain identifiably in play, our refusal to resolve or reduce it into other, more secure, "hard-edged" and intellectually manageable forms of thought and speech having received, we might suppose, the highest possible warrant. For Christians, discourse about God and with God, in liturgy, theology, or elsewhere, is bound finally to remain a matter of the image, precisely in order to be faithful to the peculiar way taken by the divine Word in God's address to us.

§6. The Object and the Mode of Knowing

To allow the images which function at the heart of Christian theology to petrify and so subject to precise determination would in practice be unfaithful to the very nature of the object we are seeking to know and to speak of, and thus, ironically perhaps, result precisely in a highly *unscientific* approach to it. This point is made forcefully in the writings of T. F.

Torrance, who reminds us repeatedly that in all properly scientific and objective procedure it is the nature of the particular object itself which must prescribe the relevant mode of knowing, and thus the form and the content of whatever knowledge arises.[38] This, he insists, is no less true of our knowledge of God than our knowledge of anything else, though its precise implications will obviously vary from field to field. Where our knowledge of God (*theo-logein*) is concerned, Torrance insists, one particular implication is that, in any true statements we make, our words are bound to possess and retain a fundamental density and resistance to precise determination, remaining fluid in their mode of signification. Theological language, he urges, is *paradigmatic*, never precisely *descriptive*; it *points to* beyond itself to God rather than attempting to picture him.[39]

Torrance prefers spatial metaphors in his articulation of this, picturing our words as physical tools, having a "side" that faces us as we handle and deploy them, and a "side" turned appropriately to make contact with the object. Theological statements, he acknowledges, must, to be sure, "be closed on our side, for we have to formulate them as carefully and exactly as we can," but on God's side they must remain "open (and therefore apposite) to the infinite objectivity and inexhaustible reality of the divine Being."[40] Only thus can our words possess an appropriate transparency, enabling us to look *through* them, rather than *at* them, and permitting our minds to "come under the compulsion of the Reality we seek to understand,"[41] rather than forcing it in a Procrustean manner into verbal and intellectual boxes already conveniently at our disposal. "It is important to see that open concepts are not irrational because they are open," Torrance writes, "for to be open vis-à-vis the eternal God is the true mode of their rationality, prescribed for them by the nature of the divine Object of knowledge—they would in fact be most imprecise and inaccurate if they were not open in this way."[42] To seek to overdetermine our meanings at this point, then, to insist on hard and precise modes of speaking, or even to permit inadvertent hardening through the familiarity of use would be a wholly inappropriate way of proceeding, irrational rather than rational and, in theological and religious terms, tantamount to idolatry. The inadequacy of the terms we use in this context is *essential to* their truth, Torrance urges,[43] rather than compromising it.

In similar vein, Colin Gunton observes that the indirectness and elusiveness of metaphor, holding together quite explicitly the affirmation that "it is" with the vital qualifier that, even so, "it is not," grants it an epistemic modesty befitting "a primary vehicle of human rationality" and superior to the hard-edged and "pure" concepts which would, in effect, finally deny reality any abiding mystery or capacity to resist our attempts to wrestle it into submission.[44] Both Torrance and Gunton would, I think, see due intellectual humility (and hence the demand for openness, indirectness, and imaginative semantic surplus in our speech and thought) as proper to all properly objective knowing, and a vital counterpoint, therefore, to whatever efforts in the direction of the precise determination and tight definition of terms may legitimately arise in our dealings with creaturely things. Only thus can we both "fix" meaning sufficiently to think and speak and write in a coherent manner about things at all, and yet, at the same time, allow reality to enforce constant modifications and adjustments to those meanings, rather than leaving them "fixed" in some once-and-for-all manner and thus blind and deaf to further insights and discoveries.[45] But it seems reasonable, nonetheless, to suggest that in the case of God in particular, and in some sense uniquely, the whisper "it is, *and it is not*" demands to have the volume cranked up to eleven on a regular basis in order to prevent us from collapsing into an inappropriate, impious, and irrational form of "rationalism."[46]

§7. Bypassing the Image in Pursuit of the Logos

Given Torrance's own inevitable reliance on figurative uses of language in writing about all this ("open" meanings which permit us to "look through" words rather than "looking at" them, or in which words are permitted to "point beyond" themselves, functioning as "tools" rather than as "pictures," etc.), it is interesting to note his general reluctance to grant the imagination much positive place in Christian theology. Of course, he admits, at one level the use of "images" drawn from the world of things familiar to us is inevitable in our talk about God if we are to think or say anything about him at all. As we have already seen, though, for Torrance, while such images are clearly "adapted to" our capacities as human knowers ("closed" on our side) so that "we may have some hold in our thought upon [God's] objective reality," they are equally certainly not "fitted to" the reality of God himself, which remains transcendent and elusive, far beyond the reach of any attempt to picture or describe it.[47]

While agreeing with the insistence of Anglican theologian Austin Farrer that we cannot discern the reality of God "except *through* the images," therefore, Torrance nonetheless demurs strongly from Farrer's further elucidation of the same point, according to which "we cannot by-pass the images to seize an imageless truth."[48] On the contrary, Torrance argues,

although we certainly cannot bypass the images, what must be recognized
and underscored is the fact that in this particular context such images do
not actually work by "imaging" at all (since the God to whom they point is
not capable of being imaged). In this sense, therefore, precisely what must
be said is that the "truth" we apprehend (and the way in which we apprehend it) is "imageless," and to forget or deny this is bound to end in some
form of idolatry. This leads Torrance quickly into seemingly paradoxical
talk about "images that do not actually image,"[49] and although faithfulness
to biblical language and practice compels him to retain the vocabulary of
the image, he gladly exchanges it on a regular basis for the less potentially
troublesome talk of "concepts," which, he urges, are closely related to
images but have been stripped down and purged of any concrete pictorial content, so that they can function now in a purer, more abstract, more
precise and "imageless" manner. At this point, Torrance appeals in what
he takes to be a biblical (and subsequently a Reformed) manner to the
pattern of auditory rather than optical experience, and to the vital qualification of the one by the other in biblical and theological understanding
of our talk about God. "In the biblical tradition image and word belong
together, and it is through word that the images are made to signify or
indicate that to which they point. It is this powerful element of word that
makes us look through the images and hear past them to what God has to
say, and so to apprehend Him in such a way that we do not have and are
not allowed to have any imaginative or pictorial representation of Him in
our thought."[50] Thus, on one hand, in this context pictures without words
are paradoxically "blind," denying us of "eyes to see," as it were, precisely
because we lack the accompanying "ears to hear." But, Torrance suggests,
words without pictures are *not* empty. Not always. We must not identify
the conceivable (let alone the rationally compelling) with states of affairs
that we can "picture" he insists, citing Frege's work on symbolic logic in
support of his case. The pure concept, stripped of all the distracting clut-
ter of perceptibility, emancipated from the inevitable opacity of the flesh,
functions "imagelessly" to penetrate successfully into deep regions of
logic lying far beyond and corresponding to nothing that we can picture
for ourselves.[51]

§8. Imagination, Reason, and Rationalism

As I shall suggest, these may not be either the most obvious or the most
helpful terms in which either to affirm what Torrance apparently wishes to
affirm or to deny what he wants to deny about the nature and functioning

of our talk about God. First, though, it is worth noting the ostensible parallels existing between his chosen terms and those associated with various forms of what Gunton refers to as "conceptual rationalism."[52] Arising in different guises across the centuries from Plato's *Republic* to the thought of G. W. F. Hegel (1770–1831), the hallmark of this philosophical tendency, Gunton observes, is its insistence "that meaning and truth are successfully conveyed only by means of concepts of an intellectual kind which have been purified as completely as possible from all imaginative or pictorial content," resulting in an overvaluing of abstract logical connections between ideas, and a relative denigration of everything else.[53]

In his *Lectures on the Philosophy of Religion* (1821–31), Hegel presents a version of this in which he distinguishes sharply between the place of *Vorstellungen* ("representations") and *Begriffen* ("concepts") in religious and theological engagements with the reality of God.[54] Religion is necessarily full to the brim with *Vorstellungen*, the "sensible forms or configurations"[55] in and through which truth is clothed for us in flesh, presented under the guise of concrete particulars and the relationships between them (pictures, stories, and the like) so that we may apprehend and grasp it readily. But this is a preliminary and provisional state of affairs as regards our dealings with the truth, and things cannot remain thus. Precisely because they are reliant on imagination and representation in this way, Hegel argues, religious traditions cannot themselves penetrate to the universal truth of things but remain trapped at the level of historical and material particularity, weighed down, as it were, by their complicity in the forms of the flesh, and prevented from any ascent beyond its regions. Thus, for Hegel, precisely what must occur is for the imaginative concretions (images, stories, etc.) of religious doctrine to be "elevated and transmuted into more adequate conceptual form,"[56] the imaginative flesh being in effect stripped away, as it were, so as to reveal the intellectually pure and logically precise skeletal framework of *Begriffen*.

At first blush the parallels between Hegel's account and that developed by Torrance are quite striking and can hardly be overlooked, even though closer inspection will at once reveal significant differences between their respective theological concerns and projects. Hegel, for instance, participates unashamedly in that intellectual prejudice according to which whatever relies on or is complicit in the realm of the particular (historical, material) has by definition a strained and problematic relationship to the truth of things and must, like the Platonic soul of old, finally be released or redeemed from its entanglement with the *kosmos aisthetos* in order to discover its true place in the realm of pure Ideas or Forms (*kosmos noetos*).

Torrance has no truck with any such dualism, being committed in a way that Hegel is not to the fact and thus the radical particularity of the incarnation,[57] that event in which, according to Christian faith, God himself "took flesh" and made the contingencies of historical and material existence his own in order to redeem them from within and to give himself to be known in and through them.[58] Indeed, for Torrance it is precisely the truth articulated in the Nicene doctrine of the *homoousion*, the consubstantiality of the incarnate Son with the Father, which both permits and compels us to deploy certain human terms in our thinking and speaking about God at all, grounding those same terms "objectively" in God.[59] But when it comes to the question of the precise epistemic force of that particular flesh which the divine Son made his own (let alone any other instance of creaturely reality falling outside the hypostatic union), when he inquires, in other words, about the significance which the particular shape and substance of this flesh has for the content and shape of our thinking and speaking about God, Torrance's case leans much further in the direction of Hegel's, in phraseology at least, and generates an apparent tension in his thought.

§9. Imagination, Imagelessness, and Invisibility

For Torrance, the "flesh" or humanity of Christ is absolutely indispensable as a starting point for theology, being precisely a vital divine accommodation to our human ways of knowing. Furthermore, Torrance insists, this flesh can never be circumvented or set aside as though it were a mere external creaturely vehicle for an inner divine content which can be grasped and held on to without it. The particular humanity of the man Jesus Christ is eternally ordained to be "God's language to man," and we cannot, Torrance insists, know God without paying constant and careful attention to it.[60] Yet we must reckon with the paradox that even here where he makes "flesh" his own, God is nonetheless known precisely through the signifying mediation of that which is "not-God" (the humanity of Jesus),[61] and if we cannot and must not seek to "get behind the back of" this *logos incarnatus* in order to know God in some direct and unmediated way, nor, therefore, must we ever mistake it for the proper object or final destination of theological knowing. The concrete human form on which our knowing depends here, even though it may and must be acknowledged and confessed as God's very own "flesh," must, in other words, like all those other creaturely forms of thought and speech which prepare the way for and duly follow on from it,[62] nonetheless be and remain "open" on its far side, the side which is turned and points us toward the eternal Being of God himself.

Even within the dynamics of the hypostatic union, in other words, for Torrance the flesh of the incarnate Son cannot function in such a way as to become the logical terminus of our knowing and speaking about God but must, like any other creaturely reality, become "transparent," functioning precisely "signitively" rather than "eidetically,"[63] merely pointing our gaze in the right direction rather than providing any picture or mimetic approximation to the Being of God.[64] Here, scandalously perhaps, we must insist that not just our vulgar human terms but even the humanity of God himself is, *in and of itself and as such*, inadequate and possessed of a certain inevitable and vital impropriety with respect to the task of making God known.[65] Inasmuch as Jesus' humanity is "not God," it participates in the inherently ambiguous condition of the sign, and if it is to function thus it must, in the very process of being assumed or appropriated, also be broken open and transfigured, acquiring a tantalizing surplus of meaning far beyond anything it ordinarily possesses, its very brokenness and open-endedness permitting it, within the Trinitarian dynamics of divine self-giving, to refer us beyond itself to that which it is not.[66]

Here, though, what Torrance certainly shares with Hegel—namely a deep suspicion of the intellectual contributions of human imagination and its products, and a self-conscious elevation within his theological method of the "pure" concept and its allegedly "imageless" and superior way of referring—generates some friction and seems finally to exist in tension with, if not to tug in a rather different direction from, the core Christian claim that the communication of divine meaning involves a radical, irreducible, and (as Torrance himself is so often at pains to remind us) *permanent* act of enfleshing.[67] Visibility is, whether we like it or not, one of the characteristics of the flesh, and we cannot strip it away to the point where it ceases to be noticed without removing it altogether, thereby effectively reversing the direction and the accomplishment of incarnation. Torrance, as we have seen, is quite emphatic that the *humanitas Christi* is both the starting point and a permanent abiding condition for our knowing and speaking of God, and insists that we cannot (and must not attempt to) go behind the back of it in a bid for some unmediated encounter with divine reality. But his talk of an ideal of "imageless" conceptuality, of "images which do not image,"[68] of words which function adequately without pictures,[69] of the purification of the image by the accompanying word so that visual content falls away to be replaced by an acoustic relation,[70] all conjures up a vision of a form of "transparency" which may finally become difficult in practice to disentangle from *invisibility*, in which case the significance for Christology of the particular shape and content of the "flesh" of Jesus (the specific things that he does and says and suffers in his ministry as the Gospels record these for us) is at risk of being attenuated in a problematic manner.

§10. Incarnation, Particularity, and Dialectic

As we saw in the previous chapter, Richard Bauckham identifies just such relative lack of attention to the particularity of Jesus in the Christology of some of the same patristic theologians whom Torrance so admires, and contrasts it with the particularizing emphasis of the New Testament writers.[71] The danger here, Bauckham suggests, is that while formally insisting upon the centrality of the "full humanity" appropriated by the eternal Word or Son in grounding and mediating all our knowing of God, in practice what occurs is that the humanity becomes insufficiently opaque to permit any imaginative purchase on it whatever, the mind's eye not "going behind the back" of the *logos incarnatus*, of course, but nonetheless effectively passing straight through the particulars of his story to a very high level of conceptual abstraction without encountering much resistance or interference. Unlike Hegel, Bauckham insists that universal significance can be had here only *in and through* (and not despite) the concrete particulars of the incarnate economy, and that the conceptually precise doctrines of incarnation and Trinity must therefore always be held closely together with the biblical stories about Jesus and not permitted in practice to become an abstract substitute for them.[72] This does not mean, of course, that the conceptual precision afforded by doctrines can be abandoned in the name of some neo-Ritschlian eschewal of "metaphysics." To do this would be to fall into the precise trap from which Torrance would rescue us, collapsing everything down to the level of a set of opaque historical and creaturely meanings in which the story of Jesus refers us *to* itself but never refers us *beyond* itself in an epiphanic manner (i.e., so that it may speak to us appropriately of God). Instead, we might say, the lesson to be learned from Christology, and applied more widely by extension from what we learn there, is that the levels of image (*eikon*) and idea/concept (*logos*) must constantly be held closely together, generating meaning precisely and only as they are maintained in a dialectic where each is constantly qualified and rejuvenated by the other. The eternal Word *takes* flesh and tabernacles with us, becoming for us (by all that he is and says and does and suffers) the very *image and likeness* of the invisible God, but this is an image which functions only as faith is granted ears and eyes to penetrate beyond (without ever letting go of) the level of what is presented to it at the level of flesh and blood, and attempts to make sense of it in terms and categories proper to that level alone are therefore bound to fail. What we are dealing with here (to pursue the christological point further) is not a stripping away or attenuation of the flesh, but a transfiguration and quickening of it in which it is appropriated by God and granted a depth and surplus of meaning which, in and of itself, it can never bear. But it is difficult to see how talk of "imagelessness" and the elevation of the "pure concept" (if such a thing exists) can secure this rather than risking its loss, in the christological context or anywhere else.

§11. Apophaticism, Images, and Concepts

Are there, then, more helpful ways of saying what Torrance apparently wishes to say? It seems to me that there are, and that they will entail the redemption of the imaginative (and hence the "image") from the purgatorial secondary state into which he typically casts it. We should remind ourselves first of Torrance's overriding concern, which, despite his direct echoing of Hegel's exaltation of the concept in theology, is in reality quite different from Hegel's own. For Hegel, Gunton suggests, the strict differentiation and disentanglement of concepts from their imaginative counterparts was to be undertaken in the conviction that the former would, once purged of fleshy impurities, be capable, in principle at least, of offering up for our contemplation reality "as it is," directly and without error.[73] For Torrance, on the other hand, it is a fundamental mistake to suppose that the reality of God could *ever* be known in this way, and the concept is to be preferred to the image precisely because it is less likely to get in the way of our knowing of God by obtruding itself as an opaque entity which we look *at* rather than looking *through*. For Torrance, we might say, there is an inherently *apophatic* impulse[74] in all our thinking and speaking about God, and concepts are precisely a means of acknowledging and preserving this circumstance rather than escaping from it in some rationalist manner. Concepts too, therefore, although they exist at a higher and "purer" level of our intellectual engagement than "images," are, on this account, nonetheless *kenotic* in nature, referring us beyond themselves in the very instant that they present themselves for consideration. We might put the same thing in literary rather than theological terms: for Torrance, concepts as well as images must finally be concluded under the rubric of the poetic whisper: "*it is, and it is not . . .*"

To suggest this, though, is to raise again the need for a more nuanced account of the relationship between concept and image, imagination and reason, than the blunt distinction so often posited. This is something that Torrance himself would almost certainly eschew but which seems to me to be both warranted and worthwhile. It affords us, I shall argue, a way of maintaining an appropriate apophatic humility in our theology without, in the process, compromising or attenuating in any way the significance of the claim that the Logos of God is, as far as we are concerned, always an *enfleshed* Logos and never a *logos nudus*.[75] The flesh is always present, and always significant, though its significance varies as we attend to it in different ways and for different purposes. In a directly related manner, I suggest, it is a mistake to suppose the existence of two distinct tiers of intellectual engagement, one in which the imagination is permitted to function freely (the sphere of the "image") and another from which it can and must be excluded at all costs in the interests of some alleged "conceptual purity." No such purity (if by that is intended precisely purity from all traces of the imaginative) is possible, as Torrance's own favorite philosopher of science, Michael Polanyi, recognizes in his unashamed reference to the importance of the "conceptual imagination" in the natural sciences, mathematics, and elsewhere.[76]

What Polanyi's phrase admits is that even concepts and precisely honed logical abstractions of the sort to which Torrance aspires for theology involve us in an act of "imagining" something, holding something in our mind's eye (though the visual connotation of this metaphor itself is misleading and demands qualification)[77] in order to look "through" it, no matter how thin or vague that something may itself be. Indeed, the very act of "looking through" an image, permitting layers of "visible" content to become epistemically transparent rather than remaining opaque, is an act of a *highly* imaginative sort rather than one from which imagination has been or ever could be purged. The attempt to "imagine nothing" is self-defeating, since in imagining "nothing" we are inevitably *imagining* something, even though the something in question may well be "nothing" (which we generally picture in terms of absence, empty space, a vacuum, or whatever). Rather than mistakenly seeking to escape from the imaginative (and the "images" it produces) into some putative imagination-free zone populated by "pure concepts" (defined precisely by their "imageless" nature), therefore, we should reckon instead both with its inescapable presence and with the remarkable variety of ways and levels in and at which it performs its given tasks, and thus the wide variety of its products, all legitimately, but in certain respects unhelpfully, concluded under the rubric of "the image." The image, it turns out, is no one-trick pony, but can be and do very different sorts of things, sometimes even managing more than one at once.

§12. Pictures and Images of Other Sorts

Despite his broad-brush disparagement of the image in relative terms, Torrance's position leaves scope for accommodating this important recognition, since, even though he often overstates his case, it is in fact to particular *sorts* of imaging relation that he directs his opprobrium. In particular, it is to that sort of imaginative activity in which we "picture" something in quite concrete terms, or allow one thing to serve as "a picture of" something else.[78] A physical picture, of course, is precisely something that we are intended to look at and attend to in its own right, even when doing so is meant precisely to stimulate our thinking about something or someone or somewhere else (e.g., in the case of a representational painting or drawing or a photograph). The relation "x is a picture of y," then, brings with it certain attendant experiences and expectations, among which we might list a high degree of visual stability (the picture is generally relatively static, and its content does not change), an expectation that it contains a high rather than a low level of representational force (in some identifiable and proper sense we expect it to "look like" that which it pictures for us, though this may not always be via any straightforward attempt at visual simulation), and a capacity to be attended to as an object in its own right (its "kenotic" aspirations are limited ones; we are expected to look *at* it, and can do so, indeed, for purposes wholly other than attending to it as "a picture of" something else). We can see at once how these expectations are hugely problematic if transferred into the context of theological imagining, resisting any notion of transparency or openness of the sort which Torrance insists is so vital, clamoring for our undivided attention, and accompanied by a strident and deafening declaration that "it is," which all but drowns out any remembrance of the fact that "it is not."

But not all "images" are of this sort. Mental images, for example, even when they are vivid and as concrete as we can possibly make them (when, for instance, we are trying to recall precisely how something looked or picture how it might look) are far more fluid and prone to spontaneous modification than we should often like; and, as Gilbert Ryle points out, despite the way in which we speak of it, the "mental image" is in any case not really a thing in its own right at all, not something we can "look at" but precisely a *way of thinking about* something else.[79] Mental images, we might say, even when we want them to perform a "picturing" function, have a built-in (and sometimes frankly infuriating) openness and transparency, resisting our attempts to firm them up and close them down. Unlike their physical counterparts, therefore, they are by nature suited to precisely the sort of breaking and chastening which Torrance advocates, though such breaking and chastening depends precisely on their place as imaginative constructs rather than betraying it. They do not, if we treat them in this manner, cease to be images but become images of a different sort, functioning now in a quite different way, enabling us to *think about* things in a quite different way and at a wholly different level. Indeed, if Ryle is correct, we cannot ever prescind wholly from the territory of the image without ceasing to "think about" anything at all. We need something, no matter how "thin" or transparent or chastened, to latch onto and work with if we are to apprehend anything at all. In Torrance's chosen terms, concepts must be "closed" on our side, even if they are radically broken open on God's side. The "flesh" assumed by the divine Word may and must indeed be chastened, transfigured, and made anew if it is to be epiphanic, but it cannot be stripped away or rendered completely invisible. Crucifixion is followed not by the absence of the flesh but by its resurrection and ascension to the Father's right hand, where it abides in its vital mediating and priestly role.

Certain sorts of verbal image, too, contain an inbuilt resistance to being dragooned inappropriately into a "picturing" role. Thus, as we have already seen, it is part of the nature of metaphor to function obliquely rather than directly, speaking of one thing in terms *suggestive of* another,[80] but with a high quotient of "contra-indication" kept constantly in play,[81] and a flickering interplay sustained between the tantalizing suggestion that "it is," and the sober and equally vital acknowledgment that "it is not." Again, we might say, such images are already broken and chastened by nature, and lend themselves well to further acts of imaginative asceticism where appropriate. Here again, though, it is not by the absence of "images" that the relevant theological concerns are safeguarded but through acts of *responsible theological imagining* in which images themselves are modified and (if we prefer) "purified" so as to fulfill a particular epistemic purpose. If it is one (widely acknowledged) function of imagination to set us free from the given constraints of the empirical, it is certainly another of its functions (though much less widely recognized) to liberate us from pictures by which we might otherwise, as Wittgenstein puts it in a closely related discussion, be "held captive" in inappropriate and damaging ways.[82] In theology, as elsewhere in our dealings with reality, it is precisely the broken or chastened image which, Gunton suggests, opens us to the world and permits the world in its turn to enforce changes in the meanings that our words bear. Thereby, in a manner that has nothing whatever to do with a precise "picturing" relation, our speech and thought become appropriately and adequately "world-shaped" (or, in the case of theology, "God-shaped").[83]

That all this occurs in the case of our God-talk only by virtue of what Karl Barth calls an "analogy of faith" rather than an "analogy of being"[84] may readily be conceded (though doubtless not all readers will feel the need to go this far). Barth's point is that a correspondence between the act of God's knowing of himself and human knowing of him arises only within the event of revelation itself, and only thus (and within this dynamic relational context for as long as it perdures)[85] is any human language granted the capacity to bear witness to the reality of God's own life and being and action. Put more simply, God himself must speak in, with, and through our human speech-acts about him if the relevant terms are actually to speak truthfully, and only within a personal relationship of faith and obedience can we begin to grasp dimly what these terms now come to mean. Otherwise they remain opaque, veiling the divine reality rather than revealing it, and leaving us only with the natural and mundane capacities of human language, with its established trajectories of vocabulary and syntax. Lest all this seem unduly technical and complex, it might be observed that some such supposition lies behind the fairly common Christian practice of praying and invoking the Spirit before embarking on readings of Scripture (or, for some, the task of theological interpretation or construction). Were it simply a matter of matching biblical words to the patterns readily traced in the best lexicons and grammars, no such deliberate petition would be thought necessary (as distinct from a mere habit or polite formality). Bruce McCormack suggests that it was Barth's adoption of "the ancient anhypostatic-enhypostatic model of Christology" in 1924 that undergirded this new emphasis in his understanding of theological language.[86] Human terms used of God lack any independent *hypostasis* or substance apart from the act in which God supplies this lack by appropriating them and taking them up into his own speaking. Quite apart from the historical point, the conceptual links between the two circumstances remain illuminating. The greater the emphasis on divine otherness with respect to the creature, the more needful some such consideration seems to be. Nevertheless, if genuine analogy or signification of any sort (rather than sheer equivocation) is to be admitted, then the fleshly term in that analogy (the flesh of the signifier) must remain within our grasp and clearly within our sights rather than being erased.[87]

§13. Image, Iconoclasm, and Revelation

Two further points demand our attention before we draw to a close. First, the rehabilitation of the category of the image proposed here does nothing to compromise the concerns lying behind that ancient biblical injunction which, admittedly, sought the wholesale removal and subsequent avoidance of "graven images" rather than their redemption.[88] To begin with, this radical surgery in the tissue of the cult was occasioned by the selfsame theological impulses we have sought carefully to preserve, elevating the wider biblical account of God's relationship to the world for which God is and remains radically other than whatever he has created, and uncircumscribed by any of its forms or processes.[89] Yet the same Old Testament which at this defining moment of Israel's history urged the abandonment of *material* representations of God elsewhere encourages and fuels an abundant and diverse poetic "imaging" of him on more or less every page (as king, shepherd, warrior, rock, lion, strength and shield, light, and so on).[90] So, the notion of a blanket biblical prohibition on all images in our dealings with God makes no sense at all. And both verbal and mental images too, we have seen, are susceptible to treatments which quickly render them unfit for religious and theological service. But images of this sort, of course, are not so easily expelled from the sanctuary or, I have suggested, from that systematic reflection which begins and remains securely earthed in what happens there. Indeed, the pervasive and central role played by verbal images, and their inextricability not only from the substance of Scripture itself but from the life of faith and the encounters of prayer and worship, seem to me sufficient to render the banishment of the image from theology inherently undesirable as well as impossible. If theology is in any sense to be held accountable to all this, then some such images at least seem bound to accompany it in some form no matter how far theology travels out from its biblical/liturgical starting point, or how often those images may have to be broken and made anew on the journey. Again, despite the superficial attractions of expulsion (and notwithstanding apparent biblical precedent for the same), what really matters here is best secured, I would contend, not by the absence of images but by their continual imaginative chastening and "making new" within the dynamics of divine self-revealing and prayerful response.

Mention of the rich stock of images supplied by Scripture and their abiding importance for theology leads conveniently to my final point in this discussion of the relationship between word and image in theology, one which, for many readers, has no doubt haunted much of our discussion to this point and must now be flushed out and tackled directly. All this talk of Christian theology as bound up irrevocably with acts of imaginative *poiesis*, as being in large measure, indeed, an image-constituted and image-constitutive set of activities, will, for some readers, seem to carry with it the implication that the substance of the faith is in some sense "made up," that it begins and ends in acts of sheer human construction and invention rather than acts of divine revelation, as if the God of which theology speaks were, in large measure at least, as we would tend to say, a mere figment of our imagination. There are, of course, theologians and theologies for whom this is indeed both a basic supposition and a positive rather than a negative judgment, and to whose names the explicit appeal to imagination in theology is often tethered in an unfortunate manner. So, for example, Gordon Kaufman[91] presents revelation and imagination as logically opposed sources for theological endeavor, and urges the latter as the only honest strategy for an age in which (he suggests) the idea of God stepping in to make himself known is no longer tenable.[92] Thus the God of our religious and theological utterance is, in the words of another writer on the subject, the "primary human Artifact,"[93] a projection of our inner reality onto the clouds rather than in any sense an objective reality breaking in from "beyond" them.

There is much in Kaufman's analysis of the structure of theological engagement that I find both persuasive and compelling, but this fundamental dichotomy between imagination and revelation is misleading and wholly unnecessary, and those who are less confident than Kaufman himself about the absence of God from the sphere of human knowing may safely choose to ignore it, premised, as it is, on a culturally familiar but entirely unwarranted identification of the *imaginative* with the purely *imaginary*. It is not my purpose here to argue the case for the abiding importance of revelation as a theological category but simply to insist unequivocally on something which others have argued persuasively and at much greater length,[94] namely, that *an account of religious and theological engagement cast in terms of the categories of the imaginative is entirely compatible with an appeal to the dynamics of revelation*, having to do chiefly with questions about the forms our knowing takes and must take, and not its ultimate source or epistemic warrant. This is a simple point, but one well worth making because of the unhelpful connotations still clinging to the word "imagination" and its cognates.

I have already spoken of the need for human images of God to be laid hold of and broken open and transfigured by their appropriation by God, and their being drawn into a wholly new semantic context (to "mean" now with respect to a divine rather than any creaturely object) sustained by the act or event of revelation. We might put the same point another way. God, we may reasonably suppose, is just as capable of taking our imaginations captive as he is of engaging our "hearts," "minds," and "wills" (insofar as these may legitimately be disentangled from the texture of imagination itself), and may give himself to be known by appropriating human activities and outputs of a highly imaginative (as well as a relatively unimaginative) sort. Indeed, if our account of revelation is informed at all by the actual forms which Christian Scripture takes and the sorts of reading it most naturally demands of us, then we appear to have good reason for insisting that this is precisely what God has done and continues to do, engaging us through texts and practices explicitly and unashamedly imaginative in nature, as well as demanding further acts of tacit but genuine *poiesis* in our more systematic theological reflections and constructions. For the sake of consistency we may refer to Torrance again at this point, according to whom "in all theological knowledge, a proper balance must be maintained between the divine Subject and the human subject" since theological knowledge "is after all a human activity" and "if the human factor is eliminated, then the whole is reduced to nonsense"; but, he adds, "unless the divine element is dominant, then man is in the last resort thrown back upon his own resources, and an impossible burden is laid upon him."[95]

If we maintain a precisely balanced and carefully ordered account of this sort in which both the fully divine and the fully human aspects of revelation are taken fully seriously, but the parabolic dynamic of revelatory action is understood to move first "from above to below" and only then "from below to above," we may in a perfectly proper sense speak of theology as a human practice of "imaginative construction"[96] and even of God as "an imagined object,"[97] without for one moment abandoning the vital claim that such imagining properly arises from and is informed, constrained, and constantly reshaped by a reality lying beyond ourselves, one our continued engagements with whom break open and "force new meanings" on the very words and images he has himself given to us as appropriate ways in which to think and speak of him. In this sense, it seems to me, Austin Farrer's claim that "divine truth is supernaturally communicated to men in an act of inspired thinking which falls into the shape of certain images"[98] is basically correct, however we may wish to gloss it and whatever we may wish to add by way of disclaimers. It follows, of course, that appeals to "revelation" therefore provide no easy escape (should anyone desire it) from the particular challenges and demands of the sort of "poetic logic" with which, I have argued in this chapter, theology, in its dealings with a God who is wholly other and thus can be spoken and thought of only under the guise of things that he is not, must grapple from beginning to end. Whether we attend to the divinely furnished images of Scripture, the concrete self-imaging of God in the flesh, or the myriad ways in which these have been taken up and responded to in the varied forms and patterns of Christian tradition across the centuries, theology is intrinsically and necessarily a "poetic" set of practices in the proper sense, and one in which the imagination is and must be kept constantly and identifiably in play.

Notes

Introduction

1 See chap. 15.

2 See Colin E. Gunton, *The One, the Three and the Many: God, Creation and the Culture of Modernity* (Cambridge: Cambridge University Press, 1993), chap. 6.

3 See, variously, chaps. 1–4, 6–7, 10 et passim.

One: Hellenization

1 See Peter L. Berger, *The Sacred Canopy: Elements of a Sociological Theory of Religion* (Garden City, N.Y.: Doubleday, 1967).

2 The claim contained in the Nicene Creed of 325 CE that the incarnate Son is ὁμοούσιος ("of one being" or "consubstantial") with the Father.

3 Eusebius, *Ecclesiastical History* 5.20. ET from *The Ecclesiastical History of Eusebius*, trans. C. F. Cruse (London: George Bell and Sons, 1908).

4 Irenaeus, *Adversus Haereses* (*Adv. Haer.*), in *Ante-Nicene Fathers* (*ANF*). All citations in English are taken from this edition unless otherwise indicated.

5 Adolf von Harnack, *History of Dogma*, vol. 2, trans. from the 3rd German ed. by Neil Buchanan (London: Williams and Norgate, 1901), 231–32.

6 The characterization is that of Charles Bigg, *The Christian Platonists of Alexandria* (Oxford: Clarendon, 1886).

7 See, e.g., Irenaeus, *Adv. Haer.* 1.8.1.

8 Harnack, *History of Dogma*, 2:234.

9 Harnack, *History of Dogma*, 2:246–47.

10 Harnack, *History of Dogma*, vol. 1, trans. from the 3rd German ed. by Neil Buchanan (London: Williams and Norgate, 1894), x.

11 Adolf von Harnack, *History of Dogma*, vol. 2, trans. from the 3rd German ed. by Neil Buchanan (London: William & Norgate, 1896), 245.

12 Harnack, *History of Dogma*, 2:17.

13 So, e.g., Irenaeus, *Adv. Haer.* 4.33.4, 3.19.1.

14 See, e.g., Irenaeus, *Adv. Haer.* 1.10.1, 2.20.3.

15 Irenaeus, *Adv. Haer.* 5.2.1, 5.16.2, 4.36.7, 3.4.2.

16 Irenaeus' polemic is directed against the gnostics; but these, he insists, borrowed most of their ideas directly from the literature of Greek poets, philosophers, and historians, and in that sense were precisely "Hellenizers" of Christian ideas. See *Adv. Haer.* 2.14. The accuracy of his claim is less important for our purposes than Irenaeus' clear intention to distance himself from the alleged theological method.

17 The question of whether the gnostics were a Christian heresy or should properly be classified otherwise need not detain us here. Irenaeus supposes that they were, and he situates his own thought and his exposition of Christian theology relative to that supposition.

18 Irenaeus, *Adv. Haer.* 1.8.1.

19 Irenaeus, *Adv. Haer.* 1.pref.1. On Scripture and meaning, see further 1.9.2, 1.9.4, 1.10.2.

20 See chap. 15. On metaphor and realism, see further the discussion of "Words and the World" in Colin E. Gunton, *The Actuality of Atonement: A Study of Metaphor, Rationality and the Christian Tradition* (Edinburgh: T&T Clark, 1988), and Paul Ricoeur, *The Rule of Metaphor: Multidisciplinary Studies of the Creation of Meaning in Language*, trans. Robert Czerny et al. (Toronto and Buffalo: Toronto University Press, 1977), passim.

21 Friedrich Loofs, *Leitfaden zum Studium der Dogmengeschichte* (Halle, 1906), 203.

22 Cf. Harnack, *History of Dogma*, 2:292.

23 See, e.g., Albrecht Ritschl, *Theologie und Metaphysik: zur Verständigung und Abwehr* (Bonn: A. Marcus, 1881). In English, "Theology and Metaphysics," in Ritschl, *Three Essays*, trans. Philip Hefner (Philadelphia: Fortress, 1972).

24 Thus: "Incorruptibility is a *habitus* which is the opposite of our present one and indeed of man's natural condition. For immortality is at once God's manner of existence and his attribute. . . . Now, the sole way in which immortality as a physical condition can be obtained is by its possessor uniting himself *realiter* with human nature." Harnack, *History of Dogma*, 2:241.

25 Robert S. Franks, *The Work of Christ: A Historical Study of Christian Doctrine* (London and New York: T. Nelson, 1962), 25.

26 Wilhelm Bousset, *Kyrios Christos: A History of the Belief in Christ from the Beginnings of Christianity to Irenaeus*, trans. John E. Steely (Nashville: Abingdon, 1970 [German, 1913]), 431–32.

27 Hastings Rashdall, *The Idea of Atonement in Christian Theology* (London: Macmillan, 1919), 238.

28 H. E. W. Turner notes the difficulty involved in constructing any single, coherent view of the idea, because the key terms involved are "patent of many different nuances" and arise in contexts indicating creative cross-fertilization with other soteriological motifs. His own treatment disentangles "eschatological," "physical,"

"metaphysical," and "mystical" variants. H. E. W. Turner, *The Patristic Doctrine of Redemption* (London: Mowbray, 1952), 70.

29　Harnack, *History of Dogma*, 2:240.

30　See Harnack, *History of Dogma*, 1:17. Cf. Martin Werner: "By speculating about the soteriological significance of the divine Logos, Hellenistic Christianity abandoned completely the original Apostolic faith and built on what was, from the doctrinal point of view, virtually new land." *The Formation of Christian Dogma: An Historical Study of Its Problem* (London: A. and C. Black, 1957), 194.

31　Maurice Wiles, "Soteriological Arguments in the Fathers," *Studia Patristica* 9 (1966): 321.

32　Four ecumenical councils are generally considered in this vein: Nicaea in 325, Constantinople in 381, Ephesus in 431, and Chalcedon in 451.

33　English text in J. Stevenson, ed., *Creeds, Councils and Controversies: Documents Illustrative of the History of the Church A.D. 337–461* (London: SPCK, 1973), 335.

34　Wiles, "Soteriological Arguments in the Fathers," 322.

35　Maurice Wiles, *Working Papers in Doctrine* (London: SCM, 1976), 119.

36　"To accept both axioms *tout court* is in effect to be committed to the Chalcedonian position.'" Wiles, "Soteriological Arguments in the Fathers," 322.

37　Wiles, "Soteriological Arguments in the Fathers," 322.

38　Wiles, "Soteriological Arguments in the Fathers," 325.

39　Wiles, "Soteriological Arguments in the Fathers," 323.

40　Wiles, "Soteriological Arguments in the Fathers," 325.

41　Patristic writers typically ground their use of the image biblically on the admittedly slender base of such texts as Psalm 82:6, John 10:35, and 2 Peter 1:4. On one classic Western source see Gerald Bonner, "Augustine's Conception of Deification," *Journal of Theological Studies*, New Series, 37, no. 2 (1986): 369–86. On Western appropriation of the theme, see further chap. 10.

42　Αὐτὸς γὰρ ἐνηνθρώπησεν, ἵνα ἡμεῖς θεοποιηθῶμεν. Athanasius, *De Incarnatione* 54.11–12. ET from *Athanasius: Contra Gentes and De Incarnatione*, ed. and trans. Robert W. Thomson (Oxford: Clarendon, 1971), 268–69.

43　Turner, *The Patristic Doctrine of Redemption*, 70.

44　See below, pp. 74–77.

45　Harnack, *History of Dogma*, 2:234.

46　Wiles, "Soteriological Arguments in the Fathers," 323.

Two: Recapitulation

1　Irenaeus, *Adv. Haer.* 4.41.2.

2　Irenaeus, *Adv. Haer.* 2.32.5.

3　Irenaeus, *Adv. Haer.* 3.6.2.

4　Irenaeus, *Adv. Haer.* 2.22.2. See further 4.28.3.

5　Irenaeus, *Adv. Haer.* 4.6.5.

6　Irenaeus, *Adv. Haer.* 4.7.5. See further 4.23.2.

7　Irenaeus, *Adv. Haer.* 4.40.1. See also 4.39.3–4. My italics.

8　Irenaeus, *Adv. Haer.* 5.14.3. See further 3.5.3.

9　Irenaeus, *Adv. Haer.* 4.33.1.

10　Irenaeus, *Adv. Haer.* 4.33.2.

11 Irenaeus, *Adv. Haer.* 5.17.3.

12 Irenaeus, *Adv. Haer.* 4.27.1.

13 Irenaeus, *Adv. Haer.* 3.28.5.

14 Gustaf Aulén, *Christus Victor* (London: SPCK, 1931), 30.

15 See, e.g., Aulén, *Christus Victor*, 6–7.

16 Irenaeus, *Adv. Haer.* 3.18.6.

17 Irenaeus, *Adv. Haer.* 3.18.7.

18 On Irenaeus' use of this image, see below, 43–53.

19 Aulén, *Christus Victor*, 22.

20 Aulén, *Christus Victor*, 33.

21 Aulén, *Christus Victor*, 34.

22 See, e.g., Irenaeus, *Adv. Haer.* 1.7.2, 1.24.3 (against Basilides), 1.26.1 (against Cerinthus). Basilides' Christ is docetic rather than dualist; Jesus (the incarnation of Nous), being incapable of suffering, he suggests, swapped places with Simon of Cyrene at the last minute and stood by, laughing at the deception involved. A greater travesty of the heart of the gospel message than this is hardly imaginable.

23 Irenaeus, *Adv. Haer.* 3.16.6.

24 Irenaeus, *Adv. Haer.* 3.16.6.

25 Irenaeus, *Adv. Haer.* 3.16.6. My italics.

26 Irenaeus, *Adv. Haer.* 3.16.6.

27 Gustaf Wingren, *Man and the Incarnation: A Study in the Biblical Theology of Irenaeus*, trans. Ross Mackenzie (Edinburgh and London: Oliver and Boyd, 1959), 113–14.

28 Wingren, *Man and the Incarnation*, 117–18. Cf. Irenaeus, *Adv. Haer.* 4.22.1: "For if he did not receive the substance of flesh from a human being, He was neither made man nor the Son of man; and if He was not made what we were, He did no great thing in what He suffered and endured."

29 On this, see chap. 4. Irenaeus is quite clear on this subject: "Every one will allow that we are [composed of] a body taken from the earth, and a soul receiving spirit from God. This, therefore, the Word of God was made, recapitulating in Himself His own handiwork." *Adv. Haer.* 4.22.1. In the same passage he insists that Christ's psychological and emotional as well as physical attributes and experiences are "tokens of the flesh (σύμβολα σαρκὸς) which had been derived from the earth." *Adv. Haer.* 4.22.2. Greek text in *A Patristic Greek Lexicon* (*PGL*) 7:958.

30 Wingren, *Man and the Incarnation*, 106.

31 See, e.g., Irenaeus, *Adv. Haer.* 4.19–20.

32 See, e.g., Irenaeus, *Adv. Haer.* 5.7.3: "As man he suffered for us, so as God he might have compassion on us, and forgive us our debts."

33 Irenaeus, *Adv. Haer.* 3.16.6.

34 Irenaeus, *Adv. Haer.* 5.1.3.

35 Irenaeus, *Adv. Haer.* 3.20.2.

36 Irenaeus, *Adv. Haer.* 5.1.1.

37 Irenaeus, *Adv. Haer.* 4.20.5.

38 Irenaeus, *Adv. Haer.* 4.20.7.

39 See, e.g., Irenaeus, *Adv. Haer.* 3.18.7, 5.14.1–2.

40 Loofs, *Leitfaden zum Studium der Dogmengeschichte*, 141–42. Loofs overplays his hand here. But Irenaeus himself testifies to the earlier existence of the theme of recapitulation in a lost work of Justin. See Irenaeus, *Adv. Haer.* 4.6.2. The influence of Justin would also seem to be evident in Irenaeus' appeal to a typological parallelism between the figures of Mary and Eve, a parallel which Justin develops in his *Dialogue with Trypho*.

41 These, though, are the only two instances of the verb in the New Testament, and it rarely appears in nonbiblical Greek. There is thus no conventional use with which to compare the apostle's use, and context is all in the task of interpreting it.

42 In fact, of course, they are not. Disagreement centers largely on whether or not use of the verb ἀνακεφαλαιόομαι should be linked to the Pauline description elsewhere of Christ as the head (κεφαλή), as, for instance, in Eph 1:22. Etymologically there is no necessary link, the noun κεφάλαιον providing the root of the verb, and suggesting a meaning more or less synonymous with κεφαλαιοῦν, "to sum up." See Heinrich Schlier in *Theological Dictionary of the New Testament* (*TDNT*), 3:681–82. The image of headship need not be excluded from Eph 1:10 by this consideration alone, however. Schlier concludes that "it is most likely that what is meant by Christ as κεφαλή led the author of Ephesians to choose this relatively infrequent but rich and varied term which agrees so well with his intention." *TDNT* 3:682. He directs our thought in particular to the force assumed by ἀνα- in addition to the normative "up." Thus: "Since every summation implies a kind of repetition, the word may sometimes have the direct sense of 'to repeat.' The ἀνα- thus assumes an iterative sense which it does not have elsewhere." *TDNT* 3:682.

43 So, e.g., J. T. Nielsen, *Adam and Christ in the Theology of Irenaeus of Lyons* (Assen: Van Gorcum, 1968), 62.

44 Irenaeus, *Adv. Haer.* 3.18.1.

45 Irenaeus, *Adv. Haer.* 5.21.1.

46 Irenaeus, *Adv. Haer.* 3.19.3.

47 Irenaeus, *Adv. Haer.* 5.1.3.

48 See, for instance, Irenaeus, *Adv. Haer.* 3.21.10.

49 Irenaeus, *Adv. Haer.* 3.21.4.

50 Irenaeus, *Adv. Haer.* 3.21.7. Cf., too, the parallelism alleged between the figures of Eve and Mary in the respective narratives of fall and redemption in 3.20.4 and 5.19.1.

51 Irenaeus, *Adv. Haer.* 5.1.2.

52 Irenaeus, *Adv. Haer.* 5.1.2.

53 Irenaeus, *Adv. Haer.* 5.14.2.

54 Irenaeus, *Adv. Haer.* 3.17.7.

55 Irenaeus, *Adv. Haer.* 1.9.3. Cf. John 1:14.

56 See, e.g., Harry Johnson, *The Humanity of the Saviour: A Biblical and Historical Study of the Human Nature of Christ in Relation to Original Sin, with Special Reference to Its Soteriological Significance* (London: Epworth, 1962), 129–32. Johnson mentions only Gregory of Nyssa among the church fathers as an advocate of the idea that the Son of God assumed "fallen (sinful) human nature." Thomas Weinandy, though, suggests that Irenaeus' soteriology more or less demands the assumption

of postlapsarian flesh in the incarnation, even if it is nowhere explicitly affirmed. See Thomas G. Weinandy, *In the Likeness of Sinful Flesh: An Essay on the Humanity of Christ* (Edinburgh: T&T Clark, 1993), 26–38. See also Thomas F. Torrance, *The Trinitarian Faith: An Evangelical Theology of the Ancient Catholic Church* (Edinburgh: T&T Clark, 1988), 166–67.

57 Weinandy, *In the Likeness of Sinful Flesh*, 29.

58 Πεπειρασμένον δὲ κατὰ πάντα καθ᾿ ὁμοιότητα χωρὶς ἁμαρτίας.

59 Irenaeus, *Adv. Haer.* 2.22.4.

60 See chap. 13.

61 Irenaeus, *Adv. Haer.* 5.23.2.

62 Irenaeus, *Adv. Haer.* 5.27.1.

63 Irenaeus, *Adv. Haer.* 3.16.6.

64 Irenaeus, *Adv. Haer.* 4.6.2.

65 Irenaeus, *Adv. Haer.* 1.10.1.

66 This phenomenon was grappled with, to some extent unhelpfully, by twentieth-century Old Testament scholars borrowing the legal and anthropological category of "corporate personality." See, e.g., Aubrey R. Johnson, *The One and the Many in the Israelite Conception of God*, 2nd ed. (Cardiff: Cardiff University Press, 1961). Despite the inadequacies of the now outmoded theory, the phenomenon itself is pervasive in the biblical texts.

67 C. F. D. Moule, *The Origin of Christology* (Cambridge: Cambridge University Press, 1977).

68 See Moule, *Origin of Christology*, 48–49.

69 Moule, *Origin of Christology*, 51.

70 Irenaeus, *Adv. Haer.* 2.22.4 et passim.

71 Irenaeus, *Adv. Haer.* 5.1.1.

72 Irenaeus, *Adv. Haer.* 3.12.3.

73 Irenaeus notes that there are four principal covenants between God and the human race in Scripture: the first under Adam, the second under Noah, the third under Moses, and "the fourth, that which renovates man and sums up all things in itself by means of the Gospel." *Adv. Haer.* 3.11.9.

74 Irenaeus, *Adv. Haer.* 3.16.6.

75 Irenaeus, *Adv. Haer.* 1.6.3.

76 See further, e.g., chap. 6.

77 Irenaeus, *Adv. Haer.* 5.8.1. Cf. 3.17.3. Christ, Irenaeus notes, having first received the Spirit as a gift from his heavenly Father, subsequently confers it on all who are partakers of himself, "sending the Holy Spirit on all the earth." 3.17.2.

78 Irenaeus, *Adv. Haer.* 5.36.3. See *PGL* 7:1224. Cf. *ANF* 1:567, which reads "confirmed and incorporated with."

79 Irenaeus, *Adv. Haer.* 3.19.1.

80 Irenaeus says: "Those who have not received the gift of adoption, but who despise the incarnation of the pure generation of the Word of God, defraud human nature of promotion into God [ἀποστεροῦντας τὸν ἄνθρωπον τῆς εἰς Θεὸν ἀνόδου] and prove themselves ungrateful to the Word of God who became flesh for them. For it was to this end that the Word of God was made man, and He who was the Son

of God became the Son of Man, that man, having been taken into the Word, and receiving the adoption, might become the son of God." *Adv. Haer.* 3.19.1. Irenaeus' original Greek phrase is preserved by Theodoret. The old Latin translators drew the sting somewhat in their rendering of the relevant phrase: *"fraudantes hominem ab ea ascensione quae est ad Dominum"* (see ANF 1:448, n. 9). But Irenaeus wasn't afraid to grasp the relevant nettle!

81 Irenaeus, *Adv. Haer.* 5.1.1.

82 Irenaeus, *Adv. Haer.* 4.36.4.

Three: Divinization

1 See Johannes Quasten, *Patrology*, vol. 3 (Westminster, Md.: Newman, 1963), 6: "This city of learning, famous for its monumental library and its schools of religion, philosophy, and sciences, was the place where Christianity came in greater contact with Hellenism than in any other metropolis of the East or West. Thus, in this setting the fundamental problem of faith arose, the problem of faith and science and the connected problem of the philosophical foundation and defense of faith."

2 On these traditions and their influence on Christianity, see, e.g., Frederick Copleston, *A History of Philosophy*, vol. 1 (London: Continuum, 2003), 451–63; Harry Austryn Wolfson, *The Philosophy of the Church Fathers: Faith, Trinity, Incarnation*, 3rd ed. (Cambridge, Mass.: Harvard University Press, 1970); Bigg, *The Christian Platonists of Alexandria*; Joseph C. McLelland, *God the Anonymous: A Study in Alexandrian Philosophical Theology* (Cambridge, Mass.: Philadelphia Patristic Foundation, 1976).

3 The main body of Plotinus' writings is to be found in *The Enneads*, ed. and trans. Stephen MacKenna (London: Faber and Faber, 1956). Citations in English are from this edition or, where indicated, from the Loeb Classical Library parallel text: Plotinus, *Ennead*, vol. 1, *Porphyry on the Life of Plotinus. Ennead I*, trans. A. H. Armstrong, LCL 440 (Cambridge, Mass.: Harvard University Press, 1969).

4 See, e.g., Plotinus, *Enneads* 5.1. For a helpful brief account, see MacKenna's "Introduction to Plotinus," in MacKenna, *Enneads*, xxiii–xxxii.

5 For the purposes of convenience, I follow the chronology offered by David Ross, *Plato's Theory of Ideas*, 2nd ed. (Oxford: Clarendon, 1953), 10.

6 Plato, *Phaedo* 74d–75e.

7 See, e.g., Plato, *Phaedo* 72b–72c.

8 Plato, *Republic* 7.514–518.

9 There is thus, as Copleston notes, no trace of the spirit of pantheism in Plotinus. "Although he makes use of metaphorical terms like *hrein* and *aporrein*, Plotinus expressly rejects the notion that God becomes in any way less through the process of emanation: He remains untouched, undiminished, unmoved." *History of Philosophy*, 1:466.

10 Plotinus, *Enneads* 5.1.6.

11 Whereas Plato ascribes creation to a lesser god (*Timaeus* 29), for Plotinus the One is the ultimate source of the world, and the transcendence of the One is the transcendence of Creator with respect to the world. So, e.g., in *Enneads* 6.8.19, with reference to the Platonic phrase "beyond Being" or "beyond Essence," he writes

of the One: "It is not merely that He generated Essence but that He is subject neither to Essence nor to Himself; His Essence is not his Principle; He is Principle to Essence and not for Himself did He make it; producing it He left it outside of Himself; He had no need of being, who brought it to be." The idea is one familiar to all students of the doctrine of creation—viz., of the Creator's alleged freedom (from all forms of necessity) in the act of creation and continuing freedom with respect to the created order.

12 On this, see J. M. Rist, *Plotinus: The Road to Reality* (Cambridge: Cambridge University Press, 1967), chap. 3, "The Plotinian One." A. Hilary Armstrong notes that "infinity" (ἀπειρία) is not posited as such of the divinity prior to Philo of Alexandria and comments: "It is indeed an idea opposed to normal Greek, and especially to the Platonic-Pythagorean way of thinking, for which the good and the divine is essentially form and definition, light and clarity, opposed to vague, formless darkness. Plotinus is the first Greek philosopher to try to work out with any precision the senses in which infinity can be predicated of the Godhead, and to distinguish them from the evil infinity of formlessness and indefinite multiplicity." Armstrong, *Plotinian and Christian Studies* (London: Variorum, 1979), 47.

13 Plotinus, *Enneads* 5.5.6.

14 Plotinus, *Enneads* 5.5.6.

15 Proclus, *In Parmenidem* 6.1074. Cited in Armstrong, *Plotinian and Christian Studies*, 81.

16 Plotinus, *Enneads* 5.6.2.

17 Plotinus, *Enneads* 3.8.9, 6.9.7–8.

18 Plotinus, *Enneads* 5.5.6.

19 See, e.g., Plotinus, *Enneads* 6.8.9.

20 *Pace* Rist, who argues that, given how much Plotinus actually has to say about the One, some sort of doctrine of analogy such as that based on efficient causality must be presumed finally to underlie his writings. Rist, *Plotinus: The Road to Reality*, 32–33.

21 "The vision baffles telling; we cannot detach the Supreme to state it; if we have seen something thus detached we have failed of the Supreme which is to be known only as one with ourselves." Plotinus, *Enneads* 6.9.10.

22 Armstrong, *Plotinus: The Road to Reality*, 83.

23 Cf., helpfully, MacKenna, "Introduction to Plotinus," in MacKenna, *Enneads*, xxviii.

24 Plotinus, *Enneads* 1.1.9.

25 Plotinus, *Enneads* 1.1.8.

26 "I am striving to give back the Divine in myself to the Divine in All." See MacKenna, "Porphyry: On the Life of Plotinus and the Arrangement of His Work," in MacKenna, *Enneads*, 2.

27 Homer, *Iliad* 2.40. Cf. Plotinus, *Enneads* 1.6.8.

28 See, e.g., Plotinus, *Enneads* 1.6.8: "The Fatherland to us is There whence we have come, and There is the Father."

29 Plotinus, *Enneads* 1.2.3 (LCL).

30 Plotinus, *Enneads* 1.2.6 (LCL).

31 Plotinus, *Enneads* 3.8.9 (LCL).

32 See, e.g., Plotinus, *Enneads* 3.8.8, 1.3.1, 4.3.4 et passim.

33 Plotinus, *Enneads* 6.9.7, 5.8.13, 1.6.9.

34 Plotinus, *Enneads* 3.8.9.

35 Plotinus, *Enneads* 3.7.1ff.

36 Plotinus, *Enneads* 6.9.8.

37 Armstrong, *Plotinus: The Road to Reality*, 128. *Pace* Paul Henry's insistence that "the latent actuality of salvation and the cold transcendence of God make it impossible [for Plotinus] . . . to conceive of any genuine doctrine of grace." See MacKenna, "Introduction to Plotinus," in *Enneads*, trans. MacKenna, xxxvii.

38 Plotinus, *Enneads* 6.7.31.

39 Salvatore R. C. Lilla, *Clement of Alexandria: A Study in Christian Platonism and Gnosticism* (London: Oxford University Press, 1971), preface.

40 Clement, *Stromateis* 1.20.98. ET from *Ante-Nicene Christian Library* (ANCL). All citations in English are taken from this edition.

41 Clement, *Stromateis* 6.8.67. See further, e.g., 1.1.18, 1.5.28, 1.7.37, 6.5.42, 6.17.153.

42 Clement, *Stromateis* 1.5.28.

43 Bigg, *Christian Platonists of Alexandria*, 47–48.

44 Rashdall, *Idea of Atonement in Christian Theology*, 222.

45 See, e.g., Clement, *Stromateis* 2.4.13, 2.4.14, 2.4.15, 2.11.48, 7.10.57, 8.3.7. Clement can also use the term πίστις to refer to that further assent granted to the results of such careful reasoning, a form of intellectual "faith" reserved for the gnostic alone, and beyond the reach of simple believers. See *Stromateis* 2.11.49. As Wolfson observes, in all this Clement departs significantly from Plato's use of πίστις to refer to a state of mind within the realm of δόξα or mere opinion, following instead the use of Aristotle and the Stoics. Wolfson, *Philosophy of the Church Fathers*, 114.

46 Sensory perception is thus the "ladder to knowledge" (ἐπιβάθα τῆς ἐπιστήμης) rather than, as for the later Plato, a slippery slope leading us away from the truth. Clement, *Stromateis* 2.4.13. See the Greek text in Die griechischen christlichen Schriftsteller der ersten drei Jahrhunderte (GCS), 17:68.

47 That "which appears evident to both the sense and the mind" must be reckoned with in knowing. Clement, *Stromateis* 8.3.7.

48 McLelland, *God the Anonymous*, 54.

49 See, e.g., Clement, *Stromateis* 5.6.39, 5.14.93.

50 See, e.g., Clement, *Stromateis* 5.1.7, 6.8.68.

51 Clement, *Stromateis* 5.11.74.

52 Clement, *Stromateis* 7.16.96.

53 Plato, *Timaeus* 28. ET from *Timaeus*, trans. Desmond Lee (Harmondsworth, UK: Penguin, 1965).

54 Clement, *Stromateis* 5.6.32; 5.4.20.

55 Clement, *Stromateis* 6.15.131. GCS 15:497–98.

56 Clement, *Stromateis* 6.15.131. GCS 15:497–98.

57 Clement, *Stromateis* 6.15.127.

58 Clement, *The Rich Man's Salvation* 5. ET from Clement of Alexandria, *The Exhortation to the Greeks. The Rich Man's Salvation. To the Newly Baptized,* trans. G. W. Butterworth, LCL 92 (Cambridge, Mass.: Harvard University Press, 1919).

59 Clement, *Stromateis* 6.15.132.

60 Clement, *Stromateis* 6.15.126.

61 See Lilla, who suggests, though, that "Clement's representation . . . goes far beyond the sphere of Platonism and Philo: it plunges directly into Gnosticism." Lilla, *Clement of Alexandria,* 175–76, 181.

62 Clement, *Stromateis* 5.6.33.

63 Clement, *Stromateis* 5.6.40.

64 Clement, *Stromateis* 5.6.37.

65 See, e.g., Henri de Lubac, *Medieval Exegesis,* vol. 1, *The Four Senses of Scripture,* trans. Mark Sebanc (Grand Rapids: Eerdmans, 1998).

66 Origen, *Contra Celsum* 4.14. ET from *Contra Celsum,* ed. and trans. Henry Chadwick (Cambridge: Cambridge University Press, 1953), 192–93.

67 For an overarching account, see Frances M. Young, *From Nicaea to Chalcedon: A Guide to the Literature and Its Background* (London: SCM, 1983).

68 Ἐναργῶς σάρξ γενόμενος. Clement, *Paidagogos* 1.3.9. ET from *ANCL.* GCS 12:95.

69 Clement, *Stromateis* 5.6.34.

70 Clement, *Paidagogos* 1.6.41.

71 Clement, *Protreptikos* 10. ET from the LCL edition of Butterworth. All citations in English are taken from this edition.

72 Clement, *Stromateis* 7.3.18.

73 Ἀνθρώποις συμπολιτεύεται θεός. Clement, *Protreptikos* 11.

74 Κατὰ πάντα ἡμῖν ἀπεικάζεσθαι. Clement, *Paidagogos* 1.5.24. GCS 12:104.

75 Clement, *Paidagogos* 1.9.85.

76 See, e.g., Bigg, *Christian Platonists of Alexandria,* 72: "If we ask 'why the birth, the passion, the cross?', why Jesus redeemed us in this way . . . Clement has no answer." His understanding of redemption is cast in very different terms and has little need of these incidents in human history.

77 Clement, *Stromateis* 4.3.9.

78 Clement, *Stromateis* 4.26.164. GCS 15:321.

79 Clement, *Stromateis* 4.26.164. GCS 15:321.

80 See, e.g., Clement, *Stromateis* 4.5.19.

81 Clement, *Stromateis* 4.3.12.

82 Clement, *Stromateis* 4.3.12.

83 See, e.g., Plato, *Phaedo* 67a–68b.

84 Plotinus' analysis, though, is different from Clement's. See above, p. 60.

85 Clement, *Paidogogos* 3.1.250. GCS 12:235.

86 Clement, *Protreptikos* 2.25.3. GCS 12:18–19.

87 Thus Clement insists that only Christ, the archtype of rationality, is the true image of God, the human mind more widely being created with the capacity (albeit one realized only by adoptive grace rather than nature) to become and be "an image of the image" (εἰκὼν δ' εἰκόνος ἀνθρώπινος νους). *Stromateis* 5.14.94. GCS 15:388. Cf. *Stromateis* 2.17.77; 6.16.136.

88 Clement, *Stromateis* 2.17.77.

89 Clement, *Stromateis* 2.16.74.

90 Clement, *Paidagogos* 1.13.101.

91 Clement, *Stromateis* 4.21.130.

92 Clement, *Paidagogos* 1.2.4.

93 Θεὸς ἐν σαρκίῳ. Clement, *Stromateis* 6.16.140. GCS 15:503.

94 Clement, *Stromateis* 6.9.71.

95 Clement, *Stromateis* 3.7.59.

96 Thus Clement refers, in good biblical vein, to Christ suffering out of his love for us (*Stromateis* 6.8.70), which might perhaps be taken to apply to a bodily suffering of scourging and death in the midst of which Christ's soul remained impassible. See Thomas F. Torrance, "The Implications of *Oikonomia* for Knowledge and Speech of God in Early Christian Theology," in *Oikonomia: Heilsgeschichte als Thema der Theologie*, ed. Felix Christ (Hamburg: Herbert Reich, 1967), 231.

97 *Stromateis* 5.6.40.

98 Clement, *Stromateis* 5.14.105.

99 Clement, *Stromateis* 6.9.72. GCS 15:467–68.

100 On Apollinaris, see Young, *From Nicaea to Chalcedon*, 182–91, esp. 186. Clement, too, can assert that Jesus had "a soul devoid of passion." Clement, *Paidagogos* 1.2.4. But the question of a distinct human soul had not yet arisen in any explicit manner and, given his anthropology, would in any case make little sense. Like Apollinaris, in the case of Jesus it was natural for Clement to picture "the Logos as providing the body's intelligence and vitality." Young, *From Nicaea to Chalcedon*, 186.

101 Clement, *Stromateis* 4.21.130.

102 Clement, *Stromateis* 5.8.83.

103 Clement, *Stromateis* 2.20.108.

104 Πνεύματι περιπατεῖτε καὶ ἐπιθυμίαν σαρκὸς οὐ μὴ τελέσητε (Gal 5:16).

105 Clement, *Stromateis* 4.22.138.

106 Clement, *Paidagogos* 1.6.26. GCS 12:105–6.

107 Clement, *Paidagogos* 1.6.27.

108 Clement, *Stromateis* 5.6.38.

109 Clement, *Stromateis* 7.2.8.

110 Clement, *Protreptikos* 10.

111 Clement, *Protreptikos* 6.

112 Progenitor of the typical Alexandrian emphasis in Christology, Clement is clear that the "person" involved in each case (albeit at different levels of engagement) is the Logos. He espouses no dualism of a proto-Nestorian sort, erring always instead in the direction of monophysitism and a "docetic" reduction of the extent of genuine assumption of "flesh" in Christ.

113 See, e.g., Clement, *Protreptikos* 11.114.4. GCS 12:81.

114 Clement, *Stromateis* 7.16.101. GCS 17:71–72.

115 Clement, *Stromateis* 7.1.3.

116 Clement, *Stromateis* 4.6.40. GCS 15:266. My italics.

117 Clement, *Paidagogos* 1.8.62. GCS 12:127.

118 Plotinus was born c. 204/5 and died in 270 CE. Clement died in c. 211–215 CE, and the period of authorship of the *Enneads* is dated by Porphyry to c. 253 CE onward.

119 Clement, *Stromateis* 5.11.71. GCS 15:373–74.

120 Clement, *Stromateis* 4.25.156.

121 Ἓν δὲ ὁ θεὸς καὶ ἐπέκεινα τοῦ ἑνὸς καὶ ὑπὲρ αὐτὴν μονάδα. Clement, *Paidagogos* 1.8.71. GCS 12:131. Cf. also *Stromateis* 4.25.156 where Clement links the economy of the Spirit to that realm which culminates in the One/Son. On his tacit identification of the One with Logos, see Lilla, *Clement of Alexandria*, 207.

122 Clement, *Stromateis* 7.2.7.

123 Clement, *Stromateis* 7.2.5.

124 See, e.g., Karl Barth, vol. 1, *The Doctrine of the Word of God*, part 2, ed. G. W. Bromiley and T. F. Torrance, trans. G. T. Thomson and Harold Knight (Edinburgh: T&T Clark, 1956), 29. Cf. chap. 9 below.

125 Clement, *Stromateis* 7.2.5.

126 R. P. Casey, "Clement and the Two Divine Logoi," *Journal of Theological Studies* 25, no. 97 (1923): 47.

127 Cited in Casey, "Clement and the Two Divine Logoi," 43.

128 See, e.g., Clement, *Protreptikos* 19.98; *Stromateis* 7.3.16.

129 Casey, "Clement and the Two Divine Logoi," 47. Casey notes a similar ambiguity in the Hellenic Judaism of Philo, leaving it unclear whether, finally, the Logos is "a property of God essential to his being and constitutive in his nature or a separate entity with hypostatic independence." "Clement and the Two Divine Logoi," 49.

130 Bigg, *Christian Platonists of Alexandria*, 64.

Four: Deification

1 See chap. 1.

2 See, e.g., Origen, *Contra Celsum* 5.39. GCS 3:43–44.

3 "Foolishness to Gentiles."

4 "For . . . Greeks desire wisdom" (1 Cor 1:22).

5 Athanasius was born in Egypt c. 293. According to a tenth-century source (the *History of the Patriarchs of Alexandria* by Severus ibn al-Muqaffaʿ), he was born into a wealthy pagan family in which idols were worshiped, receiving baptism and Christian formation only in his adolescence, and together with his mother, from Alexander, Bishop of Alexandria. He attended the Council of Nicaea in 325 as Alexander's secretary, and is best known for his subsequent staunch defense of the Nicene formulary (and its insistence that the eternal Son is "of one substance" [ὁμοούσιος] with the Father) throughout his career and until his death in 373. See further Thomas G. Weinandy, *Athanasius: A Theological Introduction* (Aldershot, UK, and Burlington, Vt.: Ashgate, 2007), 1–9.

6 Although its dating is disputed, most Athanasian scholars suppose that the compound work *Contra Gentes* and *De Incarnatione* (*CG-DI*) is among the earliest of his writings, and predates the three-volume *Orationes contra Arianos* (339–343), *De Decretis* (352–353), *Ad Serapionem* (337–339), *De Synodis* (359), and other works of significance in the development of the theology of the fourth and fifth centuries. Tradition (following the lead of seventeenth-century patristic scholar

and monk Bernard de Montfaucon) had dated *CG-DI* very early—around 319–323, prior to the Arian controversy—on the basis of the complete lack of reference to Arian ideas (and, one might add, the author's failure to clarify some of his own expressions and lines of argument which might easily lend themselves to an Arian interpretation) in the extant text. Since the late nineteenth century, it has been widely argued that such an early date cannot be taken seriously, evidence being cited of the apparent maturity of the text, a couple of passages which might in fact be taken to allude tacitly to Arianism, and an apparent literary dependence on Eusebius of Caesarea's *Theophania,* the latter generally dated to the early 330s (numerous scholars thus advocating a date in the middle of that decade for the Athanasian work). My own view, which I generally presume in this chapter, is that, despite such considerations, a pre-Arian (and certainly a pre-Nicene) date remains the most compelling way to make sense of the internal evidence of the text. For the purposes of my argument, though, a date for *CG-DI* earlier than *Contra Arianos* (and thus the more knowing perspective of the latter) is more important than the precise dates involved. For this reason I resist the suggestion made by Nordberg of a date around 362–363. See Henric Nordberg, "A Reconsideration of the Date of St Athanasius' *Contra Gentes* and *De Incarnatione,*" *Studia Patristica* 3 (1961): 262–66. I can see little likelihood at all that the author of *Contra Arianos (CA)* could subsequently have penned some of the unguarded material appearing in *CG-DI.* On the debate, see further the works by Cross, Dragas, Dräseke, Kannengiesser, Kehrhahn, Pettersen, Quasten, Slusser, Stead, and Young in the bibliography.

7 Hans von Campenhausen suggests that "Athanasius was the first Greek Father of the Church who was not at home in the academic atmosphere of Christian philosophy," in *The Fathers of the Greek Church* (London, 1963), 69. It might be more accurate to say that he was not comfortable with the ways in which Greek philosophy had sometimes been appropriated by Christian theologians. Von Campenhausen's charge that Athanasius completely ignores the "treasures" of Hellenistic culture (*Fathers of the Greek Church,* 73) thus rather misses the point. In his early works Athanasius arguably toys with Hellenism rather too much, and in the mature works he does not so much ignore as reorient what he takes mostly to be convenient intellectual utilities rather than treasures.

8 See, e.g. Athanasius, *CG* 6.1, 19.22, 21.3; *DI* 1.12, 2.16.

9 See, e.g., the echoes in Athanasius, *CG,* of Clement's *Protreptikos* noted in *Contra Gentes and De Incarnatione,* trans. Thomson, 57, 63, 67, 119.

10 See chap. 3.

11 See, e.g., Georges Voisin, "La doctrine christologique de St. Athanase," *Revue d'histoire ecclésiastique* 1 (1900): 228, where Voisin says: "Although Athanasius belongs, like Origen, to the school of Alexandria, he depends above all on Irenaeus." Specific allusions and resonances are flagged in Thomson's critical notes. See *Contra Gentes and De Incarnatione,* trans. Thomson, 11, 167, 173, 197, 215, 219. The consonance between the thought of the two theologians is, though, far deeper and wider, occluded for those who are unfamiliar with Irenaeus, perhaps, by the literary device Athanasius adopts (or the practical circumstance he faces) at the outset of his work. See *CG* 1.16–17: "Since we do not now have the works of

these teachers to hand. . . ." Cf. *Contra Gentes and De Incarnatione*, trans. Thomson, 2 n. 2.

12 Thomas F. Torrance observes that "right from the start [Athanasius'] affinities with the teaching of the early Apologists, and with Clement and Origen, were surprisingly slight, and all through his life he moved further and further away from them," in "The Hermeneutics of St Athanasius," *Ekklesiastikos Pharos* 52 (1970): 446.

13 Athanasius, *DI* 1.10–13. ET from *Contra Gentes and De Incarnatione*, trans. Thomson. All citations in English are taken from this edition.

14 Athanaisus, *DI* 1.9–10.

15 Athanaisus, *DI* 1.9–14.

16 Cf. chap. 2, on Irenaeus' use of this term. For Athanasius' use, see below.

17 So Torrance, *The Trinitarian Faith*, 189.

18 See, on the issue of date and ordering, note 6.

19 So, e.g., Athanasius, *DI* 1.9: Μακάριε καὶ ἀληθῶς φιλόχριστε. Cf. *DI* 56.3; *CG* 1.44, 1.46, 47.32. Weinandy suggests an individual named Macarius (*Athanasius: A Theological Introduction*, 12).

20 Athanasius, *CG* 56.1, 10.

21 *Pace* Weinandy, *Athanasius: A Theological Introduction*, 12.

22 Athanasius flags this duality/unity of intent early on in *CG*: "We continue then as best we can, first refuting the ignorance of the unbelievers, in order that when the lies have been refuted the truth may shine forth by itself, and you too, my friend, may be convinced that you have put your confidence in the truth and that you have not been deceived in knowing Christ. I think it proper to talk about Christ with you who love Christ, since I am convinced that you consider knowledge of him and faith in him more precious than all else." *CG* 1.44. As well as encouraging and nurturing faith, it seems likely that Athanasius hoped that the divine light shed via his apologetic/catechetical efforts might help to dispel the clouds of delusion from which unbelievers and those who worship false gods must be deemed to suffer. See *CG* 1.34–41. Cf., too, the reference to οἱ ἔξωθεν (readers "outside the Church" or non-Christians) in *DI* 25.3.

23 See, e.g., Athanasius, *CG* 7.33–5 *et passim*.

24 See, e.g., Athanasius, *DI* 2 on Platonic and gnostic notions of creation. "The divinely inspired teaching of faith in Christ," he insists, "refutes their vain talk as impiety." *DI* 1.3.

25 See, e.g., Athanasius, *DI* 41 on Greek notions of Logos, in particular the Stoic *logos spermatikos* from which as such Athanasius has already distinguished the central Christian idea (*CG* 40.23–24), but which, he insists, on its own terms makes denial of the incarnation or inhomination of a Greek "Logos" self-referentially incoherent. His claim to persuade by "reasonable" arguments (ἐκ τῶν εὐλόγων, *DI* 45.32), therefore, acknowledges different canons of reasonableness as well as certain levels of commensurability between them. Finally, though, the revealed truth about the Logos incarnate will be borne witness to by our innate powers of reason or "inner minds" (*CG* 6.18, cf. 26.24), despite the capacity of the same for generating or permitting falsehoods. This argument (redolent of Clement's insistence on the natural link between the *Logos* and that which is *logikos*) shows Athanasius to

be quite capable of embracing and endorsing Hellenic assumptions when it suits him to do so. Cf. *DI* 3.20–24.

26 Thomson, introduction to *Contra Gentes and De Incarnatione*, trans. Thomson, xxii.

27 See Thomson, introduction to *Contra Gentes and De Incarnatione*, trans. Thomson, xxii–xxiii. See further Traugott Kehrhahn, *De sancti Athanasii quae fertur Contra Gentes oratione* (Berlin: G. Schade, 1913).

28 See, e.g., Athanasius, *CG* 8.30, 11.1–23, 14.2–9, 11–39. The notes in Thomson's edition flag parallels and allusions to all Athanasius' apparent sources.

29 Τὸν ἀληθινὸν καὶ ὄντας ὄντα Θεὸν. Athanasius, *CG* 9.19.

30 See, e.g., Athanasius, *CG* 8.29–30, 18.35–40. Cf. *CG* 21.8–14.

31 Athanasius, *CG* 14.39.

32 Athanasius, *CG* 15.12, 25.3.

33 Διὸ καὶ ἡ περὶ ταῦτα θρησκεία καὶ θεοποιία οὐκ εὐσεβείας, ἀλλὰ ἀθεότητος καὶ πάσης ἀσεβείας ἐστὶν εἰσήγησις . . . Athanasius, *CG* 29.37–9.

34 Αὐτὸς γὰρ ἐνηνθρώπησεν, ἵνα ἡμεῖς θεοποιηθῶμεν. *DI* 54.11–12.

35 It is precisely a sharing κατὰ μετοχήν, a mode of relationship between God and creature, that Athanasius distinguishes carefully from the way in which the eternal, uncreated Word or Son is related to the Father in the life of God. See n. 53.

36 See, e.g., Athanasius, *CG* 6, 27.16–19; *DI* 3.1–16.

37 Τὸν ἀγένητον, Athanasius, *CG* 35.5.

38 Ὃς ἄλλος μὲν ἔστι τῶν γενητῶν καὶ πάσης τῆς κτίσεως. Athanasius, *CG* 40.29–30.

39 Athanasius, *CG* 40.12. Cf. *CG* 2.6–7, 35.3–5.

40 Φωτίσας τά τε φαινόμενα καὶ τὰ ἀόρατα πάντα, εἰς ἑαυτὸν συνέχει καὶ συσφίγγει. Athanasius, *CG* 42.3–4.

41 See Athanasius, *CG* 35–38, where he cites Rom 1:20 and Acts 14:15–17. His appeal is to the good ordering of creation as witness to the goodness as well as the "intelligence of the Creator." We might also note that it is by delving into and reckoning with the processes and order of the material creation, rather than in resolute abstraction from it, that God is thus known.

42 Athanasius, *DI* 5.2. Cf., e.g., *DI* 14.1–15, 20.1–10, 54.11.

43 Ὁ ἐκ Πατρὸς . . . προελθών. Athanasius, *CG* 41.5–8. *Contra Gentes and De Incarnatione,* trans. Thomson, 112. Cf. *CG* 45.4.

44 See, e.g., Athanasius, *CG* 42.1–2 et passim.

45 Athanasius, *CG* 41.5–8. Cf. *CG* 41.21–23: "But being good, [God] governs and establishes the world through his Word who is himself God [αὐτῷ ὄντι Θεῷ]."

46 Athanasius, *CG* 40.28–30.

47 Athanasius, *CG* 47.

48 Athanasius, *CG* 45.2–5.

49 See chap. 3.

50 Athanasius, *CG* 45.6–11. Cf., e.g., *DI* 14.28, 14.34–40.

51 See chap. 3.

52 Athanasius, *CG* 44.2.

53 Athanasius, *CG* 47.11–13, citing John 14:10. Cf. *CG* 46.54: the eternal Son is the Word of the Father not by participation (κατὰ μετοχήν—an external relationship

of the sort by which, for instance, finite creatures are said to be related to the Word himself) but directly, as "the Father's own power."

54 Athanasius, *CG* 44.20–22.

55 The prominence of Logos language in this work compared to other christological titles is striking. Dragas tabulates the following statistics: In *CG*, Logos (71), Christ (22), God (14), Savior (13), Lord (7), Son (2), Jesus (6); in *DI*, Logos (147), Christ (87), God (20), Savior (61), Lord (46), Son (22), Jesus (10). George D. Dragas, *Athanasiana: Essays in the Theology of Saint Athanasius* (London, 1980), 429–31. The disparity between Logos and Son is particularly striking, especially when compared to the relative prominence of the latter, distinctly biblical term in *CA* and Athanasius' other more mature writings.

56 E. P. Meijering, *Orthodoxy and Platonism in Athanasius: Synthesis or Antithesis?* (Leiden: Brill, 1968), 120, 131 et passim. As Rist observes, here and elsewhere "Athanasius seems to know well where, in the tradition in which he lives, Platonism ends and Christianity begins." John M. Rist, "Basil's 'Neoplatonism,'" in *Basil of Caesarea: Christian, Humanist, Ascetic*, ed. Paul J. Fedwick (Toronto: Pontifical Institute for Medieval Studies, 1981), 176.

57 Athanasius, *CG* 34.19–20. Kannengiesser notes that it is the mind as distinct from the soul per se that Athanasius considers to be created κατ᾽ εἰκόνα, and draws attention to the fact that, unlike Clement, Origen, and Eusebius of Caesarea before him, Athanasius avoids referring to the rational soul *as* an image of God or God's Logos, taking care instead to speak of it only as created *according to* or *in* the image. Like Clement, he wants to insist that the sole image of God is the Logos himself, and, he adds, it is only by virtue of our special relationship to the Logos as our Creator that we possess any likeness to God whatsoever. Charles Kannengiesser, "Athanasius of Alexandria and the Foundation of Traditional Christology," *Theological Studies* 34 (1973): 109.

58 Athanasius, *DI* 3.16–24. Cf. *CG* 2.5–15.

59 Athanasius, *CG* 46.54.

60 Athanasius, *DI* 5.5.

61 Athanasius, *CG* 46.56.

62 Athanasius, *CG* 30.4.

63 Athanasius, *DI* 3.22.

64 Athanasius, *CG* 2.19.

65 Athanasius, *CG* 8.10.

66 Athanasius, *CG* 33.30. Athanasius also dallies here with the idea that the soul is better off without the body, and at death is (temporarily at least) liberated from it.

67 Athanasius, *DI* 3.1.

68 Athanasius, *CG* 35.5. Cf. *DI* 3.5–6.

69 Πάλιν εἰς τὸ μὴ εἶναι διὰ τῆς φθορᾶς ἐπιστρέφειν. Athanasius, *DI* 6.14. Cf. *DI* 4.17–30.

70 Athanasius, *CG* 33.32–35.

71 Athanasius, *CG* 3.1–13.

72 Athanasius, *DI* 4.11–20.

73 Athanasius, *DI* 5.1.

74 Athanasius, *DI* 4.30–31, 5.1–11.

75 Athanasius, *DI* 4.17–33.

76 Athanasius, *DI* 3.24–5.27.

77 Athanasius, *DI* 5.26–7. Cf. *DI* 6.2–4, *CG* 5.

78 Athanasius, *DI* 6.7.

79 Athanasius, *DI* 13.23–25.

80 See chap. 5.

81 See, e.g., Athanasius, *DI* 44.1–18.

82 Athanasius, *DI* 8.1–28. Cf. *DI* 14.1–9.

83 Athanasius, *DI* 7.11–14. Cf. Frances Young's observation that "Athanasius has frequently been accused of being so concerned with death that he neglects the seriousness of sin and the need of salvation from guilt. Certainly his emphasis in the *De Incarnatione* is on death, but it must be remembered that death is the direct outcome of man's disobedience to God's express command." Young, *From Nicaea to Chalcedon*, 71.

84 Athanasius, *DI* 11.20.

85 Athanasius, *DI* 9.7–15.

86 Athanasius, *DI* 32.29–33.

87 Athanasius, *DI* 27.1–7.

88 Athanasius, *DI* 44.33–34.

89 Athanasius, *DI* 44.19–20.

90 Εἰς πάντα ἑαυτὸν ἥπλωσεν ὁ Λόγος. Athanasius, *DI* 44.18.

91 See Athanasius, *DI* 44.3–4.

92 Athanasius, *CG* 1.24–30.

93 See Athanasius, *DI* 17.1–12. Cf. what Athanasius has to say in *CG* 33.30 about the soul's capacity to transcend bodily existence. But whereas the latter is only by way of imaginative and intellectual engagement with things beyond the range of the embodied soul's geographical coordinates, Athanasius' idea here is that the divine Word is by definition truly present to and in all things at the same time as he exists as the man Jesus. This raises questions, of course, that would duly be grappled with in debates about whether the Son, having taken flesh, should be reckoned to have one will/mind or two; but the terms of these debates were not yet in view and we cannot expect Athanasius to address the question in this form. His concern here is merely to affirm what the later doctrine of "two natures" would insist: namely that the eternal Son remained fully God even as he became a human being, and that it was indeed this same God (in the hypostasis of the Word/Son) who was present, acted, and suffered as the man Jesus.

94 Athanasius, *DI* 17.24–28.

95 Athanasius, *DI* 8.33–34.

96 But cf. also: "He had pity on our race . . . and submitted to our corruption." Athanasius, *DI* 8.14–15. Athanasius wrestles, as Christian theologians always have, to hold together an insistence on the solidarity of Christ with those he came to save and an equal insistence that he was nonetheless different, and that it was in this very difference that his redemptive significance and impact lay. In the words of the

Epistle to the Hebrews 4:15, he was "one who in every respect has been tested as we are, yet without sin." See further chap. 11.

97 Athanasius, *DI* 8.21–35.

98 See Athanasius, *DI* 8.1–28, 9.7–15, 40.10–15.

99 Athanasius, *DI* 25.34–39.

100 See chap. 3.

101 Athanasius, *Tomus ad Antiochenos* 7, 11. ET from *Nicene and Post-Nicene Fathers* (*NPNF*). Greek text in *PGL* 26:804, 809.

102 Cf. Athanasius, *Ad Epictetum* 7: "The Saviour having in very truth become man, the salvation of the whole man was brought about . . . truly our salvation is not merely apparent, nor does it extend to the body only, but the whole man, body and soul alike, has truly obtained salvation in the Word himself." ET from *NPNF*. All citations in English are taken from this edition. For the suggestion that the evidence of the conciliar statement need not be taken as evidence "that Athanasius explicitly affirms the reality of Christ's human soul," see R. V. Sellers, *Two Ancient Christologies* (London: SPCK, 1954), 42. The two treatises *Contra Apollinarem* traditionally ascribed to Athanasius are generally accepted by scholarship as pseudonymous, and we must bracket their evidence out of consideration here. For a contrary view, though, see George D. Dragas, *St Athanasius contra Apollinarem* (Athens: Church and Theology, 1985).

103 Young, *From Nicaea to Chalcedon*, 77–78. Cf. Maurice F. Wiles, "The Nature of the Early Debate about Christ's Human Soul," *Journal of Ecclesiastical History* 16, no. 2 (1965): 147.

104 In this respect Young and others follow the influential lead of Marcel Richard, "Saint Athanase et la psychologie du Christ selon les Ariens," *Mélanges de science religieuse* 4 (1947): 4–54, and Alois Grillmeier, *Christ in Christian Tradition* (London and Oxford: Mowbray, 1965). Apollinarus' Christology was condemned formally by the Council of Constantinople in 381.

105 See Athanasius, *DI* 4.1 and 4.9. Thomson translates both as "incarnation," obscuring the potential differences of connotation.

106 Athanasius, *DI* 8.17.

107 Athanasius, *DI* 18.3–5, 31.28.

108 Athanasius, *DI* 31.25–26.

109 Athanasius, *DI* 44.30–49.

110 Athanasius, *DI* 1.29–30.

111 Athanasius, *DI* 9.12.

112 Athanasius, *DI* 8.24.

113 Athanasius, *DI* 22.25. Cf. *DI* 8.25, 45.2.

114 Ὡς ἄνθρωπος ἐν ἀνθρώποις, ἀναστρέφεται, καὶ τὰς αἰσθήσεις πάντων ἀνθρώπων προσλαμβάνει. Athanasius, *DI* 15.12–13. Cf. his statement in *DI* 44.11 that the Word "became a man and used the body as a human instrument" (γέγονε δὲ ἄνθρωπος διὰ τοῦτο, καὶ ἀνθρωπείῳ ὀργάνῳ κέκρηται τῷ σώματι).

115 Athanasius, *DI* 16.5–6.

116 Ὡς ἄνθρωπος εἰς τὸν θάνατον καταβάς. Athanasius, *DI* 50.16. Cf. *DI* 14.35.

117 Athanasius, *CA* 2.46. *PGL* 26:245.

118 Athanasius, *CA* 2.74. ET from *Select Treatises of St. Athanasius in Controversy with the Arians*, vol. 2, trans. John Henry Newman (London: Longmans, Green, 1903); all citations in English are from this edition. *PGL* 26:305.

119 Athanasius, *CA* 2.66.

120 Athanasius, *CA* 2.65, 2.70. *PGL* 26:285, 296. Cf. *CA* 2.47.

121 See, e.g., Athanasius, *CA* 1.50, 2.53, 3.33.

122 See, e.g., Athanasius, *CA* 3.35.

123 Ἄνθρωπος δὲ γέγονε, καὶ οὐκ εἰς ἄνθρωπον ἦλθε. Athanasius, *CA* 3.30. *PGL* 26:388.

124 See, e.g., Athanasius, *CA* 1.41, 1.43, 3.33.

125 Athanasius, *CA* 3.30. Cf. *Epistola ad Epictetum* 8: "To say 'the Word became flesh' is equivalent [ἴσος] to saying 'the Word has become man.'" ET from *NPNF*. *PGL* 26:1064.

126 Irenaeus, as we saw in chap. 2, appears to use "flesh" in precisely this way. Georges Voisin, who insists on the influence of Irenaeus and the theological tradition of Asia Minor on Athanasius, argues for the latter having adopted a similarly broad range of meaning for the term in his Christology. See Voisin, "La doctrine christologique de St. Athanase."

127 Dragas identifies only 6 "Christological" uses of σάρξ over against 126 of σῶμα, whereas in *CA* the comparable statistics are σάρξ 199 to σῶμα 97. Dragas, *Athanasiana*, 12–13. ET is that of Dragas.

128 Dragas, *Athanasiana*, 12–13. ET is that of Dragas.

129 So, e.g., Athanasius, *CA* 3.34: Ὡς γὰρ ὁ κύριος, ἐνδυσάμενος τὸ σῶμα, γέγονεν ἄνθρωπος, οὕτως ἡμεῖς οἱ ἄνθρωποι παρὰ τοῦ Λόγου τε θεοποιούμεθα. *PGL* 26:397.

130 See Grillmeier, *Christ in Christian Tradition*.

131 Thus, Richard is correct to insist that "that which it is necessary to determine is the sense attributed by the bishop of Alexandria to the expression 'to become man'" (and, we might add, to the expression "assume flesh"). Richard, "Saint Athanase et la psychologie du Christ selon les Ariens," 17.

132 *Pace* Young, *From Nicaea to Chalcedon*, 185.

133 So, for instance, "The human race is not saved by the assumption of a mind and a whole man, but by the taking of flesh.... An immutable mind [ἄτρεπτος νοῦς] was needed which would not fail through the weakness of understanding." Apollinaris, Fragment 76, in *Apollinaris von Laodicea und seine Schule, Texte und Untersuchungen*, ed. H. Lietzmann (Tübingen: Mohr, 1904), 222; cited in Young, *From Nicaea to Chalcedon*, 185.

134 Gregory Nazianzen, Epistle 101. Cf. Cyril of Alexandria (c. 375–444), Commentary on John, *PGL* 74:89: Ὁ γὰρ μὴ προσείληπται, οὐδὲ σέσωσται.

135 *Pace* Grillmeier, *Christ in Christian Tradition*, 326.

136 According to the confession of the Council of Chalcedon (451) the one "person" (*hypostasis*) of the Savior subsists in two distinct "natures" (*ousiai*): "without confusion, without change, without division, without separation [ἀσυγχύτως, ἀτρέπτως, ἀδιαιρέτως, ἀχωρίστως]; the distinction of natures being in no way abolished because of the union, but rather the characteristic property of each nature being preserved, and concurring into one Person and one subsistence, not as if Christ were parted or divided into two persons, but one and the same Son and

only-begotten God, Word, Lord, Jesus Christ." ET from Stevenson, *Creeds, Councils and Controversies*, 335.

137 See, e.g., the helpful critique of this tendency in Rowan Williams, "'Person' and 'Personality' in Christology," *Downside Review* 94 (1976): 253–60.

138 E. L. Mascall, *Theology and the Gospel of Christ: An Essay in Reorientation* (London: SPCK, 1977), 156.

139 Mascall, *Theology and the Gospel of Christ*, 157.

140 Mascall, *Theology and the Gospel of Christ*, 154.

141 Williams, "'Person' and 'Personality' in Christology," 255.

142 See *A Patristic Greek Lexicon*, ed. G. Lampe (Oxford: Oxford University Press, 1961), 164 (*APGL*).

143 Williams, "'Person' and 'Personality' in Christology," 257–58.

144 Athanasius, *DI* 15.12.

145 See, e.g., Athanasius, *CA* 3.26.

146 Athanasius, *DI* 54.14.

147 Athanasius, *CA* 3.27.

148 Athanasius, *CA* 3.31.

149 Athanasius, *DI* 18.6–9.

150 Athanasius, *CA* 2.11. *PGL* 26:172.

151 Athanasius, *CA* 1.45. *PGL* 26:104–5.

152 Athanasius, *DI* 19.12–16.

153 Athanasius, *CA* 3.57.

154 Athanasius, *CA* 3.43.

155 See, e.g., Voisin, "La doctrine christologique de St. Athanase," 231: "Is it necessary to take the terms 'sarx' and 'soma' literally, or are they there simply expressions consecrated by use, serving to show the human nature of the Saviour? The latter interpretation appears to us the better founded." Translation mine.

156 Richard, "Saint Athanase et la psychologie du Christ selon les Ariens," 12.

157 Grillmeier, *Christ in Christian Tradition*, 315. We might note, though, that Irenaeus (whose probable influence on Athanasius' theology we have already noted) does precisely the same, ascribing to Christ's sorrow and fear as well as various physical weaknesses the status of "tokens of the flesh [σύμβολα σαρκὸς] which . . . he had recapitulated in himself, bearing salvation to his own handiwork." Irenaeus, *Adv. Haer.* 3.22.2. *PGL* 7:931.

158 Athanasius, *CA* 3.35.

159 Athanasius, *CA* 3.38.

160 Thus, the Word, having come in our body, was "conformed to our condition," such that he, too, having been made a creature, called the Father "Lord." Athanasius, *CA* 3.57. Cf. *CA* 2.47, 2.50, 2.55. As well as being the one who pours out grace, therefore, the incarnate Word is also a natural recipient of it. *CA* 1.45. And as well as the one who, as God, bestows the Spirit on all flesh, in respect of his humanity he is himself inferior to and dependent on the Spirit. *CA* 1.50.

161 Athanasius, *CA* 2.11.

162 Athanasius, *CA* 3.32.

163 Athanasius, *CA* 3.32. *PGL* 26.389.

164 Origen, *De Principiis* 2.6.2. ET from *ANCL*. GCS 22:140–41. See further McLelland, *God the Anonymous*, 120–21.

165 Origen, *De Principiis* 2.6.3.

166 Origen, *De Principiis* 2.6.3.

167 Origen, *De Principiis* 2.6.3. Cf. Origen, *Contra Celsum* 5.39.

168 J. N. D. Kelly, *Early Christian Doctrines*, 5th ed. (London: Black, 1977), 156–57.

169 Origen, *Contra Celsum* 4.15. Elsewhere Origen appeals to relevant Gospel texts such as Matt 26:38 and John 12:27 to reinforce the point. See *De Princ.* 4.4.4. Cf. Kelly, *Early Christian Doctrines*, 156.

170 Origen, *Commentary in John* 1.28. ET from *ANCL*.

171 Mascall, *Theology and the Gospel of Christ*, 156.

172 See Athanasius, *Ad Epictetum* 8. On date, see, e.g., Weinandy, *Athanasius: A Theological Introduction*, 7.

173 Athanasius, *Ad Epictetum* 7.

174 Athanasius, *CA* 2.54.

175 Athanasius, *CA* 2.56.

176 Athanasius, *CA* 2.65.

177 Athanasius, *CA* 3.39.

178 Athanasius, *CA* 2.7. *PGL* 26:121. Newman has "propitiating God," which seems to sit less well with the context where a positive offering of self is intended. Cf. *CA* 1.64: Ὁ Λόγος σὰρξ ἐγένετο . . . καὶ ἐγένετο ἱλασμός. *PGL* 26:145.

179 See chap. 3.

180 Athanasius, *CA* 2.69.

181 Athanasius, *CA* 1.49.

182 Athanasius, *CA* 1.41, 3.31.

183 Athanasius, *CA* 2.70.

184 Athanasius, *CA* 3.48.

185 Athanasius, *CA* 2.53, 2.65.

186 Athanasius, *CA* 1.42, 3.33.

187 See, e.g., Wiles, *Working Papers in Doctrine*, chap. 9; George S. Hendry, *The Gospel of the Incarnation* (London: SCM, 1959), 59–62.

188 Athanasius, *CA* 1.41.

189 Athanasius, *CA* 2.9.

190 Melville Scott, *Athanasius on the Atonement* (Stafford, UK: J. and C. Mort, 1914), 33.

191 Scott, *Athanasius on the Atonement*, 51.

192 Athanasius, *CA* 2.65. *PGL* 26:293. The italicized words are Scott's own English translation rather than Newman's (which the citation otherwise follows).

193 Scott, *Athanasius on the Atonement*, 62.

194 Scott, *Athanasius on the Atonement*, 79.

195 See chap. 11.

196 See, e.g., Athanasius, *DI* 20.10–13, 31–33.

197 Athanasius, *CA* 1.47.

198 Athanasius, *CA* 1.49.

199 See, for instance, the paraphrase of John 17:19 in Athanasius, *CA* 1.46: "I, being the Father's Word, I give to myself, when become man, the Spirit; and in the same Spirit do I sanctify myself when become man, that henceforth in me . . . all men may be sanctified." Cf. *CA* 1.49: "Through whom then and from whom behoved it that the Spirit should be given but through the Son, whose also is the Spirit? and when were we enabled to receive it, except when the Word became man? . . . [for] not otherwise should we have partaken of the Spirit and been sanctified, save that the giver of the Spirit, the Word himself, had spoken of himself as anointed with the Spirit for us. And therefore did we securely receive it, because he was declared to be anointed in the flesh; for the flesh being first sanctified in him, and he being said, as man, to have received the gift in behalf of his flesh, we have after him the Spirit's grace, receiving 'out of his fulness.'"

200 See above, 354, n. 102.

201 Grillmeier, *Christ in Christian Tradition*, 326.

202 So, e.g., Wiles, "Soteriological Arguments in the Fathers." See, more widely, chap. 1 above.

203 Athanasius, *DI* 54.11–12; *CA* 1.38, 2.70, 3.34 et passim.

204 Irenaeus, *Adv. Haer.* 4.33.4, 3.19.1. See more widely chap. 2 above.

205 Athanasius, *CA* 3.24. Cf. 1.58: "The Son is different in kind and different in substance from things created, and on the contrary belongs to the Father's substance and is one in nature with it." Newman, *Select Treatises of St. Athanasius*, 241.

206 Athanasius, *CA* 2.74.

207 Athanasius, *CA* 1.38.

208 Athanasius, *CA* 2.61.

209 Athanasius, *CA* 3.24. Cf. *CA* 1.49.

210 Athanasius, *CA* 2.64. *PGL* 26:284.

211 Athanasius, *CA* 1.39. *PGL* 26:93.

212 Athanasius, *CA* 1.43.

Five: Satisfaction

1 Isa 42:1, NRSV.

2 *The Scottish Book of Common Prayer* (Edinburgh: Cambridge University Press, 1929), 337.

3 Cf. C. Gunton, *The Actuality of Atonement.*

4 As far as this doctrine is concerned, Tertullian's theological and apologetic writings occasionally echo themes we have already seen to be characteristic of the Christian East. So, e.g., *Adversus Marcionem* 2.27. As Daniélou notes in another connection, Tertullian clearly knew and was happy to depend on the works of Irenaeus. Jean Daniélou, *The Origins of Latin Christianity*, trans. David Smith and John Austin Baker, ed. John Austin Baker (Philadelphia: Westminster, 1977), 377. His more typical allusions to the atonement, though, anticipate the orientation of later Western theology, being focused on the death of Christ and, as Turner notes, they do "not go much further than the quotation of metaphors derived from Scripture." *The Patristic Doctrine of Redemption*, 102–3. Cf. Reinhold Seeberg, *Text-book of the History of Doctrines* (Grand Rapids: Baker, 1964), 131.

5 Hermann Schultz, "Der sittliche Begriff des Verdienstes und seine Anwendung auf das Verständniss des Werkes Christi," *Theologische Studien und Kritiken* (1894): 1–50, 245–314, 554–614. Cf. Franks, *The Work of Christ*, 78.

6 Schultz, "Der sittliche Begriff des Verdienstes," 79. "In Ambrose," Schultz notes, "the transference of the merits of martyrs (and virgins) is quite axiomatic." "Der sittliche Begriff des Verdienstes," 86.

7 Tertullian, *De Pudicitia* ("On Modesty") 22. ET from *ANF*.

8 Namely, "death" (θάνατος), which, according to the apostle Paul, is the "wages of sin." Rom 6:23.

9 Tertullian, *De Poenitentia (De Poen.)* 5.

10 Franks, *The Work of Christ*, 79.

11 It is true, of course, that the imagery of sacrifice has sometimes been made sense of in penal terms, as though the sacrificial victim were first identified with and then put to death (punished) in the place of the sinful offerer. Scripture offers no clear explanation of the efficacy of sacrifice. The only unambiguous instance of the identification of the victim with sin, though, seems to be the case of the scapegoat or goat "for Azazel" (Lev 16:7–10), which is precisely *not* put to death, but bears the sins of the nation "outside the camp" into the wilderness. The shedding of blood in the temple seems to be more about the voluntary offering of the force of life on the altar, which in some way compensates for or symbolizes in liturgy the "return" to Yahweh of a life which ought to have been devoted to him but has not been, and thereby "covers" the sin. Sacrifice is, in any event, a multifaceted sacrament which includes thanksgiving as well as penitence among its modes.

12 God is *"auctor et defensor"* of the very works that provide *satisfactio. De Poen.* 2.9. Latin text in *Tertullien: De Paenitentia, De Pudicitia*, ed. and trans. Pierre de Labriolle (Paris: Alphonse Picard et Fils, 1906), 6.

13 Tertullian, *De Poen.* 2.7. Labriolle, *Tertullien: De Paenitentia, De Pudicitia* 6. Thus, Tertullian writes, "whatever defilement inveterate error had imparted, whatever contamination in the heart of man ignorance had engendered, that *poenitentia* should sweep and scrape away, and cast out of doors, and thus prepare the home of the heart, by making it clean, for the Holy Spirit." *De Poen.* 2.6. ET from *ANF*. All citations in English are from this edition. Labriolle, *Tertullien: De Paenitentia, De Pudicitia*, 6.

14 Tertullian, *De Poen.* 9.3. Labriolle, *Tertullien: De Paenitentia, De Pudicitia*, 40.

15 Tertullian, *De Poen.* 9.2: "paenitentia Deus mitigatur." Labriolle, *Tertullien: De Paenitentia, De Pudicitia*, 40.

16 Tertullian, *De Poen.* 9.3: *"temporali afflictione aeterne supplicia . . . sed expungat."* Labriolle, *Tertullien: De Paenitentia, De Pudicitia*, 40.

17 John McIntyre, *St. Anselm and His Critics: A Re-interpretation of the Cur Deus Homo* (Edinburgh: Oliver and Boyd, 1954), 83–84.

18 McIntyre, *St. Anselm and His Critics*, 85.

19 See, e.g., the insightful treatment in Janet Martin Soskice, *Metaphor and Religious Language* (Oxford: Clarendon, 1985). See further George Lakoff and Mark Johnson, *Metaphors We Live By* (Chicago: University of Chicago Press, 2003). See also chap. 15 below.

20 It is possible, of course, that penal resonances were carried across to the practice of confession from a legal use which bore the connotations both of merit and of penalty. It is also possible that, Tertullian using the term *satisfactio* as Schultz suggests in the sense of "meritorious offering," the penal overtones were ones picked up precisely from its application to a theological use around the confessional, where ideas of both merit and penalty were to be found.

21 See Gunton, *The Actuality of Atonement*.

22 See John R. W. Stott, *The Cross of Christ* (Leicester, UK, and Downers Grove, Ill.: InterVarsity Press, 1986), 142–43.

23 "*Dei naturam nulla vis iniuriosae perturbationis offenderet: tamen suscepta voluntarie est, officio quidem ipsa satisfactura poenali, non tamen poenae sensu laesura patientem: non quod illa laedendi non habuerit pro ipsa passionis qualitate naturam; sed quod dolorem divinitatis natura non sentit.*" Hilary, *Commentary on Psalm liii.12*. Hilary makes the same point about punishment in *De Trinitate* 10.23. Christ, he argues, "suffered the violence of punishment without its consciousness" (*sine sensu poenae vim poenae*). PGL 10:362a. Turner mistakenly conflates these two passages in his discussion. See Turner, *The Patristic Doctrine of Redemption*, 104. Cf. Franks, *The Work of Christ*, 85. My thanks are due to Dr. Peter Maxwell-Stuart of the University of St. Andrews for helpful advice on the translation of the former extract.

24 Ambrose, *De fuga saeculi* 7.44. Cited in Franks, *The Work of Christ*, 84.

25 Anselm, *Cur Deus Homo* pref. ET from *Why God Became Man; and The Virgin Conception and Original Sin*, trans. Joseph M. Colleran (Albany, N.Y.: Magi, 1969). Citations of *Cur Deus Homo* in English are from this version unless otherwise indicated.

26 McIntyre, *St. Anselm and His Critics*, 44.

27 What McIntyre refers to as "the sustained attempt on the part of the Christian to relate the *credo* to the rest of his beliefs." The resultant pattern will include many ideas or beliefs which, at some level, are shared with unbelievers. McIntyre, *St. Anselm and His Critics*, 44.

28 As McIntyre notes, these will include "certain ideas commonly accepted in [Anselm's] time but not self-evident to any other age of human thought, particularly our own." *St. Anselm and His Critics*, 47.

29 McIntyre, *St. Anselm and His Critics*, 47.

30 Or, we might add, "word" or "image."

31 McIntyre, *St. Anselm and His Critics*, 46.

32 McIntyre, *St. Anselm and His Critics*, 52.

33 See, e.g., Timothy Gorringe, *God's Just Vengeance: Crime, Violence, and the Rhetoric of Salvation* (Cambridge and New York: Cambridge University Press, 1996), 87–99.

34 See, e.g., David Hogg, *Anselm of Canterbury: The Beauty of Theology* (Aldershot, UK, and Burlington, Vt.: Ashgate, 2004), 164.

35 Adolf von Harnack, *History of Dogma*, vol. 6, trans. from the 3rd German ed. by William McGilchrist (London: William & Norgate, 1899), 56, n. 3; McIntyre, *St. Anselm and His Critics*, 85–86.

36 McIntyre's reference to "an entirely new conception" and a scheme of atonement "autonomous in its logic" exaggerates the matter unduly, but his insistence on attending primarily to what Anselm *does* with the words, ideas, and images that he chooses to appropriate, rather than their significances in prior contexts, is sound. *St. Anselm and His Critics*, 87, 95.

37 McIntyre, *St. Anselm and His Critics*, 85.

38 Hogg, *Anselm of Canterbury*, 183, n. 39.

39 Anselm, *Cur Deus Homo* 1.1.

40 So, Gorringe, *God's Just Vengeance*, 93: "The same act, let us say a blow, directed against a peasant, a knight, a nobleman, or the king, is not the same act. A blow exchanged between two peasants might call for nothing but a mutual pardon, but if directed by a peasant against a king would threaten the integrity of the whole social order and demand the death sentence."

41 Anselm, *Cur Deus Homo* 1.11.

42 Anselm, *Cur Deus Homo* 1.11.

43 Anselm, *Cur Deus Homo* 1.20. Here, of course, Anselm breaks directly with the suggestion of Tertullian's penitential theology that a penitent return to God, exemplified in concrete acts of penance, can make good the damage done by postbaptismal sin. For Anselm, all this (and the whole course of our future life lived in complete dedication to God) is already owed to God, and thus not available as spiritual capital with which to make good our debt. This does not mean, though (*pace* McIntyre, *St. Anselm and His Critics*, 87), that the wider connotations of "penitence," in duly modified form, are not applicable to his understanding of Christ's *satisfactio*. Christ's offering to the Father may not be related to an individual sense of sin and guilt, but may certainly be understood as a penitential response made on behalf of the sinful race, and realized all the more fully and sharply precisely *because* he "feels" the weight and the horror of sin as others do not and cannot.

44 Anselm, *Cur Deus Homo* 1.21.

45 Anselm, *Cur Deus Homo* 1.12.

46 Anselm, *Cur Deus Homo* 2.6.

47 Anselm, *Cur Deus Homo* 2.7.

48 Anselm, *Cur Deus Homo* 2.18. My italics.

49 Anselm, *Cur Deus Homo* 1.13: "*Necesse est ergo ut aut ablatus honor solvatur, aut poena sequitur.*" *PGL* 158: 379A.

50 Anselm, *Cur Deus Homo* 1.14.

51 Anselm, *Cur Deus Homo* 1.9.

52 For details see Peter Kenneth Stevenson, *God in Our Nature: The Incarnational Theology of John McLeod Campbell* (Carlisle, UK: Paternoster, 2004); James B. Torrance, "The Contribution of McLeod Campbell to Scottish Theology," *Scottish Journal of Theology* 26, no. 3 (1973): 295–311; George M. Tuttle, *So Rich a Soil: John McLeod Campbell on Christian Atonement* (Edinburgh: Handsel, 1986).

53 The Whole Proceedings before the Presbytery of Dumbarton, and Synod of Glasgow and Ayr, in the Case of the Rev. John McLeod Campbell, Minister of Row (Greenock, UK: Lusk, 1831), 1.

54 Whole Proceedings, 8.

55 George Carey, *The Gate of Glory* (London: Hodder and Stoughton, 1986), 130. See also Stott, *The Cross of Christ*, 141–42; Robert S. Paul, *The Atonement and the Sacraments* (London: Hodder and Stoughton, 1961), 140–41.

56 John McLeod Campbell, *The Nature of the Atonement and Its Relation to Remission of Sins and Eternal Life,* 6th ed. (London: Macmillan, 1886 [1st ed. 1855]), 20.

57 Campbell, *The Nature of the Atonement,* 25.

58 Campbell, *The Nature of the Atonement,* 22. My italics.

59 Campbell, *The Nature of the Atonement,* 16.

60 John McLeod Campbell, *Sermons and Lectures,* 3rd ed. (Greenock, UK: Lusk, 1832), 13.

61 Campbell, *Sermons and Lectures,* 13.

62 Campbell, *The Nature of the Atonement,* 116.

63 Campbell, *The Nature of the Atonement,* 116.

64 "In Christ's honouring of the righteous law of God, the sentence of the law was included, as well as the mind of God which that sentence expressed. In this light are we to see the death of Christ, as connected with his redeeming those that were under the law." Campbell, *The Nature of the Atonement,* 260.

65 Campbell, *The Nature of the Atonement,* 267. My italics.

66 Campbell, *Sermons and Lectures,* 70.

67 I.e., one informed by the new perspective provided by the reality of the saving activity of God in the fulfillment of the messianic promises made to God's people.

68 Campbell, *The Nature of the Atonement,* 99.

69 Campbell, *The Nature of the Atonement,* 100. My italics.

70 Campbell, *The Nature of the Atonement,* 102. My italics.

71 Campbell, *The Nature of the Atonement,* 102.

72 Jonathan Edwards, "Concerning the Necessity and Reasonableness of the Christian Doctrine of Satisfaction for Sin," in *The Works of Jonathan Edwards,* ed. Edward Hickman, vol. 2 (London: William Ball, 1829), 565–78, 567.

73 The oft-made complaint that the notion of a sinless Christ "repenting" for others is meaningless fails to see that, for Campbell, Christ's sinlessness, far from disqualifying him from such "repentance," is actually that which *enables* him to confess the sins of the race, and that this "repentance" culminates precisely in a oneness of mind with the divine judgment on sin, and a submission to the sentence of death.

74 Campbell, *The Nature of the Atonement,* 125.

75 Campbell, *The Nature of the Atonement,* 117.

76 Campbell, *The Nature of the Atonement,* 226.

77 Campbell, *The Nature of the Atonement,* 261.

78 Campbell, *The Nature of the Atonement,* 101.

79 Stott's objection, in *The Cross of Christ,* that "penitent substitution" is not really substitutionary in the proper sense would seem to rest on a misunderstanding of what Campbell means by "penitence."

80 It is on this basis that Campbell rejects the interpretation of Matthew 27:46 as evidence of any real God-forsakenness in the cross, insisting on a reading of Psalm 22:1 within the larger context of the whole psalm, in which the mood duly alters to one of assurance and praise. It would certainly seem to be necessary to refute

any notion of God-forsakenness which implies a separation of the Son from the Father within the eternal Trinity, or which posits any other attitude than that of love between the Father and the Son. To this extent Campbell provides a necessary corrective. Yet it would seem to be possible to distinguish between an *actual* God-forsakenness (which would require either a Nestorian Christology or a tritheistic theology of the Trinity) and the incarnate Son's human *experience* of that separation from the Father which is the consequence of human sin. Likewise, while we must affirm the love of the Father for the Son and the Son for the Father in the midst of the suffering of Calvary, it is not meaningless to speak of the incarnate Son experiencing that darkness which is the manifestation of divine wrath toward sin. What we must hold onto in both cases is the fact that the Cross causes the Father pain as well as the Son, and that, concerning the Son's enduring it for the salvation of humankind, both are of one mind and will.

81 The verb ὑψόω can mean both "lift up" and "exalt," and in John (3:14, 12:32) it is closely associated with the crucifixion as a paradoxical epiphany of the glory of God (see, obliquely, 3:12–13 and, more directly, 12:28), a key theme with which John effectively bookends his Gospel (1:14–18, 19:1–19, 30). I am grateful to Richard Bauckham for this latter observation.

82 Alexander John Scott, "The Kingdom of Christ," Lecture 1 of *Social Systems of the Present Day Compared to Christianity*, reprinted in Scott, *Discourses* (London: Macmillan, 1866), 88.

83 See Campbell, *The Nature of the Atonement*, 11–12.

84 See Hogg, *Anselm of Canterbury*, 165–72.

85 Gen 1:4, 10, 12, 18, etc.

86 So, e.g., Ps 104:31.

87 See Ps 19:1, 7, 13–14.

88 So, e.g., Lev 11:44–45, 19:2, 20:26, etc.

89 Matt 6:9–10.

90 *Perichoresis* is the Greek term employed in classical Trinitarian theology to refer to the interpenetration of the three "persons" within the Godhead, by virtue of which they are nonetheless one God, so that to refer to one of the three is, by implication, to refer also and equally to the other two.

91 See, e.g., Lev 16 and 17.

92 P. T. Forsyth, "Reconciliation: Philosophic and Christian," in *The Work of Christ* (London: Hoder and Stoughton, 1910), 90.

93 See, e.g., Exod 20:2 where the delivery of the "ten words" is prefaced by a statement of Yahweh's electing and redemptive activity.

94 Jer 31:1; Ezek 36:28.

95 So, e.g., Amos 5:12–13.

96 On this theme see, helpfully, J. B. Torrance, "The Place of Jesus Christ in Worship," in Ray S. Anderson, ed., *Theological Foundations for Ministry: Selected Readings for a Theology of the Church of Ministry* (Grand Rapids: Eerdmans, 1979), 370–89.

97 See Heb 4:14–5:10, 7:23–25.

98 For an extended discussion of this point and its importance, see Thomas F. Torrance, "The Mind of Christ in Worship: The Problem of Apollinarianism in the

Liturgy," in his *Theology in Reconciliation: Essays Towards Evangelical and Catholic Unity in East and West* (London: G. Chapman, 1975), 139–214.

Six: Substitution

1 Louis Bouyer, *The Spirit and Forms of Protestantism*, trans. A. V. Littledale (London: Collins, 1963).

2 Bouyer, *Spirit and Forms of Protestantism*, 152.

3 See, e.g., Adelbert Denaux, Nicholas Sagovsky, and Charles Sherlock, eds., *Looking Towards a Church Fully Reconciled: The Final Report of the Second Anglican-Roman Catholic International Commission 1983–2005 (ARCIC II)* (London: Society for Promoting Christian Knowledge, 2016), 3–34. The relevant section of the report, titled "Salvation and the Church," was first published in 1987.

4 Cf., for example, Alister McGrath, in *Iustitia Dei: A History of the Christian Doctrine of Justification*, vol. 1 (Cambridge: Cambridge University Press, 1986), 2: "Wherever the church commemorates, celebrates and proclaims the passion of her redeemer, and *the benefits which she thereby receives,* she rehearses her faith in the reconciliation he accomplished on her behalf, and which called her into being." My italics.

5 See chap. 4.

6 The terms, referring to what God saves us *from* on one hand and what God saves us *for* on the other, are those employed by Campbell in *The Nature of the Atonement.* See chap. 4.

7 See, e.g., John Calvin, *Institutes of the Christian Religion*, ed. John T. McNeill, trans. Ford Lewis Battles, Library of Christian Classics, vols. 20–21 (Louisville: Westminster John Knox, 1960), 3.11.6.

8 John Calvin, *Commentary on Hebrews* 9.12. ET from *Commentary on Hebrews, I and II Peter*, trans. W. B. Johnston (Edinburgh: Oliver and Boyd, 1963).

9 Calvin, *Commentary on John* 3.16. ET from *The Gospel according to St John 1-10*, trans. T. H. L. Parker (Edinburgh: Oliver & Boyd, 1959). See further *Commentary on Colossians* 1.14.

10 Calvin, *Sermon on Luke* 1.39–44, quoted in Ronald S. Wallace, *Calvin's Doctrine of the Word and Sacraments* (Edinburgh: Oliver and Boyd, 1953), 168.

11 Calvin, *Commentary on Hebrews* 5.7.

12 Calvin, *Institutes* 1.1.2.

13 Calvin, *Commentary on John* 3.6.

14 Calvin, *Commentary on John* 3.3.

15 Calvin, *Commentary on Ephesians* 1.16–18. ET from *Galatians, Ephesians, Philippians and Colossians*, trans. T. H. L. Parker (Edinburgh: Oliver and Boyd, 1965).

16 Calvin, *Commentary on 1 Corinthians* 15.3–4. ET from *The First Epistle of Paul to the Corinthians*, trans. John W. Fraser (Edinburgh: Oliver & Boyd, 1960).

17 Calvin, *Commentary on Hebrews* 5.7.

18 Calvin, *Commentary on Romans* 10.7. ET from *Epistles of Paul the Apostle to the Romans and to the Thessalonians*, trans. Ross Mackenzie (Edinburgh: St Andrew Press, 1961).

19 Calvin, *Commentary on Romans* 4.25.

20 Calvin, *Institutes* 4.17.2.

21 Calvin, *Commentary on 1 Corinthians* 1.30; see further *Commentary on Romans* 8.13, etc.

22 Calvin, *Institutes* 3.14.17.

23 Calvin, *Commentary on Colossians,* introduction to the theme of the Epistle. My italics.

24 Calvin, *Commentary on John* 6.51.

25 Calvin, *Institutes* 2.15.5.

26 Calvin, *Commentary on 1 Corinthians* 2.12. My italics.

27 See Calvin, *Institutes* 3.11.4–12.

28 Calvin, *Institutes* 3.11.6.

29 See chap. 1.

30 Calvin, *Institutes* 3.11.9. My italics.

31 Calvin, *Institutes* 3.11.11.

32 Calvin, *Institutes* 3.11.11.

33 Calvin, *Institutes* 3.11.11. My italics.

34 Calvin, *Institutes* 3.11.23.

35 Calvin, *Commentary on Hebrews* 5.2. See, further, 5.17.

36 John Calvin, *A Treatise on the Sacraments of Baptism and the Lord's Supper* (Edinburgh, 1838), 109. Cf. *Institutes* 4.17.2.

37 Calvin, *Institutes* 3.15.5. My italics.

38 "I do not understand my own actions. For I do not do what I want, but I do the very thing I hate." Rom 7:15.

39 Calvin, *Institutes* 3.2.24.

40 Calvin, *Sermon on Titus* 1.7–9.

41 Calvin, *Commentary on II Corinthians* 1.20.

42 Calvin, *Commentary on John* 3.16.

43 Paul M. van Buren, *Christ in Our Place: The Substitutionary Character of Calvin's Doctrine of Reconciliation* (Edinburgh: Oliver and Boyd, 1957), 9.

44 Calvin, *Commentary on John* 17.23.

45 Calvin, *Commentary on 1 Timothy* 3.16, in *Tracts and Treatises,* with a short life of Calvin by Theodore Beza, translated by Henry Beveridge, historical notes and introduction added to the present ed. by Thomas F. Torrance, 3 vols. (Grand Rapids: Eerdmans, 1958).

46 Calvin, *Institutes* 2.12.1.

47 See, e.g., *Commentary on I Corinthians* 3.23.

Seven: Mediation

1 Charles Rogers, *Life of George Wishart, the Scottish Martyr* (Edinburgh, 1876), 66.

2 George Steiner, *After Babel: Aspects of Language and Translation,* 2nd ed. (Oxford and New York: Oxford University Press, 1992), 121.

3 Steiner, *After Babel,* 125.

4 See chap. 8.

5 See, on this aspect of the theme of election, H. H. Rowley, *The Biblical Doctrine of Election* (London: Lutterworth, 1950), 42–43, and Lesslie Newbigin, *The Open Secret: Sketches for a Missionary Theology* (Grand Rapids: Eerdmans, 1978), 75–87.

6 Walther Eichrodt, *Theology of the Old Testament,* vol. 1 (London: SCM, 1960), 54.

7 Eichrodt, *Theology of the Old Testament,* 1:56.

8 Eichrodt, *Theology of the Old Testament,* 1:403–4.

9 Eichrodt, *Theology of the Old Testament,* 1:164.

10 Eichrodt, *Theology of the Old Testament,* 1:439, 454.

11 See, e.g., especially Deut 17:14–20.

12 Eichrodt, *Theology of the Old Testament,* 1:69.

13 It is true that chapter 2 of the Confession adverts to God as Trinity, but the formal reiteration of classic orthodoxy here is frankly little more than an awkward *Quicumque vult* tacked on to a doctrine of God otherwise largely unqualified by its presence. It is also true that Christ is mentioned both in the context of election and that of covenant. My point is simply that the incarnation as such does not seem to be formative in the elaboration and discussion of these themes.

14 Both Ussher's Irish Articles of 1615 and the Canons of Dort of 1619, both of which are widely assumed to have had a substantial influence on the Westminster divines, do essentially the same thing.

15 Perry Miller, *The New England Mind: The Seventeenth Century* (Cambridge, Mass.: Harvard University Press, 1954), 378.

16 See, e.g., Jens G. Møller, "The Beginnings of Puritan Covenant Theology," *Journal of Ecclesiastical History* 14, no. 1 (1963): 46–67. Møller traces the distinctives of the covenant scheme in Britain as early as the prologue to William Tyndale's 1534 edition of the New Testament.

17 John Lumsden, *The Covenants of Scotland* (Paisley, UK: Gardner, 1914).

18 See, on this, James B. Torrance, "Covenant or Contract?: A Study of the Theological Background of Worship in Seventeenth-Century Scotland," *Scottish Journal of Theology* 23, no. 1 (1970): 51–76, and "The Covenant Concept in Scottish Theology and Politics and Its Legacy," *Scottish Journal of Theology* 34, no. 3 (1981): 225–43.

19 Eichrodt, *Theology of the Old Testament,* 1:38.

20 Cited in Møller, "The Beginnings of Puritan Covenant Theology," 53.

21 John Preston, cited in Miller, *The New England Mind,* 389.

22 Miller, *The New England Mind,* 389.

23 See, e.g., Robert S. Paul, *The Assembly of the Lord: Politics and Religion in the Westminster Assembly and the "Grand Debate"* (Edinburgh: T&T Clark, 1985), 82: "The religious situation of the country provided a very plausible excuse for debating the Church of England's doctrinal standards, for challenging the errors that had infiltrated through the Arminian opinions of Laudian divines, and for refuting the Pelagianism that Calvinists discovered under the covers of every prayer book. On the other side there were the equally horrendous heresies among the sectarians."

24 Miller, *The New England Mind,* 368.

25 "The condition is faith, but covenant faith has in the law a way prescribed for it to walk in, and faith as the fulfilment of a covenant obliges the believer so to walk, whereas unsophisticated piety naively supposes that faith in itself is adequate for salvation regardless of how it walks." Miller, *The New England Mind,* 385.

26 Samuel Rutherford, *Christ Dying and Drawing Sinners to Himself, or, A Survey of Our Saviour in His Soule-suffering, His Lovelynesse in His Death, and the Efficacie Thereof* (London, 1647).

27 Rutherford, *Christ Dying*, 78. My italics. Thomas F. Torrance appears to read this passage incorrectly when, citing what is actually a quotation from Saltmarsh that Rutherford subsequently rejects, he presents it as Rutherford's own view. See Torrance, *Scottish Theology from John Knox to John McLeod Campbell* (Edinburgh: T&T Clark, 1996), 100.

28 Rutherford, *Christ Dying*, 79.

29 Rutherford, *Christ Dying*, 418.

30 Rutherford, *Christ Dying*, 262–63.

31 Notably Edward Fisher, whose *The Marrow of Moderne Divinity* (London, 1645) offers an alternative emphasis to that of Rutherford yet still espouses the covenant scheme. So, for example, "in this covenant there is not any condition or law to be performed on man's part by himself. No: there is no more for him to do, but only to know and believe that Christ hath done all for him. . . . And so shall you obtain forgiveness of sins, righteousness and eternal happiness, not as an agent but as a patient, not by doing but by receiving" (111).

32 See chap. 5.

33 Fisher, *The Marrow of Moderne Divinity*, 137.

34 Rutherford, *Christ Dying*, 258. Cf. Fisher, *The Marrow of Moderne Divinity*, 126–27.

35 Fisher, *The Marrow of Moderne Divinity*, 123. Cf. Rutherford, *Christ Dying*, 250.

36 A use of logic intended to relate assurance of salvation constructively to the external evidences of it in a believer's life. For instance:

> Good works are an evidence of genuine faith.
> I can identify good works in my life.
> Therefore, I am among those having genuine faith.

Eight: Sanctification

1 P. T. Forsyth, *Positive Preaching and the Modern Mind*, 3rd ed. (London: Independent Press, 1949), 193.

2 See, e.g., P. T. Forsyth, *The Old Faith and the New* (Leicester, UK: Midland Educational Company), 25.

3 P. T. Forsyth, "The Cross as the Final Seat of Authority" (1899), in Marvin W. Anderson, ed., *The Gospel and Authority: A P. T. Forsyth Reader* (Minneapolis: Augsburg, 1971), 165.

4 Forsyth, *Positive Preaching*, 48.

5 P. T. Forsyth, "Christ's Person and His Cross," *Methodist Review* 66 (January 1917): 15.

6 P. T. Forsyth, *The Cruciality of the Cross*, Expositor's Library (London and New York: Hodder and Stoughton, 1909), 121.

7 Forsyth, *The Cruciality of the Cross*, 121.

8 Forsyth, *The Cruciality of the Cross*, 119.

9 Forsyth, *Positive Preaching*, 207–8.

10 Cf. P. T. Forsyth, *The Church, the Gospel and Society* (London: Independent Press, 1962), 19.

11 Forsyth, *The Cruciality of the Cross*, 116.

12 Forsyth, "Christ's Person and His Cross," 8.

13 P. T. Forsyth, *The Preaching of Jesus and the Gospel of Christ* (Blackwood, Australia: New Creation, 1987; originally published as articles in the *Expositor*, 1915), 88.

14 Forsyth, "Christ's Person and His Cross," 8; cf. P. T. Forsyth, *The Work of Christ*, Expositor's Library (London and New York: Hodder and Stoughton, 1910), 166.

15 P. T. Forsyth, contribution to *The Atonement in Modern Religious Thought: A Theological Symposium* (London: James Clarke, 1900), 86.

16 Forsyth, *The Preaching of Jesus*, 209.

17 Forsyth, *The Preaching of Jesus*, 240.

18 See P. T. Forsyth, "The Preaching of Jesus and the Gospel of Christ: The Meaning of a Sinless Christ," *Expositor*, 8th ser., 25 (1923): 298.

19 Forsyth, "The Preaching of Jesus and the Gospel of Christ," 299.

20 See P. T. Forsyth, *The Justification of God: Lectures for War-time on a Christian Theodicy* (London: Duckworth, 1916), 3.

21 P. T. Forsyth, *God the Holy Father* (London: Independent Press, 1957), 5.

22 Forsyth, "The Cross as the Final Seat of Authority," in Anderson, *The Gospel and Authority*, 152.

23 Forsyth, "The Cross as the Final Seat of Authority," in Anderson, *The Gospel and Authority*, 152.

24 Forsyth, *The Work of Christ*, 10.

25 Forsyth, *The Church, the Gospel and Society*, 100.

26 Forsyth, *The Church, the Gospel and Society*, 102.

27 Forsyth, *The Preaching of Jesus*, 234.

28 Forsyth, *The Church, the Gospel and Society*, 115.

29 See, e.g., Forsyth, *The Preaching of Jesus*, 45.

30 See, e.g., Forsyth, *God the Holy Father*, 10.

31 Forsyth, "The Preaching of Jesus and the Gospel of Christ," 298–99.

32 Forsyth, "Christ's Person and His Cross," 8.

33 See, e.g., Forsyth, *The Work of Christ*, 122.

34 Forsyth, *The Work of Christ*, 123.

35 Forsyth, *The Cruciality of the Cross*, 131.

36 Forsyth, *The Cruciality of the Cross*, 32.

37 Forsyth, "The Cross as the Final Seat of Authority," in Anderson, *The Gospel and Authority*, 173.

38 Forsyth, *The Work of Christ*, 28.

39 Forsyth, *The Work of Christ*, 23.

40 Forsyth, *The Justification of God*, 80.

41 Forsyth, *The Justification of God*, 77.

42 Forsyth, *The Work of Christ*, 18.

43 Forsyth, *The Old Faith and the New*, 17.

44 So, e.g., Forsyth, *The Church, the Gospel and Society*, 10.

45 Forsyth, *The Church, the Gospel and Society*, 12, 21.

46 Forsyth, *The Justification of God*, 156.

47 See Forsyth, *The Work of Christ*, 77.

48 Forsyth, *The Cruciality of the Cross*, 111, 204.

49 F. H. Bradley, *Ethical Studies*, 2nd rev. ed. (Oxford: Clarendon, 1962 [1876]), 28.

50 Forsyth acknowledged his debt to Kant in this regard in a short article in *The Christian World*, September 24, 1908: "In respect of the place of law ... if Hooker was my first teacher ... my second was Burke, ... But my greatest was the father of modern thought—Kant. ... I will add that to my mind the thing most needful in our theological education, after a knowledge of the Bible, is that each student should be examined in Kant, 'the philosopher of Protestantism,' before he begins the study of theology at the plastic time when mind is made or not at all."

51 Forsyth, *The Preaching of Jesus*, 243.

52 Forsyth, in *The Atonement in Modern Religious Thought*, 66.

53 Forsyth, *God the Holy Father*, 9–10.

54 Forsyth, "The Preaching of Jesus and the Gospel of Christ," 298.

55 Forsyth, in *The Atonement in Modern Religious Thought*, 66.

56 Forsyth, *The Preaching of Jesus*, 118.

57 Forsyth, *The Preaching of Jesus*, 213.

58 Forsyth, *The Preaching of Jesus*, 213.

59 E.g., Forsyth, *The Justification of God*, 136.

60 Forsyth, "The Cross of Christ as the Moral Principle of Society," *Methodist Review* 99 (January 1917): 11.

61 Forsyth, *The Justification of God*, 130, 171; *The Work of Christ*, 160–61.

62 Forsyth, *God the Holy Father*, 8.

63 Forsyth, in *The Atonement in Modern Religious Thought*, 79.

64 Forsyth, *The Justification of God*, 152.

65 Forsyth, *The Old Faith and the New*, appendix, ii.

66 Forsyth, *The Old Faith and the New*, 17.

67 Forsyth, *The Church, the Gospel and Society*, 12.

68 See Paul S. Fiddes, *Past Event and Present Salvation: The Christian Idea of Atonement* (London: Darton, Longman & Todd, 1989), chapters 2 and 5.

69 Forsyth, *Missions in State and Church: Sermons and Addresses* (London: Hodder and Stoughton, 1908), 72.

70 Forsyth, *Missions in State and Church*, 73.

71 Forsyth, *The Cruciality of the Cross*, 203.

72 Forsyth, *The Cruciality of the Cross*, 205.

73 Cf. Forsyth, *The Work of Christ*, 162–63.

74 Forsyth, in *The Atonement in Modern Religious Thought*, 84.

75 Forsyth, in *The Atonement in Modern Religious Thought*, 85, 68.

76 Forsyth, "The Preaching of Jesus and the Gospel of Christ," 301.

77 Forsyth, *God the Holy Father*, 25–26. Cf. Forsyth, in *The Atonement in Modern Religious Thought*, 64: "The Son could not suffer without the Father suffering."

78 Cf. Forsyth, *The Work of Christ*, 204, 205.

79 Forsyth, *Missions in State and Church*, 52.

80 Forsyth, *The Work of Christ*, 126; cf. *The Church, the Gospel and Society*, 82.

81 Forsyth, *The Justification of God*, 172.

82 Cf. Forsyth, in *The Atonement in Modern Religious Thought*, 67.

83 Forsyth, *The Cruciality of the Cross*, 181.

84 Forsyth, *The Work of Christ*, 157.

85 Forsyth, *The Cruciality of the Cross*, 116.

86 Forsyth, *The Old Faith and the New*, appendix, iv.

87 Forsyth, "The Preaching of Jesus and the Gospel of Christ," 299.

88 Forsyth, *The Old Faith and the New*, 14.

89 Forsyth, "The Preaching of Jesus and the Gospel of Christ," 298

90 Forsyth, *The Work of Christ*, 195.

91 Forsyth, *The Work of Christ*, 192

92 Forsyth, *The Work of Christ*, 226.

93 Forsyth, *The Work of Christ*, 195.

94 Forsyth, *The Work of Christ*, 130.

95 Forsyth, *The Justification of God*, 125.

96 Forsyth, *The Justification of God*, 169–70.

Nine: Revelation

1 D. M. Baillie, *God Was in Christ: An Essay on Incarnation and Atonement* (London: Faber and Faber, and New York: Scribners, 1948).

2 This is my, rather than Baillie's own, way of describing it.

3 Baillie, *God Was in Christ*, 28.

4 Baillie, *God Was in Christ*, 54.

5 See Baillie, *God Was in Christ*, esp., e.g., 17–18, 36–37, 48–50, 53.

6 Baillie, *God Was in Christ*, 53.

7 R. H. Roberts, "Karl Barth's Doctrine of Time: Its Nature and Implications," in S. W. Sykes, ed., *Karl Barth: Studies of His Theological Method* (Oxford: Clarendon, 1979), 88–146.

8 Roberts, "Karl Barth's Doctrine of Time," 144, 145.

9 Graham Ward, *Barth, Derrida and the Language of Theology* (Cambridge: Cambridge University Press, 1995), esp. chap. 11.

10 Baillie, *God Was in Christ*, 20.

11 See S. W. Sykes, "The Theology of the Humanity of Christ," in *Christ, Faith and History: Cambridge Studies in Christology*, ed. S. W. Sykes and J. P. Clayton (Cambridge: Cambridge University Press, 1972), 53–72.

12 Karl Barth, *The Göttingen Dogmatics: Instruction in the Christian Religion*, vol. 1, ed. Hannelotte Reiffen, trans. Geoffrey W. Bromiley (Grand Rapids: Eerdmans, 1991), 136; *Unterricht in der christlichen Religion*, vol. 1, ed. Hannelotte Reiffen (Zurich: Theologischer Verlag, 1985), 166.

13 Barth, *Church Dogmatics*, 1/2:750, 839.

14 Barth, *Church Dogmatics*, 1/1:214, 224.

15 See, e.g., Barth, *Church Dogmatics*, 1/2:29.

16 Barth, *Church Dogmatics*, 1/2:238, 246.

17 Barth, *Göttingen Dogmatics*, 1:144; *Unterricht in der christlichen Religion*, 1:177.

18 Barth, *Church Dogmatics*, 1/2:29.

19 Barth, *Church Dogmatics*, 1/1:158.

20 Barth, *Göttingen Dogmatics*, 1:444.

21 Barth, *Göttingen Dogmatics*, 1:366; *Unterricht in der christlichen Religion*, vol. 2 (Zurich, 1990), 66.

22 Barth, *Göttingen Dogmatics*, 1:151.

23 See, e.g., Barth, preface to the second edition, in *The Epistle to the Romans*, trans. Edwyn C. Hoskyns (Oxford: Oxford University Press, 1933), 10–11.

24 Barth, *Church Dogmatics*, 1/2:31.

25 Barth, *Göttingen Dogmatics*, 1:359.

26 Barth, *Göttingen Dogmatics*, 1:329.

27 Barth, *Göttingen Dogmatics*, 1:136; *Unterricht in der christlichen Religion*, 1:166.

28 For a discussion of the earlier writings, see Bruce L. McCormack, *Karl Barth's Critically Realistic Dialectical Theology: Its Genesis and Development, 1909–1936* (Oxford: Clarendon, 1995), esp. 130–31 and 207–8.

29 Rowan Williams, "'Person' and 'Personality' in Christology," *Downside Review* 94, no. 317 (1976): 255.

30 Barth, *Church Dogmatics*, 1/1:133.

31 Barth, *Göttingen Dogmatics*, 1:168; *Church Dogmatics*, 1/2:204.

32 Barth, *Church Dogmatics*, 1/1:166.

33 See, on this, Richard Harries, *Art and the Beauty of God: A Christian Understanding* (London: Mowbray, 1993), 6–7.

34 Barth, *Unterricht in der christlichen Religion*, 1:110; cf. *Göttingen Dogmatics*, 1:91.

35 Barth, *Church Dogmatics*, 1/2:17.

36 Barth, *Göttingen Dogmatics*, 1:192–93.

37 Barth, *Church Dogmatics*, 1/2:155–56.

38 This criticism is made and substantiated by Alan J. Torrance in *Persons in Communion: An Essay on Trinitarian Description and Human Participation, with Special Reference to Volume One of Karl Barth's* Church Dogmatics (Edinburgh: T&T Clark, 1996), 100–119.

39 Barth, *Church Dogmatics*, 1/1:242.

40 Barth, *Göttingen Dogmatics*, 1:374.

41 Barth, *Church Dogmatics*, 1/1:216.

Ten: Filiation

1 See chaps. 1–4. For an account of the doctrine's place in a classic Western source, see Gerald Bonner, "Augustine's Conception of Deification," *Journal of Theological Studies*, New Series, 37, no. 2 (1986): 369–86. Modern advocates of the theme in East and West respectively include the Russian Orthodox Vladimir Lossky and the Anglo-Catholic theologian Eric Mascall. See Vladimir Lossky, *The Mystical Theology of the Eastern Church*, trans. the Fellowship of St. Alban and St. Sergius (London: James Clarke, 1957), 67–90, and *In the Image and Likeness of God*, ed. John H. Erickson and Thomas E. Bird (Crestwood, N.Y.: St. Vladimir's Seminary Press, 1974), 97–110. For Mascall's account, see, e.g., E. L. Mascall, *Christ, the Christian and the Church: A Study of the Incarnation and Its Consequences* (London: Longmans, Green, 1946), 97ff., and *Via Media: An Essay in Theological Synthesis* (London: Longmans, Green, 1956), 121–65.

2 See, e.g., Thomas F. Torrance, *Theology in Reconstruction* (London: SCM, 1965), 243. Torrance expresses a preference for *theopoiesis* over *theosis*, since its accommodation of the verb *poieo* keeps clear the creaturely nature of the verb's object as well as the full deity of its subject.

3 In what follows I have deliberately restricted my consideration to a handful of core sources in order to make the task of the reader wishing to pursue matters further a manageable one.

4 Torrance, *The Mediation of Christ*, 2nd ed. (Edinburgh: T&T Clark, 1992), 64.

5 See, e.g., Torrance, *Theology in Reconstruction*, 132.

6 See, e.g., Torrance, *The Mediation of Christ*, 40; Torrance, "Karl Barth and the Latin Heresy," *Scottish Journal of Theology* 39, no. 4 (1986): 473–74.

7 For a discussion of examples, see, e.g., Fiddes, *Past Event and Present Salvation*.

8 See, for instance, the discussion of this difference in Hans Küng, *Justification: The Doctrine of Karl Barth and a Catholic Reflection* (London: Burns and Oates, 1966).

9 See, e.g., Torrance, *The Mediation of Christ*, 10ff.

10 For the relevant distinction, see Michael Polanyi, *Personal Knowledge: Towards a Post-Critical Philosophy* (London: Routledge and Kegan Paul, and Chicago: University of Chicago Press, 1958).

11 See, e.g., Torrance, *Theology in Reconstruction*, 249: "It is through the same Spirit who came down at Pentecost that we are united to Christ in his identification with us, and joined to him in his self-consecration and self-offering for us once and for all on earth and eternally prevalent in heaven. . . . The Spirit which Christ breathes upon us then becomes the Spirit of our response to him and through him to the Father."

12 Torrance, *The Mediation of Christ*, 54.

13 Torrance, *The Mediation of Christ*, 24–25.

14 Torrance, *Theology in Reconstruction*, 132–33.

15 Torrance, *The Mediation of Christ*, 26.

16 See, e.g., his essay "Justification: Its Radical Nature and Place in Reformed Doctrine and Life," in Torrance, *Theology in Reconstruction*, 150–68. On the specific question of the relationship between his thought and Catholic theology see, e.g., his essay "The Roman Doctrine of Grace from the Point of View of Reformed Theology," in Torrance, *Theology in Reconstruction*, 169–91.

17 See, e.g., Torrance, *Theology in Reconstruction*, 132–33.

18 See esp. the essay "The Mind of Christ in Worship: The Problem of Apollinarianism in the Liturgy," in Torrance, *Theology in Reconciliation*, 139–214.

19 Torrance, *The Mediation of Christ*, 56.

20 Torrance, *The Mediation of Christ*, 65.

21 See Torrance, *The Trinitarian Faith*, 154ff.

22 Torrance, "Karl Barth and the Latin Heresy," 474.

23 Torrance, "Karl Barth and the Latin Heresy," 475.

24 See, e.g., Torrance, "Karl Barth and the Latin Heresy," 476–77.

25 Torrance, *The Mediation of Christ*, 29.

26 See, e.g., Torrance, *Theology in Reconciliation*, 136; cf. Torrance, *The Mediation of Christ*, 94.

27 On the supposed influence of philosophical ideas on "mystical" and "metaphysical" notions of redemption in the patristic East, see, e.g., H. E. W. Turner, *The Patristic Doctrine of Redemption: A Study of the Development of Doctrine During the First Five Centuries* (London: Mowbray, 1952). For appeals to "primitive" anthropological categories in making sense of biblical ideas of redemptive solidarity, see the classic study by H. Wheeler Robinson, *Corporate Personality in Ancient Israel*, rev. ed. (Edinburgh: T&T Clark, 1981).

28 Torrance, *Theology in Reconciliation*, 111.

29 "Thus our receiving of the Spirit is objectively grounded in and derives from the self-sanctification of Christ through his own Spirit, and is not a different receiving of the Spirit from his." Torrance, *Theology in Reconciliation*, 235.

30 "God is God and not man, and yet in the incarnation God has become man, this particular Man, Jesus Christ, without ceasing to be God." Torrance, *Theology in Reconciliation*, 130.

31 See, esp., the essay "Come Creator Spirit, for the Renewal of Worship and Witness," in Torrance, *Theology in Reconstruction*, 240–58.

32 "By *theosis* the Greek fathers wished to express the fact that in the new coming of the Holy Spirit we are up against God in the most absolute sense, God in his ultimate holiness or Godness." Torrance, *Theology in Reconstruction*, 243. See also *The Trinitarian Faith*, 191–251. On *Ad Serapionem*, see Torrance, *Theology in Reconciliation*, 231–32.

33 Torrance, *Theology in Reconstruction*, 241.

34 For a classic example, see Adolf von Harnack, *What Is Christianity?* 2nd ed. (London: Williams and Norgate, and New York: Putnam, 1901).

35 See Torrance, *The Trinitarian Faith*, 189.

Eleven: Impeccability

1 H. P. Owen, "The Sinlessness of Jesus," in *Religion, Reason, and the Self: Essays in Honour of Hywel D. Lewis*, ed. Stewart R. Sutherland and T. A. Roberts (Cardiff: University of Wales Press, 1989).

2 See Sykes, "The Theology of the Humanity of Christ," 56–57.

3 L. W. Grensted, *The Person of Christ* (London: Nisbet, 1933), 274.

4 Sykes, "The Theology of the Humanity of Christ," 61.

5 P. T. Forsyth, *The Person and Place of Jesus Christ* (London: Hodder and Stoughton, 1909).

6 Forsyth, *The Person and Place of Jesus Christ*, 301.

7 See William Sanday, *Christologies Ancient and Modern* (Oxford: Clarendon, 1910), chaps. 6 and 7.

8 See, further, J. L. Mackie, *Ethics: Inventing Right and Wrong* (London: Penguin, 1977), chap. 9: "Determinism, Responsibility, and Choice." See also Richard Swinburne, *Responsibility and Atonement* (Oxford: Clarendon, 1989), chap. 3: "The Relevance of Free Will." Mackie admits that certain elements in particular views of human freedom are incompatible with determinism as he understands it but argues that it is perfectly possible (and desirable) to construct a meaningful view of human morality and responsibility that omits these elements (see 225–26).

9 David Wiggins, "Towards a Reasonable Libertarianism," in *Essays on Freedom of Action*, ed. Ted Honderich (London: Routledge and Kegan Paul, 1973), 37.

10 Mackie, *Ethics*, 218–19.

11 On this, see, further, R. S. Downie and Elizabeth Telfer, *Respect for Persons* (London: Allen and Unwin, 1969), 97–98.

12 See Swinburne, *Responsibility and Atonement*, 52. Cf. the judgment of Wiggins that "compatibilist resolutions to the problem of freedom must wear an appearance of superficiality, however serious or deep the reflections from which they originate, until what they offer by way of freedom can be compared with something else, whether actual or possible or only seemingly imaginable, which is known to be the best that any indeterminist or libertarian could describe." "Towards a Reasonable Libertarianism," 33.

13 Swinburne, *Responsibility and Atonement*, 52.

14 Swinburne, *Responsibility and Atonement*, 51.

15 Swinburne, *Responsibility and Atonement*, 63.

16 See Downie and Telfer, *Respect for Persons*, 106.

17 Friedrich Nietzsche, *The Genealogy of Morals* 1:13, cited in Swinburne, *Responsibility and Atonement*, 63.

18 See Swinburne, *Responsibility and Atonement*, 63, n. 21, citing Nietzsche's *Thus Spake Zarathustra*.

19 Donald M. Baillie, "Philosophers and Theologians on the Freedom of the Will," in *The Theology of the Sacraments, and Other Papers*, ed. John Baillie (London: Faber and Faber, 1957), 128.

20 Baillie, "Philosophers and Theologians on the Freedom of the Will," 134.

21 See Mackie, *Ethics*, 224.

22 Downie and Telfer, *Respect for Persons*, 106.

23 Jean-Paul Sartre, "Itinerary of a Thought," *New Left Review* 58 (1969), cited in Wiggins, "Towards a Reasonable Libertarianism," 53.

24 Wiggins, "Towards a Reasonable Libertarianism," 53.

25 See George Hall, "D. M. Baillie: A Theology of Paradox," in *Christ, Church and Society: Essays on John Baillie and Donald Baillie*, ed. David Fergusson (Edinburgh: T&T Clark, 1993), 81. Baillie's treatment of the "paradox of grace" is to be found in chap. 5 of *God Was in Christ*.

26 See Forsyth, *The Person and Place of Jesus Christ*, 301–2.

27 I am grateful to Professor Paul Helm for his observation that, since in theory there might be supposed to be more than one "sinless" choice in a given set of moral circumstances, it is not *necessary* to embrace a strict philosophical determinism in order to affirm the doctrine of *non posse peccare*. Nonetheless, determinism in its compatibilist versions does claim to offer a coherent philosophical account of how every sinful choice was absolutely excluded from Christ's moral life while yet leaving the language of freedom and responsibility intact. Its attractions for those wishing to maintain the doctrine, therefore, would seem to be considerable.

Twelve: Universality

1 Robinson's autobiography was published under the title *The Roots of a Radical* (London: SCM, 1980). He had first coined the phrase (and owned the label) in

the title of a public talk broadcast by the BBC and published in *The Listener* in February 1963. See Eric James, *A Life of Bishop John A. T. Robinson: Scholar, Pastor, Prophet* (London: Collins, and Grand Rapids: Eerdmans, 1987), 113. I am indebted to this work for several factual details in what follows.

2 For a sensitive account of the whole *Lady Chatterley* affair, see James, *A Life of Bishop John A. T. Robinson*, 85–109.

3 Robinson was suffragan Bishop of Woolwich from 1959 to 1969. His involvement in the *Chatterley* trial earned Robinson a rebuke (both private and public) from the Archbishop of Canterbury Geoffrey Fisher, and Fisher's successor, Michael Ramsey, publicly distanced himself from *Honest to God*, referring to its argument as misleading and potentially damaging.

4 In the wake of the publication of *Honest to God*, Robinson appeared as a guest on the Saturday night TV current affairs show *That Was the Week That Was*.

5 John A. T. Robinson, "Universalism—Is It Heretical?" *Scottish Journal of Theology* 2, no. 2 (1949): 139, quoting Emil Brunner, *Dogmatik*, Band 1, 363. Robinson was aware that the doctrine may have been formally denounced as heretical by the fifth ecumenical council, but he was equally conscious of the acknowledgment in the twenty-first of the Church of England's Thirty-nine Articles of Religion that such councils "may err and sometimes have erred, even in things pertaining unto God," and therefore happy to weigh conciliar doctrine in the light of biblical exegesis.

6 According to Robinson's own recollection, his arguments on universalism had first been worked out in 1942 or 1943 while he was still an undergraduate at Cambridge. See John A. T. Robinson, *In the End, God . . . : A Study of the Christian Doctrine of the Last Things*, rev. ed. (London: Collins Fontana, 1968), 1.

7 T. F. Torrance, "Universalism or Election?" *Scottish Journal of Theology* 2, no. 3 (1949): 310–18.

8 John A. T. Robinson, "Universalism—A Reply," *Scottish Journal of Theology* 2, no. 4 (1949): 378–380.

9 Robinson, *In the End, God . . .*, 13.

10 The pun is Robinson's own, taken from the later edition of his book, though he insists it is "no mere verbal trick," since there remains a genuine connection between questions of divine teleology and what we believe about the import of the word "God" itself. See Robinson, *In the End, God. . .*, 3.

11 Robinson published an article in the London newspaper the *Evening Standard* on July 11, 1963 titled "South Bank Religion—What I'm Trying to Do." See James, *A Life of Bishop John A. T. Robinson*, 133.

12 Torrance, "Universalism or Election?" 310.

13 Torrance, "Universalism or Election?" 318.

14 It must not be forgotten that Torrance's response is to Robinson's case as made in the article, and not to the slightly more developed account in the book. For reviews of the latter, see, e.g., Alec Whitehouse in *Scottish Journal of Theology* 5 (1952): 313–16; Reginald Fuller, "Book Review: *In the End, God . . .*," *Theology* 54, no. 373 (1951): 269–70; and an editorial review in *The Expository Times* 62, no. 6 (1951): 161–62.

15 Alan Richardson, *Christian Apologetics* (London: SCM, 1947), 40–64. Richardson's account was heavily influenced by A. D. Ritchie, *Scientific Method* (London: Kegan Paul, and New York: Harcourt Brace, 1923), and the application of such thinking to theology in Leonard Hodgson, *Theology in an Age of Science* (Oxford: Clarendon, 1944).

16 Richardson, *Christian Apologetics*, 54. Cf. Robinson, *In the End, God...*, 25–26.

17 Richardson, *Christian Apologetics*, 58.

18 See Robinson, *In the End, God...*, 31.

19 Robinson, *In the End, God...*, 63.

20 Robinson, *In the End, God...*, 30.

21 Robinson, *In the End, God...*, 34.

22 Following the lead of Rudolf Bultmann's 1941 essay "Neues Testament und Mythologie" (which appeared in English for the first time in 1953, but Robinson had good German and was probably familiar with it), Robinson uses the term "myth" to describe such constructs, but his immediate comparison with "myths" deployed in science suggests that "model" or "hypothesis" might better fit the epistemic bill. His concern is with imaginative extrapolation on the basis of something known to be true to circumstances lying beyond the reach of experimental verification.

23 Robinson, *In the End, God...*, 31. In a footnote Robinson adds: "This 'must' ... is a scientific rather than a metaphysical necessity. The formulations of theology, here as elsewhere, are hypothetical rather than final.... They are hypotheses which require to be verified, and can be verified, objectively, by reference to the data to be explained."

24 Robinson, *In the End, God...*, 31.

25 Robinson, *In the End, God...*, 37–39.

26 Kierkegaard's notion of truth as subjectivity and Martin Buber's I-Thou (mediated through the theological personalism of his doctoral supervisor and mentor H. H. Farmer) both had a profound shaping impact on Robinson's early theological development. Chris Partridge notes that, for Farmer, too, an understanding of revelation as present encounter is nonetheless accompanied by an insistence on the indispensability and normative role of the Bible, since it is precisely through biblical witness to the events of salvation history that the living encounter with Christ arises and takes shape. See Christopher H. Partridge, *H. H. Farmer's Theological Interpretation of Religion: Towards a Personalist Theology of Religions* (Lewiston, N.Y.: E. Mellen, 1998), 45–51.

27 See Robinson, "Universalism—Is It Heretical?" 139–40; Robinson, *In the End, God...*, 99–101.

28 Robinson, *In the End, God...*, 99.

29 On the term "myth," see n. 22 above.

30 Robinson lists, inter alia, Rom 5:8, 8:19–21; 1 Cor 15:22, 24–28; Eph 1:10; Col 1:20; 1 Tim 2:4. The scale of his coverage does not permit him, nor does he deem it necessary, to engage in a detailed exegesis of these texts.

31 From other publications it is clear that Robinson considered some of the key passages to originate in the preaching of the church rather than the teaching of Jesus

himself, but he makes no convenient theological capital out of this, treating the passages in question in their final form. See, e.g., Robinson, "The 'Parable' of the Sheep and the Goats," *New Testament Studies* 2, no. 4 (1956): 225–37.

32 Robinson, *In the End, God...*, 100.

33 Torrance, "Universalism or Election?" 310.

34 Robinson, *In the End, God...*, 102. There is an irony (one which Robinson no doubt enjoyed!) in laying this charge back at the door of Torrance, who, together with Paul Althaus and Emil Brunner, he identifies as advocates of this view.

35 Robinson, *In the End, God...*, 102.

36 Robinson, *In the End, God...*, 105.

37 Torrance, "Universalism or Election?" 311.

38 See Robinson, "Universalism—Is It Heretical?" esp. 141.

39 Robinson, "Universalism—A Reply," 378.

40 Robinson, *In the End, God...*, 107.

41 Robinson, *In the End, God...*, 108.

42 "If universalism is true, is a necessity, then every road whether it had the Cross planted on it or not would lead to salvation." Torrance, "Universalism or Election?" 312. This is true of those versions of universalism that secure it only by relativizing the particulars of the Christian story, but it hardly applies to Robinson's argument, predicated as it is precisely on the conviction that God has planted the cross on every "road" as an objective fact to which all must respond. See, further, Trevor Hart, "Universalism: Two Distinct Types," in *Universalism and the Doctrine of Hell*, ed. Nigel M. de S. Cameron (Carlisle, UK: Paternoster, and Grand Rapids: Baker, 1992).

43 See n. 26 above.

44 See, e.g., Robinson, "Universalism—Is It Heretical?" 152. Cf. the discussion of divine justification, election, and regeneration in Friedrich Schleiermacher, *The Christian Faith*, trans. H. R. Mackintosh from the 2nd German ed. (Edinburgh: T&T Clark, 1928), 496–505, 532–60.

45 *Kierkegaard's Concluding Unscientific Postscript*, trans. David F. Swenson (Princeton, N.J.: Princeton University Press, 1941), 221. See Robinson, *In the End, God...*, 109.

46 This emphasis on subjectivity does not occlude or undermine what Robinson has already said, of course, about the thoroughly objective nature of God's logically prior redemptive work in Christ. His point is simply that the objective moment in redemption (accomplished for all) must finally be fulfilled in a "subjective" moment in which God is equally involved and which embraces each in their turn. On the wider treatment of "truth as subjectivity" in Kierkegaard, see, briefly and helpfully, Patrick L. Gardiner, *Kierkegaard* (Oxford: Oxford University Press, 1988), 66–100.

47 Robinson, "Universalism—A Reply," 379.

48 Cf. the sort of imaginative remodeling undertaken by Jeremy Begbie, drawing on insights from the world of music and suggesting, for example, that our thinking about the incarnation and the co-inherence of two discrete "natures" might benefit from an articulation in the categories of aural rather than visual space since,

in the former, two or more tones naturally overlap and indwell one another and, far from trespassing on or compromising the integrity of either, the outcome is an enhancement of each. See, e.g., Jeremy Begbie, ed., *Beholding the Glory: Incarnation through the Arts* (Grand Rapids: Baker, 2000), 138–54. The point of this sort of appeal is not, of course, to ground or demonstrate the truth of doctrine, but to suggest an alternative conceptuality or "logic" in terms of which it might be explored, and which might render some of its distinctive claims less baffling or contradictory than they have sometimes appeared. Elsewhere, Begbie has pursued the same imaginative approach further and with more significant heuristic (as distinct from primarily illustrative) force, engaging deep-rooted issues of divine and creaturely temporality. See Jeremy Begbie, *Theology, Music, and Time* (Cambridge and New York: Cambridge University Press, 2000).

49 Robinson, *In the End, God...*, 110.

50 "As for my use of analogy I base nothing on it at all. . . . The only use I make of human analogy is not to establish this position, but to try and show that it is not in fact so utterly contradictory as it sounds. . . . But if the analogies do not help, scrap them: nothing rests on them." Robinson, "Universalism—A Reply," 379.

51 Torrance, "Universalism or Election?" 312.

52 Partridge notes how, for theological "personalists" such as Farmer (who was, we recall, Robinson's doctoral supervisor in Cambridge), the "world of persons" constitutes in effect a relational continuum embracing "God, the neighbour and the self," so that discussion of God as personal can and must properly begin with our experience of human personhood, since this is already meshed securely into "the ultimate nature of reality." See Partridge, *H. H. Farmer's Theological Interpretation of Religion*, 6–11.

53 "How these two realities can be held together without lessening the seriousness of either may," Robinson acknowledges, "be beyond our imagination, as it certainly is beyond our logic." Robinson, "Universalism—A Reply," 380. His contention, though, is that in fact it is *not*: we *can* imagine a state of affairs in which the relevant juxtaposition makes good sense. He claims no more, but no less, than that.

54 Torrance, "Universalism or Election?" 312.

55 See Robinson, "Universalism—Is It Heretical?" 152. Cf. Robinson, *In the End, God...*, 115.

56 Baillie, *God Was in Christ*, 114–18. Robinson makes no reference to Baillie's thought, though it is possible that he was familiar with it. The theme of paradox, and the importance of faith holding together the terms of apparent antinomies while struggling imaginatively for "fuller light and deeper experience" which renders the antinomies "less acute," had already been aired in the last of Baillie's 1926 Kerr Lectures. See Baillie, *Faith in God and Its Christian Consummation*, Kerr Lectures (Edinburgh: T&T Clark, 1964), 300–308. And while his appeal to the "paradox of grace" was subsequently criticized as an attempt, in effect, to found the doctrine of the incarnation on a feature of shared Christian experience (thereby robbing it of its uniqueness), a closer reading of his argument suggests that he may have been intending an exercise of precisely the same sort as Robinson's, viz., a way of remodeling some of the "paradoxical" claims of that doctrine in terms of certain

finite and familiar realities, demonstrating that sense can at least be made of them. That he intended to "explain" the incarnation by means of the model seems wholly unlikely. See, further, McIntyre, "The Christology of Donald Baillie in Perspective," in Fergusson, *Christ, Church and Society*, 102–11.

57 This is, he insists by way of deference to his chosen intellectual lights, Kierkegaard and Buber, precisely an instance of "truth as subjectivity" that can only be known in the breach of an I-Thou encounter. Robinson, *In the End, God. . .*, 114.

58 Torrance, "Universalism or Election?" 312.

59 According to Augustine, *Enchiridion* 98, God can indeed "change the evil wills of human beings, whichever, whenever, and wheresoever he chooses, and direct them to what is good." Cited in George Hunsinger, *Disruptive Grace: Studies in the Theology of Karl Barth* (Grand Rapids: Eerdmans, 2000), 249.

60 Robinson, *In the End, God. . .*, 117–18.

61 Cf. Barth's discussion of chaos (*tohu wa-bohu*) and ungodliness as that which, in his primordial creative purpose and act, God has "not-chosen," and the "reality" of which (available for the foolish creature to choose) is wholly contingent on and related to its deliberate and gracious exclusion from his positive purpose. Karl Barth, *Church Dogmatics*, vol. 3, *The Doctrine of Creation*, part 1, ed. G. W. Bromiley and T. F. Torrance, trans. G. W. Bromiley et al. (Edinburgh: T&T Clark, 1957), 101–9.

62 Robinson, *In the End, God. . .*, 120.

63 Robinson, *In the End, God. . .*, 118.

64 Robinson, *In the End, God. . .*, 119.

65 Robinson, *In the End, God. . .*, 122.

66 Robinson, *In the End, God. . .*, 122

67 See Torrance, *The Mediation of Christ*, 59.

68 See n. 26 above.

69 Cf. Richard J. Bauckham and Trevor Hart, *Hope against Hope: Christian Eschatology in Contemporary Context* (London: Darton, Longman and Todd, and Grand Rapids: Eerdmans, 1999), chap. 4.

70 Cf. Hunsinger, *Disruptive Grace*, 237.

71 Fuller, "Book Review: *In the End, God. . .*," 270.

72 Robinson, *In the End, God. . .*, 111. Hunsinger is correct to point to this shortfall but overstates the case considerably when he suggests that "sin is an idea . . . conspicuous mostly by its absence" from Robinson's argument and his God "nothing if not meek and mild." See Hunsinger, *Disruptive Grace*, 238. Cf., e.g., Robinson, *In the End, God. . .*, 80–81, 104.

73 See, e.g., Robinson, *In the End, God. . .*, 58. Cf., though, his criticism of notions of "immortality" and "survival" on precisely this score. *In the End, God. . .*, 80.

74 Robinson, *In the End, God. . .*, 80.

75 See Hunsinger, *Disruptive Grace*, 242–49.

76 Robinson, *In the End, God. . .*, 123.

77 Robinson, *In the End, God. . .*, 123.

Thirteen: Particularity

1 This chapter first appeared as a contribution to a Festschrift for Richard Bauckham.

2 Richard Bauckham, "Christology Today," *Scriptura* 27 (1988): 20–28.

3 The careful use of the category of "identity" in discussions of Christology in preference both to the classical language of "substance" and "persons" and to the long-established distinction typically drawn between "ontological" and "functional" Christologies by New Testament scholars is one of the distinctives of Bauckham's work over the period since the 1980s. It has successfully recast the terms in which christological questions may helpfully be asked and answered, and opened up new possibilities for serious conversation between biblical and systematic theology, not least by contradicting the assumption that "high" dogmatic Christology was something that only eventually emerged (legitimately or otherwise) from a "low" biblical starting point. While the immediate concerns of the earlier piece are different ones ("to bring together constructively . . . a concern about the meaning of the doctrine of the incarnation . . . and a concern to put the praxis of the historical Jesus back at the centre of Christology"), the categorical precursor to such use is already to be found in its central thesis that, in Jesus' identification of himself with the Father's will and his concrete identification with the plight of other people, God "identifies himself in identifying with us." Bauckham, "Christology Today," 20, 25.

4 Gunton, *The One, the Three and the Many*, 17.

5 Gunton, *The One, the Three and the Many*, 46.

6 Gunton, *The One, the Three and the Many*, 21.

7 See Jürgen Moltmann, "The Knowing of the Other and the Community of the Different," in his *God for a Secular Society: The Public Relevance of Theology* (Minneapolis: Fortress, 1999), 135–52. Bauckham's engagement with Moltmann's work over several decades makes the latter a particularly appropriate resource to draw on at this point.

8 As Paul Ricoeur observes in his 1991 Gifford Lectures, the phenomenology of everyday experience suggests that each of us actually encounters "otherness" *within ourselves* too, a point drawn attention to by habits of speech in which, without any apparent sense of risk, we straddle ourselves awkwardly in syntax between grammatical subject and object—in such phrases as "I look after myself," "She caught herself staring at him," and so on. French, Ricoeur reminds us, admits this internal opposition more consistently through its widespread use of pronominal verbs (conjugated by prefixing the reflexive noun *se* to the infinitive form—*Elle se promené, Tu te baigne, Nous nous habillons*, etc.). Paul Ricoeur, *Oneself as Another*, trans. Kathleen Blamey (Chicago: University of Chicago Press, 1992). Ricoeur's discussion of the nature of personal identity in this work, his development of the distinction between *idem*- and *ipse*- identity, and of categories as "identification as" and "identification with," seems likely to have fed constructively into Bauckham's own distinctive appropriation and development of the terms in his writings since the 1996 Didsbury Lectures, duly published as *God Crucified: Monotheism and Christology in the New Testament* (Carlisle, UK: Paternoster, and Grand Rapids: Eerdmans, 1998).

9 For a discussion of the nature of identity and the origins of contemporary concern with it, see, helpfully, Zygmunt Bauman, *Identity: Conversations with Benedetto Vecchi* (Cambridge, UK, and Malden, Mass.: Polity, 2004).

10 Moltmann, *God for a Secular Society*, 139.

11 Moltmann, *God for a Secular Society*, 140.

12 It might also be noted that such putative "shared" perspectives frequently end up looking very much like an assemblage of fundamental and particular convictions held by the dominant party or power group within the plural exchange, and thus amount in reality to a form of colonialism by stealth. Genuinely shared territories of meaning can only be established or identified when all the differences that divide are taken fully into consideration and allowed full play, and not despite these.

13 Moltmann, *God for a Secular Society*, 144.

14 Moltmann, *God for a Secular Society*, 145.

15 For a more developed consideration of the issues treated in this section, see Trevor Hart, "Conversation after Pentecost? Theological Musings on the Hermeneutic Motion," *Literature and Theology* 28, no. 2 (2014): 164–78.

16 For what follows, see esp. Daphne Hampson, *Theology and Feminism* (Oxford: Blackwell, 1990), 50–80.

17 Strictly speaking, therefore, it is specificity rather than maleness here that is the problem for Hampson. Though she does not say so, the drift and terms of her argument would have to apply equally had God become a woman.

18 Hampson, *Theology and Feminism*, 51.

19 Bauckham, "Christology Today," 22–23.

20 N.b., Hampson acknowledges that, for example, a similar case might be made by gentiles on the basis of Jesus' Jewishness. See Hampson, *Theology and Feminism*, 55.

21 Hampson, *Theology and Feminism*, 53–58.

22 It is clear, though, that Irenaeus continues to feel the force of the sort of problem Hampson poses; thus his rather awkward insistence that, in order to sanctify all people regardless of their age, the Son of God became an infant in order to sanctify infants, a child for children, a youth for youths, and "an old man for old men" (*Adv. Haer.* 2.22.4). Why particularity of age should be reckoned significant and other dimensions of human particularity (gender, race, etc.) not so is an avenue which that Irenaeus (perhaps wisely) leaves unexplored.

23 Although Hampson does not draw attention to the fact, most of the fathers place due weight on the events of Jesus' passion and resurrection, which, they insist, he endured and experienced "in our nature" and thus "for us." Some, following Irenaeus (and the New Testament), also place considerable weight on the importance of Jesus' obedience to the Father as displacing our disobedience in fashioning a "new humanity." These, though, tend to be addressed precisely as qualities of a shared human condition, empirical and promised. Other events in Jesus' history—particular things he did, conversations he had with others, ways in which he was treated by his friends and his enemies, his responses to those who encountered him, and so on (i.e., the very things of which, notwithstanding the weight

afforded to the passion narratives, the canonical Gospels largely consist)—tend to fall into the background of consideration for soteriological and christological purposes.

24 Significantly, suffering and death are, among those experiences available to humanity, some of those most resistant to postmodern skepticism about a "shared human condition." As Terry Eagleton notes, we all die, and "it is, to be sure, a consoling thought for pluralists that we meet our end in such a richly diverse series of ways, that our modes of exiting from existence are so splendidly heterogeneous, that there is no drearily essentialist 'death' but a diffuse range of cultural styles of expiring. . . . But we die anyway." Terry Eagleton, *Sweet Violence: The Idea of the Tragic* (Oxford: Blackwell, 2003), xiii.

25 Bauckham, "Christology Today," 24.

26 See, e.g., Torrance, *Theology in Reconstruction*, 20; Thomas F. Torrance, *Theological Science* (London: Oxford University Press, 1969), 20; and Thomas F. Torrance, *God and Rationality* (London: Oxford University Press, 1971), 23. For a full development of the point, see chap. 15 below.

27 Ludwig Feuerbach, *The Essence of Christianity* (*Das Wesen des Christentums*, 3rd ed., 1849), trans. George Eliot (London: Kegan Paul, Trench, Trübner, 1893).

28 Bauckham, "Christology Today," 26.

29 Bauckham, "Christology Today," 26.

30 Bauckham, "Christology Today," 25.

31 Bauckham, "Christology Today," 28.

32 Bauckham, "Christology Today," 21–22.

33 Bauckham, "Christology Today," 24.

34 Bauckham, "Christology Today," 21.

35 It is, of course, through an encounter with the Risen Christ that this occurs, but it occurs nonetheless through our engagement with the particulars of his human story, and not otherwise. See Bauckham, "Christology Today," 25.

36 See, e.g., John Hick, *God and the Universe of Faiths: Essays in the Philosophy of Religion* (London: Macmillan, 1973), chap. 9, and John Hick, ed., *The Myth of God Incarnate* (London: SCM, 1977), chap. 9.

37 See Vernon White, *Atonement and Incarnation: An Essay in Universalism and Particularity* (Cambridge: Cambridge University Press, 1991).

38 See, for example Jürgen Moltmann, *The Coming of God: Christian Eschatology,* trans. Margaret Kohl (London: SCM, 1996), 116–18.

39 For discussion of the issues, see Bauckham and Hart, *Hope against Hope*, chap. 4.

Fourteen: Availability

1 Ingolf U. Dalferth, *Becoming Present: An Inquiry into the Christian Sense of the Presence of God* (Leuven, Belgium, and Dudley, Mass.: Peeters, 2006), 33.

2 George Steiner, *Real Presences: Is There Anything in What We Say?* (London: Faber and Faber, 1989), 3.

3 Cf. Dalferth, *Becoming Present*, 51, and Steiner, *Real Presences*, 39.

4 In a related vein, Kant refers to the "wise adaptation" of our cognitive faculties to the demands of our "practical vocation" rather than to "that power of insight or enlightenment which we would like to possess." See Immanuel Kant, *Critique of*

Practical Reason, trans. Lewis White Beck (New York: Liberal Arts Press, 1956), §IX, 151–52. Cf. also John Baillie, *The Sense of the Presence of God*, Gifford Lectures (London: Oxford University Press, 1962), 162. Such considerations are, needless to say, hardly adequate by way of response in contexts where the sense of divine *absence* is one bound up inextricably with our suffering of life's horrors and terrors. Despite this, though, for wider purposes they are important to bear in mind.

5 Samuel Terrien, *The Elusive Presence: Toward a New Biblical Theology* (San Francisco: Harper and Row, 1978).

6 Terrien, *The Elusive Presence*, 27, 31.

7 Terrien, *The Elusive Presence*, 29.

8 Dalferth, *Becoming Present*, 50.

9 Cf. Moltmann's insistence that the experience of the Spirit's presence with us is always "historical" and "eschatological," viz., shaped by the flow of time, situated (consciously rather than merely de facto) "between remembered past and expected future." Jürgen Moltmann, *The Spirit of Life: A Universal Affirmation*, trans. Margaret Kohl (London: SCM, 1992), 17.

10 Dalferth, *Becoming Present*, 50.

11 For what follows see Steiner, *Real Presences*, esp. 39–42.

12 Steiner, *Real Presences*, 40.

13 Steiner, *Real Presences*, 40.

14 Steiner, *Real Presences*, 122.

15 Steiner, *Real Presences*, 122.

16 Steiner, *Real Presences*, 3–4 et passim.

17 Cf. Dalferth, *Becoming Present*, 55. For a helpful discussion of the different kinds of things there are "present" to us, and the different ways in which we are compelled (by what they are) to apprehend them, see Nicholas Lash, "On What Kinds of Things There Are," in *The Beginning and End of "Religion"* (Cambridge: Cambridge University Press, 1996), 93–111. See also Baillie, *The Sense of the Presence of God*, 41–59.

18 As Dalferth observes, "presence" is always a matter of relativity, i.e., of that which is present to (though not necessarily apprehended by) *someone* in a particular spatio-temporal situation. Dalferth, *Becoming Present*, 57.

19 Moltmann, *The Spirit of Life*, 39.

20 See H. H. Farmer, *The World and God: A Study of Prayer, Providence and Miracle in Christian Experience*, 2nd ed. (London: Nisbet, 1936), 15. Farmer borrows the term from F. R. Tennant, who uses it to refer to a mode of apprehension that, while anything but positivistic (again, we must learn to trust our apprehensions and to weigh them), is nonetheless distinct from that of logical inference. Hence, where our apprehension of nonmaterial realities is concerned, even though it is mostly mediated by (given in, with, and under) our experience of material things, it is nonetheless "immediate" in the relevant sense. According to Tennant, our apprehension of the reality ("presence") of other persons (i.e., as distinct from their bodily presentation) is of precisely this sort, and Farmer duly argues for something directly parallel in the case of our apprehension of the presence of God.

21 Dalferth notes that originally "presence" signified "a specific mode of co-existence, a special way of being together of one thing with another," viz., one involving the immediacy of an agent to the acts which he performs. Dalferth, *Becoming Present*, 57.

22 So, e.g., Baillie, *The Presence of God*, 33. The adequacy of so-called "presentism" (i.e., the view that the present is the only time that actually exists) is challenged by the absolute, decentered conceptions of modern physics, but it reflects well enough the patterns of our experience of temporality from the point of view of living. See the discussion in Dalferth, *Becoming Present*, 52ff. Cf. Richard Bauckham and Trevor Hart, "The Shape of Time," in *The Future as God's Gift: Explorations in Christian Eschatology*, ed. David Fergusson and Marcel Sarot (Edinburgh: T&T Clark, 1999).

23 Moltmann, *The Spirit of Life*, 39.

24 See Moltmann, *The Spirit of Life*, 148. In his helpful discussion of the notion of "tradition" in theology, Stephen Holmes argues on these grounds that being situated in a particular time and place (and thus heir to a very particular past) is precisely a creaturely good rather than a constraint from which we should aspire to free ourselves. See Stephen R. Holmes, *Listening to the Past: The Place of Tradition in Theology* (Grand Rapids: Baker Academic, 2002).

25 Dalferth, *Becoming Present*, 242. On theological construals of human life as a drama "performed" (consciously or otherwise) in the presence of God, see Trevor Hart, "The Sense of an Ending: Finitude and the Authentic Performance of Life," in *Faithful Performances: Enacting Christian Tradition*, ed. Steven R. Guthrie and Trevor Hart (Aldershot, UK: Ashgate, 2007), 167–98.

26 Thus, for instance, T. F. Torrance appeals to the Nicene theologians in support of his own insistence on "the transcendence of God over all space and time for [these] were produced along with His creation." *Space, Time and Incarnation* (London: Oxford University Press, 1969), 2. Cf. also Augustine, classically, *Confessions* 11, ET in Saint Augustine, *Confessions*, trans. Henry Chadwick (Oxford: Oxford University Press, 1991), and *City of God* 11.6, ET in Saint Augustine, *Concerning the City of God against the Pagans*, trans. Henry Bettenson (London: Penguin, 1984).

27 See, e.g., Dalferth, *Becoming Present*, 75. I do not wish here to raise questions about whether God might have his own uncreated "space" and "time" analogous to but utterly distinct from those which he has invested in creation. My concern is limited to the latter, and God's relation to them as the uncreated Creator. If the heavens "cannot contain him," it is not because God is too big (though this may be a helpful way of picturing the otherwise difficult-to-grasp idea) but because God is not spatially situated relative to the cosmos at all.

28 So, e.g., Torrance, *Space, Time and Incarnation*, 72. Cf. Farmer, *The World and God*, 102ff.

29 Thomas Aquinas, *Summa theologiae* 1a, q. 8, a. 1. ET from *Summa Theologiae*, vol. 2, ed. and trans. Timothy McDermott (London: Blackfriars, 1964).

30 Dalferth, *Becoming Present*, 39.

31 Dalferth, *Becoming Present*, 39. Cf. Aquinas: "God exists in everything . . . as an agent is present to that in which its action is taking place," *ST* 1a, q. 8, a. 1.

32 For what follows see Dalferth, *Becoming Present*, 152–55.

33 Italics original.

34 Aquinas, *ST* 1a, q. 8, a. 2. McDermott, *Summa Theologiae*, 2:115.

35 For what follows in this section, see Moltmann, *God in Creation: A New Theology of Creation and the Spirit of God*, trans. Margaret Kohl (London: SCM, 1985), 72–93.

36 Moltmann, *God in Creation*, 87. "He 'creates' the preconditions for the existence of his creation." Moltmann is paraphrasing the view of Scholem here, but he does so without demurral. The scare quotes suffice to indicate the ambiguity of the term's use. Cf. Gershom Scholem, "Schöpfung aus Nichts und Selbstverschränkung Gottes," *Eranos Jahrbuch* 25 (1956): 87–119. There is, of course, a long tradition of Jewish and Christian exegesis of Gen 1:2 that posits a "two-stage" creation, God first calling into being the *tohu wabohu* before displacing it with an ordered cosmos. So, e.g., Calvin: "The world was not perfected at its very commencement, in the manner in which it is now seen, but . . . was created an empty chaos." John Calvin, *Commentaries on the First Book of Moses Called Genesis*, vol. 1, trans. John King (Edinburgh, 1848), 70. Barth, meanwhile, interprets the *tohu wabohu* to signify imaginatively a state of affairs which God deliberately *excludes*, a creative option which, because it is hostile to his sovereign purpose, he does not choose, and thus does not permit to exist. See Karl Barth, *Church Dogmatics*, 3/1:102ff.

37 I.e., a circumstance in which God permits (by limiting himself) something essentially destructive (nonbeing or antibeing) to exist in his presence, and to threaten the survival of his creation from the first, thus arguably compromising the notion of creation as such as something essentially good, and relativizing the significance of the Fall. (It was for reasons such as these that Irenaeus, for example, rejected all suggestion that God could ever have created a "formless void" before creating the world itself. Such, he insisted, would be wholly unfitting of God.)

38 Thus "God's self-humiliation does not begin merely with creation, inasmuch as God commits himself to this world; it begins beforehand, and is the presupposition that makes creation possible." Moltmann, *God in Creation*, 88.

39 "*Creatio ex nihilo* in the beginning is the preparation and promise of the redeeming *annihilatio nihili*, from which the eternal being of creation proceeds. . . . So the resurrection and the kingdom of glory are the fulfillment of the promise which creation itself represents." Moltmann, *God in Creation*, 90.

40 Torrance, *Space, Time and Incarnation*, 78.

41 Torrance, *Space, Time and Incarnation*, 16.

42 Torrance, *Space, Time and Incarnation*, 13.

43 Calvin, *Commentary on Ephesians* 1.16–18. ET from *Galatians, Ephesians, Philippians and Colossians*, trans. Parker.

44 Moltmann, *The Spirit of Life*, 48.

45 Moltmann, *The Spirit of Life*, 48.

46 Moltmann, *The Spirit of Life*, 50.

47 See Dalferth, *Becoming Present*, 143–44.

48 Dalferth, *Becoming Present*, 50.

49 Dalferth, *Becoming Present*, 51.

50 Dalferth, *Becoming Present*, 52.

51 Farmer, *The World and God*, 243.

52 Farmer, *The World and God*, 100–101.

53 Farmer, *The World and God*, 243.

54 John 19:30: Ἰησους εἶπεν τετέλεσται, και . . . παρέδωκεν τὸ πνεῦμα.

55 Moltmann, *God in Creation*, 91.

56 On the essential ambiguity and dialectical nature of the *triduum* at the heart of the Easter narrative, see, authoritatively, Alan E. Lewis, *Between Cross and Resurrection: A Theology of Holy Saturday* (Grand Rapids: Eerdmans, 2001), passim.

57 Dalferth, *Becoming Present*, 36.

58 Cf. Dalferth, *Becoming Present*, 49.

59 Dalferth, *Becoming Present*, 220, 241.

60 Dalferth, *Becoming Present*, 130–32.

61 See David Brown, *God and Enchantment of Place: Reclaiming Human Experience* (Oxford: Oxford University Press, 2004); David Brown, *God and Grace of Body: Sacrament in Ordinary* (Oxford: Oxford University Press, 2007); and David Brown, *God and Mystery in Words: Experience through Metaphor and Drama* (Oxford: Oxford University Press, 2008).

62 Brown, *God and Enchantment of Place*, 8.

63 Brown, *God and Enchantment of Place*, 9.

64 Brown, *God and Enchantment of Place*, 33.

65 Rudolf Otto, *The Idea of the Holy: An Inquiry into the Non-rational Factor in the Idea of the Divine and Its Relation to the Rational*, trans. John W. Harvey (London: Oxford University Press, 1923)

66 Baillie, *The Presence of God*, 83–84.

67 For what follows, see, e.g., Farmer, *The World and God*, 39–67.

68 Farmer, *The World and God*, 81.

69 Farmer, *The World and God*, 79.

70 Farmer, *The World and God*, 73.

71 Farmer, *The World and God*, 71.

72 Farmer, *The World and God*, 88.

73 Farmer, *The World and God*, 88–89.

74 Farmer, *The World and God*, 88.

75 Dalferth, *Becoming Present*, 42.

76 Dalferth continues: "It is the former which determines the truth and appropriateness of the latter, and it is the latter which determines the mode and clarity of our sense of the presence of God . . . [and] the appropriateness of our apprehensions of God's presence." Dalferth, *Becoming Present*, 220. "Perspectives involve interpretation, and different perspectives different interpretations. Thus if we apprehend what we apprehend (feel, perceive, experience, believe etc.) with the horizon of the Christian doxastic practice, we apprehend it in a specific way and in a specific (re-) interpretation." Dalferth, *Becoming Present*, 226.

77 See Dalferth, *Becoming Present*, 130–32, 220, 226.

78 Hendrik Kraemer, *The Christian Message in a Non-Christian World* (New York: Harper, 1938), 125–26.

79 As Lesslie Newbigin notes, there is no particular reason to assume "that it is religion among all the activities of the human spirit which is the sphere of God's saving action." Newbigin, *The Open Secret*, 195. One might say the same about "morality," except insofar as it is shot through the texture of everything we do and suffer in the world. In this regard, theological reckonings with the wider spread of human experience (such as Brown's) seem to me to be welcome and an important advance on concentration on "theologies of religion."

80 Newbigin, *The Open Secret*, 73–101.

81 Dalferth, *Becoming Present*, 36.

Fifteen: Imagination

1 Undermining the dichotomy commonly supposed to exist between evidence-based and "rational" procedures on one hand and the spheres of operation of imagination on the other has been an important contribution of recent theory, reinforcing the observation made more than a century ago now by the Scots poet, novelist, and preacher George MacDonald, that imagination, far from needing to be rendered subservient to reason or even maintained in a perpetual critical dialectic with it, actually furnishes the logical and linguistic conditions under which alone reason may perform even its "coolest" tasks. See George MacDonald, *A Dish of Orts* (Whitehorn, Calif.: Johannesen, 1996), 11–15. (The relevant essay was first published in 1867.) Cf., e.g., Mark Johnson, *The Body in the Mind: The Bodily Basis of Meaning, Imagination, and Reason* (Chicago and London: University of Chicago Press, 1987), and George Lakoff and Mark Johnson, *Philosophy in the Flesh: The Embodied Mind and Its Challenge to Western Thought* (New York: Basic Books, 1999).

2 For a helpful discussion of the connection between these two strands of Lewis' literary output, see Michael Ward, "The Good Serves the Better and Both the Best: C. S. Lewis on Imagination and Reason in Apologetics," in *Imaginative Apologetics: Theology, Philosophy and the Catholic Tradition*, ed. Andrew Davison (London: SCM, 2011).

3 The key text is "Bluspels and Flalansferes," in C. S. Lewis, *Rehabilitations and Other Essays* (London: Oxford University Press, 1939), 135–58. Cf. Kant's discussion of the transcendental and empirical imagination in Immanuel Kant, *Critique of Pure Reason*, trans. Norman Kemp Smith (London: Macmillan, 1929), A115–30. Kant's concern is with the formation of the *Objekt* of knowledge in perception and its subsequent classification and retrieval, whereas Lewis concentrates specifically on the role of language in shaping and reshaping meaningful wholes for our indwelling. In other respects, though, their accounts are consonant.

4 Lewis, *Rehabilitations*, 157.

5 Nelson Goodman, *Languages of Art: An Approach to a Theory of Symbols* (London: Oxford University Press, 1969), 68.

6 See, on this, Richard Boyd, "Metaphor and Theory Change: What Is 'Metaphor' a Metaphor For?" in *Metaphor and Thought*, ed. Andrew Ortony (Cambridge: Cambridge University Press, 1993).

7 See, e.g., Johnson, *The Body in the Mind*, 98, 157 et passim, and Ricoeur, *The Rule of Metaphor*, 246.

8 R. S. Thomas, *Collected Poems 1945–1990* (London: Phoenix, 1995), 324.

9 The relevant discussion is in Aquinas, *ST* 1a, q. 12–13, ET in St. Thomas Aquinas, *Summa Theologiae*, vol. 3, ed. and trans. Herbert McCabe (London: Blackfriars, 1964). All citations in English are from this edition.

10 Aquinas, *ST* 1a, q. 12, a. 4.

11 McCabe, "Signifying Imperfectly" (editorial appendix), in McCabe, *Summa Theologiae*, 3:104.

12 See esp. Aquinas, *ST* 1a, q. 12, a. 4, and 1a, q. 12, a. 11.

13 "*Non enim possumus nominare Deum nisi ex creaturis, ut supra dictum est.*" Aquinas, *ST* 1a, q. 13, a. 5.

14 Aquinas, *ST* 1a, q. 13, a. 5. This observation arises as the premise for one of the arguments *in contrarium*, but Aquinas' *responsio* endorses it as a ground for rejecting univocal predication, while denying that equivocation is the only logical alternative. Cf. McCabe, *Summa Theologiae*, 3:67.

15 See the discussion of this difference in Aquinas, *ST* 1a, q. 13, a. 3 and a. 6.

16 See, e.g., Aquinas, *ST* 1a, q. 13, a. 2: "Any creature, in so far as it possesses any perfection, represents God and is like to him, for he, being simply and universally perfect, has pre-existing in himself the perfections of all his creatures." Cf. Aquinas, *ST* 1a, q. 12, a. 12. In these passages Aquinas echoes the metaphysical principle first aired in the fifth century CE by the Neoplatonist Proclus, according to whom "everything which by its existence bestows a character on others, itself primitively possesses that character, which it communicates to the recipient." Proclus, *The Elements of Theology*, trans. E. R. Dodds (Oxford: Clarendon, 1953), 21. For Aquinas, though, the more significant point is that such perfections exist in creatures atypically and imperfectly, and exist in God "in a higher way than we can understand or signify." McCabe, *Summa Theologiae*, 3:55.

17 See Soskice, *Metaphor and Religious Language*, 64–65.

18 "*Hoc dicendum est quod quantum ad rem significatam per nomen per prius dicuntur de Deo quam de creaturis.*" Aquinas, *ST* 1a, q. 13, a. 6. McCabe, *Summa Theologiae*, 3:70.

19 See esp. Aquinas, *ST* 1a, q. 13, a. 3.

20 "*Omnia nomina quae metaphorice de Deo dicuntur, per prius de creaturis dicuntur quam de Deo.*" Aquinas, *ST* 1a, q. 13, a. 6. McCabe, *Summa Theologiae*, 3:68.

21 "Thus it is part of the meaning of 'rock' that it has its being in a merely material way. Such words can be used of God only metaphorically." McCabe, *Summa Theologiae*, 3:59.

22 See Aquinas, *ST* 1a, q. 13, a. 3 and a. 6.

23 Aquinas, *ST* 1a, q. 13, a. 6. My italics.

24 This perhaps unduly extravagant and indulgent image was suggested to me both by a quick scan for biblical metaphors (see Hos 5:12, NIV) and by stumbling inadvertently again across "The Empty Church" in Thomas, *Collected Poems*, 349.

25 Sallie McFague, *Metaphorical Theology: Models of God in Religious Language* (Philadelphia: Fortress, 1982), 12, 15.

26 Soskice, *Metaphor and Religious Language,* 65–66. Soskice's book remains the most thorough and helpful overall treatment of the subject available.

27 Goodman, *Languages of Art,* 69.

28 Goodman, *Languages of Art,* 69.

29 McFague, *Metaphorical Theology,* 13. Cf. Ricoeur, *The Rule of Metaphor,* 224.

30 Hos 5:12, NRSV. KJV and NIV both have "moth."

31 On this, see, helpfully, McFague, *Metaphorical Theology,* 13. Metaphors, we ought to note, are not stable, and do not all function on the same level. Indeed, it is precisely those that prove most rich and fruitful in opening up territories of meaning that tend, eventually, to pass into "literal" use and so surrender their metaphorical status. In linguistic terms, both "Son" and "rock" are metaphors as applied to God, but the profundity and semantic excess attaching to the former place it on a quite different level than the latter.

32 Gunton, *The Actuality of Atonement,* 34.

33 Gunton, *The Actuality of Atonement,* 35. Here Gunton draws on Ricoeur's account of the relevant distinction. See Ricoeur, *The Rule of Metaphor,* 291.

34 See Soskice, *Metaphor and Religious Language,* 71–74.

35 It is not difficult to imagine a semantic (and religious/theological) past where these two terms and other alleged instances of analogical use were ones the application of which to God had once fallen fairly clearly outside rather than comfortably within their established domain of use, and where this fact was seen in the ability of native speakers, on reflection, to identify a certain sense of disturbance at their theological application. That they apply to God naturally or properly is a metaphysical claim, and a controvertible one at that.

36 I am indebted to my colleague Richard Bauckham for suggesting this example.

37 Ricoeur, *The Rule of Metaphor,* 224.

38 See, e.g., Torrance, *Theological Science,* 13–14 et passim. Cf. Torrance, *Theology in Reconstruction,* 53–54.

39 Torrance, *Theological Science,* 20.

40 Torrance, *God and Rationality,* 186–87.

41 Torrance, *God and Rationality,* 187.

42 Torrance, *God and Rationality,* 187

43 Torrance, *God and Rationality,* 187–88.

44 See Gunton, *The Actuality of Atonement,* 39.

45 On the metaphorical "fixing" of meaning and its implications see Gunton, *The Actuality of Atonement,* 45. For the same basic point cast in other terms, cf. Torrance, *God and Rationality,* 19.

46 On "rationalism" in the relevant sense, see Gunton, *The Actuality of Atonement,* 1–25.

47 Torrance, *Theological Science,* 20.

48 See Austin Farrer, *The Glass of Vision* (Westminster, UK: Dacre, 1948), 110. For Torrance's discussion see Torrance, *Theological Science,* 19.

49 Torrance, *Theological Science,* 20.

50 Torrance, *Theological Science,* 20.

51 Cf. Torrance, *God and Rationality,* 23.

52 See Gunton, *The Actuality of Atonement,* 16ff.

53 Gunton, *The Actuality of Atonement,* 17.

54 See, e.g., G. W. F. Hegel, *Lectures on the Philosophy of Religion,* vol. 1, ed. Peter C. Hodgson, trans. R. F. Brown, P. C. Hodgson, and J. M. Stewart (Berkeley: University of California Press, 1984), 396ff. For a full discussion, see further Charles Taylor, *Hegel* (Cambridge: Cambridge University Press, 1975), 465–533.

55 A more familiar term, Hegel notes, is simply *Bilder* ("images"). See Hegel, *Lectures on the Philosophy of Religion,* 1:397.

56 Gunton, *The Actuality of Atonement,* 22.

57 For Hegel the doctrine of the incarnation is to be understood as a pictorial representation whereby the universal truth that "the divine nature is the same as the human" is imaginatively mediated and grasped at a lower level than its philosophical realization. See G. W. F. Hegel, *Phenomenology of Spirit,* trans. A. V. Miller (Oxford: Clarendon, 1977), 459–60, 475. For a helpful account, cf. Colin E. Gunton, *Yesterday and Today: A Study of Continuities in Christology* (London: Darton, Longman and Todd, 1983), 40–43.

58 This doctrine, Torrance insists, constitutes the very "antithesis of any radical dichotomy between intelligible and sensible worlds. It is the doctrine of the coming of God into our human existence in space and time, and his affirming of its validity in relation to himself as Creator and Redeemer." Torrance, *Theology in Reconstruction,* 52.

59 See Torrance, *Theology in Reconstruction,* 39, cf. 52.

60 Torrance, *Theology in Reconstruction,* 129–30.

61 Here Torrance follows Barth who puts the matter thus: "What if God," he inquires, "be so much God that without ceasing to be God he can also be, and is willing to be, not God as well [?]" Karl Barth, *The Göttingen Dogmatics,* 1, 136.

62 Torrance speaks of Israel's history as the divinely furnished matrix for interpreting the person and work of Christ, the divine Word being here already "on the road to becoming flesh," and providing conceptual tools for its own proper articulation. See, e.g., Thomas F. Torrance, *The Mediation of Christ,* 1–23.

63 Torrance, *Theology in Reconstruction,* 19–20.

64 For Torrance, any denial of this would amount to a serious compromising of the insights of Chalcedonian Christology, according to which the two "natures" of the incarnate Son are *inseparabiliter* and *indivise,* but equally vitally *inconfuse* and *immutabiliter.* See Torrance, *Theology in Reconstruction,* 130.

65 Torrance, *Theology in Reconstruction,* 31.

66 Torrance's account of the signitive relation concurs with Barth's notion of an *analogia fidei* rather than an *analogia entis.* See below, 208–9. There is also a parallel with Aquinas' insistence that terms used analogously of God merely point us toward God rather than granting us any comprehension of their meaning as it pertains to his essence; for Torrance and Barth, though, the analogy arises strictly within the context of revelation, whereas for Aquinas its source is one rooted firmly in creation and our capacity of reasoning. See above, 314–15.

67 The presence of Jesus' risen and ascended body (as part of his full sharing in our nature) at the right hand of the Father is basic to Torrance's theology of the

priesthood of Christ. For a full elaboration, see Thomas F. Torrance, *Space, Time and Resurrection* (Edinburgh: Handsel, 1976), 106–58.

68 Torrance, *Theological Science*, 20.

69 Torrance, *God and Rationality*, 23.

70 Torrance, *Theology in Reconstruction*, 20.

71 See Bauckham, "Christology Today."

72 Bauckham, "Christology Today," 23–24. On the relationship between universality and particularity in theology, see, helpfully, Gunton, *The One, the Three and the Many*, esp. chap. 5.

73 Gunton, *The Actuality of Atonement*, 22–23, 38.

74 By "apophatic" in this context I intend not the sort of radical undercutting of the status of theological statements which denies them any purchase whatever on the reality of God and ends thus in a form of devout agnosticism or a mystical experience which eschews the cognitive altogether, but rather the constant acknowledgment that even the most carefully formulated and precise uses of language about God are inadequate and fall short of defining or comprehending his reality even as they are taken up and made new within the dynamic event of revelation itself.

75 This seems to me to be the epistemic significance of the doctrines of resurrection and ascension (where the incarnation is affirmed as a permanent state of affairs in the divine economy rather than a merely temporary manifestation), and the pursuit of a Word whose flesh has been rendered practically invisible in the process of our knowing and speaking inevitably calls it into question.

76 Polanyi, *Personal Knowledge: Towards a Post-Critical Philosophy*, 46.

77 A mental "image" (if we take this now to refer to any product of acts of imagination) may not be visual at all, but aural, or related to others of our five senses. I can imagine a taste or a sound just as readily as something "seen." In this sense, of course, appeal to experiences of audition (in relation to the theological category of a "Word" which speaks to us) may equally be an appeal to an "image," albeit one of a sort distinct from those to which Torrance refers when using the term.

78 See, e.g., his insistence that in theology, as in mathematics, we must not identify "the conceivable with the picturable." Torrance, *God and Rationality*, 23. Cf. his allusion to "the fatal mistake of treating . . . images as pictorial representations or reproductions" in theology. Torrance, *Theology in Reconstruction*, 51.

79 Gilbert Ryle, *The Concept of Mind* (London: Penguin, 1963), chap. 8. Cf. the discussion in Jean-Paul Sartre, *The Psychology of Imagination* (London: Methuen, 1972).

80 Soskice, *Metaphor and Religious Language*, 15.

81 Goodman, *Languages of Art*, 69.

82 Ludwig Wittgenstein, *Philosophical Investigations: The German Text, with a Revised English Translation*, 3rd ed., trans. G. E. M. Anscombe (Oxford: Blackwell, 2001), 1. §115. Wittgenstein's point has to do with one particularly unhelpful "picture" of how language itself is related to reality, i.e., as though it in its turn in some sense *pictured* the things it speaks of.

83 See, e.g., Gunton, *The Actuality of Atonement*, 45–47.

84 See Barth, *Church Dogmatics*, 1/1:243–47. For a helpful brief elucidation, see Bruce McCormack, *Karl Barth's Critically Realistic Dialectical Theology*, 16–19.

85 For Barth the relevant analogy never passes over into human hands or control but depends continually on the gracious action of divine self-giving.

86 McCormack, *Karl Barth's Critically Realistic Dialectical Theology*, 19.

87 An issue which we cannot consider here but which merits mention is that of the nature and scale of the relevant transformation of our terms in the "analogy of faith." Barth's tendency is to suggest that, prior to the divine appropriation of our language, no such analogy exists (rather than claiming that our language in and of itself lacks any created capacity to point us to God). If, though, this emphasis is pushed too far, it seems to entail the idea that the relationship between the meanings attaching ordinarily to our terms and images and those which they acquire through their chastening and making anew in the analogy of faith is *equivocal* rather than analogical or metaphorical, which presents its own set of serious theological concerns. If what we ordinarily mean by "goodness," "love," etc. has no proper relationship to the meanings obtaining when such terms are taken up into the act of revelation, then we quickly find ourselves in a quite peculiar theological territory. It would seem more satisfactory to indicate that such terms bear a particular surplus of meaning which cannot be apprehended by the creature apart from the context of divine speaking and the response of faith and obedience.

88 Exod 20:3–5; Deut 27:15.

89 So, e.g., Gerhard von Rad, *Old Testament Theology*, vol. 1, *The Theology of Israel's Historical Traditions*, trans. D. M. G. Stalker (Edinburgh: Oliver and Boyd, 1962), 212–19.

90 Cf. Tryggve N. D. Mettinger, *No Graven Image? Israelite Aniconism in Its Ancient Near Eastern Context* (Stockholm: Almqvist and Wiksell International, 1995), 15.

91 See Gordon D. Kaufman, *The Theological Imagination: Constructing the Concept of God* (Philadelphia: Westminster, 1981), esp. 21–57, 263–79. An essentially similar approach is found in McFague, *Metaphorical Theology*.

92 Kaufman, *The Theological Imagination*, 30.

93 Elaine Scarry, *The Body in Pain: The Making and Unmaking of the World* (Oxford: Oxford University Press, 1985), 181–243.

94 See, e.g., Tony Clark, *Divine Revelation and Human Practice: Responsive and Imaginative Participation* (Eugene, Oreg.: Cascade, 2008); Bruce McCormack, "Divine Revelation and Human Imagination: Must We Choose between the Two?" *Scottish Journal of Theology* 37, no. 4 (1984): 431–55.

95 Torrance, *Theology in Reconstruction*, 27.

96 Kaufman, *The Theological Imagination*, 263–64.

97 Scarry, *The Body in Pain*, 184.

98 Farrer, *The Glass of Vision*, 57. Not all biblical images, of course, carry equal weight within Christian tradition, and some serve within the canonical pattern and subsequently in the work of theological interpretation and construction to inform our understanding of others.

Works Cited

Anselm. *Cur Deus Homo*. ET from *Why God Became Man; and The Virgin Conception and Original Sin*. Translated by Joseph M. Colleran. Albany, N.Y.: Magi, 1969.

Ante-Nicene Christian Library (ANCL). Edited by Alexander Roberts and James Donaldson. Edinburgh: T&T Clark, 1867ff. Reprinted by Wentworth Press, 2016.

The Ante-Nicene Fathers (ANF). Edited by Alexander Roberts and James Donaldson. 1885–1887. 10 vols. Repr., Peabody, Mass.: Hendrickson, 1994.

Apollinaris. *Apollinaris von Laodicea und seine Schule, Texte und Untersuchungen*. Edited by H. Lietzmann. Tübingen: Mohr, 1904.

Aquinas. *Summa Theologiae*. ET from vol. 3, *Knowing and Naming God*. Edited and translated by Herbert McCabe. London: Blackfriars, 1964.

Armstrong, H. A. *Plotinian and Christian Studies*. London: Variorum Reprints, 1979.

Athanasius. *Ad Epictetum*. NPNF, Second Series, vol. 4.

———. *Contra Gentes*. ET from *Athanasius: Contra Gentes and De Incarnatione*. Edited and translated by Robert W. Thomson. Oxford: Clarendon, 1971.

———. *De Incarnatione*. ET from *Athanasius: Contra Gentes and De Incarnatione*. Edited and translated by Robert W. Thomson. Oxford: Clarendon, 1971.

———. *Orationes contra Arianos* or *Contra Arianos*. ET from *Select Treatises of St. Athanasius in Controversy with the Arians*, vol. 2. Translated by John Henry Newman. London: Longmans, Green, 1903.

Augustine. *Confessions*. ET from *Saint Augustine Confessions*. Translated by Henry Chadwick. Oxford: Oxford University Press, 1991.

————. *City of God*. ET from *Saint Augustine Concerning the City of God against the Pagans*. Translated by Henry Bettenson. London: Penguin, 1984.

Aulén, Gustaf. *Christus Victor*. London: SPCK, 1931.

Baillie, D. M. *Faith in God and Its Christian Consummation*. Kerr Lectures. Edinburgh: T&T Clark, 1964.

————. *God Was in Christ: An Essay on Incarnation and Atonement*. London: Faber and Faber; New York: Scribners, 1948.

————. "Philosophers and Theologians on the Freedom of the Will." In *The Theology of the Sacraments, and Other Papers*, edited by John Baillie. London: Faber and Faber, 1957.

Baillie, John. *The Sense of the Presence of God*. Gifford Lectures. London: Oxford University Press, 1962.

Barth, Karl. *Church Dogmatics*. Vol. 3, *The Doctrine of Creation*. Part 1. Edited by G. W. Bromiley and T. F. Torrance. Translated by G. W. Bromiley et al. Edinburgh: T&T Clark, 1957.

————. *The Doctrine of the Word of God*. Vol 1. Part 2. Edited by G. W. Bromiley and T. F. Torrance. Translated by G. T. Thomson and Harold Knight. Edinburgh: T&T Clark, 1956.

————. *The Epistle to the Romans*. 2nd ed. Translated by Edwyn C. Hoskyns. Oxford: Oxford University Press, 1933.

————. *The Göttingen Dogmatics: Instruction in the Christian Religion*. Vol. 1. Edited by Hannelotte Reiffen. Translated by Geoffrey W. Bromiley. Grand Rapids: Eerdmans, 1991.

————. *Unterricht in der christlichen Religion*. Vol. 1. Edited by Hannelotte Reiffen. Zurich: Theologischer Verlag, 1985.

————. *Unterricht in der christlichen Religion*. Vol. 2. Zurich: Theologischer Verlag, 1990.

Bauckham, Richard. "Christology Today." *Scriptura* 27 (1988): 20–28.

————. *God Crucified: Monotheism and Christology in the New Testament*. 1996 Didsbury Lectures. Carlisle, UK: Paternoster, and Grand Rapids: Eerdmans, 1998.

Bauckham, Richard J., and Trevor Hart. *Hope against Hope: Christian Eschatology in Contemporary Context*. London: Darton, Longman and Todd; Grand Rapids: Eerdmans, 1999.

————. "The Shape of Time." In *The Future as God's Gift: Explorations in Christian Eschatology*, edited by David Fergusson and Marcel Sarot. Edinburgh: T&T Clark, 1999.

Bauman, Zygmunt. *Identity: Conversations with Benedetto Vecchi*. Cambridge, UK, and Malden, Mass.: Polity, 2004.

Begbie, Jeremy. *Beholding the Glory: Incarnation through the Arts*. Grand Rapids: Baker, 2000.

————. *Theology, Music, and Time*. Cambridge and New York: Cambridge University Press, 2000.

Berger, Peter L. *The Sacred Canopy: Elements of a Sociological Theory of Religion*. Garden City, N.Y.: Doubleday, 1967.

Bigg, Charles. *The Christian Platonists of Alexandria*. Oxford: Clarendon, 1886.

Bonner, Gerald. "Augustine's Conception of Deification." *Journal of Theological Studies*, New Series 37, no. 2 (1986): 369–86.

Bousset, Wilhelm. *Kyrios Christos: A History of the Belief in Christ from the Beginnings of Christianity to Irenaeus*. Translated by John E. Steely. Nashville: Abingdon, 1970.

Bouyer, Louis. *The Spirit and Forms of Protestantism*. Translated by A. V. Littledale. London: Collins, 1963.

Boyd, Richard. "Metaphor and Theory Change: What Is 'Metaphor' a Metaphor For?" In *Metaphor and Thought*, edited by Andrew Ortony. Cambridge: Cambridge University Press, 1993.

Bradley, F. H. *Ethical Studies*. 2nd rev. ed. Oxford: Clarendon, 1962 [1876].

Brown, David. *God and Enchantment of Place: Reclaiming Human Experience*. Oxford: Oxford University Press, 2004.

———. *God and Grace of Body: Sacrament in Ordinary*. Oxford: Oxford University Press, 2007.

———. *God and Mystery in Words: Experience through Metaphor and Drama*. Oxford: Oxford University Press, 2008.

Calvin, John. *Commentaries on the First Book of Moses Called Genesis*. Vol. 1. Translated by John King. Edinburgh, 1848.

———. *Commentary on 1 Corinthians*. ET from *The First Epistle of Paul to the Corinthians*. Translated by John W. Fraser. Edinburgh: Oliver & Boyd, 1960.

———. *Commentary on 1 Timothy*. ET from *Tracts and Treatises*. With a short life of Calvin by Theodore Beza. Translated by Henry Beveridge. Historical notes and introduction added to the present ed. by Thomas F. Torrance. 3 vols. Grand Rapids: Eerdmans, 1958.

———. *Commentary on the Second Epistle of Paul the Apostle to the Corinthians and the Epistles to Timothy, Titus and Philemon*. Translated by T. A. Smail. London: Oliver and Boyd, 1964.

———. *Commentary on Ephesians*. ET from *Galatians, Ephesians, Philippians and Colossians*. Translated by T. H. L. Parker. Edinburgh: Oliver and Boyd, 1965.

———. *Commentary on Hebrews*. ET from *Commentary on Hebrews, I and II Peter*. Translated by W. B. Johnston. Edinburgh: Oliver and Boyd, 1963.

———. *Commentary on John*. ET from *The Gospel according to St John 1–10*. Translated by T. H. L. Parker. Edinburgh: Oliver & Boyd, 1959.

———. *Commentary on Romans*. ET from *Epistles of Paul the Apostle to the Romans and to the Thessalonians*. Translated by Ross Mackenzie. Edinburgh: St Andrew Press, 1961.

———. *Institutes of the Christian Religion*. Edited by John T. McNeill and translated by Ford Lewis Battles. Library of Christian Classics, vols. 20–21. Louisville: Westminster John Knox, 1960.

———. *A Treatise on the Sacraments of Baptism and the Lord's Supper*. Edinburgh, 1838.

Campbell, John McLeod. *The Nature of the Atonement and Its Relation to Remission of Sins and Eternal Life*. 6th ed. London: Macmillan, 1886.

———. *Sermons and Lectures*. 3rd ed. Greenock, UK: Lusk, 1832.

Carey, George. *The Gate of Glory*. London: Hodder and Stoughton, 1986.

Casey, R. P. "Clement and the Two Divine Logoi." *Journal of Theological Studies* 25, no. 97 (1923).

Clark, Tony. *Divine Revelation and Human Practice: Responsive and Imaginative Participation*. Eugene, Oreg.: Cascade, 2008.

Clement of Alexandria. *Protreptikos*. ET from *The Exhortation to the Greeks. The Rich Man's Salvation. To the Newly Baptized*. Translated by G. W. Butterworth. Loeb Classical Library 92. Cambridge, Mass.: Harvard University Press, 1919.

Copleston, Frederick. *A History of Philosophy*. Vol. 1. London: Continuum, 2003.

Dalferth, Ingolf U. *Becoming Present: An Inquiry into the Christian Sense of the Presence of God*. Leuven, Belgium, and Dudley, Mass.: Peeters, 2006.

Daniélou, Jean. *The Origins of Latin Christianity*. Translated by David Smith and John Austin Baker and edited by John Austin Baker. Philadelphia: Westminster, 1977.

de Lubac, Henri. *Medieval Exegesis*. Vol. 1. *The Four Senses of Scripture*. Translated by Mark Sebanc. Grand Rapids: Eerdmans, 1998.

Denaux, Adelbert, Nicholas Sagovsky, and Charles Sherlock, eds. *Looking towards a Church Fully Reconciled: The Final Report of the Second Anglican-Roman Catholic International Commission 1983–2005 (ARCIC II)*. London: Society for Promoting Christian Knowledge, 2016.

Die griechischen christlichen Schriftsteller der ersten drei Jahrhunderte (GCS). 53 vols. Leipzig: Hinrichs, 1897–1969.

Downie, R. S., and Elizabeth Telfer. *Respect for Persons*. London: Allen and Unwin, 1969.

Dragas, George D. *Athanasiana: Essays in the Theology of Saint Athanasius*. London, 1980.

———. *St Athanasius contra Apollinarem*. Athens: Church and Theology, 1985.

Eagleton, Terry. *Sweet Violence: The Idea of the Tragic*. Oxford: Blackwell, 2003.

Edwards, Jonathan. "Concerning the Necessity and Reasonableness of the Christian Doctrine of Satisfaction for Sin." In *The Works of Jonathan Edwards*, edited by Edward Hickman. Vol. 2. London: William Ball, 1829.

Eichrodt, Walther. *Theology of the Old Testament*. Vol. 1. London: SCM, 1960.

Farmer, H. H. *The World and God: A Study of Prayer, Providence and Miracle in Christian Experience*. 2nd ed. London: Nisbet, 1936.

Farrer, Austin. *The Glass of Vision*. Westminster, UK: Dacre, 1948.

Feuerbach, Ludwig. *The Essence of Christianity*. Translated by George Eliot. London: Kegan Paul, Trench, Trübner, 1893.

Fiddes, Paul S. *Past Event and Present Salvation: The Christian Idea of Atonement*. London: Darton, Longman & Todd, 1989.

Fisher, Edward. *The Marrow of Moderne Divinity*. London, 1645.

Forsyth, P. T. *The Church, the Gospel and Society*. London: Independent Press, 1962.

———. "Christ's Person and His Cross." *Methodist Review* 66 (January 1917).

———. Contribution to *The Atonement in Modern Religious Thought: A Theological Symposium*. London: James Clarke, 1900.

———. "The Cross as the Final Seat of Authority." In *The Gospel and Authority: A P. T. Forsyth Reader*, edited by Marvin W. Anderson. Minneapolis: Augsburg, 1971.

———. "The Cross of Christ as the Moral Principle of Society." *Methodist Review* 99 (January 1917).

———. *The Cruciality of the Cross*. Expositor's Library. London and New York: Hodder and Stoughton, 1909.

———. *God the Holy Father*. London: Independent Press, 1957.

———. *The Justification of God: Lectures for War-time on a Christian Theodicy*. London: Duckworth, 1916.

———. *Missions in State and Church: Sermons and Addresses*. London: Hodder and Stoughton, 1908.

———. *The Old Faith and the New*. Leicester, UK: Midland Educational Company.

———. *The Person and Place of Jesus Christ*. London: Hodder and Stoughton, 1909.

———. *Positive Preaching and the Modern Mind*. 3rd ed. London: Independent Press, 1949.

———. *The Preaching of Jesus and the Gospel of Christ*. Blackwood, Australia: New Creation, 1987.

———. "The Preaching of Jesus and the Gospel of Christ: The Meaning of a Sinless Christ." *Expositor*, 8th ser., 25 (1923).

———. *The Work of Christ*. Expositor's Library. London and New York: Hodder and Stoughton, 1910.

Franks, Robert S. *The Work of Christ: A Historical Study of Christian Doctrine*. London and New York: T. Nelson, 1962.

Fuller, Reginald. Review of *In the End, God . . . A Study of the Christian Doctrine of the Last Things*, by John Robinson. *Theology* 54, no. 373 (1951).

Gardiner, Patrick L. *Kierkegaard*. Oxford: Oxford University Press, 1988.

Goodman, Nelson. *Languages of Art: An Approach to a Theory of Symbols*. London: Oxford University Press, 1969.

Gorringe, Timothy. *God's Just Vengeance: Crime, Violence, and the Rhetoric of Salvation*. Cambridge and New York: Cambridge University Press, 1996.

Gregory Nazianzen. Epistle 101. Available online at http://www.newadvent.org/fathers/3103a.htm.

Grensted, L. W. *The Person of Christ*. London: Nisbet, 1933.

Grillmeier, Alois. *Christ in Christian Tradition*. London and Oxford: Mowbray, 1965.

Gunton, Colin E. *The Actuality of Atonement: A Study of Metaphor, Rationality and the Christian Tradition*. Edinburgh: T&T Clark, 1988.

————. *The One, the Three and the Many: God, Creation and the Culture of Modernity.* Cambridge: Cambridge University Press, 1993.

————. *Yesterday and Today: A Study of Continuities in Christology.* London: Darton, Longman and Todd, 1983.

Hall, George. "D. M. Baillie: A Theology of Paradox." In *Christ, Church and Society: Essays on John Baillie and Donald Baillie,* edited by David Fergusson. Edinburgh: T&T Clark, 1993.

Hampson, Daphne. *Theology and Feminism.* Oxford: Blackwell, 1990.

Harries, Richard. *Art and the Beauty of God: A Christian Understanding.* London: Mowbray, 1993.

Hart, Trevor. "Conversation after Pentecost? Theological Musings on the Hermeneutic Motion." *Literature and Theology* 28, no. 2 (2014): 164–78.

————. "The Sense of an Ending: Finitude and the Authentic Performance of Life." In *Faithful Performances: Enacting Christian Tradition,* edited by Steven R. Guthrie and Trevor Hart. Aldershot, UK: Ashgate, 2007.

————. "Universalism: Two Distinct Types." In *Universalism and the Doctrine of Hell,* edited by Nigel M. de S. Cameron. Carlisle, UK: Paternoster; Grand Rapids: Baker, 1992.

Hegel, G. W. F. *Introduction and the Concept of Religion.* Vol. 1, *Lectures on the Philosophy of Religion,* edited by Peter C. Hodgson and translated by R. F. Brown, P. C. Hodgson, and J. M. Stewart. Berkeley: University of California Press, 1984.

————. *Phenomenology of Spirit.* Translated by A. V. Miller. Oxford: Clarendon, 1977.

Hendry, George S. *The Gospel of the Incarnation.* London: SCM, 1959.

Hick, John. *God and the Universe of Faiths: Essays in the Philosophy of Religion.* London: Macmillan, 1973.

————. *The Myth of God Incarnate.* London: SCM, 1977.

Hodgson, Leonard. *Theology in an Age of Science.* Oxford: Clarendon, 1944.

Hogg, David. *Anselm of Canterbury: The Beauty of Theology.* Aldershot, UK, and Burlington, Vt.: Ashgate, 2004.

Holmes, Stephen R. *Listening to the Past: The Place of Tradition in Theology.* Grand Rapids: Baker Academic, 2002.

Hunsinger, George. *Disruptive Grace: Studies in the Theology of Karl Barth.* Grand Rapids: Eerdmans, 2000.

James, Eric. *A Life of Bishop John A. T. Robinson: Scholar, Pastor, Prophet.* London: Collins; Grand Rapids: Eerdmans, 1987.

Johnson, Aubrey R. *The One and the Many in the Israelite Conception of God.* 2nd ed. Cardiff: Cardiff University Press, 1961.

Johnson, Harry. *The Humanity of the Saviour: A Biblical and Historical Study of the Human Nature of Christ in Relation to Original Sin, with Special Reference to Its Soteriological Significance.* London: Epworth, 1962.

Johnson, Mark. *The Body in the Mind: The Bodily Basis of Meaning, Imagination, and Reason.* Chicago and London: University of Chicago Press, 1987.

Kannengiesser, Charles. "Athanasius of Alexandria and the Foundation of Traditional Christology." *Theological Studies* 34 (1973).

Kant, Immanuel. *Critique of Practical Reason*. Translated by Lewis White Beck. New York: Liberal Arts Press, 1956.

———. *Critique of Pure Reason*. Translated by Norman Kemp Smith. London: Macmillan, 1929.

Kaufman, Gordon D. *The Theological Imagination: Constructing the Concept of God*. Philadelphia: Westminster, 1981.

Kehrhahn, Traugott. *De sancti Athanasii quae fertur Contra Gentes oration*. Berlin: G. Schade, 1913.

Kelly, J. N. D. *Early Christian Doctrines*. 5th ed. London: Black, 1977.

Kierkegaard, Søren. *Kierkegaard's Concluding Unscientific Postscript*. Translated by David F. Swenson. Princeton, N.J.: Princeton University Press, 1941.

Kraemer, Hendrik. *The Christian Message in a Non-Christian World*. New York: Harper, 1938.

Küng, Hans. *Justification: The Doctrine of Karl Barth and a Catholic Reflection*. London: Burns and Oates, 1966.

Labriolle, Pierre de, ed. and trans. *Tertullien: De Paenitentia, De Pudicitia*. Paris: Alphonse Picard et Fils, 1906.

Lakoff, George, and Mark Johnson. *Metaphors We Live By*. Chicago: University of Chicago Press, 2003.

———. *Philosophy in the Flesh: The Embodied Mind and Its Challenge to Western Thought*. New York: Basic Books, 1999.

Lampe, G. W., ed. *A Patristic Greek Lexicon (PGL)*. Oxford: Oxford University Press, 1961.

Lash, Nicholas. "On What Kinds of Things There Are." In *The Beginning and End of "Religion."* Cambridge: Cambridge University Press, 1996.

Lewis, Alan E. *Between Cross and Resurrection: A Theology of Holy Saturday*. Grand Rapids: Eerdmans, 2001.

Lewis, C. S. *Rehabilitations and Other Essays*. London: Oxford University Press, 1939.

Lilla, Salvatore R. C. *Clement of Alexandria: A Study in Christian Platonism and Gnosticism*. London: Oxford University Press, 1971.

Loofs, Friedrich. *Leitfaden zum Studium der Dogmengeschichte*. Halle, 1906.

Lossky, Vladimir. *In the Image and Likeness of God*. Edited by John H. Erickson and Thomas E. Bird. Crestwood, N.Y.: St. Vladimir's Seminary Press, 1974.

———. *The Mystical Theology of the Eastern Church*. Translated by the Fellowship of St. Alban and St. Sergius. London: James Clarke, 1957.

Lumsden, John. *The Covenants of Scotland*. Paisley, UK: Gardner, 1914.

MacDonald, George. *A Dish of Orts*. Whitehorn, Calif.: Johannesen, 1996.

Mackie, J. L. *Ethics: Inventing Right and Wrong*. London: Penguin, 1977.

Mascall, E. L. *Christ, the Christian and the Church: A Study of the Incarnation and Its Consequences*. London: Longmans, Green, 1946.

——. *Theology and the Gospel of Christ: An Essay in Reorientation*. London: SPCK, 1977.

——. *Via Media: An Essay in Theological Synthesis*. London: Longmans, Green, 1956.

McCormack, Bruce L. "Divine Revelation and Human Imagination: Must We Choose between the Two?" *Scottish Journal of Theology* 37, no. 4 (1984): 431–55.

——. *Karl Barth's Critically Realistic Dialectical Theology: Its Genesis and Development, 1909–1936*. Oxford: Clarendon, 1995.

McFague, Sallie. *Metaphorical Theology: Models of God in Religious Language*. Philadelphia: Fortress, 1982.

McGrath, Alister. *Iustitia Dei: A History of the Christian Doctrine of Justification*. Vol. 1. Cambridge: Cambridge University Press, 1986.

McIntyre, John. "The Christology of Donald Baillie in Perspective." In *Christ, Church and Society*, edited by David Fergusson. New York: T&T Clark, 2004.

——. *St. Anselm and His Critics: A Re-interpretation of the Cur Deus Homo*. Edinburgh: Oliver and Boyd, 1954.

McLelland, Joseph C. *God the Anonymous: A Study in Alexandrian Philosophical Theology*. Cambridge, Mass.: Philadelphia Patristic Foundation, 1976.

Meijering, E. P. *Orthodoxy and Platonism in Athanasius: Synthesis or Antithesis?* Leiden: Brill, 1968.

Mettinger, Tryggve N. D. *No Graven Image? Israelite Aniconism in Its Ancient Near Eastern Context*. Stockholm: Almqvist and Wiksell International, 1995.

Miller, Perry. *The New England Mind: The Seventeenth Century*. Cambridge, Mass.: Harvard University Press, 1954.

Møller, Jens G. "The Beginnings of Puritan Covenant Theology." *Journal of Ecclesiastical History* 14, no. 1 (1963).

Moltmann, Jürgen. *The Coming of God: Christian Eschatology*. Translated by Margaret Kohl. London: SCM, 1996.

——. *God in Creation: A New Theology of Creation and the Spirit of God*. Translated by Margaret Kohl. London: SCM, 1985.

——. "The Knowing of the Other and the Community of the Different." In *God for a Secular Society: The Public Relevance of Theology*. Minneapolis: Fortress, 1999.

——. *The Spirit of Life: A Universal Affirmation*. Translated by Margaret Kohl. London: SCM, 1992.

Moule, C. F. D. *The Origin of Christology*. Cambridge: Cambridge University Press, 1977.

Newbigin, Lesslie. *The Open Secret: Sketches for a Missionary Theology*. Grand Rapids: Eerdmans, 1978.

Nicene and Post-Nicene Fathers (NPNF). Series 1. Edited by Philip Schaff. 1886–1889. 14 vols. Repr., Peabody, Mass.: Hendrickson, 1994.

Nicene and Post-Nicene Fathers (NPNF). Series 2. Edited by Philip Schaff. 1904–1916. 14 vols. Repr., Peabody, Mass: Hendrickson, 1996.

Nielsen, J. T. *Adam and Christ in the Theology of Irenaeus of Lyons*. Assen: Van Gorcum, 1968.

Nordberg, Henric. "A Reconsideration of the Date of St Athanasius *Contra Gentes* and *De Incarnatione*." *Studia Patristica* 3 (1961): 262–66.

"Notes of Recent Exposition." *The Expository Times* 62, no. 6 (1951): 161–62.

Otto, Rudolf. *The Idea of the Holy: An Inquiry into the Non-rational Factor in the Idea of the Divine and Its Relation to the Rational*. Translated by John W. Harvey. London: Oxford University Press, 1923.

Owen, H. P. "The Sinlessness of Jesus." In *Religion, Reason, and the Self: Essays in Honour of Hywel D. Lewis*, edited by Stewart R. Sutherland and T. A. Roberts. Cardiff: University of Wales Press, 1989.

Partridge, Christopher H. *H. H. Farmer's Theological Interpretation of Religion: Towards a Personalist Theology of Religions*. Lewiston, N.Y.: E. Mellen, 1998.

Patristic Greek Lexicon. Edited by Geoffrey W. H. Lampe. Oxford: Clarendon, 1961.

Paul, Robert S. *The Assembly of the Lord: Politics and Religion in the Westminster Assembly and the "Grand Debate."* Edinburgh: T&T Clark, 1985.

———. *The Atonement and the Sacraments*. London: Hodder and Stoughton, 1961.

Plato. *Timaeus*. Translated by Desmond Lee. Harmondsworth, UK: Penguin, 1965.

Plotinus. *Ennead*. Vol. 1, *Porphyry on the Life of Plotinus. Ennead I*. Translated by A. H. Armstrong. LCL 440. Cambridge, Mass.: Harvard University Press, 1969.

———. *The Enneads*. Edited and translated by Stephen MacKenna. London: Faber and Faber, 1956.

Polanyi, Michael. *Personal Knowledge: Towards a Post-Critical Philosophy*. London: Routledge and Kegan Paul; Chicago: University of Chicago Press, 1958.

Proclus. *The Elements of Theology*. Translated by E. R. Dodds. Oxford: Clarendon, 1953.

Quasten, Johannes. *Patrology*. Vol. 3. Westminster, Md.: Newman, 1963.

Rashdall, Hastings. *The Idea of Atonement in Christian Theology*. London: Macmillan, 1919.

Richard, Marcel. "Saint Athanase et la psychologie du Christ selon les Ariens." *Mélanges de science religieuse* 4 (1947): 4–54.

Richardson, Alan. *Christian Apologetics*. London: SCM, 1947.

Ricoeur, Paul. *Oneself as Another*. Translated by Kathleen Blamey. Chicago: University of Chicago Press, 1992.

———. *The Rule of Metaphor: Multidisciplinary Studies of the Creation of Meaning in Language*. Translated by Robert Czerny et al. Toronto and Buffalo: Toronto University Press, 1977.

Rist, John M. "Basil's 'Neoplatonism.'" In *Basil of Caesarea: Christian, Humanist, Ascetic*, edited by Paul J. Fedwick. Toronto: Pontifical Institute for Medieval Studies, 1981.

———. *Plotinus: The Road to Reality*. Cambridge: Cambridge University Press, 1967.

Ritchie, A. D. *Scientific Method*. London: Kegan Paul; New York: Harcourt Brace, 1923.

Ritschl, Albrecht. *Theologie und Metaphysik: zur Verständigung und Abwehr*. Bonn: A. Marcus, 1881.

———. "Theology and Metaphysics." In *Three Essays*, translated by Philip Hefner. Philadelphia: Fortress, 1972.

Roberts, R. H. "Karl Barth's Doctrine of Time: Its Nature and Implications." In *Karl Barth: Studies of His Theological Method*, edited by S. W. Sykes. Oxford: Clarendon, 1979.

Robinson, H. Wheeler. *Corporate Personality in Ancient Israel*. Rev. ed. Edinburgh: T&T Clark, 1981.

Robinson, John A. T. *In the End, God . . . : A Study of the Christian Doctrine of the Last Things*. Rev. ed. London: Collins Fontana, 1968.

———. "The 'Parable' of the Sheep and the Goats." *New Testament Studies* 2, no. 4 (1956): 225–37.

———. *The Roots of a Radical*. London: SCM, 1980.

———. "South Bank Religion—What I'm Trying to Do." *Evening Standard*, July 11, 1963.

———. "Universalism—A Reply." *Scottish Journal of Theology* 2, no. 4 (1949): 378–80.

———. "Universalism—Is It Heretical?" *Scottish Journal of Theology* 2, no. 2 (1949): 139–55.

Rogers, Charles. *Life of George Wishart, the Scottish Martyr*. Edinburgh, 1876.

Ross, David. *Plato's Theory of Ideas*. 2nd ed. Oxford: Clarendon, 1953.

Rowley, H. H. *The Biblical Doctrine of Election*. London: Lutterworth, 1950.

Rutherford, Samuel. *Christ Dying and Drawing Sinners to Himself, or, A Survey of Our Saviour in His Soule-suffering, His Lovelynesse in His Death, and the Efficacie Thereof*. London, 1647.

Ryle, Gilbert. *The Concept of Mind*. London: Penguin, 1963.

Sanday, William. *Christologies Ancient and Modern*. Oxford: Clarendon, 1910.

Sartre, Jean-Paul. "Itinerary of a Thought." *New Left Review* 58 (1969).

———. *The Psychology of Imagination*. London: Methuen, 1972.

Scarry, Elaine. *The Body in Pain: The Making and Unmaking of the World*. Oxford: Oxford University Press, 1985.

Schleiermacher, Friedrich. *The Christian Faith*. 2nd ed. Translated by H. R. Mackintosh. Edinburgh: T&T Clark, 1928.

Scholem, Gershom. "Schöpfung aus Nichts und Selbstverschränkung Gottes." *Eranos Jahrbuch* 25 (1956): 87–119.

Schultz, Hermann. "Der sittliche Begriff des Verdienstes und seine Anwendung auf das Verständniss des Werkes Christi." *Theologische Studien und Kritiken* (1894): 1–50, 245–314, 554–614.

Scott, Alexander John. "The Kingdom of Christ." Lecture 1 of *Social Systems of the Present Day Compared to Christianity*, reprinted in Scott, *Discourses*. London: Macmillan, 1866.

Scott, Melville. *Athanasius on the Atonement*. Stafford, UK: J. and C. Mort, 1914.

The Scottish Book of Common Prayer. Edinburgh: Cambridge University Press, 1929.

Seeberg, Reinhold. *Text-book of the History of Doctrines*. Grand Rapids: Baker, 1964.

Sellers, R. V. *Two Ancient Christologies*. London: SPCK, 1954.

Soskice, Janet Martin. *Metaphor and Religious Language*. Oxford: Clarendon, 1985.

Steiner, George. *After Babel: Aspects of Language and Translation*. 2nd ed. Oxford and New York: Oxford University Press, 1992.

———. *Real Presences: Is There Anything in What We Say?* London: Faber and Faber, 1989.

Stevenson, J., ed. *Creeds, Councils and Controversies: Documents Illustrative of the History of the Church A.D. 337–461*. London: SPCK, 1973.

Stevenson, Peter Kenneth. *God in Our Nature: The Incarnational Theology of John McLeod Campbell*. Carlisle, UK: Paternoster, 2004.

Stott, John R. W. *The Cross of Christ*. Leicester, UK and Downers Grove, Ill.: InterVarsity Press, 1986.

Swinburne, Richard. *Responsibility and Atonement*. Oxford: Clarendon, 1989.

Sykes, S. W. "The Theology of the Humanity of Christ." In *Christ, Faith and History: Cambridge Studies in Christology*, edited by S. W. Sykes and J. P. Clayton. Cambridge: Cambridge University Press, 1972.

Taylor, Charles. *Hegel*. Cambridge: Cambridge University Press, 1975.

Terrien, Samuel. *The Elusive Presence: Toward a New Biblical Theology*. San Francisco: Harper and Row, 1978.

Theological Dictionary of the New Testament (TDNT). Edited by Gerhard Kittel and Gerhard Friedrich. Translated by Geoffrey W. Bromiley. 10 vols. Grand Rapids: Eerdmans, 1964–1976.

Thomas, R. S. *Collected Poems 1945–1990*. London: Phoenix, 1995.

Torrance, Alan J. *Persons in Communion: An Essay on Trinitarian Description and Human Participation, with Special Reference to Volume One of Karl Barth's "Church Dogmatics."* Edinburgh: T&T Clark, 1996.

Torrance, James B. "The Contribution of McLeod Campbell to Scottish Theology." *Scottish Journal of Theology* 26, no. 3 (1973): 295–311.

———. "The Covenant Concept in Scottish Theology and Politics and Its Legacy." *Scottish Journal of Theology* 34, no. 3 (1981): 225–43.

———. "Covenant or Contract? A Study of the Theological Background of Worship in Seventeenth-Century Scotland." *Scottish Journal of Theology* 23, no. 1 (1970): 51–76.

———. "The Place of Jesus Christ in Worship." In *Theological Foundations for Ministry: Selected Readings for a Theology of the Church of Ministry*, edited by Ray S. Anderson. Grand Rapids: Eerdmans, 1979.

Torrance, Thomas F. *God and Rationality*. London: Oxford University Press, 1971.

———. "The Hermeneutics of St. Athanasius." *Ekklesiastikos Pharos* 52 (1970).

———. "The Implications of *Oikonomia* for Knowledge and Speech of God in Early Christian Theology." In *Oikonomia: Heilsgeschichte als Thema der Theologie*, edited by Felix Christ. Hamburg: Herbert Reich, 1967.

———. "Karl Barth and the Latin Heresy." *Scottish Journal of Theology* 39, no. 4 (1986).

———. *The Mediation of Christ*. 2nd ed. Edinburgh: T&T Clark, 1992.

———. *Scottish Theology from John Knox to John McLeod Campbell*. Edinburgh: T&T Clark, 1996.

———. *Space, Time and Incarnation*. London: Oxford University Press, 1969; Edinburgh: Handsel, 1976.

———. *Theological Science*. London: Oxford University Press, 1969.

———. *Theology in Reconciliation: Essays Towards Evangelical and Catholic Unity in East and West*. London: G. Chapman, 1975.

———. *Theology in Reconstruction*. London: SCM, 1965.

———. *The Trinitarian Faith: An Evangelical Theology of the Ancient Catholic Church*. Edinburgh: T&T Clark, 1988.

———. "Universalism or Election?" *Scottish Journal of Theology* 2, no. 3 (1949): 310–18.

Turner, H. E. W. *The Patristic Doctrine of Redemption: A Study of the Development of Doctrine During the First Five Centuries*. London: Mowbray, 1952.

Tuttle, George M. *So Rich a Soil: John McLeod Campbell on Christian Atonement*. Edinburgh: Handsel, 1986.

Van Buren, Paul M. *Christ in Our Place: The Substitutionary Character of Calvin's Doctrine of Reconciliation*. Edinburgh: Oliver and Boyd, 1957.

Voisin, Georges. "La doctrine christologique de St. Athanase." *Revue d'histoire ecclésiastique* 1 (1900): 224–48.

von Campenhausen, Hans. *The Fathers of the Greek Church*. London, 1963.

von Harnack, Adolf. *History of Dogma*. Vol. 1. Translated by Neil Buchanan. London: Williams and Norgate, 1894.

———. *History of Dogma*. Vol. 2. Translated by Neil Buchanan. London: Williams and Norgate, 1901.

———. *What Is Christianity?* 2nd ed. London: Williams and Norgate; New York: Putnam, 1901.

———. *History of Dogma*. Vol. 6. Translated by William M'Gilchrist. London: William & Norgate, 1899.

von Rad, Gerhard. *Old Testament Theology*. Vol. 1, *The Theology of Israel's Historical Traditions*, translated by D. M. G. Stalker. Edinburgh: Oliver and Boyd, 1962.

Wallace, Ronald S. *Calvin's Doctrine of the Word and Sacraments*. Edinburgh: Oliver and Boyd, 1953.

Ward, Graham. *Barth, Derrida and the Language of Theology*. Cambridge: Cambridge University Press, 1995.

Ward, Michael. "The Good Serves the Better and Both the Best: C. S. Lewis on Imagination and Reason in Apologetics." In *Imaginative Apologetics: Theology, Philosophy and the Catholic Tradition*, edited by Andrew Davison. London: SCM, 2011.

Weinandy, Thomas G. *Athanasius: A Theological Introduction*. Aldershot, UK, and Burlington, Vt.: Ashgate, 2007.

———. *In the Likeness of Sinful Flesh: An Essay on the Humanity of Christ*. Edinburgh: T&T Clark, 1993.

Werner, Martin. *The Formation of Christian Dogma: An Historical Study of Its Problem*. London: A. and C. Black, 1957.

White, Vernon. *Atonement and Incarnation: An Essay in Universalism and Particularity*. Cambridge: Cambridge University Press, 1991.

Whitehouse, Alec. *Scottish Journal of Theology* 5 (1952): 313–16.

The Whole Proceedings before the Presbytery of Dumbarton, and Synod of Glasgow and Ayr, in the Case of the Rev. John McLeod Campbell, Minister of Row. Greenock, UK: Lusk, 1831.

Wiggins, David. "Towards a Reasonable Libertarianism." In *Essays on Freedom of Action*, edited by Ted Honderich. London: Routledge and Kegan Paul, 1973.

Wiles, Maurice F. "The Nature of the Early Debate about Christ's Human Soul." *Journal of Ecclesiastical History* 16, no. 2 (1965): 321–25.

———. "Soteriological Arguments in the Fathers." *Studia Patristica* 9 (1966): 321–25.

———. *Working Papers in Doctrine*. London: SCM, 1976.

Williams, Rowan. "'Person' and 'Personality' in Christology." *Downside Review* 94 (1976): 253–60.

Wingren, Gustaf. *Man and the Incarnation: A Study in the Biblical Theology of Irenaeus*. Translated by Ross Mackenzie. Edinburgh and London: Oliver and Boyd, 1959.

Wittgenstein, Ludwig. *Philosophical Investigations: The German Text, with a Revised English Translation*. 3rd ed. Translated by G. E. M. Anscombe. Oxford: Blackwell, 2001.

Wolfson, Harry Austryn. *The Philosophy of the Church Fathers: Faith, Trinity, Incarnation*. 3rd ed. Cambridge, Mass.: Harvard University Press, 1970.

Young, Frances M. *From Nicaea to Chalcedon: A Guide to the Literature and Its Background*. London: SCM, 1983.

Credits

The chapters of this book are for the most part based straightforwardly on the earlier publications listed below. All have been adjusted slightly to suit their inclusion in a single volume. Some of the early essays have been significantly reworked to accomplish consistency of style and to suit the needs of the larger volume more satisfactorily. In chapters 1–4 I have also drawn on and developed unpublished material from my doctoral thesis completed in the University of Aberdeen ("Two Views of Salvation in Relation to Christological Understanding in the Patristic East," 1989).

"Humankind in Christ and Christ in Humankind: Salvation as Participation in Our Substitute in the Theology of John Calvin." *Scottish Journal of Theology* 42, no. 1 (1989): 67–84. Used by permission.

"Irenaeus, Recapitulation and Physical Redemption." In *Christ in Our Place: The Humanity of God in Christ for the Reconciliation of the World*, edited by Trevor Hart and Daniel Thimell, 152–81. Exeter, UK: Paternoster, 1989. Used by permission.

"The Two Soteriological Traditions of Alexandria." *Evangelical Quarterly* 6, no. 3 (1989): 239–59.

"Anselm and McLeod Campbell: Where Opposites Meet?" *Evangelical Quarterly* 62, no. 4 (1990): 311–33.

"Atonement and Worship." *Anvil* 11, no. 3 (1994): 203–14.

"Morality, Atonement and the Death of Jesus." In *Justice the True and Only Mercy: Essays on the Life and Theology of Peter Taylor Forsyth*, edited by Trevor Hart. Edinburgh: T&T Clark, 1995. Used by permission.

"Sinlessness and Moral Responsibility: A Problem in Christology." *Scottish Journal of Theology* 48, no. 1 (1995): 37–54. Used by permission.

"Was God in Christ? Revelation, History and the Humanity of God." In *Regarding Karl Barth: Essays Toward a Reading of His Theology*, 1–27. Carlisle, UK: Paternoster, 1999, and Downers Grove, Ill: IVP, 2000. Used by permission.

"Christ the Mediator." In *Reformed Theology in Contemporary Perspective: Westminster: Yesterday, Today—and Tomorrow?* edited by Lynn Quigley, 66–86. Edinburgh: Rutherford House, 2005. Used by permission.

"Atonement, the Incarnation, and Deification: Transformation and Convergence in the Soteriology of T. F. Torrance." *Princeton Theological Review* 14, no. 2 (2008): 79–90.

"*In the End, God. . .* : The Christian Universalism of J. A. T. Robinson (1919–1983)." In *"All Shall Be Well": Explorations in Universal Salvation and Christian Theology, from Origen to Moltmann*, edited by Gregory MacDonald, 355–81. Eugene, Oreg.: Wipf and Stock, 2011. Used by permission.

"Complicating Presence: Interdisciplinary Perspectives on a Theological Question." In *Divine Presence and Absence in Exilic and Post-Exilic Judaism*, edited by Nathan MacDonald and Isaak de Hulster. Tübingen: Mohr Siebeck, 2013. Used by permission.

"Between the Image and the Word." In *Between the Image and the Word: Theological Engagements with Imagination, Language and Literature*, 13–42. Farnham, UK: Ashgate, 2013. Used by permission.

"Parmenides, Particularity and *Parousia*: Identifying the One Who Will Come to Judge the Living and the Dead." In *In the Fullness of Time: Essays on Christology, Creation, and Eschatology in Honor of Richard Bauckham*, edited by Daniel M. Gurtner, Grant Macaskill, and Jonathan T. Pennington, 49–64. Grand Rapids: Eerdmans, 2016. Used by permission.

Index

Alexandrian theology, 32, 55, 62, 64, 77, 87, 99–105, 106, 155, 209, 223, 343n2, 347n112, 400

Ambrose of Milan, 121, 359n6, 360n24

Anaxagoras, 280

Anselm of Canterbury, 11, 46, 89, 122–29, 130, 133–34, 139, 201, 359nn17–18, 360nn25–29, 360nn31–32, 360nn34–35, 361nn36–39, 361nn41–51, 363n84, 393, 398, 400, 407

Apollinarianism, 28, 97, 101, 173, 247, 363n98, 372

Apollinaris of Laodicea, 11, 28, 68, 72, 93, 94, 97, 107, 347n100, 355n133, 393

Apologists, 2, 76, 82, 350n12

Aquinas, Thomas, 15, 225, 265–66, 269, 295–96, 312–19, 384n29, 385n31, 385n34, 388nn9–16, 18–23, 390n66, 393

Arianism, 42, 76–77, 99–104, 349, 355n118, 393

Aristotle, 63, 265, 280, 281, 345n45

Arius, 11, 28, 29, 68, 77, 86, 99, 110

Arminianism, 183–85

Armstrong, A. H., 60, 62, 343n3, 344n12, 344n15, 344n22, 345n37, 393, 401

Athanasius, 11, 13, 20, 29–32, 80–111, 227, 238, 339n42, 348nn5–6, 349nn6–9, 349n11, 350nn12–16, 350nn19–25, 351nn27–48, 351n50, 351nn52–53, 352nn54–73, 353nn74–79, 353nn81–96, 354nn97–99, 354nn101–2, 354nn104–17, 355nn118–29, 355n131, 356nn144–63, 357nn172–78, 357nn180–86, 357nn188–94, 357nn196–98, 358n199, 358nn203–12, 393, 396, 399, 400, 401, 403, 404, 405

Augustine, 60, 271, 339n41, 371n1, 379n59, 384n26, 393, 394, 395

Aulén, Gustaf, 38–42, 340nn14–15, 340nn19–21, 394

Baillie, D. M., 12, 205–10, 251–54, 270, 370nn1–6, 370nn10, 374nn19–20, 374n25, 378n56, 379n56, 394, 398, 400

Baillie, John, 304–6, 383n4, 383n17, 384n22, 386n66, 394, 398

Barth, Karl, 13, 76, 207–26, 231, 306, 332, 348n124, 370nn7–9, 370nn12–19, 371nn20–28, 371nn30–32, 34–41, 372n6, 372n8, 372nn22–24, 379n59, 379n61, 385n36, 390n61, 390n66, 392nn84–87, 394, 398, 399, 400, 402, 403, 404, 405, 408

Bauckham, Richard, 14, 277–90, 327, 363n81, 379n69, 379n1, 380nn2–3, 380nn7–8, 381n19, 382n25, 382n28–35, 382n39, 384n22, 389n36, 391nn71–72, 394, 408

Bauman, Zygmunt, 381n9, 394

Baur, F. C., 96

Begbie, Jeremy, 377n48, 378n48, 394

Berger, Peter, 19, 337n1, 394

Bigg, Charles, 63, 77, 337n6, 343n2, 345n43, 346n76, 348n130, 394

Blake, William, 60

Bonner, Gerald, 339n41, 371n1, 395

Bousset, Wilhelm, 26, 338n26, 395

Bouyer, Louis, 152, 364nn1–2, 395

Boyd, Richard, 387n6, 395

Bradley, F. H., 197, 369n49, 395

Brown, David, 304–6, 386nn61–64, 387n79, 395

Buber, Martin, 376n26, 379n57

Bultmann, Rudolf, 220, 376n22

Calvin, John, 11, 154–66, 180, 187, 299, 364nn7–20, 365nn21–28, 365nn30–37, 365nn39–47, 385n36, 385n43, 395, 404, 405, 407

Campbell, John McLeod, 11, 122, 129–38, 139, 361n52–54, 362nn56–66, 362nn68–71, 362nn73–80, 363n80, 363n83, 364n6, 367n27, 396, 403, 404, 405, 407

Cappadocian fathers, 32, 46, 97, 227, 282

Carey, George, 362n55, 396

Casey, R. P., 77, 348nn126–27, 348n129, 396

Celsus, 67

Chalcedon, council and formula of, 29, 98–99, 109, 111, 155, 160, 208–9, 216, 238–39, 279, 339nn32–33, 339n36, 355n136, 390n64

Clark, Tony, 392n94, 396

Clement of Alexandria, 10, 20, 22, 30, 32, 62–77, 80–82, 85–86, 345nn39–42, 345nn45–47, 345nn49–52, 345nn54–57, 346nn58–64, 346nn68–82, 346nn84–87, 347nn88–103, 347nn105–17, 348nn118–23, 348nn125–29, 349n9, 350n12, 350n25, 352n57, 396, 399

Copleston, Frederick, 343n2, 343n9, 396

Cranmer, Thomas, 122

Dalferth, Ingolf, 292, 295–96, 300, 302–3, 307, 382n1, 382n3, 383n8, 383n10, 384nn21–22, 384n25, 384n27, 384n30, 385nn31–32, 385n47, 386nn48–50,

386nn57–60, 386nn75–77,
  387n81, 396
Daniélou, Jean, 358n4, 396
Downie, R. S., 252, 374n11, 374n16,
  374n22, 396
Dragas, George, 96–97, 101, 349n6,
  352n55, 354n102, 355nn127–28,
  396

Eagleton, Terry, 382n24, 396
Edwards, Jonathan, 130, 136–37,
  362n72, 396
Eichrodt, Walther, 175, 179, 182,
  365n6, 366nn7–10, 366n12,
  366n19, 396
Euripides, 280
Eusebius of Caesarea, 21, 349, 352

Farmer, H. H., 301, 305–6, 376n26,
  378n52, 383n20, 384n28,
  386nn51–53, 386nn67–74, 396,
  401
Farrer, Austin, 15, 322, 336, 389n48,
  392n98, 396
Feuerbach, Ludwig, 211, 215, 226,
  382n27, 396
Fiddes, Paul, 200, 369n68, 372n7, 396
Fisher, Edward, 187, 367n31,
  367nn33–35, 396
Forsyth, P. T., 3, 12, 174, 189–204,
  246–50, 253–56, 288, 363,
  367–70, 373, 374, 397, 408
Franks, Robert S., 26, 117–18,
  120, 338n25, 359n5, 359n10,
  360nn23–24, 397
Fuller, Reginald, 274, 375n14,
  379n71, 397

Gardiner, Patrick, 377n46, 397
Gnosticism, 21–25, 36, 40, 45, 47,
  52, 85, 231, 338nn16–17, 345n39,
  346n61, 350n24, 399

Goodman, Nelson, 317, 387n5,
  389nn27–28, 391n81, 397
Gorringe, Timothy, 360n33,
  361n40, 397
Gregory Nazianzen, 355n134, 397
Gregory of Nyssa, 341n56
Grensted, L. W., 245, 373n3, 397
Grillmeier, Alois, 96, 101–2,
  354n104, 355n130, 355n135,
  356n157, 358n201, 397
Gunton, Colin, 9, 278, 318–19,
  321–22, 324, 328, 332, 337n2,
  338n20, 358n3, 360n21,
  380nn4–6, 389nn32–33,
  389nn44–46, 390nn52–53,
  390nn56–57, 391nn72–73,
  391n83, 397–98

Hall, George, 253–54, 374n25, 398
Hampson, Daphne, 282–83,
  381nn16–18, 381nn20–23, 398
Harnack, Adolf, 21–23, 25–27,
  29, 32, 37, 337n5, 337nn8–10,
  338nn11–12, 338n22, 338n24,
  339nn29–30, 339n45, 360n35,
  373n34, 404
Harries, Richard, 371n33, 398
Hart, Trevor, 377n42, 379n69,
  381n15, 382n39, 384n22,
  384n25, 394, 398
Hegel, G. W. F., 12, 192, 193,
  324–28, 390nn54–55, 390n57,
  398, 403
Hegelianism, 96, 210, 285, 292
Helm, Paul, 374n27
Heraclitus, 278
Hick, John, 287–88, 382n36, 398
Hilary of Poitiers, 121, 360n23
Hodgson, Leonard, 376n15, 398
Hogg, David, 125, 360n34, 363n84,
  398
Holmes, Stephen R., 384n24, 398

Hopkins, Gerard Manley, 220
Hunsinger, George, 379n59,
    379n70, 379n72, 379n75, 398

image, imagery (mental, verbal,
    poetic), 2–12, 15, 20, 24, 25,
    27, 30, 31, 36, 37, 43, 44, 49, 50,
    59, 62, 72, 88, 93, 106, 115–24,
    129–34, 139, 143–45, 152, 157,
    167–70, 179, 180, 201, 202, 226,
    229, 285, 297, 312–36, 339n41,
    340n18, 341n42, 359n11,
    360n30, 361n36, 388n24,
    390n55, 391n77, 391n78,
    392n87, 392n90, 392n98, 399,
    400, 408
image of God (Christological,
    soteriological, anthropological),
    23, 42, 45, 46, 52, 56, 69–71, 84,
    87–91, 106–8, 141, 176, 192, 206,
    229, 279, 285, 346n87, 352n57,
    371n1
Irenaeus of Lyons, 10, 20–33,
    35–53, 64, 81, 85, 109, 227, 283,
    337n4, 337n7, 338nn13–19,
    338n26, 339nn1–10,
    340nn11–13, 340nn16–18,
    340nn22–29, 340nn31–39,
    341n40, 341nn43–56,
    342nn59–65, 342nn70–80,
    343nn80–82, 349n11, 350n16,
    355n126, 356n157, 358n204,
    358n4, 381nn22–23, 385n37,
    395, 401, 405, 407

James, Eric, 375nn1–2, 375n11, 398
Johnson, Aubrey R., 342n66, 398
Johnson, Harry, 341n56, 398
Johnson, Mark, 359n19, 387n1,
    388n7, 398, 399

Kähler, Martin, 206
Kannengiesser, Charles, 349n6,
    352n57, 399
Kant, Immanuel, 60, 195, 197–98,
    210, 212, 251, 263, 310, 369n50,
    382n4, 387n3, 399
Kaufman, Gordon, 334,
    392nn91–92, 392n96, 399
Kierkegaard, Søren, 220, 262,
    267, 312, 376n26, 377nn45–46,
    379n57, 397, 399
Kraemer, Hendrik, 306–7, 387n78,
    399

Lakoff, George, 359n19, 387n1, 399
Lewis, Alan E., 386n56, 399
Lewis, C. S., 310–11, 387nn2–4,
    399, 405
Lilla, Salvatore, 62, 345n39, 346n61,
    348n121, 399
Loofs, Friedrich, 25–26, 44, 338n21,
    341n40, 399
Lossky, Vladimir, 371n1, 399
Lumsden, John, 181, 366n17, 399
Luther, Martin, 152, 186

MacDonald, George, 387n1, 399
MacKenna, Stephen, 343nn3–4,
    344n23, 344n26, 345n37, 401
Mackey, James, 219
Mackie, J. L., 248–49, 252, 373n8,
    374n10, 374n21, 399
Macmurray, John, 221
Mascall, E. L., 98, 104,
    356nn138–40, 357n171, 371n1,
    400
McCabe, Herbert, 313, 388n9,
    388n11, 388n14, 388n16,
    388n18, 388nn20–21, 391
McCormack, Bruce, 332, 371n28,
    392n84, 392n86, 392n94, 400

McFague, Sallie, 317, 388n25, 389n29, 389n31, 392n91, 400
McGrath, Alister, 364n4, 400
McIntyre, John, 120, 123–25, 359nn17–18, 360nn26–29, 360nn31–32, 360n35, 361nn36–37, 361n43, 379n56, 400
Meijering, E. P., 87, 352n56, 400
metaphor, 1–8, 43, 49, 61, 88, 118, 119, 120, 139–44, 167–70, 174, 175, 180–82, 201, 226, 231, 297, 311–21, 329, 331, 338, 343, 358, 359, 386–92, 395–403
Mettinger, Trygve N. D., 392n90, 400
Miller, Perry, 180–81, 366n15, 366nn21–22, 366nn24–25, 400
Møller, Jens, 366n16, 366n20, 400
Moltmann, Jürgen, 201, 279–81, 288, 297–300, 302, 380n7, 381nn10–11, 381nn13–14, 382n38, 383n9, 383n19, 384nn23–24, 385nn35–39, 385nn44–46, 386n55, 400
Moule, C. F. D., 50, 342nn67–69, 400

Nestorianism, 12, 29, 40, 42, 101–4, 173, 205, 347n112, 363n80
New Age, 228
Newbigin, Lesslie, 307, 365n5, 365nn79–80, 400
Nietzsche, Friedrich, 251, 374nn17–18
Nordberg, Henric, 349n6, 401

Origen, 32, 62, 67, 103–4, 346n66, 348n2, 349n11, 350n12, 352n57, 357nn164–67, 357n170, 408
Osiander, 12, 160–62, 163

Otto, Rudolf, 304, 386n65, 401
Owen, H. P., 243, 373n1, 401

Pantaenus, 63
Parmenides, 57, 278, 408
Partridge, Christopher H., 376n26, 378n52, 401
Paul, Robert S., 362n55, 366n23, 401
Philo, 55, 64, 65, 344n12, 346n61, 348n129
Photius, 76–77
Plato, 56–58, 62–66, 69–70, 75, 85, 286, 324, 343nn5–8, 343n11, 345nn45–46, 345n53, 346n83, 401, 402
Platonism, 10–11, 22, 32, 42, 55–67, 69–70, 73–75, 77, 79, 85–86, 104, 106, 109, 283, 337n6, 343n2, 343n11, 344n12, 345n39, 345n43, 346n61, 346n76, 348n130, 350n24, 352n56, 388n16, 394, 399, 400, 402
Plotinus, 55–62, 64, 68–69, 74–75, 85, 343nn3–4, 343nn9–11, 344nn12–14, 344nn16–30, 345nn31–38, 346n84, 348n118, 401, 402
Polanyi, Michael, 231, 329, 372n10, 391n76, 401
Porphyry, 60, 343n3, 344n26, 348n118, 401
Proclus, 59, 344n15, 388n16, 401

Quasten, Johannes, 343, 349, 401

Rashdall, Hastings, 27, 63, 338n27, 345n44, 401
Richard, Marcel, 101, 102, 354n104, 355n131, 356n156, 401

Richardson, Alan, 260–61, 376nn15–17, 401

Ricoeur, Paul, 317, 320, 338n20, 380n8, 388n7, 389n29, 389n33, 389n37, 401

Rist, John M., 344n12, 344n20, 352n56, 402

Ritchie, A. D., 376n15, 402

Ritschl, Albrecht, 12, 25, 26, 338n23, 402

Ritschlianism, 190, 192, 199, 210, 327

Roberts, Richard H., 207–9, 370nn7–8, 402

Robinson, J. A. T., 13, 257–76, 374n1, 375nn1–6, 8–11, 14, 376nn16, 18–28, 30–31, 377nn31–32, 377nn34–36, 377nn38–42, 377nn44–47, 378nn49–50, 378nn52–53, 378nn55–56, 379n57, 379n60, 379nn62–66, 379nn72–74, 379nn76–77, 397, 398, 402, 408

Rowley, H. H., 365n5, 402

Rutherford, Samuel, 183–85, 187, 367n26–30, 367n34, 402

Ryle, Gilbert, 330–31, 391n79, 402

Saltmarsh, John, 184, 367n27

Sanday, William, 247, 373n7, 402

Sartre, Jean-Paul, 252, 374n23, 391

Scarry, Elaine, 392n93, 392n97, 402

Scott, A. J., 138–39, 363n82, 403

Scott, Melville, 106–8, 357n190, 357nn193–94, 403

Schleiermacher, F. D. E., 210, 221, 267, 377n44, 403

Schlier, Heinrich, 341n42

Scholem, Gershom, 385n36, 403

Schultz, Hermann, 117–20, 359nn5–6, 360n20, 403

Seeberg, Reinhold, 358n4, 403

Sellers, R. V., 354n102, 403

Soskice, Janet, 15, 314, 317, 319, 359n19, 388n17, 389n26, 389n34, 391n80, 403

Steiner, George, 172–73, 293–94, 305, 365nn2–3, 382nn2–3, 383nn11–16, 403

Stevenson, Peter K., 361n52, 403

Stott, John W., 360n22, 362n55, 362n79, 403

Studdert Kennedy, Geoffrey, 145

Swinburne, Richard, 250–51, 373n8, 374nn12–15, 374n18, 403

Sykes, Stephen W., 210, 244–46, 370n7, 370n11, 373n2, 373n4, 402, 403

Taylor, Charles, 390n54, 403

Telfer, Elizabeth, 252, 374n11, 374n16, 374n22, 396

Terrien, Samuel, 292, 383nn5–7, 403

Tertullian, 11, 117–21, 124–25, 128–29, 154, 358n4, 358n7, 358n9, 358nn12–16, 360n20, 361n43

Thomas, R. S., 312, 388n24, 403

Thomson, R. W., 83, 349n9, 349n11, 351n28, 354n105

Torrance, Alan J., 371, 403

Torrance, J. B., 6, 366, 403

Torrance, T. F., 13, 15, 227–39, 258, 259, 264–74, 285, 299, 321–31, 335, 342, 347–50, 361–65, 367, 372–85, 389–95, 404, 408

Turner, H. E. W., 31, 338n28, 339n28, 339n43, 358n4, 360n23, 373n27, 404

Tuttle, George M., 361n52, 404

Tyndale, William, 183, 366n16, 366n20

Van Buren, Paul M., 165, 365n43,
    404
Voisin, Georges, 101, 349n11,
    355n126, 356n155, 404
von Campenhausen, Hans, 349n7,
    404
von Rad, Gerhard, 392n89, 404

Ward, Graham, 208, 370n9, 405
Ward, Michael, 387n2, 405
Weinandy, Thomas G., 341n56,
    342nn56–57, 348n5, 350n19,
    350n21, 357n172, 405
Werner, Martin, 339n30, 405
White, Vernon, 287, 382n37, 405
Whitehouse, Alec, 375n14, 405
Wiggins, David, 248, 253, 374n9,
    374n12, 374nn23–24, 405
Wiles, Maurice, 28–30, 32–33,
    339n31, 339nn34–40, 339n46,
    354n103, 357n187, 358n202, 405

Williams, Rowan, 98, 216, 356n137,
    356n141, 356n143, 371n29, 405
Wingren, Gustaf, 41–42,
    340nn27–28, 340n30, 405
Wishart, George, 168, 365n1, 402
Wittgenstein, Ludwig, 225, 331,
    391n82, 405
Wolfson, H. A., 343n2, 345n45, 405

Young, Frances, 94, 346n67,
    347n100, 349n6, 353n83,
    354nn103–4, 355nn132–33, 405